MONEY AND FINANCE IN ECONOMIC GROWTH AND DEVELOPMENT

BUSINESS ECONOMICS AND FINANCE

a series of monographs and textbooks

Executive Editor

Arthur B. Laffer

Department of Economics
University of Chicago
Graduate School of Business
Chicago, Illinois

Volume 1
Common Globe or Global Commons: Population
Regulation and Income Distribution   *John C. G. Boot*

Volume 2
Lags in the Effects of Monetary Policy: A Nonparametric
Analysis   *Gene C. Uselton*

Volume 3
Demand for Money in Israel   *Lewis Mandell*

Volume 4
Key Issues in International Monetary
Reform   *Edited by Randall Hinshaw*

Volume 5
Private Short-Term Capital Flows   *Arthur B. Laffer*

Volume 6
International Trade and Distortions in
Factor Markets   *Stephen P. Magee*

Volume 7
Money and Finance in Economic Growth
and Development   *Edited by Ronald I. McKinnon*

Other Volumes in Preparation.

MONEY AND FINANCE IN ECONOMIC GROWTH AND DEVELOPMENT

Essays in Honor of Edward S. Shaw

Proceedings of the conference held at Stanford University

edited by RONALD I. McKINNON

Center for Research in Economic Growth
Stanford University
Stanford, California

MARCEL DEKKER, INC.   New York and Basel

The Bank of America provided generous financial support for the publication of the proceedings under the auspices of the Center for Research in Economic Growth, Stanford University.

MARCEL DEKKER, INC.

270 Madison Avenue, New York, New York 10016

LIBRARY OF CONGRESS CATALOG CARD NUMBER: 75-21191

ISBN: 0-8247-6366-1

Current Printing (last digit)

10 9 8 7 6 5 4 3 2 1

PRINTED IN THE UNITED STATES OF AMERICA

CONTENTS

Contributors   ix

1. Introduction   1
   Ronald I. McKinnon

Part I Money and Finance in Economic Development

2. Economic Growth and Financial Intermediation   11
   Lewis J. Spellman
   Comment   23
   Claudio Gonzalez-Vega

3. Inflation, Financial Repression,
   and Capital Formation in Latin America   35
   Robert C. Vogel
   Stephen A. Buser

v

Comment   71

    Clark W. Reynolds

4. Saving Propensities and the Korean
   Monetary Reform in Retrospect   75

    Ronald I. McKinnon

Comment   92

    Tibor Scitovsky

Part II   Alternatives to Domestic Financial Intermediation

5. Capital Markets in the Less Developed Countries:
   The Group Principle   97

    Nathaniel H. Leff

Comment   123

    Frank C. Child

6. International Financial Intermediation
   for Developing Countries   127

    Charles P. Kindleberger

Comment   138

    Hugh T. Patrick

7. Concepts, Causes, and Cures of Instability
   in Less Developed Countries   143

    David C. Cole

Comment   172

    Charles R. Blitzer

Part III   Inflation and Deflation: The Short-Run Dynamics

8. Some Dynamic Aspects of the Welfare Cost
   of Inflationary Finance   177

    Jacob A. Frenkel

Comment 196
John L. Scadding

9. Two Approaches to Ending Inflation 199
Basant K. Kapur

Comment 222
Joseph J. Bisignano

Part IV Aspects of International Economic Integration

10. Some Policy Implications of Foreign
Capital Flows in Certain Developing Countries 227
Richard T. Stillson

Comment 251

Walter S. Salant

11. Trade Credit and Other Forms of Inside Money 259
Arthur B. Laffer

Comment 277
Donald J. Mathieson

12. International Financial Integration:
Long-Run Policy Implications 281
Michael G. Porter

Comment 298
Harry G. Johnson

13. Coordination of European Macroeconomic Policies 303
Donald R. Hodgman

Comment 319
Edward J. Ray

Author Index 323
Subject Index 327

CONTRIBUTORS

JOSEPH J. BISIGNANO, Federal Reserve Bank of San Francisco, San Francisco, California.

CHARLES R. BLITZER, International Bank for Reconstruction and Development, Development Research Center, Washington, D.C.

STEPHEN A. BUSER, Department of Finance, Ohio State University, Columbus, Ohio.

FRANK C. CHILD, Department of Economics, University of California at Davis, Davis, California.

DAVID C. COLE, Harvard Institute for International Development, Harvard University, Cambridge, Massachusetts.

JACOB A. FRENKEL, Department of Economics, University of Chicago, Chicago, Illinois; and Department of Economics, Tel-Aviv University, Tel-Aviv, Israel.

CLAUDIO GONZALEZ-VEGA, Department of Economics, Stanford University, Stanford, California; and Department of Economics, University of Costa Rica, San José, Costa Rica.

DONALD R. HODGMAN, Department of Economics, University of Illinois, Urbana, Illinois.

HARRY G. JOHNSON, Department of Economics, University of Chicago, Chicago, Illinois.

BASANT K. KAPUR, Department of Economics, University of Singapore, Republic of Singapore.

CHARLES P. KINDLEBERGER, Department of Economics, Massachusetts Institute of Technology, Cambridge, Massachusetts.

ARTHUR B. LAFFER, Graduate School of Business, University of Chicago, Chicago, Illinois.

NATHANIEL H. LEFF, Graduate School of Business, Columbia University, New York, New York.

DONALD J. MATHIESON, International Monetary Fund, Washington, D.C.

RONALD I. McKINNON, Center for Research in Economic Growth, Stanford University, Stanford, California.

HUGH T. PATRICK, Department of Economics, Yale University, New Haven, Connecticut.

MICHAEL G. PORTER,* Department of Economics, Australian National University, Canberra, Australia.

EDWARD J. RAY, Department of Economics, Ohio State University, Columbus, Ohio.

CLARK W. REYNOLDS, Food Research Institute, Stanford University, Stanford, California.

WALTER S. SALANT, The Brookings Institution, Washington, D.C.

JOHN L. SCADDING, Council of Economic Advisers, Washington, D.C.

TIBOR SCITOVSKY, Department of Economics, Stanford University, Stanford, California.

RICHARD T. STILLSON, International Monetary Fund, Washington, D.C.

LEWIS J. SPELLMAN, Department of Finance, University of Texas at Austin, Austin, Texas.

ROBERT C. VOGEL, Department of Economics, Southern Illinois University, Carbondale, Illinois.

---

*Present address: Department of Economics, Monash University, Clayton, Australia.

Chapter 1

Introduction

RONALD I. McKINNON

Center for Research in Economic Growth
Stanford University
Stanford, California

Edward Shaw's views on money and finance—as best reflected in *Money, Income, and Monetary Policy* (1950), *Money in a Theory of Finance* (with J. G. Gurley) 1960, and *Financial Deepening in Economic Development* 1973—have significantly influenced economic thinking while never being really fashionable. Shaw was very early concerned that, in attempting to stabilize nominal rates of interest, the Federal Reserve Bank introduced pronounced cyclical fluctuations into the money supply. He argued vigorously that the cycles in output, unemployment, and inflation, experienced in the postwar period were not wholly endogenous, but reflected unstable American monetary policy. Yet during the 1950s, such views on monetary theory and policy were eclipsed by the Keynesian revolution in income-expenditure theory that emphasized the importance of fine tuning the economy through fiscal policy.

When monetarism, emanating chiefly from the University of Chicago, became generally recognized in scholarly writings in the mid-1960s, its theoretical structure differed from Shaw's although its stress on the importance of stabilizing short-run monetary policy was similar. Eminent Chicago economists such as Milton Friedman, Harry Johnson, and Robert Mundell adhered to a "wealth view" of money, where real cash balances competed with physical capital in the portfolios of wealthholders over prolonged periods of time, an approach to long-run monetary theory also espoused by neo-Keynesians such as James Robin. In effect, this view generated a second-best justification for inflation as means of encouraging new investment because continuous price inflation reduces the perceived yields on money so as to induce private wealthholders to acquire real assets instead of cash balances. In addition, if at least a portion of this unlegislated inflation tax is collected by governments, they may be trusted to spend the proceeds for real capital formation. To be sure, writers in the Chicago tradition—although not so much in the Keynesian—stress the substantial inefficiencies resulting from distorting the payments mechanism by using inflation to stimulate real investment.

An alternative to this generally accepted wealth view of money is what Shaw calls the debt-intermediation view. In recognizing the importance of money as a means of payment, numeraire, and store of value, Shaw holds that real cash balances are a debt, i.e., liabilities of the banks, associated with real capital accumulation on the asset side of the economy's aggregate balance sheet. Hence, he holds that real cash balances are not a distinct form of wealthholding apart from physical capital, but rather are a portion of the debt arising out of the process of capital accumulation itself. This debt-intermediation view of money implies that capital markets can operate at optimum efficiency only if the monetary system is fully deployed as a financial intermediary between savers and investors—a point that seems obvious in less developed countries where commercial banks may be the sole "organized" capital market, and only slightly less obvious in advanced countries. The liabilities of the monetary system are peculiarly attractive to small savers but serve everybody as an important repository for savings that can, and should, be transmuted into productive new investment. Hence, the neoclassical and neo-Keynesian view that considers money to be kind of a liquidity trap that inhibits investment is rejected by Shaw.

Do such conceptual differences in matters of theory have policy implications? After all, Chicago monetarists, with Shaw, stress the importance of stabilizing short-run monetary policy as measured by the growth of monetary aggregates. Both schools of thought are in favor of price stability in the long run as a first-best economic policy. However, Shaw's debt-intermediation approach is more irreconcilably opposed to prolonged price inflation (induced by expansion in the nominal stock of money) as a device for stimulating capital formation, output, and employment. On the one hand, prolonged price inflation (with the intent of extracting an inflation tax by maintaining ceilings on nominal deposit rates of interest) typically reduces the size of real cash balances relative to gross national product, thereby constricting capital accumulation via bank intermediation. On the other hand, Shaw would suggest that high inflation is necessarily uncertain inflation, and primary securities markets themselves become disorganized, particularly at longer term, in an inflationary environment. (In the neoclassical world, in contrast, there is a "perfect" capital market in primary securities that equates all yields on nonmonetary assets—suitably discounted for "objective" risk—irrespective of events occurring in the monetary sector.) Because of this disruption in both the monetary and nonmonetary means of finance, Shaw rules out even a second-best argument for stimulating investment and employment through inflation.

While Shaw has thus managed over most of forty years to stay intellectually out of step with mainline theory developed in the context of advanced industrial economies, he never even received the correct marching orders in what every economist should know about less developed countries—despite innumerable visits and advisory missions to Africa, Asia, and Latin America.

He remained a steadfast free trader during the postwar boom in "Third World" countries of forced draft industralization through restraining manufactured imports by tariffs, quotas, foreign-exchange restrictions, and so on. Concomittantly, he opposed turning the terms of trade against agriculture to extract an "economic surplus" by involuntary nonfinancial means. More generally, he resisted the introduction of detailed fiscal and budgetary planning techniques to substitute for decentralized financial processes in allocating his clients investable capital—whether such capital resulted from domestic saving or from foreign aid. From the beginning, he viewed input-output, linear, and dynamic programming techniques with gentle skepticism to be used by younger colleagues mainly in scholarly pursuits.

On the positive side, Shaw pushed hard for the development of an efficient *domestic* capital market in all but the tiniest less developed countries. He believes that savings can be coaxed from rural and urban households by a healthy financial system providing liquid assets at attractive real yields, and that expropriation of rural income by fiscal or other means is undesirable. The wherewithal to pay this reward to savers, small and large, can come from aggressive lending to farmers of all classes, and to urban entrepreneurs, at high market rates of interest reflecting the prevailing scarcity of capital. He opposed interest ceilings and other measures to reduce the price of capital to favored investors (including the government) that in turn reduced the yield to small savers—advice not likely to win many popularity contests. Indeed, he considers uniformly high real interest rates on financial assets and high real yields on physical assets to be a *sine qua non* of a successful development policy.

In completing this circle, Shaw's debt-intermediation view of money is crucial. In most less developed countries, money (broadly defined to include saving deposits as well as currency and demand deposits) might well be the only marketable financial asset because of its peculiarly attractive liquidity properties in an otherwise uncertain world. In less developed countries, therefore, Shaw is even more opposed to using an inflation tax that saps the lending capacity of the banking system. Concomittantly, Shaw has always been very sympathetic to "informal" capital markets—rural cooperatives, money lenders, pawn brokers, trade credit, and so forth— that can be very important in the early stages of development, but then fade naturally if a more competitive organized financial-banking sector is allowed to grow. Shaw considers much of foreign aid and other forms of international development assistance to be a rather poor substitute for a vigorous domestic capital market.

Organization: A Brief Reader's Guide

Let us now turn to the organization of the chapters in this volume. Rather than being a general *festschrift* in which a diverse set of papers is offered to the honored recipient, the focus here is much narrower. Indeed, the chapters contained herein were first presented to a conference held at Stanford University in April of 1974 on "Money and Finance in Economic Growth and Development." Hence most do build on, or are critical of, financial processes. The conference format has the additional advantage of providing a formal discussant for each chapter—a few of whom recorded some of the more general comments from the floor. While no attempt was made to transcribe all the proceedings, several of the authors used the general commentary in making their written revisions. Since analytical content is not always accurately predictable from the initial assignment of topics, I have taken the liberty in this book of regrouping the chapters somewhat differently from the order of presentation of papers at the conference.

Part I, "Money and Finance in Economic Development," contains three chapters that extend and formalize Shaw's work on domestic financial processes as they influence private propensities to save and invest.

Part II, "Alternatives to Domestic Financial Intermediation," contains three chapters that are more critical in the sense of not assigning the same primacy to organized finance based on the domestic monetary system that might be assigned by Shaw.

While Parts I and II deal mainly with longer-run financial policies in developing countries, *Part III*, "Inflation and Deflation: The Short-Run Dynamics," addresses the extremely important short-run problem of what happens at the time when deflation (a sharp reduction in the rate of experienced price inflation) is imposed by alternative policy measures.

Part IV, "Aspects of International Economic Integration," is less of a unified package, but these four chapters make a series of interesting points on how the international economy impinges on domestic fiscal and monetary policies.

Lewis Spellman's chapter, the first in Part I, portrays the macroeconomic impact of financial innovations in a one-sector economy in long-run growth equilibrium. In order to sharply focus the issues involved, he compares an economy completely dependent on self-finance—each saver acquiring physical assets and managing them directly—to the same economy that becomes fully financed where savers hold claims on a depository intermediary. This financial innovation permits two kinds of technical improvement. First, increased asset liquidity shifts the stock demand for wealth upward. Secondly, the improved investment allocation reduces dispersion in real yields and potentially raises the average yield seen by savers. In a "comment" that is virtually a chapter in itself, Claudio Gonzales-Vega shows the precise conditions under which this technical improvement on the investment allocation side will increase the long-run return to capital seen by holders of wealth. Both authors then analyze technical regression arising from the imposition of interest ceilings on the deposit or on the lending activities of the financial intermediaries.

The Vogel-Busser chapter looks more explicitly at the problem of optimum portfolio choice when capital markets are very imperfect. Indeed, in less developed countries where open primary securities markets may not exist, a reasonable abstraction is to assume that savers hold only money, productive physical assets, or inflation hedges—excess inventories of goods that are easily stored and that maintain their real value in an inflationary environment. The authors then examine the plausible conjunction of risk-return characteristics of these assets when money and productive physical capital are complementary: That is, reducing the rate of price inflation increases the flow of self-financed productive investment (apart from the increased availability of bank credit). The second part of their chapter uses Latin American data to test various facets of their provocative theoretical propositions on portfolio choice, although, unfortunately, one cannot distinguish inflation hedges from productive capital in the statistics on real investment.

In the last paper of Part I, McKinnon reviews the Korean monetary and saving experience during several years after a successful financial innovation occurred: the 1965 reforms that were strongly influenced by Edward Shaw's written reports and direct contacts with the Korean authorities in collaboration with David Cole, John Gurley, and Hugh Patrick. The unusually high real monetary growth from 1965 to 1972 is linked to the jump in the private domestic propensity to save; and the financial feasibility of further increases in private saving is also investigated. The difficult problem of controlling the monetary base after the reform is analyzed, and the influence that inflation has on shortening the term structure of finance is also discussed.

In Part II, Nathaniel Leff develops the "group principle" of repressed financial markets in less developed countreis. If price inflation, or usury restrictions, or both truncate the banking system and suppress primary securities markets, reversion to pure self-finance within individual small enterprises may be mitigated by the formation of large industrial conglomerates, i.e., groups, that can extract savings and allocate investments among their components. Aside from the adverse consequences for income distribution mentioned by the discussant, Frank Child, Leff analyzes the advantages and disadvantages of allowing such groups to substitute for an open capital market. Charles Kindleberger wonders if too much stress isn't being placed on domestic financial reforms when the international capital market may be available, whereas David Cole suggests that stability and growth from successful financial deepening as per Shaw may be swamped in less developed economies by other sources of instability.

In Part III, some readers may find the chapters by Frenkel and Kapur on the short-run dynamics of inflation more complex mathematically than the other contributions. Hence a reader's guide may be somewhat more in order if only because those authors take such different approaches to the same basic problem: the fairly immediate welfare consequences of slowing down or speeding up the rate of price inflation. Since some of the preceding chapters—and Shaw's own work on financial deepening—argue for a low or zero rate of price inflation to encourage real financial growth, what are the alternative economic strategies for bringing rampant inflation to a halt?

Jacob Frenkel's chapter is a nice, rather complete statement of the "wealth view" of deflating or inflating. Real cash balances bear zero nominal yield and compete with nonmonetary assets, which bear a uniform nominal rate of interest, in the portfolios of wealthholders. Price inflation is socially costly because it escalates nominal rates of interest on nonmonetary assets and hence reduces the real cash balances that individuals are willing to hold. The resulting decline in welfare is seen as an inverse function of the size of real case balances because of the reduced social efficiency in making *current* monetary transactions and the impaired standard-of-value function of money. However, Frenkel's chapter ignores the process of capital accumulation or decumulation itself, as it is directly influenced by the banks as financial intermediaries when real cash balances change due to inflationary pressure. Open markets in primary securities function independently of the rate of inflation, be it high or low. In these respects, Frenkel ignores the debt-intermediation view of money in his formal theorizing—as do most economists.

In considering the short-run dynamics of deflating (or inflating), Frenkel explores the consequences of sharply reducing rate of monetary expansion μ. He defines money sufficiently narrowly that the nominal deposit rate of interest d is not a policy variable and is simply set at zero. Because individuals do not adjust their inflationary expectations downward and inflation does not cease immediately when μ is reduced, a reduction in real cash balances may occur when the rate of nominal monetary expansion falls—the well known "liquidity squeeze" associated with deflationary policies. An immediate loss in welfare ensues because of the impairment of the payments mechanism. It is not difficult to drop Frenkel's assumption of full employment and consider social losses in employment and output as money wages continue to rise in the face of reduced aggregate demand. Frenkel then suggests that these immediate welfare losses must be weighed against the longer-term welfare gains from moving to a lower inflation rate where real cash balances are larger. The mirror image of Frenkel's analysis suggests that there exist short-term gains from inflation that must be weighed against longer-term losses—a view that is strongly criticized by the discussant, John Scadding.

In contrast to Jacob Frenkel, Basant Kapur examines the problem of short-run deflation in the theoretical context of the debt-intermediation view and for an economy with imperfect capital markets—such as those in a typical less developed country. Past inflation in Kapur's economy has repressed the banking system as a financial intermediary, an effect accentuated by low official ceilings on both deposit and lending rates of interest that create excess demand for bank credit. In addition, inflation has eradicated open-market trading in primary securities so that self-finance within enterprises is the principal alternative to the banks. The long-run rates of productive capital accumulation and growth in real output are thereby reduced. The problem faced by the government, therefore, is to lower the long-run rate of inflation in order to move to a higher growth path without suffering the full consequences of a liquidity squeeze that reduces short-run output and employment. Since the banking system, even in its repressed state, is the principal source of finance for the net accumulation of working capital, including advance payments to workers in industrial enterprises, a liquidity squeeze from a curtailment of monetary growth and real bank credit will indeed reduce short-run output and employment.

Besides considering the need to reduce μ (the rate of nominal money expansion) as did Frenkel, Kapur puts much stress on increasing d (the nominal rate of interest on bank deposits) as an alternative means of deflating in the short run. In order for the banks to find the wherewithal to pay for a sharp increase in the returns to their depositors, an increase in d implies that the government must cease covering fiscal deficits by borrowing from the banks and that private recipients of bank credit pay market-clearing rates of interest—that is, a nominal rate of interest that reflects anticipated inflation inherited from the past. With these not insignificant reforms to support it, an increase in d then raises the demand for money in terms of goods and hence reduces short-run price inflation for any given μ or inherited set of inflationary expectations. Instead of a liquidity squeeze, however, the size of the banking system *expands* as both real cash balances (deposits) and real bank credit to rural and urban enterprises increase. Hence, the increased net accumulation of working capital allows more workers to be hired (and raw materials to be purchased) and potentially increases short-run employment and output that itself further reduces the rate of price inflation.

While more complex and subtle than the scenario described above, Kapur's analysis is a conscious attempt to formally model a monetary reform of the type that Shaw presided over in Korea in 1965. The issues involved are important in a world of high inflation if one can establish that there are inefficient and efficient ways of deflating according to the selection among the instruments of economic policy.

In Part IV, the chapter by Richard Stillson unearths an interesting fiscal problem in inflation control for those countries whose governments receive a high proportion of tax revenue or other budgetary support from abroad. Then, an aggregate balance between revenues and expenditures, or even a large budgetary surplus, may still lead to high domestic inflation associated with excessive monetary expansion. Stillson distinguishes between a domestic and a foreign budget in terms of sources of income and allocation of expenditures, and between tradable and nontradable producing sectors, in order to define the conditions under which a given fiscal policy may be judged inflationary or deflationary—issues that are further clarified by the discussant Walter Salant. Stillson then applies his accounting techniques to Indonesia, Jordan, and Oman.

The chapters by Arthur Laffer and Michael Porter both emphasize the endogenous character of the domestic supply of nominal money in fixed exchange-rate regimes. For Porter, full discretionary control over the nominal stock of money in an open economy implies that the government neither pegs the exchange rate nor has a separate target for the nominal rate of interest, which is determined in foreign capital markets in conjunction with expectations of future exchange-rate movements. For Laffer, even these strong conditions are insufficient to achieve firm control over the nominal stock of money. Deposits in foreign currency, and domestic-currency deposits in foreign banks, can substitute for domestic money as can a rather elastic supply of unutilized trade credit. In effect, "inside" money (to use Gurley-Shaw terminology), in Laffer's judgment, is now —uncomfortably enough—in such elastic supply that national or international monetary authorities can easily by stymied in exercising effective short-run monetary control. Donald Hodgman then reminds us of how difficult international policy coordination is to achieve—judging from the recent experience of the European Common Market.

In discussing Michael Porter's paper, Harry Johnson took extra time to pay tribute to Shaw for keeping the importance of financial intermediation based on the monetary system in sharp focus when prevailing formal theorizing—Keynesian or Monetarist—had virtually discarded it.

For financial help that made the conference possible, we are thankful for the efforts of Leland Prussia, William Hurst and John B. Ross of the Bank of America, and Alan Weeden of Weeden Associates. Stanford University provided agreeable conference facilities and Nellie Neil and Lillian Zabohon gave indispensable administrative support.

Part 1

**Money and Finance in
Economic Development**

Economic Growth and
Financial Intermediation

LEWIS J. SPELLMAN

Department of Finance
University of Texas at Austin
Austin, Texas

This chapter presents a macroeconomic growth model that exhibits many of the features of the Shavian models of *Money in a Theory of Finance* and *Financial Deepening in Economic Development*. The model analyzes the growth equilibrium of the investment share of output, the capital intensity, the interest rate, per capita output, and per capita consumption. In an extension it indicates how these variables are influenced by the introduction of a financial system.

The basic model is set out in Section I, it is solved in Section II, and the equilibrium values are analyzed in Section III. The financial system is added in Section IV and the aggregate effects of deposit and loan rate ceilings are discussed in Section V.

I. The Wealth Demand Model

This model will describe an economy that for the sake of simplicity, is assumed to produce a single homogeneous good. A part of the net output of this economy is consumed and a part of it is saved. The portion saved is then placed back into the production process by producers and constitutes net additions to the capital stock. All capital is thus self-employed by producers and the single form of wealth is the real capital stock. A monetary asset does not yet exist. These simplifying assumptions are made at this point in order to focus on the macroeconomic interrelationships. In later sections some of these assumptions will be altered.

The microeconomic technology is utilized efficiently by many atomistic producers and yields a macroeconomic production function in which net output Y is linear homogeneous in the two substitutable factors, capital and labor, K and L, respectively.

$$\lambda Y = Y(\lambda K, \lambda L) \tag{1}$$

The standard technological assumption of diminishing returns to each factor is made where the partial derivatives are

$$Y_K, Y_L > 0 \qquad Y_{KK}, Y_{LL} < 0 \tag{2}$$

In the case of a linear homogeneous technology the marginal products of capital and labor depend on the capital/labor ratio only

$$Y_K = Y_K(k) \qquad Y_L = Y_L(k) \tag{3}$$

where $Y_{Kk} < 0$ and $Y_{Lk} > 0$.
The labor force is assumed to grow at the natural rate of growth n.

$$\frac{\dot{L}}{L} = n \tag{4}$$

The labor force is inelastically supplied on the labor market and is thus fully employed at all times. Competition prevails and output is distributed according to the marginal contribution of each factor of production.

It is assumed that the demand for the capital stock by the community of private wealthowners depends on the rate of return to capital r and net real income Y

$$K = w(r, Y) \tag{5}$$

Furthermore it is assumed that the demand for capital is linear homogeneous in income and can be written

$$K = W(r)Y \qquad \infty > W_r > 0 \tag{6}$$

The desired stock of capital increases with capital's rate of return, which indicates that wealthowners accumulate capital relative to income as the incentive to hold capital increases.[1]

This aggregate demand for capital might also be viewed by wealthowners as the desired ratio of their stock of capital to their flow of income. This desired capital/income ratio is interest elastic.

$$\frac{K}{Y} = W(r) \tag{7}$$

Since at this point all capital in this economy is self-employed, the rate of return r may be considered either the marginal product of capital or

$$r = Y_K \tag{8}$$

an *average* rate of return for each capital intensity. Dispersion in yields is common where all physical capital is necessarily self-employed due to the absence of a financial system that would permit saving and investing to be specialized activities. The capital demand function then becomes

$$K = W(Y_K)Y \tag{6a}$$

II.   The Capital/Labor Ratio, the Investment Share of Output, and Per Capita Consumption

The simultaneous solution to the model is obtained in the following way. First we differentiate the production function and the capital demand function with respect to time.

$$\dot{Y} = Y_K\dot{K} + Y_L\dot{L} \tag{9}$$

$$\dot{K} = W(Y_K)\dot{Y} + YW_r\dot{Y}_K \tag{10}$$

If we substitute (9) into (10) and solve for $\dot{K}$ we derive a simultaneous solution for net capital accumulation.

$$\dot{K} = \frac{W(Y_K)Y_L}{1 - W(Y_K)Y_K}\dot{L} + \frac{YW_r}{1 - W(Y_K)Y_K}\dot{Y}_K \tag{11}$$

The capital growth process thus involves parameters reflecting wealth preferences and the technology, and it is solved in terms of the exogenous growth in the labor force and changes in the marginal product of capital. In equilibrium the capital/labor ratio is constant and thus the term reflecting changes in the marginal product becomes zero, as the marginal product of capital depends on the capital/labor ratio only. Hence in balanced growth capital accumulation is a multiple of the increase in the labor force.

$$\dot{K} = \frac{W(Y_K)Y_L}{1 - W(Y_K)Y_K}\dot{L} \tag{12}$$

When the growth rate of capital matches the natural growth rate of the labor force

$$\frac{\dot{K}}{K} = \frac{\dot{L}}{L} \quad \text{or} \quad k = \frac{K}{L} \tag{13}$$

where k is the capital/labor ratio or what is commonly called the capital intensity. Hence from (12) and (13) the equilibrium capital intensity is

$$k = \frac{W(Y_K)Y_L}{1 - W(Y_K)Y_K} \tag{14}$$

With natural growth rates of inputs along with a linear homogeneous technology, the economic system produces natural growth rates of output as well.

Once the model has been solved for k, it is then possible to solve for the investment share of output i in terms of k and n. The equilibrium investment share is simply derived from (12) by dividing through by Y.

$$i = \frac{I}{Y} = \frac{W(Y_K)Y_L}{[1 - W(Y_K)Y_K] Y(K,L)} \dot{L} \tag{15}$$

By factoring L from the production function (which is permissible with a linear homogeneous production function) and substituting the value n for the population growth rate, the investment share becomes a function of n and k only.

$$i(n,k) = \frac{n[W(Y_K(k)) Y_L(k)]}{[1 - W(Y_K(k))] Y(k,1)} \tag{16}$$

Per capita consumption c in steady-state growth is simply derived from per capita output $Y(k,1)$ less steady state per capita investment requirements nk.[2]

$$c(n,k) = Y(k,1) - nk \tag{17}$$

A Diagrammatic Solution of the Model

A diagrammatic interpretation of the model can be seen in Fig. 1. Equations (1) and (6) are represented by what is labeled the T curve and the W curve, respectively.

The T curve represents the rate of return yielded by the production function for each K/Y ratio.[3] The W curve indicates the community's desired capital holdings relative to income (or output) at successive rates of return to capital. The intersection indicates the single capital-output ratio for which the technology generates a sufficient rate of return to satisfy the tastes of wealth-owners. Since the capital intensity is monotonically related to the marginal product by Eq. (3) this intersection determines the capital intensity as well.

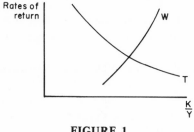

FIGURE 1

III. Analysis of the Model

A. Saving Behavior

The equilibrium values of k, i, r, and c are rooted in the structural saving behavior. The structural saving equation was obtained by differentiating the demand for capital, Eq. (6), with respect to time

$$\dot{K} = W(Y_K)\dot{Y} + YW_r\dot{Y}_K \tag{10}$$

and the wealthowner's desired saving proportion from current income s can be deduced simply by dividing (10) by Y.

$$s = \frac{\dot{K}}{Y} = W(Y_K)\frac{\dot{Y}}{Y} + W_r\dot{Y}_K \tag{18}$$

The desired saving proportion is thus a function whose parameters derive in turn from the parameters of the wealth demand function, $W(Y_K)$. In equilibrium growth, where $\dot{Y}_K = 0$, the desired saving proportion simply depends on the desired capital/income ratio $W(K_K)$ times the rate of growth of income.

$$s = W(Y_K)\frac{\dot{Y}}{Y} \tag{19}$$

For example if the desired capital/income ratio $W(Y_K)$ were equal to 3, an income growth rate of 3 percent would result in a 9 percent desired saving proportion, a 2 percent income growth rate would result in a 6 percent desired saving proportion, etc. Thus any factor that would cause a spurt in the rate of income growth will also tend to increase the desired saving proportion as wealthowners strive to maintain their wealth portfolios in proportion to higher income levels. This saving rate reaction to income growth has especially been noted by McKinnon [10], as producing a self-reinforcing effect in economic development.

The role of interest rates in stimulating saving rates has long been a question in economic theory. In this model the rate of return to capital influences desired saving proportions both by its level as well as changes in its level. *High* rates of return on capital produce large desired capital/income ratios. *Increasing* rates of return also have a positive effect on the desired saving proportion, as the W_r term is positive. Thus both high (low) and rising (falling) rates of return due to a capital scarcity (abundance) stimulate (depress) the desired saving proportion. Hence the interest rate provides an equilibrating mechanism for capital growth in the model.

This model is also useful in analyzing shifts in the underlying functions that are common in economic development. For example a rightward shift in the W curve, the demand for capital, would increase desired saving proportions due to an increase in the desired capital/income ratio $W(r)$.

Technical changes perhaps due to a "green revolution" represented by a rightward shift in the T curve would also raise the desired saving proportion by increasing the marginal product of capital and by increasing the income growth rate, and hence technical change stimulates desired saving proportions both through a rate effect as well as an income effect.

B.   Population Growth and the Capital Intensity

It should be noted that the equilibrium capital intensity given by Eq. (14) depends on wealth demands and the technology and is independent of the population growth rate. As a result the model has the property that for any two economies that possess the same technologies and the same predilections to accumulate capital, we would find the same equilibrium capital intensity and the same equilibrium real interest rate. Thus we have a growth analog to the static Fisherian system in which the capital intensity and interest rate are determined by productivity and thrift alone.

In order for the capital intensity and interest rate to be independent of the population growth rate, the investment share of income as seen by Eq. (16) needs to be directly proportional to the population growth rate. As a result, if population growth rates were to increase and if all members of society were to maintain the same capital endowments, the investment share would have to increase in proportion to population growth rates. The converse is of course also true and, if a stationary population were to emerge, the capital intensity would be maintained, as the (net) investment share of output would fall to zero. Thus the independence of the capital intensity and interest rate from population growth rates is due to the responsiveness of the investment share to population growth rates.

The mechanism that causes these adjustments to take place is somewhat indirect. An increase in the population growth rate increases the amount of labor relative to capital and thus lowers the capital intensity and hence raises the rate of return to wealth. As noted above, the high and rising rate of return increases desired saving proportions.[4]

The policy implication for an economy that behaved in this manner is clear. Population control would not influence the capital intensity, the interest rate, or per capita output; whereas, in direct contrast, policies to increase desired capital/income ratios relative to the rate of interest would increase the capital intensity, the investment share, and would—during a transitory period—raise the income growth rate from one steady-state growth path to another. Thus in economies described by this model, the centerpiece of economic policy would be measures to shift the W curve by stimulating wealthowning.

IV. Capital Accumulation Through a Financial System

The model presented in Section I must be interpreted as self-financed production since wealthowners directly utilize capital in production and earn capital's marginal product. The model of completely self-financed production could be usefully contrasted to a model of completely financed production. If production were undertaken by firms that borrow real physical capital, this capital would be transferred from surplus to deficit units on financial markets. Knowledge of the precise financial intermediary channel for connecting surplus and deficit units along with its accompanying financial institutions, financial instruments, and financial markets is less significant than noting the fact that every financial intermediary channel, whether direct or indirect, uses real factor inputs and incurs real factor costs.[5] These real factor costs per unit of capital will be denoted by c.

When savings are placed in a financial intermediary that invests this capital with deficit units, the financial system achieves a separation of the ownership and the use of capital. Presumably this process, which Gurley and Shaw [4] have termed "intermediary effects," allocates capital resources to earn an average yield much higher than under self-finance. This financial intermediation raises the marginal product of capital for each capital intensity. The marginal product of capital when investment is "financed" is shown in Fig. 2 and is labeled Y_K^f. It is contrasted to the marginal product under self-finance Y_K^s, previously called the T curve.

Where financial intermediation is performed by a depository financial institution and where the sector is sufficiently competitive so that there are no monopoly profits in financial intermediation, the wealthowners rate of return is given by

$$r = Y_K^f - c \tag{20}$$

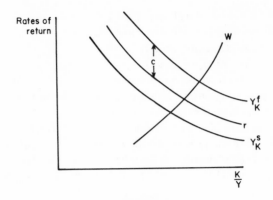

FIGURE 2

where r is now a deposit rate, Y^f_K is the marginal product of capital of the financed economy, and c, as previously noted, is the real unit cost of finance per period. In Fig. 2 the unit financial costs are the difference between the marginal product of capital and the deposit rate, as in Eq. (20).

The solution to the model for the capital intensity and the investment share could be analyzed through equations analogous to Eqs. (1) and (5) by the substitution of the new wealth demand curve and the new production function.[6] Diagrammatically, the solution is seen as the intersection of the r and W curves of Fig. 2.

From this figure it is clear that the more efficient the financial intermediary in terms of lower unit financial costs, the higher will be the r curve and the greater will be the equilibrium capital intensity. Further real effects on the capital intensity will also be felt, as in the previous section, if the financial system is able to achieve a rightward shift in the W curve, as compared to wealth demands under self-finance. Such an increase in the capital intensity rests on the presumption that the financial system is able, through specialized financial instruments, to provide a more desirable form of wealthowning as compared to self-employment of capital and that wealthowners respond to these incentives by permanent shifts in the desired $W(r)$ ratios. Financial intermediaries have been especially touted in this regard by Gurley and Shaw as stimulating saving rates by offering a risk diversified, liquid asset tailored to the needs of wealthowners.

In summary, the financial system can influence the capital intensity and output by achieving an allocation of capital resources that places productive resources with the most efficient producers and thus alters the aggregate production function of the economy. An efficient financial system will produce financial services at low unit financial costs and will tend to raise the capital intensity. Finally, the financial system with more desirable features or services will raise the desired wealth/income ratio and increase the capitalization and output of the economy.

V.   Financial and Economic Repression from Deposit and Loan Rate Ceilings

It is a simple extension of the framework to analyze the real economic and financial impacts from an imposed loan or deposit rate ceiling. Both cases are contained in Fig. 3. If a loan rate ceiling is imposed at the rate level r_1, the intermediary must cover its unit costs and is then only able to pay a deposit rate of r_2. At this deposit rate the financial sector will only attract a capital/income ratio of K/Y_1. Since the intermediary must charge r_1 for its capital, there is an excess demand for capital by firms. This capital must then be rationed by the financial intermediary. If the amount of capital K/Y_1 is available for investment and it is allocated to its highest use it will earn a marginal product equal to r_3, for which firms pay r_1 and the differential would accrue to the firm. This differential would no doubt give rise to efforts on the part of firms to secure the rationed capital, as it could be usefully employed for all projects for which the marginal productivity exceeds or is equal to r_1. Thus loan rate ceilings not only cause an undercapitalization, but also present the possibility of a misallocation of scarce capital.

For the deposit rate ceiling imposed at r_2 this rate would again only attract a deposit/income ratio of K/Y_1. As before, this amount of capital would be allocated to firms and with no loan rate ceiling, the intermediary

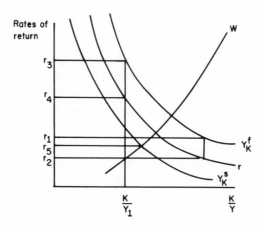

FIGURE 3

could charge r_3 and earn r_4 after its financial costs are covered. Thus the financial firm could possibly earn economic profits amounting to the difference between r_4 and r_2. The disposition of this surplus could take many forms. If competition prevails among intermediaries, it is possible that this surplus could be expended for demand-increasing costs such as advertising, or for excessively lavish bank buildings, or it could be paid to depositors in ancillary financial services.

In summary, both cases of rate ceilings are similar in that they tend to result in a lower deposit rate, a shrunken financial system, a lower capital intensity, and an increased rate spread between capital's marginal product in production and the real deposit rates paid to wealthowners. Hence, as deposit rates do not accurately reflect the scarcity of capital, a state of undercapitalization prevails in the economy.

It should also be noted that the result, particularly for the case of the loan rate ceiling, is decidedly the converse of what one with Keynesian reflexes would anticipate. Depressed loan rates due to a ceiling are *not* consistent with a high capital intensity and a high investment level.

In addition to a low capital intensity, another far-reaching impact of deposit and loan rate ceilings might occur. If the rate of return received by wealthowners is less than what they could earn under self-finance, one might expect not only a shrinkage of the financial sector, but a return to self-financed production techniques. Incentives for the return to self-financed investment would exist when the intersection of Y_K^s and the W curve produces rates of return greater than the regulated yield to depositors in financial intermediaries, as, for example, in Fig. 3. This return to self-finance would partially mitigate the adverse economic effects of repressing the financial system.

NOTES

1. This derivative indicates that for a sufficiently large number of wealthowners, the intertemporal allocation of their income exhibits a stronger substitution effect than income effect due to an increase in capital's rate of return.

2. The derivation of steady state per capita consumption has been derived by Phelps [12].

3. The T curve is constructed from the production function. Since the production function is linear homogeneous, we can divide through both sides of the equation by K to obtain the output/capital ratio.

$$\frac{Y}{K} = Y\left(1, \frac{L}{K}\right) = Y\left(1, \frac{1}{k}\right)$$

Thus each capital/output ratio corresponds to a capital/labor ratio.

$$\frac{K}{Y} = \frac{1}{Y(1, l/k)}$$

With the linear homogeneous technology, the level of the marginal product of capital also corresponds to the level of the capital/labor ratio as expressed in Eq. (3). Thus the T curve is a locus of points each of which corresponds to a capital/labor ratio. From the above it can be seen that as the capital/labor ratio increases, this corresponds to a higher capital/output ratio and a lower marginal product of capital. Thus the T curve has a negative slope. Since each point on the T curve corresponds to a capital/labor ratio, the intersection of the T curve and the W curve also determines the system's equilibrium capital intensity.

4. This behavior is in direct contrast to the fixed saving proportion models where saving rates are inflexible with respect to the interest rate and where investment shares are inflexibly responsive to population growth. In a fixed-saving share model, rates of return do not matter and the population growth rate affects the capital intensity and interest rate. For a more detailed explanation of this see Spellman [14].

5. The derivation of capital and labor allocations to financial intermediation are worked out in greater detail by Spellman [16].

6. This solution is analyzed by Spellman [16].

REFERENCES

1. Andrew F. Brimmer, "Central Banking and Economic Development," *Journal of Money, Credit, and Banking,* **3**, 4, November 1971, pp. 780-792.

2. Milton Friedman, "Government Revenue from Inflation," *Journal of Political Economy,* **79**, 4 (July/August 1971), pp. 846-856.

3. John G. Gurley, "The Savings-Investment Process and the Market for Loanable Funds," in L. Ritter (ed.), *Money and Economic Activity,* 3rd edition, Houghton Mifflin, Boston, 1967, pp. 50-55.

4. John G. Gurley, and Edward S. Shaw, *Money in a Theory of Finance,* Brookings Institution, Washington, D.C., 1960, pp. xiv, 371.

5. John G. Gurley, "Financial Aspects of Economic Development," *American Economic Review,* **45**, September 1955, pp. 515-538.

6. John G. Gurley, "Financial Intermediaries and the Savings-Investment Process," *The Journal of Finance,* **9**, May 1956, pp. 257-276.

7. John G. Gurley, "The Growth of Debt and Money in the United States: A Suggested Interpretation," *The Review of Economics and Statistics,* August 1957.

8. John G. Gurley, "Financial Structure and Economic Development," *Economic Development and Cultural Change,* **15**, 3, April 1967, pp. 257-268.

9. Harry G. Johnson, "Inside Money, Outside Money, Income, Wealth and Welfare in Monetary Theory," *Journal of Money, Credit, and Banking,* **1**, February, 1969, pp. 30-45.

10. Ronald I. McKinnon, *Money, Capital and Economic Development,* The Brookings Institution, Washington, D.C., 1973, Chap. 9, p. 320.

11. Ronald I. McKinnon, "Money, Growth, and the Propensity to Save: An Iconoclastic View," in G. Horwich and P. Samuelson, Eds., *Trade, Stability and Macroeconomics: Essays in Honor of Lloyd A. Metzler,* Academic Press, New York, 1974, pp. 487-502.

12. Edmund S. Phelps, *Golden Rules of Economic Growth: Studies of Efficient and Optimal Investment,* Norton, New York, 1966, pp. xv, 189.

13. Edward S. Shaw, *Financial Deepening in Economic Development,* Oxford, New York, 1973.

14. Lewis Spellman, *Fixed and Flexible Savings Shares in Economic Growth,* Working Paper 72-37, Bureau of Business Research, Graduate School of Business, University of Texas at Austin, 1972.

15. Lewis Spellman, "A Financial System," *Financial Structure and Economic Output,* Working Paper 73-41, Bureau of Business Research, The University of Texas at Austin, June, 1973.

16. Lewis Spellman, *Finance As An Industry: A Simple Model of Growth,* Ph.D. Dissertation, Stanford University, 1971.

17. James, Tobin, "Notes on Optimal Monetary Growth," *Journal of Political Economy,* **76**, July/August 1968, pp. 833-859.

Comment

CLAUDIO GONZALEZ-VEGA

Department of Economics
Stanford University
Stanford, California

and

Department of Economics
University of Costa Rica
San José, Costa Rica

Lewis J. Spellman's chapter is very ambitious. It contains a neoclassical one-sector growth model with a mechanism of adjustment that, based on wealth demands, permits the endogenous determination of the savings ratio. It discusses the impact of financial intermediation on the steady-state growth configuration of the system, and it examines some of the consequences of ceilings imposed on rates of interest.

Spellman has managed to include in his chapter a large number of Edward S. Shaw's contributions and, for that reason, it is most welcome. In order to cover so many aspects, however, he has been forced to leave out some key pieces of the argument. Also, assumptions introduced in some sections of the chapter are not necessarily consistent with the results obtained in others. Some of these problems are discussed here, and possible ways to overcome the deficiencies are indicated.

I.   The Basic Model

The model contained in the first section of Spellman's chapter is another attempt to deal with the "completely arbitrary and theoretically indefensible assumption of a fixed savings ratio, an analytical relic of naive Keynesianism," as Harry G. Johnson called it in 1966 [1]. Then, Johnson assumed that the average individual saves from current income a constant fraction of the difference between his desired and his actual capital stock over and above what must be saved to maintain the current capital/income ratio.[1]

In contrast, Spellman postulates, following the Shaw tradition, that the desire to accumulate wealth is a function of the rate of interest (the rate of return on capital); but he leaves the speed at which the savings ratio changes —in order to eliminate the discrepancies between the desired and the actual capital/output ratios—unspecified.

One important result of Spellman's model is that the equilibrium labor/capital ratio is independent of the rate of growth of the labor force and of the steady-state rate of growth of the economy.[2] In this model, the interaction of the production function and of the wealth-demand function determines the marginal productivity of capital. This equilibrium marginal productivity of capital is consistent with only one labor/capital ratio, independent of the rate of growth of the labor force. The savings ratio, instead, adjusts to changes in this rate of growth.

These results, illustrated in Fig. 1, explicitly represent the simultaneous satisfaction of the two conditions of equilibrium in Spellman's model: (a) the

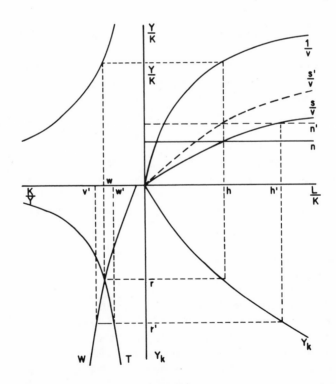

FIGURE 1

equality of the desired and the actual capital/output ratios, and (b) the equality of the rates of growth of the labor force and of the capital stock.

The production function $1/v$ is depicted in the first quadrant of Fig. 1 as the average productivity of capital Y/K, for every labor/capital ratio L/K. The rate of growth of the stock of capital is given by s/v, and the rate of growth of the labor force is given by n; the technique employed is well known [2]. In the second quadrant, a rectangular hyperbola is used to transform the average productivity of capital Y/K into its inverse, the capital/output ratio K/Y.

The third quadrant contains (a) Spellman's wealth-demand function W and (b) Spellman's production function T. The W function relates the desired capital/output ratios w to the marginal productivity of capital Y_k.

The T function has been derived from the first and the fourth quadrants as a technological relationship between the marginal productivity of capital and the capital/output ratio v or, indirectly, as a relationship between the former and the inverse of the latter, i.e., the average productivity of capital. The fourth quadrant relates the marginal productivity of capital and the labor/capital ratio.

The equilibrium marginal productivity of capital r is determined by the intersection of the W and the T curves and it is consistent with only one labor/capital ratio h, independently of the rate of growth of the labor force. Steady-state equilibrium is given, in turn, by the intersection of the n and the s/v curves. The savings ratio s is thus endogenously determined.

In this model, if the rate of growth of the labor force increases to n', the labor/capital ratio would tend to increase to h' and the marginal productivity of capital would tend to increase to r'. The desired capital/output ratio w' would be higher than the actual capital/output ratio v'. The savings ratio has to increase to s' in order to close this gap.

In the new position of equilibrium, given by the intersection of the n' and s'/v curves, the labor/capital ratio h is the same as before the change in the rate of growth of the labor force. It will remain at that same level as long as the W and the T curves do not shift.

II. Consumption Per Capita and the Rate of Growth of the Labor Force

The policy implications of Spellman's model are that population control would not influence the capital intensity of the economy, the interest rate, or per capita output. Instead, policies that affect the desired capital/output ratios are recommended. Although these results very usefully highlight the importance of financial policies, particularly in terms of their impact on the wealth-demand function, some qualifications are necessary.

One limitation of Spellman's analysis is that the wealth-demand function is not explicitly derived from the maximizing behavior of individual units. Saving and asset accumulation, however, are not undertaken for their own sake but, mostly for the sake of future consumption.

Aggregate wealth-demand functions derived from the optimization of consumption per capita over time may be dependent on the rate of growth of the labor force [3, 4, 5].[3] In this cases, the capital intensity of the economy is not independent of the rate of growth of the labor force. Changes in this rate would affect the position of Spellman's W curve and therefore affect the equilibrium level of the labor/capital ratio. A policy of population control could then be used to affect the capital intensity of the economy.

More importantly, even under the specifications of Spellman's model, the rate of growth of the labor force affects a more interesting magnitude from the point of view of policy: consumption per capita.[4]

In this model, a shift in the rate of growth of the labor force to a new, permanently higher, level does not induce a change in output per capita, even though it also increases the savings ratio.[5] Since neither the equilibrium labor/capital ratio nor the equilibrium output/capital ratio are affected by the change in the rate of growth of the labor force, it is not possible for output per capita to change. The greater number of workers will merely produce, combining labor and capital in the same proportion as before, the same output per worker.

Consumption per capita, however, necessarily falls. Since output per capita has not changed and, since a higher proportion of output per capita is saved, consumption per capita has to decline. As new workers, that are not equipped with capital, are added to the labor force at a greater speed than before, it becomes necessary to consume less and to save more in order to provide these additional workers with the same amount of capital as the old workers.

Formally, this result can be derived from the relationship: $c(n,k) = Y/L - nk$.[6] Neither output per capita Y/L nor the capital/labor ratio k changes as the rate of growth of the labor force increases. As a result, consumption per capita c declines. A policy of population control, therefore, could be used, even under the conditions of Spellman's model, to affect consumption per capita.

III.   The Impact of Technological Progress

Spellman asserts that technological progress, perhaps due to a green revolution, shifts the production function T outward and so increases the savings ratio. This is not necessarily true. The impact of technological change on the savings ratio depends on the nature of that change. Actually, only one type of technological progress—labor saving in a Hicksian sense—unambiguously induces the impact on the rate of accumulation posited by Spellman.

Changes in the production function that leave the competitive share of capital unchanged, for every labor/capital ratio, do not shift the T curve, since it is

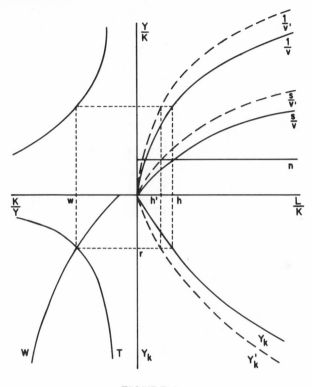

FIGURE 2

obvious that the area under the T curve is the share of income going to capital, rK/Y.

This result is illustrated in Fig. 2. When technological change is neutral in the Hicksian sense, the relationship between the marginal productivity of capital and the average productivity of capital remains unchanged. As a result, the T curve does not shift. The equation of the desired and the actual capital/output ratios determines the same equilibrium marginal productivity of capital r as before.

Neutral technological change, however, shifts the production function upward to $1/v'$ and it shifts the relationship between the marginal productivity of capital and the labor/capital ratio outward, to Y_k'. As a consequence, the equilibrium labor/capital ratio declines to h'. Since the changes in output per unit of capital and in savings per unit of capital are proportional, the savings ratio s remains unchanged.

When technological progress is labor saving in the Hicksian sense, the proportional increase in the marginal productivity of capital is higher than the proportional increase in the average productivity of capital for every labor/capital ratio. In Fig. 3, the proportional increase from $1/v$ to $1/v'$ is smaller

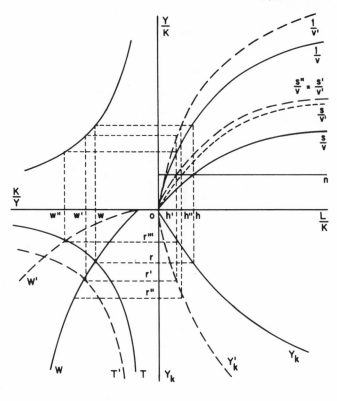

FIGURE 3

than the proportional increase from Y_k to Y_k'. As a consequence, the share of income going to capital increases and Spellman's T function shifts outward toward T'.

In the new position of equilibrium, the marginal productivity of capital r' is higher than before and, as a consequence of the shift of the Y_k curve, it is associated with a lower labor/capital ratio h'.

Furthermore, the condition for steady-state equilibrium requires that the savings ratio increase to s'. If the savings ratio remained constant, the intersection of the s/v' curve and the n curve would result in a labor/capital ratio h'' compatible only with a rate of return on capital r'' higher than the equilibrium marginal productivity of capital r'. Given this rate of return on capital, the desired capital/output ratio would be higher than the actual capital/output ratio. Therefore, the savings ratio has to increase to s', in order to close the gap. Steady-state equilibrium is thus given by the equation $n = s'/v'$.

Alternatively, when technological change is capital saving in the Hicksian sense, the T curve shifts inward, despite the fact that the $1/v$ curve and the Y_k curve shift outward. The equilibrium marginal productivity of capital declines and the labor/capital ratio declines, but not by as much as when technological change is labor saving, and the savings ratio also declines.

Harrod labor-augmenting technological change, on the other hand, shifts the T curve outward, if the elasticity of substitution is less than one; and it shifts the T curve inward, if the elasticity of substitution is greater than one.

IV.   The Impact of Financial Intermediation

Spellman extends his model to include financial intermediation. This transition presents some fundamental problems. His basic model belongs to the world of one-commodity asset, no risk, no uncertainty, no indivisibilities, and linear homogeneous production functions that characterize the wealth-view models that Shaw has criticized. According to Shaw, in these models there can be no money wealth unless the services of money generate a demand for it. However, services for money to perform cannot be detected in those regimes and rational bases for nonmonetary financial intermediation do not exist [6, 7].

Keeping this difficulty in mind, Spellman's model can still be used an an approximation to an economy where differences in individual production functions and in original endowments of capital and labor, combined with some form of market imperfection, indivisibility, transaction costs, or economies of scale, result in divergences among the individual rates of return on capital and create a role for financial intermediation.[7]

Spellman recognizes three impacts of financial intermediation: (a) a better allocation of investment (the allocation effect); (b) an increased desire to hold financial wealth per unit of output (the intermediation effect); and (c) a separation of the rate of return on capital earned by firms and the rate of deposit earned by the holders of financial assets (the cost effect). Each of these effects will be examined separately.

Spellman does not discuss the way in which the allocation effect shifts the aggregate production function (specifically, the $1/v$, the Y_k, and the T curves). The integration of the capital market, in fact, augments both the aggregate average and the aggregate marginal productivities of capital.[8]

Furthermore, for the T curve to shift outward, as Spellman posits, it is necessary that the proportional change in the marginal productivity of capital be higher than the proportional change in the average productivity of capital. This is precisely what happens when the impact of financial intermediation is to reallocate capital from units for which the marginal productivity of capital is low to units for which it is high.[9] That is, *the allocation effect of intermediation is equivalent to a labor-saving technological change.*

As shown in Fig. 3, if the allocation effect is considered independently, it shifts the T curve to T', the $1/v$ curve to $1/v'$, and the Y_k curve to Y_k'. This outward shift of the production function is a consequence of the greater efficiency induced by intermediation. As a result, the equilibrium marginal productivity of capital increases to r', the equilibrium labor/capital ratio declines to h', and the savings ratio increases to s'.

The impact of the intermediation effect—an increased demand for financial assets—shifts the W curve outward to W' in Fig. 3. Independently considered, this effect reduces the equilibrium labor/capital ratio from h to h' —and it reduces the equilibrium marginal productivity of capital from r to r'''—while it increases the savings ratio from s to s''.[10]

The impacts of the allocation effect and of the intermediation effect on the equilibrium labor/capital ratio (that declines) and on the savings ratio (that increases) reinforce each other. Their impacts on the equilibrium marginal productivity of capital, however, are opposite in direction.

If the intermediation effect dominates, the marginal productivity of capital declines. More likely, the allocation effect (net of the cost effect) will dominate and the rate of deposit paid to the holders of financial assets, and consequently the equilibrium marginal productivity of capital, will be higher than the rate of return on capital under conditions of self-finance.

When the cost effect is added, as shown in Fig. 4, equilibrium is given, not by the intersection of the W curve and the T curve, but by the intersection of the W curve and the $(T - c)$ curve, which indicates the rate of deposit that can be paid to holders of financial assets for each capital/output ratio.

As a consequence of the cost of intermediation, the equilibrium marginal productivity of capital increases, but the rate of deposit paid to the holders of financial assets declines. The equilibrium labor/capital ratio increases and the savings ratio declines.

The likely combined impact of the three effects is to increase the equilibrium marginal productivity of capital, to reduce the equilibrium labor/capital ratio, and to increase the savings ratio.

V. The Impact of Interest Rate Ceilings

Spellman uses his model to examine some of the effects of ceilings on deposit and loan rates of interest. The consequence of ceilings is to generate an excess demand for credit, represented in this model as an excess of the actual capital/output ratio v' over the desired capital/output ratio w'.

That is, given the rate of deposit to be paid to the holders of financial assets d, they will save just enough, $s''Y$, to maintain the capital/output ratio

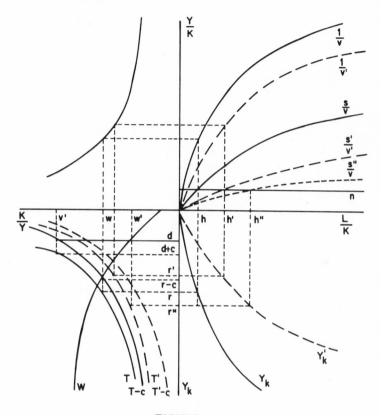

FIGURE 4

at the lower w' level, as shown in Fig. 4. At the same time, given the resulting cost of credit of $(d + c)$, investors can find profitable opportunities that imply a higher capital/output ratio v' and will demand credit accordingly. This discrepancy is solved through rationing.

Although the impact of interest rate ceilings depends on the type of rationing that is used to clear the market, Spellman does not explicitly consider alternative rationing mechanisms [8].

Two possible rationing mechanisms are: (a) to grant loans to some units and not to others, and (b) to grant loans to all units, but in proportion to the available funds.[11] In the latter case, individual demands for credit are only partially satisfied, while in the first case these demands are totally satisfied in the case of some units and not at all in the case of other units.

In the first case, for those privileged borrowers that receive all the credit that they demand at the loan rate of $(d + c)$, the labor/capital ratio declines, in view of the lower price of capital.[12] This result, called "Keynesian reflex" by Spellman, is not applicable to the whole economy, since one must also consider the capital intensity of projects not financed with credit. For those units that revert to self-finance, the labor/capital ratio increases. In the second case, all projects are partly self-financed and partly credit-financed.

In both cases, the aggregate labor/capital ratio increases to h', because the aggregate production function shifts downward to $1/v'$. There are also inward shifts toward T', toward $(T' - c)$, and toward Y_k', as shown in Fig. 4. This contraction occurs as the efficiency of the financial intermediation process is reduced, in view of the excess demands for credit generated and of the rationing and self-finance that accompany them.

Equilibrium is given by the intersection of the W curve and of the new $(T' - c)$ curve that represents a combination of credit and self-finance. The equilibrium marginal productivity of capital declines to r', the equilibrium labor/capital ratio in creases to h', and the savings ratio declines to s'. The amount of savings $s''Y$ is mobilized through the financial market, while the amount of savings $(s' - s'')Y$ is self-invested.

Contrary to what is assumed by Spellman, if the marginal productivity of capital under self-finance is higher than the ceiling imposed on the rate of deposit paid to the holders of financial assets (i.e., if the ceiling is effective), production will not be completely credit-financed, and self-finance has to be added to the model. The addition of self-finance somewhat reduces the negative impact of the ceiling, in comparison to Spellman's result for a model of completely credit-financed production.

Edward Shaw will probably regret the absence, in Spellman's analysis, of a market in which one could see the value of the privilege that loan officers have in rationing loans. This "charter" is valuable, while there may be an undercover market in which some of the excess demand for loans is dissipated by bribes [6].

Alternatively, Milton Friedman might claim that financial intermediaries would tend to increase the effective rate of deposit by several means, thus circumventing the ceiling [9]. This mechanism would increase the cost of intermediation and it would shift the $(T' - c)$ curve further inward. On the other hand, the additional services offered by intermediaries may increase the desire to hold wealth in the form of financial assets and the wealth-demand function would shift outward. This process could continue until the new W and $(T' - c)$ curves intersected at the level of the ceiling imposed on the rate of deposit.

Such developments would have a favorable impact on the allocation of resources. Actually, this effect would shift the $1/v'$ curve, the Y_k' curve, and the T' and $(T' - c)$ curves outward, but not to their original levels. This shift would limit, however, the increment in the labor/capital ratio and the reduction in the savings ratio. That is, successful attempts to circumvent interest-rate restrictions have a favorable impact on the allocation of resources and on the rate of capital accumulation.

NOTES

1. In an alternative approach, Johnson defined wealth in a broad sense, as the capitalized value of the productive services of both nonhuman and human wealth [1].

2. This result differs from the result of a neoclassical model with a fixed savings ratio, namely in that the labor/capital ratio increases as the rate of growth of the labor force increases. For the purposes of the figures, the capital intensity of the economy is represented by the labor/capital ratio h, which is the inverse of Spellman's capital/labor ratio k.

3. Cass and Yaari attempted to fuse the Modigliani-Brumberg life-cycle theory of savings into Solovian growth theory [3].

4. No optimization rule, equivalent to a golden rule, is explicitly presented in Spellman's paper. Presumably, policies designed to affect the wealth demand function could be used to move the system to a golden rule path of growth. This path would be characterized by the equation of the equilibrium marginal productivity of capital and the steady-state rate of growth of the system, that is, by the condition that $r = n = s/v$ [10].

5. In the Solow model, an increase in the rate of growth of the labor force increases the output/capital ratio and the labor/capital ratio and decreases output per capita. An increase in the savings ratio, on the other hand, decreases the output/capital ratio and the labor/capital ratio, while output per capita increases.

6. Eq. (17) in Spellman's chapter.

7. The role of intermediation is to facilitate the mobilization of resources from units for which the marginal productivity of capital is low to units for which it is high. Given the assumptions of a neoclassical steady-state one-sector model of growth, it is difficult to justify the differences in individual marginal productivities posited. On the other hand, the algebraic simplicity of the one-sector model has many advantages and the introduction of capital markets through the dispersion assumption turns out to be very fruitful.

8. With respect to individual units, the integration of the capital market increases the average and marginal productivities of capital in the case of surplus units and lowers them in the case of deficit units. The aggregate productivities increase, however, as a consequence of the gain in overall efficiency.

9. If the marginal productivity of capital is a decreasing function of the capital/labor ratio, as the capital/labor ratio changes it is mathematically inevitable that the proportional change in the average productivity of capital be smaller than the proportional change in the marginal productivity of capital. That is, $d(Y/K)/d(K/L) < d(Y_k)/d(K/L)$ if $Y_{kk} < 0$.

10. As shown in Fig. 3, a shift in the W curve that reduced the labor/ capital ratio to the same extent that a given shift in the T curve would, e.g. to h', would increase the savings ratio by more (from s to s'' instead of to s') because the production function does not shift as the W curve shifts and, as a consequence, output per capita does not increase by as much as with an equivalent shift in the T curve.

11. An alternative mechanism of rationing, a combination of these two is for the banks to supply only a proportion of the amount demanded on the basis of the different costs of administering different types of loans [8].

12. If a ceiling is imposed on the rate of deposit only, financial intermediaries could charge a loan rate as high as the marginal productivity of capital that corresponds to the capital/output ratio w', induce a reduction in the demand for credit, and earn a rent. Additional production would be self-financed.

REFERENCES

1. Harry G. Johnson, "The Neo-classical One-sector Growth Model: A Geometrical Exposition and Extension to a Monetary Economy," *Economica*, 33, 131, August 1966. Also, "Money in a Neo-classical One-sector Growth Model," *Essays in Monetary Economics*, Unwin and Brothers, London, 1967.

2. Robert M. Solow, *Growth Theory*, Oxford, New York, 1970.

3. David Cass and Menahem E. Yaari, "Individual Saving, Aggregate Capital Accumulation and Efficient Growth," in Karl Shell (ed.), *Essays on the Theory of Optimal Economic Growth*, MIT Press, Cambridge, 1967.

4. Miguel Sidrausky, "Inflation and Economic Growth," *Journal of Political Economy*, December 1967. Also "Rational Choice and Patterns of Growth in a Monetary Economy," *American Economic Review*, Papers and Proceedings, May 1967.

5. Henry Y. Wan, *Economic Growth*, Harcourt-Brace-Jovanovich, New York, 1971.

6. Edward S. Shaw, *Financial Deepening in Economic Development*, Oxford, New York, 1973.

7. Ronald I. McKinnon, *Money and Capital in Economic Development*, Brookings Institution, Washington, D.C., 1973.

8. Claudio Gonzalez-Vega, *The Iron Law of Interest Rate Restrictions*, Ph.D. dissertation, Stanford University, 1975.

9. Milton Friedman, *The Optimum Quantity of Money and Other Essays*, Aldine, Chicago, 1969, p. 38.

10. Edmund S. Phelps, *Golden Rules of Economic Growth*, Norton, New York, 1966.

Chapter 3

Inflation, Financial Repression, and Capital Formation in Latin America

ROBERT C. VOGEL

Department of Economics
Southern Illinois University
Carbondale, Illinois

STEPHEN A. BUSER

Department of Finance
Ohio State University
Colombus, Ohio

In their recent works McKinnon [1] and Shaw [2] challenge the traditional view adopted by such economists as Tobin [3], Johnson [4], and Levarhi and Patinkin [5] that money and capital are substitutes in the portfolios of private wealthholders and in the aggregate economy. In rejecting the traditional view, the two authors propose and defend the thesis that money and capital are likely to be complements in less developed, fragmented economies where the financial sector has been severely repressed due to explicit government policy. As McKinnon and Shaw note, policymakers in less developed countries typically offer a myriad of reasons for disregarding prices and intervening directly in financial markets in an attempt to "improve" the allocation of resources. This intervention generally takes the form of controls over interest rates, which reduce the rates of return on financial assets (thus depressing saving and capital formation), and which also increase the demand for loans (leading to some form of rationing to allocate among investment projects).

Both McKinnon [1, Ch. 7] and Shaw [2, Chs. 4 and 6] also emphasize the intimacy of the relationship between financial repression and inflation. Since deposit and loan rates are set in nominal terms, any appreciable rate of inflation can readily make real rates of interest on loans and real rates of return on financial assets negative. Johnson [6] had previously identified two major evils of inflation in less developed countries: (1) a high rate of inflation appears to lead inevitably to a highly variable rate of inflation, making it impossible for economic agents to anticipate and to adjust adequately to inflation, and (2) other prices, as well as interest rates, are likely to be controlled, so

that inflation leads to distortions in the allocation of resources, and higher
rates of inflation to greater distortions.[1] It remained for McKinnon and Shaw,
by elucidating the importance of the real size of the financial sector for the
process of capital accumulation, to identify a third adverse impact of inflation
on economic development. In less developed countries, where the market for
primary securities is likely to be underdeveloped, the role of indirect financial
assets (especially the liabilities of the monetary system) is particularly important in promoting capital formation, so that the results of financial repression
augmented by inflation are likely to be particularly severe.

The present chapter extends the thesis of complementarity between
money and capital by analyzing the influences of both risk and return in the
process of portfolio selection. In addition to examining the behavior of individual portfolios, some of the specifically macroeconomic implications of
financial repression and liberalization discussed by McKinnon and Shaw are
extended in the first section of the chapter. In the second section the relationships between inflation and financial repression, and between real financial
growth and capital accumulation, are examined empirically for a sample of
16 Latin American countries over the period 1950-1971.

I.   Risk, Return, and the Complementarity Hypothesis

Money and capital cannot be complements when they are the only two assets
held in the portfolio and when the constraint on total assets is fixed.[2] Thus,
it is not surprising that the complementarity hypothesis has been overlooked
in growth models where money is grafted onto the economy as the second
of only two assets.[3] However, the consideration of additional classes of assets
introduces the possibility of limited complementarity. For McKinnon
and Shaw, the additional assets considered are stores of goods or finished inventories labeled as inflation hedges.[4] Both authors argue that self-financed
investment projects are apt to dominate the process of capital formation in
less developed, fragmented economies where the financial sector has been
severely repressed. Under this "regime of self-finance" the prior accumulation
of stocks of money and/or inflation hedges is a necessary precondition for
investment whenever the scale of an investment project exceeds the resources
provided by current income flows. Given the appropriate time lag, one
should thus expect to find strong complementarity between money and
capital, and/or between inflation hedges and capital, with strong substitutability
between money and inflation hedges.

McKinnon and Shaw reinforce the complementarity hypothesis by establishing a direct relationship between the demand for money and the total asset
constraint. Shaw focuses on the relationship between increased holdings of

bank deposits and the flow of credit, while McKinnon considers the effect of the portion of seigniorage from currency issue that the government returns to the private sector via transfer payments. Both authors also argue in support of a number of indirect links between money and the constraint on total assets, such as the effects of changes in the availability and scale of financing, the method of project selection, and so forth, on the rate of return on investments and hence on saving.

McKinnon and Shaw defend the complementarity hypothesis admirably within the context of a single-parameter (expected value) analysis. However, the complementarity issue can be broadened and extended by considering the effects of risk as well as return within the context of a two-parameter (mean and standard deviation) portfolio model. Even the concept of financial repression itself has a broader meaning within this context. For McKinnon and Shaw the term "financial repression" means that the real rate of return on money is suppressed (the nominal deposit rate is decreased relative to the rate of inflation), but repression can also take the form of increased riskiness of the return on money (increased variability of the deposit rate and/or the rate of inflation). Given this interpretation, financial liberalization can mean either raising the real rate of return on money (e.g., Korea) or stabilizing the rate at some (perhaps low) level (e.g., Brazil). In this section, the two forms of repression are examined independently. For each form of repression, both the direct effects on capital formation and the indirect effects, via other parameters in the model, are analyzed. However, as is shown in the second part of the chapter, both forms of repression typically occur together, so that the separate effects explored in Theorems 1 through 5 are often reinforcing.

A standard result in the mean and standard deviation portfolio model is that, in general, the demand for any one asset depends on the mean and standard deviation of the return on each asset, and on the covariance between the returns on each pair of assets in the portfolio. Thus, for any wealth-holder, the optimal investment in capital K, inflation hedges H, money M, or any other asset in the portfolio depends on:

γ The expected real rate of return on money (which depends positively on the nominal deposit rate and negatively on the expected rate of inflation)

r The expected real rate of return on capital

θ The expected real rate of return on inflation hedges

$\sigma_M, \sigma_K, \sigma_H$ The standard deviations of the real rates of return on money, capital, and inflation hedges, respectively

$\sigma_{MK}, \sigma_{MH}, \sigma_{HK}$ The covariances between the real rates of return on money and capital, money and inflation hedges, and inflation hedges and capital, respectively

In general, the absolute level of the demand for any asset also depends on the investor's preferences for risk and return, but under suitable conditions the optimal relative mix of nonmonetary assets is independent of the investor's preferences for risk and return. This "separation property" of portfolio theory has been demonstrated by Tobin [10] and Lintner [11] in the restricted case where money is assumed to be riskless. However, the separation property holds more generally, as illustrated in Fig. 1, for the case where $\gamma < \theta < r$ and $\sigma_M < \sigma_H < \sigma_K,$[5] and where some but not all of available wealth is held in the form of money.[6]

If points B and C represent portfolios consisting entirely of inflation hedges and capital, respectively, then the line BC represents the set of portfolios generated by combining varying proportions of inflation hedges and capital but excluding money. A movement toward (away from) C reflects an increase (decrease) in capital's share in the mix of nonmonetary assets. If point A represents a portfolio consisting entirely of money, then each dotted line from A to a point on BC represents the set of portfolios generated by combining, in varying proportions, money and the fixed-proportion mixture of capital and inflation hedges determined by the position of the end point of the dotted line on BC. A movement along any one of these dotted lines toward (away from) BC reflects an increase (decrease) in the allocation to nonmonetary assets.

The collection of all such dotted lines traces out the set of feasible combinations of risk and return. The portion of the efficient frontier of this set, which corresponds to positive monetary holdings ($M > 0$), is represented

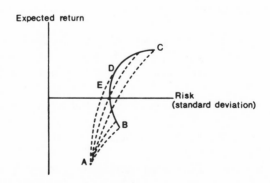

FIGURE 1

by the dotted line AD, which is tangent to BC. Point E, which corresponds to the optimal portfolio, depends on the investor's preferences and can lie anywhere along the efficient frontier ADC, but whenever money is held in the portfolio, E is restricted to AD. By construction, all points on AD represent portfolios with the same relative mix of nonmonetary assets. This mix is determined by the position of D along BC and is independent of the investor's preferences for risk and return, thus confirming (for $M > 0$) the generalized separation property.

Capital's share α of the total investment in all nonmonetary assets N is defined as $\alpha \equiv K/N$. Accordingly, any change in the demand for capital can be expressed as a change in capital's share, with a fixed investment in all nonmonetary assets, and/or a change in the scale of investment in all non-monetary assets, with capital's share remaining fixed:

$$dK = N \, d\alpha \; + \; \alpha \, dN \tag{1}$$

Since any change in the scale of investment in all nonmonetary assets must equal the change in total assets minus the change in money, Eq. (1) can also be expressed as:

$$dK = N \, d\alpha \; + \; \alpha(dV \, - \, dM) \tag{2}$$

where

$$V \equiv M + N$$

By virtue of the generalized separation property, the change in capital's share in response to a change in any of the parameters can be determined on purely technical grounds and is reflected graphically by a movement of the point of tangency D along the curve BC. The change in the scale of invest-ment in all nonmonetary assets in response to a parameter change is reflected by a movement of point E along the efficient frontier ADC, but the direction of this movement cannot be determined without knowing the investor's preferences for risk and return. The following theorems give the necessary and sufficient conditions for determining the combined share and scale effects on the demand for capital when each of five repression-related variables is changed. The first two theorems examine the direct effects of financial re-pression and liberalization, that is, the impact of changes in γ and σ_M on the demand for capital. Theorems 3, 4, and 5, respectively, examine the indirect effects of repression and liberalization through changes in r, σ_K, and V.

A.   Complementarity Via the Expected Real Rate
of Return on Money

THEOREM 1: *Ceteris paribus,* the demand for capital is positively (negatively) related to the expected real rate of return on money whenever the ratio of nonmonetary to monetary assets is greater (less) than the ratio of the elasticities of money and capital's share, each with respect to the expected real rate of return on money.

Proof: On the basis of Eq. (2), the response of the demand for capital to a change in γ, with all other parameters held constant, is given by:

$$\frac{\partial K}{\partial \gamma} = N \frac{\partial \alpha}{\partial \gamma} - \alpha \frac{\partial M}{\partial \gamma} \tag{3}$$

As shown in Fig. 2, capital's share is positively related to γ (for $M > 0$). As γ increases, point A moves to A', and the line AD becomes $A'D$. If AD is tangent to BC at D, then the slope of $A'D$ must be less than the slope of BC at D. Hence the tangency between BC and the new set of lines from A' to BC must be at some point D' above D. Accordingly, the new efficient frontier is $A'D'C$, and (for $M > 0$) the movement from D to D' implies an increase in capital's share. Dividing each term in Eq. (3) by M $\partial\alpha/\partial\gamma > 0$ produces the desired result:

$$\frac{\partial K}{\partial \gamma} \gtreqless 0 \quad <=> \quad \frac{N}{M} \gtreqless \frac{\xi_\gamma^M}{\xi_\gamma^\alpha} \tag{4}$$

where

$$\xi_\gamma^M \equiv \frac{\partial M/M}{\partial \gamma/\gamma} \quad \text{and} \quad \xi_\gamma^\alpha \equiv \frac{\partial \alpha/\alpha}{\partial \gamma/\gamma}$$

are, respectively, the elasticities of money and capital's share with respect to γ. As indicated in Fig. 2, the elasticity of capital's share ξ_γ^α is necessarily

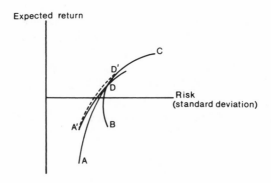

FIGURE 2

positive (for $M > 0$); and, except when money is an inferior asset with respect to its own rate of return, the elasticity of money ξ_γ^M is also positive. Thus, the shift between monetary and nonmonetary assets typically works against the change in capital's share (the ratio of the two elasticities is positive), and the net effect on the demand for capital depends on the relative magnitudes of the two ratios in Eq. (4). The ratio of nonmonetary to monetary assets N/M provides an intuitive index of the extent of financial repression. The more severely repressed the financial sector, the greater should be the ratio of nonmonetary to monetary assets. Equation 4 shows that, *ceteris paribus*, the positive relationship between the demand for capital and γ predicted by the complementarity hypothesis is more likely to hold: (1) the greater is the index of financial repression N/M; (2) the more responsive is capital's share to γ; and (3) the less responsive is money to γ.

It should be noted that condition 3, as well as condition 1, may be related to the extent of financial repression. For lower levels of γ, a decrease in risk aversion may be more likely to accompany an increase in portfolio return, that is, individuals made wealthier by an increase in γ may become less averse to risk and may therefore shift increasingly into riskier nonmonetary assets. Such an effect would reduce the elasticity of money ξ_γ^M and might even make money an inferior asset. In this extreme case the effects of changes in capital's share and in the scale of nonmonetary assets are reinforcing (the ratio of the two elasticities is negative), and the positive relationship between the demand for capital and γ is assured. Theorem 1 can thus be interpreted as supporting the McKinnon-Shaw hypothesis, and the likelihood of complementarity increases with the degree of financial repression.

B.   Complementarity Via the Variability of the Real Rate of Return on Money

THEOREM 2: *Ceteris paribus,* the demand for capital is negatively (positively) related to the standard deviation of the real rate of return on money whenever the ratio of nonmonetary to monetary assets is greater (less) than the ratio of the elasticities of money and capital's share, each with respect to the standard deviation of the real rate of return on money.

Proof: On the basis of Eq. (2), the response of the demand for capital to a change in σ_M, with all other parameters held constant, is given by:

$$\frac{\partial K}{\partial \sigma_M} = N \frac{\partial \alpha}{\partial \sigma_M} - \alpha \frac{\partial M}{\partial \sigma_M} \tag{5}$$

As shown in Fig. 3, capital's share is inversely related to σ_M (for $M > 0$).

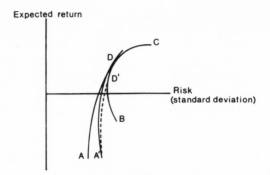

FIGURE 3

As σ_M increases, point A moves to A' and the line AD becomes $A'D$. If AD is tangent to BC at D, then the slope of $A'D$ must be greater than the slope of BC at D. Accordingly, the new tangency must be at some point D' below D on the new efficient frontier, $A'D'C$, and (for $M > 0$) the movement from D to D' implies a decrease in capital's share. Dividing each term in Eq. (5) by $M\ \partial\alpha/\partial\sigma_M < 0$ produces the desired result:

$$\frac{\partial K}{\partial\sigma_M} \gtreqless 0 \quad <=> \quad \frac{N}{M} \gtreqless \frac{\xi^M_{\sigma_M}}{\xi^\alpha_{\sigma_M}} \tag{6}$$

where

$$\xi^M_{\sigma_M} \equiv \frac{\partial M/M}{\partial\sigma_M/\sigma_M} \quad \text{and} \quad \xi^\alpha_{\sigma_M} \equiv \frac{\partial\alpha/\alpha}{\partial\sigma_M/\sigma_M}$$

are respectively, the elasticities of money and capital's share with respect to σ_M.

The McKinnon-Shaw complementarity hypothesis as extended in the present study predicts that in financially repressed economies the demand for capital will be inversely related to σ_M. Equation 6 shows that this inverse relationship holds whenever the index of financial repression N/M is large relative to the ratio of the two elasticities. As indicated in Fig. 3, the elasticity of capital's share $\xi^\alpha_{\sigma_M}$ is necessarily negative (for $M > 0$); and, except when money is an inferior asset with respect to σ_M, the elasticity of money $\xi^M_{\sigma_M}$ is also negative. Thus the shift between monetary and nonmonetary assets typically works against the change in capital's share (the ratio of the two elasticities is positive), and the net effect on the demand for capital depends on the relative magnitudes of the two ratios in Eq. (6). *Ceteris paribus,* the inverse relationship between the demand for capital and σ_M is more likely to hold: (1) the greater is the index of financial repression N/M; (2) the more responsive is capital's share to σ_M; and (3) the less responsive is money to σ_M.

Condition 3, as well as condition 1, may be related to financial repression. To the extent that risk aversion increases with the level of risk (a relationship that may be intensified by financial repression), an increase in σ_M will tend to induce a shift into relatively safe monetary assets. In the extreme case, when money is an inferior asset with respect to σ_M, the effects of changes in the scale of nonmonetary assets and in capital's share are reinforcing (the ratio of the two elasticities is negative), and the inverse relationship between the demand for capital and σ_M is assured. Therefore, Theorem 2 can also be interpreted as supporting the extended McKinnon-Shaw hypothesis, and the likelihood of complementarity increases with the degree of financial repression.

C. Complementarity Via the Expected Real Rate of Return on Capital

By disrupting intermediation, financial repression restricts the financing of individual investment projects; and, in the absence of a well developed market for primary securities, each individual is thus primarily limited to his own self-financed investment projects. By restricting the method of finance, repression biases investment against high-yielding, large-scale, and long-term projects, and away from new projects (many of which might have high rates of return) in favor of extensions of existing projects, even if these projects have low or negative rates of return. Financial repression is thus likely to have an adverse effect on the expected real rate of return on capital. Intuitively one would expect that the demand for capital will be positively related to its own expected real rate of return, and Theorem 3 demonstrates that this is true in all but extreme cases.

THEOREM 3: *Ceteris paribus,* the demand for capital is positively (negatively) related to its own expected real rate of return whenever the ratio of nonmonetary assets to monetary assets is greater (less) than the ratio of the elasticities of money and capital's share, each with respect to the expected real rate of return on capital.

Proof: Through a geometric analysis similar to that employed in Theorems 1 and 2, it can be shown that capital's share is positively related to r. Given this relationship, the desired result follows from a procedure analogous to that used in the preceding theorems:

$$\frac{\partial K}{\partial r} \gtreqless 0 \iff \frac{N}{M} \gtreqless \frac{\xi_r^M}{\xi_r^\alpha} \tag{7}$$

where

$$\xi_r^M \equiv \frac{\partial M/M}{\partial r/r} \quad \text{and} \quad \xi_r^\alpha \equiv \frac{\partial \alpha/\alpha}{\partial r/r}$$

are, respectively, the elasticities of money and capital's share with respect to r.

The elasticity of capital's share ξ_r^α is necessarily positive, but the elasticity of money ξ_r^M can be of either sign. However, the income effect of a change in r on the demand for money would have to be both positive and large to offset completely the negative substitution effect. Thus, the ratio of the two elasticities in Eq. (7) will typically be negative, and the positive relationship between the demand for capital and r will be assured. Moreover, even in extreme cases when ξ_r^M is positive, it must be large relative to ξ_r^α in order for the ratio of the elasticities to exceed the index of financial repression N/M and to reverse the positive relationship between the demand for capital and r. Theorem 3, like Theorems 1 and 2, generally supports the McKinnon-Shaw complementarity hypothesis, and the strength of this support again increases with the degree of financial repression, as measured by the ratio of nonmonetary to monetary assets.

D. Complementarity Via the Variability of the Real Rate of Return on Capital

Even in an economy dominated by self-finance, some investment projects will have a long duration. To the extent that repression interferes with the certainty of future means of finance, the risk associated with these long-term investment projects will be increased. Through this impact on the variability of the real rate of return on capital, financial repression can have a further effect on the demand for capital. The intuitive expectation is that the demand for capital will be negatively related to the variability of its own real rate of return, and Theorem 4 demonstrates that this is true in all but extreme cases.

THEOREM 4: *Ceteris paribus,* the demand for capital is negatively (positively) related to the standard deviation of its own real rate of return whenever the ratio of nonmonetary assets to monetary assets is greater (less) than the ratio of the elasticities of money and capital's share, each with respect to the standard deviation of the real rate of return on capital.

Both the proof and discussion of Theorem 4 are analogous to the preceding theorems and are therefore omitted. However, it should be noted that, like the preceding theorems, the support of Theorem 4 for the extended complementarity hypothesis increases with the severity of financial repression.

E.   Complementarity Via the Portfolio Constraint

In the traditional textbook approach, both money and debt intermediation play important roles in the economy by promoting efficient production and exchange and by smoothly channeling saving into investment. However, as McKinnon and Shaw point out, these roles are denied under the perfect-market assumptions pervading many of the existing models of money and growth. Shaw's debt-intermediation view rejects these perfect-market assumptions as particularly inappropriate for less developed countries and thus revives the traditional roles for money and debt. In Shaw's institutional environment, financial repression, by interfering with the monetary and debt intermediation processes, can increase transactions costs and reduce efficiency. As a result, the constraint governing both consumption and asset selection is tightened.

McKinnon and Shaw also argue that financial repression will reduce saving in favor of consumption, thus further tightening the constraint governing asset selection. This reduction in saving is due to the limitations on both the number and desirability of the alternatives to consumption. McKinnon and Shaw argue that in less developed countries nonmonetary financial assets and markets for primary securities are likely to be underdeveloped or entirely absent, so that the only options open to an individual for disposing of his income are his personal investment projects, increased holdings of nonproductive inflation hedges, increased holdings of money, and consumption. Under conditions of financial repression the real rate of return on money will be low and/or uncertain. The low expected return on money is the only factor that McKinnon and Shaw consider, but the uncertainty of this return is potentially an important factor as well. This extension of the complementarity hypothesis reflects the view that the consumption-saving decision involves a trade-off between certainty and uncertainty, as well as a trade-off between present and future. Theorem 5 shows that, except in extreme cases, a reduction in the demand for capital results from the tightening of the constraint governing asset selection.

THEOREM 5: *Ceteris paribus,* the demand for capital is positively (negatively) related to an increase in the asset constraint whenever the partial derivative of money with respect to the asset constraint is less (greater) than unity.

Proof: On the basis of Eq. (2), the response of the demand for capital to a change in the asset constraint, with all other parameters held constant, is given by:

$$\frac{\partial K}{\partial V} = N \frac{\partial \alpha}{\partial V} + \alpha \left(1 - \frac{\partial M}{\partial V} \right) \tag{8}$$

The desired result follows directly from Eq. (8), based on the standard result from portfolio theory that the relative shares of nonmonetary assets are independent of the scale of the portfolio ($\partial\alpha/\partial V = 0$).

$$\frac{\partial K}{\partial V} \gtreqless 0 \quad <=> \quad \frac{\partial M}{\partial V} \gtreqless 1 \tag{9}$$

Under the assumption that risk aversion is inversely related to wealth, an increase in wealth would tend to induce a shift out of relatively safe monetary assets. Moreover, even when risk aversion increases with wealth, the investor's preferences would have to change abruptly in response to an increase in the asset constraint before the increase in the demand for money could exceed the increase in V. Thus, a positive relationship between the demand for capital and the asset constraint can normally be expected, so that Theorem 5, like the preceding theorems, supports the McKinnon-Shaw complementarity hypothesis. In addition, Theorems 1 through 4 indicate that the likelihood of complementarity between money and capital increases with the severity of financial repression, as measured by the ratio of nonmonetary assets to monetary assets.

F.   Complementarity in the Aggregate Economy

In addition to reflecting the aggregate behavior of individual private wealth-holders, the accumulation of private capital in the economy as a whole involves a distinctly macroeconomic feature. The impact of changes in the asset constraint on the demand for capital is examined in Theorem 5 (following a discussion of some forces that could influence the asset constraint), but the analysis stops short of making this variable endogenous. The constraint governing total assets becomes an important endogenous variable at the aggregate level when two additional factors are considered. First, if the seigniorage from the issue of fiat money is returned to the private sector via transfer payments, as in the models of Tobin [3] and McKinnon [1], then increases in the real value of fiat money can augment disposable income and loosen the constraint on total assets. A more general assumption is adopted herein, that some portion t ($0 \leqslant t \leqslant 1$) of seigniorage is returned to the private sector. Second, and perhaps even more important from the standpoint of financial repression and liberalization, is the impact of increased bank deposits on the asset constraint. Under a fractional reserve system of banking, where bank credit is a function of private deposits and reserve ratios, an increase in bank deposits can lead to an increase in credit and an easing of the asset constraint.

To incorporate these distinctly macroeconomic elements, an adjustment must be made in the framework used in the microeconomic analysis. In

Theorems 1 through 5 it was assumed that only one form of money existed. While this assumption is convenient for the microeconomic analysis, it can be misleading at the macroeconomic level. Financial repression need not have the same impact on the demand for each form of money, and the different forms of money need not have identical impacts on the asset constraint (and hence on capital formation).[7] In fact, the concepts of financial repression and liberalization are no longer as well defined when more than one form of money exists. Currency has no deposit rate, and increased holdings of currency do not contribute directly to private financial intermediation. In addition, the deposit rates and reserve ratios for demand deposits and time and savings deposits are not necessarily the same, and these forms of deposits need not contribute equally to the process of private financial intermediation.

In order to incorporate these distinctions, changes in aggregate monetary holdings are separated into components:

$$dM = d\frac{CC}{P} + d\frac{DD}{P} + d\frac{TS}{P} \tag{10}$$

where

$$d\frac{CC}{P} \qquad d\frac{DD}{P} \qquad d\frac{TS}{P}$$

are, respectively, the changes in the real value of currency, demand deposits, and time and savings deposits.

If ρ_D and ρ_T are, respectively, the reserve ratios for demand deposits and time and savings deposits, then $t\,d(CC/P)$ represents the real value of seigniorage returned to the private sector, and $(1 - \rho_D)\,d(DD/P)$ and $(1 - \rho_T)\,d(TS/P)$ represent the real value of the credit flows generated by changes in holdings of demand deposits and time and savings deposits, respectively. Based on these monetary components, changes in the aggregate (private-nonbank) asset constraint resulting from saving, seigniorage, and credit flows can be expressed as follows:

$$dV = S + t\,d\frac{CC}{P} + (1 - \rho_D)\,d\frac{DD}{P} + (1 - \rho_T)\,d\frac{TS}{P} \tag{11}$$

where S is real current saving.

As in the microeconomic analysis, the accumulation of private capital at the aggregate level can be broken down into the change in capital's share in the mix of nonmonetary assets and/or the change in the scale of nonmonetary assets. Substituting for the change in the scale of nonmonetary assets, Eq. (11) minus Eq. (10), in the aggregate version of Eq. (2) yields the following expression for the aggregate accumulation of capital:

$$dK = N\,d\alpha + \alpha\left[S - (1 - t)\,d\frac{CC}{P} - \rho_D\,d\frac{DD}{P} - \rho_T\,d\frac{TS}{P}\right] \quad (12)$$

Equation (12) indicates that the aggregate accumulation of capital can be attributed to changes in any of five parameters. The effect of a change in capital's share α on capital formation can be viewed as essentially an aggregation of the microeconomic effects of financial repression and liberalization examined in Theorems 1 through 4. Similarly, the effect of saving can be viewed in part as an aggregation (over private wealthholders) of the various effects examined in Theorem 5. The effects of changes in the monetary variables embody the endogenous elements in the asset constraint, which become relevant at the aggregate level.

Due to the credit flows generated, an increase in bank deposits does not necessitate, for the economy as a whole, an equal reduction in the holdings of other assets. In contrast to the analysis based on individual portfolios, only that fraction of the increase in bank deposits that banks retain as reserves is competitive in the aggregate with nonmonetary assets.[8] The link between currency and the asset constraint, and hence between currency and capital formation, is through the portion of seigniorage returned to the private sector. To the extent that the portion of seigniorage returned is small ($t \simeq 0$), currency holdings will tend to be more competitive with the holding of non-monetary assets. However, as the portion increases, this competition decreases; and, in the limit where all seigniorage is returned ($t = 1$), increases in currency holdings need not constrict the holding of nonmonetary assets at all.

The fact that neither currency nor bank deposits are necessarily competitive with capital on a dollar for dollar basis at the aggregate level makes the conditions for complementarity at the aggregate level even less stringent than those derived on the basis of the analysis of individual portfolios. Moreover, high reserve requirements and the seigniorage retained by the government contribute to financial repression in two ways: (1) they reduce the rate of return on currency (if seigniorage can feasibly be returned to currency holders) and reduce the rates of return that banks can pay on deposits; and (2) they tighten the constraint on total assets.

II.   Inflation and Financial Repression in Latin America

According to Theorems 1 and 2, an increase in the expected real rate of return on money is likely to increase the demand for capital, while an increase in the variability of this return is likely to decrease the demand. Under a regime of financial repression, with controls over nominal rates of interest, an increase in the expected rate of inflation will have an adverse impact on the expected real rate of return on money. Moreover, to the extent that the rate of inflation and its variability are highly correlated, an increase in the rate of inflation will also tend to reduce the demand for capital through the impact of inflation on the variability of the real rate of return on money. Because of the link between inflation and financial repression, an increase in the rate of inflation will also tend to reduce the demand for capital through the indirect effects presented in Theorems 3 through 5 and in the discussion of complementarity in the aggregate.

Widespread controls over nominal rates of interest on loans and deposits, together with many instances of high rates of inflation, make Latin America an ideal place to examine the relationships among inflation, financial repression, and capital formation discussed in the preceding section. Latin American countries have provided McKinnon and Shaw with numerous examples of financial repression and its link with inflation. However, the empirical work in both McKinnon [1] and Shaw [2] is primarily illustrative, and econometric techniques have not been used to test rigorously the hypotheses suggested. Their examples of financial repression and financial reform have been selected to illustrate the relationships among inflation, financial growth, and economic development, and not to test if such relationships are general and widespread phenomena.

Other studies have estimated the impact of inflation on the demand for money in various Latin American countries, especially those countries with high rates of inflation.[9] The present study goes beyond these studies by differentiating among the demands for currency, demand deposits, and time and savings deposits because, as indicated in the preceding analysis, the demand for each form of money is likely to respond differently to inflation and to have different implications for capital formation. Because of the link between inflation and financial repression, the present study also estimates the impact of inflation on the share of investment in national income. Finally, the impact of financial repression and liberalization on the share of investment in national income is estimated on the basis of Eq. (12), with particular attention to the effects of changes in the real holdings of each form of money, reserve requirements, and the ratio of nonmonetary to monetary assets. In examining these relationships among inflation, the real size of the financial sector, and capital formation, the present study makes primary use of pooled regressions for 16 Latin American countries, but also uses time-series regressions for each country to test for homogeneity.

To provide as much comparability as possible among countries, all data used in the present study are taken from *International Financial Statistics.* The rate of inflation is measured by the consumer price index; real national income is nominal gross domestic product deflated by the consumer price index; and investment is gross fixed capital formation. The monetary variables are: currency outside banks, demand deposits at commercial banks, and time

and savings deposits at commercial banks.[10] The Latin American countries
included in the present study are those listed in Table 1, which also indicates
the time period covered (and hence the number of observations available) for
each of the 16 countries.[11] Deficiencies in data for less developed countries,
even data compiled by international organizations, are well known, so that the
usual warnings need not be repeated here.

Some tentative conclusions about inflation, financial repression, and
capital formation can be reached by examining the country averages presented
in Table 1. First, the myth that all countries in Latin America have been experiencing rampant inflation can be dispelled. The countries in Table 1 are
listed according to rates of inflation, from highest to lowest, and only 5 of
the 16 countries have had average rates of inflation greater than 25 percent
per year; four have had moderate inflation, between 4 and 10 percent per
year; and seven have had low inflation, less than 3 percent per year. The
standard deviation in the rate of inflation for each country shows, however,
that all countries have not had consistently high or low rates of inflation. For
example, Bolivia's rate of inflation dropped sharply after 1957, and Paraguay's
rate fell somewhat beginning in 1961. Uruguay, on the other hand, experienced substantial increases in its rate of inflation in 1958 and again in
1963, while the dramatic changes in Brazil's inflationary experience are well
known. However, once-and-for-all shifts in inflationary behavior cannot alone
explain the pattern that clearly emerges in Table 1: that countries with
higher rates of inflation have more variable rates of inflation. This pattern
strongly confirms the point made by Johnson, McKinnon, Shaw, and others
that high rates of inflation go hand-in-hand with uncertain rates of inflation,
with all the undesirable consequences of such uncertainty for financial
growth and the allocation of resources.

Table 1 also suggests that inflation may have some impact on real
financial growth and capital accumulation. Although growth rates of currency
in real terms are not appreciably different for the three groups of countries,
growth rates of real demand deposits and of real time and savings deposits are
highest for low-inflation countries (7.3 and 18.6 percent per year, respectively),
lowest for high-inflation countries (5.0 and 8.0 percent), and intermediate for
moderate-inflation countries (5.8 and 12.6 percent). Differences in financial
structure among the three groups are also evident. The ratio of currency to
demand deposits rises from the low inflation group to the high inflation group
(.98, 1.01, 1.66), while the ratio of time and savings deposits to demand
deposits falls (.78, .71, .70).[12] On the other hand, there seem to be no consistent differences among the three groups of countries in the share of investment in national income, although real investment appears to have grown more
rapidly in low- and moderate-inflation countries (7.5 and 6.9 percent, per year,
respectively) than in high-inflation countries (4.7 percent). Table 1 thus provides

TABLE 1

Inflation, Financial Growth, and Capital Formation in Latin America

	Rate of inflation[a]	Growth rates[a]						
		$\dfrac{CC}{DD}$	$\dfrac{TS}{DD}$	$\dfrac{CC}{P}$	$\dfrac{DD}{P}$	$\dfrac{TS}{P}$	$\dfrac{I}{P}$	$\dfrac{I}{Y}$
Uruguay	40.9	2.372	1.653	3.4	2.3	-3.7	1.2	.120
1957-71	(32.6)	(.589)	(.652)	(16.9)	(25.5)	(19.3)	(21.1)	(.024)
Brazil	36.2	.425	.132	-0.6	3.5	4.1	3.7	.161
1952-69	(21.0)	(.096)	(.075)	(7.2)	(11.2)	(41.9)	(12.9)	(.014)
Bolivia	35.8	3.797	.313	5.2	3.4	17.3	4.9	.149
1952-71	(52.7)	(1.051)	(.328)	(15.0)	(18.2)	(37.3)	(32.5)	(.027)
Chile	26.3	.699	.701	12.7	13.6	19.6	10.1	.144
1957-71	(11.4)	(.050)	(.156)	(19.8)	(21.7)	(23.1)	(14.3)	(.024)
Argentina	25.5	.986	.690	-0.2	2.1	2.9	3.6	.187
1952-70	(23.7)	(.122)	(.076)	(11.6)	(15.4)	(16.3)	(13.3)	(.017)
Colombia	9.4	.687	.271	5.9	8.2	9.4	8.0	.170
1952-69	(9.1)	(.083)	(.052)	(7.2)	(10.7)	(24.7)	(9.1)	(.014)
Peru	8.4	1.075	1.323	5.6	2.9	7.2	4.7	.193
1952-67	(3.2)	(.226)	(.414)	(4.6)	(8.3)	(11.0)	(14.0)	(.030)
Paraguay	8.0	1.421	.890	5.5	4.6	23.5	6.4	.143
1954-71	(8.1)	(.079)	(.757)	(7.7)	(10.1)	(27.5)	(23.2)	(.023)
Mexico	4.8	.858	.347	4.8	7.3	10.1	8.6	.162
1952-71	(4.5)	(.144)	(.072)	(5.9)	(8.1)	(9.5)	(11.2)	(.024)
Ecuador	2.9	1.014	.488	5.9	9.5	12.7	10.5	.134
1952-71	(2.8)	(.175)	(.088)	(7.9)	(9.2)	(10.9)	(14.3)	(.030)
Costa Rica	1.9	.724	.379	5.4	9.7	15.7	8.9	.196
1952-71	(1.8)	(.145)	(.079)	(6.3)	(12.1)	(20.5)	(11.4)	(.021)
Honduras	1.7	1.238	.910	4.5	5.7	17.6	6.5	.146
1952-71	(2.7)	(.214)	(.524)	(8.8)	(9.1)	(14.4)	(14.0)	(.022)
Nicaragua	1.6	.837	.335	2.7	4.8	27.5	5.2	.156
1955-69	(4.3)	(.158)	(.230)	(9.9)	(12.5)	(32.4)	(13.6)	(.020)
Venezuela	1.2	.604	.762	4.4	9.7	18.0	6.5	.223
1952-71	(2.1)	(.140)	(.230)	(5.2)	(13.2)	(18.7)	(12.8)	(.045)
Guatemala	0.6	1.526	1.072	4.1	7.3	18.4	7.5	.117
1952-71	(1.5)	(.418)	(.751)	(6.0)	(13.4)	(15.9)	(18.9)	(.023)
El Salvador	0.6	.946	1.514	2.7	4.3	20.2	7.5	.129
1960-71	(1.6)	(.129)	(.389)	(6.9)	(8.9)	(18.6)	(15.7)	(.017)

Note: Figures are averages for the period indicated for each country; standard deviations are given in parentheses. Inflation is measured by the consumer price index, *P*. *CC* is currency outside banks; *DD* is demand deposits at commercial banks; *TS* is time and savings deposits at commercial banks; *I* is gross fixed capital formation; and *Y* is gross domestic product.
[a]Percent per year.
Source: Ref. 35.

some evidence for the relationships suggested in the preceding theoretical analysis, but confirmation of these relationships, and in particular the links between real financial growth and capital formation, requires more rigorous statistical analysis.

A. Inflation and the Demand for Real Monetary Assets

This more rigorous analysis begins with regressions to estimate the impact of inflation on the real size of the financial sector. The equation used in these regressions is based on earlier studies of the demand for money and on the theoretical analysis in Section I of this chapter, that is, the demand for real balances is a function of the constraint on total assets, the expected yields on monetary assets and alternative assets, and the risk associated with each of these yields. The constraint on total assets is typically represented by real national income, and in the present analysis this is measured by real gross domestic product. Measures of yields on real assets are seldom available, and in the case of Latin American countries even yields on nonmonetary financial assets are largely unavailable because, as suggested above, the availability of such financial assets is highly restricted.

For 5 of the 16 countries in the study, no interest-rate data are included in *International Financial Statistics,* and for most of the remaining countries only the central bank discount rates are given. Widespread controls over nominal rates of interest in Latin American countries further limit the usefulness of even these published data. In particular, it is not clear whether an increase in the central bank discount rate indicates a movement toward financial liberalization or the imposition of a traditional stabilization program (resulting in increased financial repression), and whether an increase in the discount rate represents a relative increase or decrease in the yields on monetary versus nonmonetary assets.[13] The rate of inflation is thus the main observable variable that affects the yield on monetary assets relative to the yields on alternative assets. Moreover, because of the high correlation between the rate of inflation and its standard deviation shown in Table 1, the rate of inflation indicates not only the relative yield on monetary assets but also the risk associated with holding money.

Since expectations are not likely to be based entirely on the most recent experience (and adjustment may not be instantaneous), the demand for real balances will not in general depend only on current values of the rate of inflation and other independent variables. There are a number of procedures, generally involving lagged dependent variables and elaborate estimation techniques, for estimating such lags due to adjustment and the formation of expectations.[14] In the present study, however, the less complex approach of simply adding lagged independent variables proves to be feasible. The lags due to adjustment and the formation of expectations do not appear to be long (requiring independent variables for only the current and preceding year), and the use of pooled regressions provides 286 observations, so that multicolinearity and loss in degrees of freedom do not present serious problems.[15] The use of pooled regressions covering the 16 Latin American countries over the period 1950 through 1971 also offers an opportunity to test whether the relationships among inflation, the real size of the financial sector, and capital formation are homogeneous throughout Latin America. Although obvious differences among Latin American countries necessitate the introduction of dummy variables to allow for differing country intercepts, slope coefficients do not necessarily differ among countries, and individual country regressions are used to test whether countries respond homogeneously to the independent variables.[16]

The regression results presented in Table 2 show the impact of inflation on the real size of the financial sector. The dependent variables are limited to currency, demand deposits, and time and savings deposits because of the restricted availability of nonmonetary financial assets in Latin America, as well as the lack of comparable data on such assets for a sufficient number of countries. These dependent variables are expressed as ratios to gross domestic product because the real size of the financial sector is most appropriately measured relative to national income, and the use of ratios also facilitates the pooling of data among countries. Regressions using as dependent variables the ratios of currency and time and savings deposits to demand deposits are also reported in Table 2 to illustrate further the impact of inflation, although these results could be inferred from the other regressions. The rate of inflation, as indicated above, is the principal independent variable, and real gross domestic product is used to represent the constraint on total assets.[17] All variables are expressed as logarithms because this form provides better explanatory power and coefficients with higher significance levels than untransformed data, as well as yielding constant elasticities.

The R^2's for the regressions in Table 2 show that 78 to 94 percent of the variation in the real size of the financial sector is explained, and averaging the independent variables for the current and preceding year has no appreciable effect on this explanatory power.[18] Although much of the explanatory power is due to the dummy variables for individual country intercepts, both the rate of inflation and real gross domestic product have a highly significant impact on the real size of the financial sector. A higher rate of inflation significantly reduces the ratios of both currency and demand deposits to gross domestic product, although the coefficients indicate that the elasticities are quite low. On the other hand, the negative impact of inflation on the ratio of time and savings deposits to gross domestic product is not only highly significant but also approximately unit elastic.[19] These high levels of

TABLE 2

The Real Size of the Financial Sector as a Function of Inflation and Real Gross Domestic Product: Pooled Regressions for 16 Latin American Countries, 1950-1971

Dependent variable	Intercept	$\left(\dfrac{\Delta P}{P}\right)_t$	$\left(\dfrac{\Delta P}{P}\right)_{t-1}$	$\dfrac{\left(\dfrac{\Delta P}{P}\right)_t + \left(\dfrac{\Delta P}{P}\right)_{t-1}}{2}$
$\dfrac{CC}{Y}$	−.780	−.097** (3.9)	−.082** (3.8)	
$\dfrac{CC}{Y}$	−.738			−.162** (6.7)
$\dfrac{DD}{Y}$	−1.632	−.072* (2.4)	−.050 (1.9)	
$\dfrac{DD}{Y}$	−1.595			−.106** (3.5)
$\dfrac{TS}{Y}$	−4.784	−.518** (7.0)	−.463** (7.1)	
$\dfrac{TS}{Y}$	−4.618			−.958** (13.3)
$\dfrac{CC}{DD}$	.852	−.025 (1.0)	−.032 (1.5)	
$\dfrac{CC}{DD}$	.859			−.055* (2.3)
$\dfrac{TS}{DD}$	−3.156	−.446** (6.9)	−.413** (7.2)	
$\dfrac{TS}{DD}$	−3.026			−.852** (13.5)

Note: Each regression has 286 observations, and all variables are expressed as logarithms. CC is currency outside banks; DD is demand deposits at commercial banks; and TS is time and savings deposits at commercial banks. Y is gross domestic product; $\Delta P/P$ is the rate of inflation; and P is the consumer price index. Subscripts indicate current or lagged variables. Intercepts are averages of

$\left(\dfrac{Y}{P}\right)_t$	$\left(\dfrac{Y}{P}\right)_{t-1}$	$\dfrac{\left(\dfrac{Y}{P}\right)_t + \left(\dfrac{Y}{P}\right)_{t-1}}{2}$	R^2	S_e
−.557** (4.4)	.281* (2.2)		.79	.063
		−.293** (8.9)	.78	.064
−.276 (1.8)	.432** (2.7)		.89	.078
		.142** (3.5)	.89	.079
−.064 (0.2)	1.330** (3.4)		.81	.191
		1.190** (12.1)	.81	.190
−.273* (2.2)	−.159 (1.2)		.94	.063
		−.436** (13.4)	.94	.063
.219 (0.7)	.892** (2.6)		.82	.167
		1.050** (12.3)	.82	.166

the intercepts for individual countries. The t values are given in parentheses below each coefficient: those marked with one asterisk (*) are significant at the 5 percent level, and those marked with two asterisks (**) at the 1 percent level. R^2 and S_e are the multiple correlation coefficient and the standard error of the estimate.

significance confirm the contribution of inflation to financial repression, while
the low elasticities for currency and demand deposits (especially relative to
time and savings deposits) strongly support Shaw's view [2, pp. 84-85] that
financial repression may proceed to the point where the willingness to hold
those assets that are used for transactions purposes is no longer very responsive
to inflation, because of the high costs of reversion to barter.

The regressions in Table 2 also show that real currency holdings rise
somewhat less than proportionately and real demand deposits rise slightly more
than proportionately with increases in real gross domestic product, while the
increase in real holdings of time and savings deposits is substantially more than
proportionate. Because of the high degree of responsiveness to both the rate
of inflation and real gross domestic product, the role of time and savings
deposits in financial repression and liberalization is doubly important. If the
attempts of individuals to accumulate more real time and savings deposits in
response to a reduction in the rate of inflation result, as McKinnon and Shaw
suggest, in a higher rate of saving, which in turn results in a higher rate of
growth, then the demand for real time and savings deposits will be further
stimulated. The last four regressions in Table 2 illustrate the effects of inflation and growth on financial structure. Growth in real gross domestic product
decreases currency holdings and increases time and savings deposits relative to
demand deposits, while higher rates of inflation cause a substantial shift from
time and savings deposits to demand deposits and a slight shift from currency
holdings to demand deposits.

F-tests were run to determine if individual country regressions (in which
slope coefficients as well as intercepts are allowed to differ among countries)
significantly reduce the residual sums of squares compared to the pooled regressions with dummy variables (in which only the country intercepts are
allowed to differ). The F-ratios range from 4.9 to 17.3 for the various regressions in Table 2, and thus reveal significant heterogeneity in slope coefficients
among countries. In an earlier study by Hanson and Vogel [24, pp. 367-369],
slope coefficients did not differ significantly among countries when only
current and lagged rates of inflation were used as independent variables, but
significant differences among countries arose when real gross domestic product
per capita and the ratio of currency to currency plus demand deposits were
added as independent variables.[20] Thus, the heterogeneity of slope coefficients
in the present study seems more likely to result from differing responses to
changes in real gross domestic product than from differing responses to inflation.
In any event, it is not surprising to find heterogeneity among countries, given
that the specific nature of controls over interest rates and the financial sector
differs widely among Latin America countries.

B.   Inflation and Capital Formation

The preceding empirical analysis has shown that inflation significantly reduces the real size of the financial sector, and thereby makes a substantial contribution to financial repression, so that the logical next step is to estimate the impact of inflation on capital formation. Since capital stock data are non-existent in most Latin American countries, data on investment are used for these estimates. However, as McKinnon [25] points out, these investment data are likely to include not only investment undertaken for productive purposes, but also investment undertaken as a hedge against inflation. According to the hypothesis under examination, real financial assets are substitutes for inflation hedges and complements of productive investment, so that the impact of inflation and the real size of the financial sector on productive investment will be underestimated. Since inventories are likely to be particularly attractive as inflation hedges, the measure of investment used in the present study includes only gross fixed capital formation.

According to the complementarity hypothesis, inflation will reduce the demand for capital, especially under a regime of financial repression with controls over nominal rates of interest. However, to the extent that controls over nominal rates of interest are not completely effective (or the controls are changed in response to inflation), the link between inflation and financial repression will be weakened and the impact of inflation on the demand for capital will be reduced.[21]

To estimate the impact of inflation on the demand for capital, one might proceed as in estimating the demand for monetary assets and use the same equation as in Table 2. However, as previously mentioned, data on investment, rather than data on the capital stock, are available for these estimates. A lower expected rate of inflation implies, according to the complementarity hypothesis, a greater demand for capital, but investment will only be higher during the period of adjustment to the larger capital stock.[22] A higher level of investment will only continue after the capital stock adjusts to this new equilibrium if the expected rate of inflation continues to fall. Thus, it is not the expected rate of inflation, but the change in the expected rate of inflation that influences the equilibrium level of investment. However, it would be surprising if the link between expected and past *changes* in the rate of inflation were as close as the link between expected and past *levels* of the rate of inflation. As a result, changes in the rate of inflation may be largely unexpected, and the impact on investment of such unexpected changes is less clear.[23]

Various equations have been used in an attempt to detect any impact of inflation on investment resulting from either a new equilibrium level of

investment or the adjustment to a new equilibrium capital stock in response to
changes in inflationary behavior. In order to take into account the formation
of expectations as well as lags in adjustment, both levels and changes in the
rate of inflation for both current and past time periods have been used in
various combinations as independent variables. The dependent variable in all
the regressions is the share of gross fixed capital formation in gross domestic
product. For regressions in either linear or logarithmic form, none of the inflation variables has a significant impact on the share of investment in gross
domestic product. In some of these regressions the R^2's are as high as .58, but
this explanatory power is due almost entirely to the dummy variables for individual country intercepts. The failure of inflation to affect capital formation
might be attributed to any of several factors (such as the inclusion of inflation
hedges in gross fixed capital formation, the circumvention of controls over
nominal rates of interest, or inadequacies in dealing with expectations and adjustment), but a more satisfactory explanation can be offered only after an
examination of the impact of financial repression and financial growth on
capital formation.

C.   Financial Repression, Financial Growth, and
Capital Formation

Equation 12 provides a basis for estimating the effects of financial repression
and financial growth on capital formation. As previously indicated, a change
in the demand for capital can be broken down into the change in capital's
share in the mix of nonmonetary assets and the change in the scale of
nonmonetary assets. The change in capital's share in response to
financial repression and liberalization is essentially the result of the microeconomic effects examined in Theorems 1 through 4. These theorems
indicate that the ratio of nonmonetary to monetary assets provides an
index of the extent of financial repression. The change in the scale of
nonmonetary assets is equal to the change in the asset constraint minus
the change in the real holdings of monetary assets. At the macroeconomic
level, changes in the real holdings of currency, demand deposits, and time
and savings deposits have differing effects on the asset constraint, according
to the portion of seigniorage that the government returns to the private
sector and the reserve requirements that it imposes on the banking system.
In addition, as indicated by Theorem 5, financial repression and liberalization also have an effect on the asset constraint through the effect on
saving.

   The dependent variable used in the following regressions is the share
of gross fixed capital formation in gross domestic product. The primary

independent variables are the changes in the ratios of currency holdings, demand deposits, and time and savings deposits to gross domestic product; these independent variables represent not only financial repression and liberalization, but also the differing effects of each form of money on the asset constraint. As shown in Eq. (12), the differing effects of the three forms of money on capital formation are due in part to differing reserve requirements (as well as to the portion of seigniorage returned to the private sector). However, most Latin American countries have so many different categories of bank deposits, each with its own reserve requirements, that assembling and correctly aggregating the necessary information is beyond the scope of the present chapter. Instead, a proxy has been used, the ratio of commercial bank reserves to demand deposits plus time and savings deposits, in order to incorporate at least the overall variations among countries and over time in aggregate reserve requirements.[24] The last independent variable is the ratio of nonmonetary to monetary assets, the index of financial repression suggested by Theorems 1 through 4. However, since no data are available for nonmonetary assets, it becomes necessary to make the heroic (but not unusual) assumption that there is a stable monotonic relationship between nonmonetary assets and output, so that gross domestic product can be used as a proxy for nonmonetary assets.[25]

Because of the lack of adequate data, the other relationships discussed above cannot be estimated. The survey of saving behavior by Mikesell and Zinser [29] points out not only the paucity of any concrete findings, but also the serious data problems that arise in most less developed countries from calculating saving as a residual. The amount of seigniorage that the government returns to the private sector is another variable for which no adequate data are available.

To allow for lags in adjustment, the changes in the ratios of currency holdings, demand deposits, and time and savings deposits to gross domestic product for both the current and preceding year are introduced as independent variables. Since there is no particular reason to think that such short lags should be adequate, values for these independent variables lagged two years were also introduced, but they failed to be significant. As in Table 2, the regressions in Table 3 are also run using averages of the current and preceding year for each of these independent variables. For the other two independent variables (the ratio of commercial bank reserves to demand deposits plus time and savings deposits, and the ratio of gross domestic product to monetary assets), values for only the current year are introduced because these ratios generally vary little from year to year. As in the regressions to estimate the impact of inflation on capital formation, all variables are expressed in both linear and logarithmic form.

The regressions in Table 3 yield R^2's of .61 to .63, and this explanatory power is not appreciably reduced by averaging independent variables for the

TABLE 3

Capital Formation as a Function of Growth in Monetary Assets, the Ratio of Gross Domestic Product to Monetary Assets, and Bank Reserve Ratios: Pooled Regressions for 16 Latin American Countries, 1950-1971

	Linear	Logarithmic	Linear	Logarithmic
Intercept	.167	−.521	.095	−.540
$\left(\Delta \dfrac{CC}{Y}\right)_t$	.142 (0.5)	.077 (0.5)		
$\left(\Delta \dfrac{CC}{Y}\right)_{t-1}$	−.289 (1.1)	−.214 (1.5)		
$\dfrac{\left(\Delta \frac{CC}{Y}\right)_t + \left(\Delta \frac{CC}{Y}\right)_{t-1}}{2}$			−.208 (0.8)	−.215 (1.1)
$\left(\Delta \dfrac{DD}{Y}\right)_t$	−.181 (0.9)	−.173 (1.4)		
$\left(\Delta \dfrac{DD}{Y}\right)_{t-1}$	.316 (1.5)	.162 (1.4)		
$\dfrac{\left(\Delta \frac{DD}{Y}\right)_t + \left(\Delta \frac{DD}{Y}\right)_{t-1}}{2}$			.153 (0.6)	.005 (0.1)
$\left(\Delta \dfrac{TS}{Y}\right)_t$	.559** (2.6)	.243* (2.0)		
$\left(\Delta \dfrac{TS}{Y}\right)_{t-1}$	.145 (0.6)	.047 (0.4)		
$\dfrac{\left(\Delta \frac{TS}{Y}\right)_t + \left(\Delta \frac{TS}{Y}\right)_{t-1}}{2}$			.770** (2.6)	.333* (2.0)
$\dfrac{R}{CC + DD + TS}$	−.0012* (2.0)	−.195** (4.0)	−.0012* (2.0)	−.193** (4.0)
$\dfrac{Y}{DD + TS}$	−.0011 (0.9)	−.010 (0.6)	−.0011 (0.9)	−.009 (0.6)
R^2	.62	.63	.61	.62
S_e	.024	.065	.024	.066

current and preceding year. Although the dummy variables for individual country intercepts again account for much of this explanatory power, several of the independent variables are highly significant. An increase in the ratio of gross domestic product to monetary assets significantly reduces the share of gross fixed capital formation in gross domestic product; but the ratio of commercial bank reserves to demand deposits plus time and savings deposits is not significant, although the coefficients are consistently negative. Neither changes in the ratio of currency holdings to gross domestic product nor changes in the ratio of demand deposits to gross domestic product have a significant impact on capital formation; but the coefficients for the former tend to be negative, and the coefficients for the latter tend to be positive. On the other hand, changes in the ratio of time and savings deposits to gross domestic product have a significant positive impact on capital formation. The F-ratios comparing the explanatory power of individual country regressions with the pooled regressions in Table 3 range from 2.3 to 4.0. These are substantially lower than the F-ratios for the regressions in Table 2, but they still reveal significant heterogeneity among countries.

The regression results in Table 3 strongly support the complementarity hypothesis as extended in this chapter. Although the coefficients of the independent variables are not always significant, their signs and relative magnitudes are consistent with the expectations based on Eq. (12). The index of financial repression indicates that repression significantly reduces capital formation. The significant positive impact of growth in real time and savings deposits on capital formation, in contrast to the negligible effects of growth in real currency holdings and demand deposits, emphasizes the importance of financial intermediation and the crucial role of time and savings deposits in this process. The failure of growth in real demand deposits to stimulate capital formation significantly is not surprising, given the higher reserve requirements that governments typically impose on demand deposits. The tendency for growth in real currency holdings to have negative, though insignificant, coefficients suggests, not surprisingly, that governments do not return a large portion of seigniorage to the private sector. The importance of effects on the asset constraint stemming from increased holdings of real monetary assets is also

---

Note: Each regression has 286 observations, and the dependent variable is the ratio of gross fixed capital formation to gross domestic product. CC is currency outside banks; DD is demand deposits at commercial banks; and TS is time and savings deposits at commercial banks. Y is gross domestic product; and R is commercial bank reserves. Δ indicates changes; and subscripts indicate current or lagged variables. Intercepts are averages of the intercepts for individual countries. The t values are given in parentheses below each coefficient; those marked with one asterisk (*) are significant at the 5-percent level, and those marked with two asterisks (**) at the 1 percent level. R^2 and S_e are the multiple correlation coefficient and the standard error of the estimate.

suggested by the consistently negative coefficients of the proxy for overall reserve requirements, although these coefficients fail to be significant.

The only paradoxical result is that inflation fails to affect capital formation, in spite of the impact of inflation on the real size of the financial sector and the impact of financial repression and financial growth on capital formation. The most likely explanation for this apparent paradox lies in the type of policies that have generally been undertaken in Latin America to curb inflation. As McKinnon [1, pp. 80-88] and Kapur (see Chapter 9) point out, orthodox anti-inflation policies do not stress financial liberalization (with the accompanying growth in real holdings of financial assets) to curb inflation, but rather emphasize the restriction of credit. It has been argued that such orthodox policies may appreciably reduce aggregate supply as well as aggregate demand; this not only makes it more difficult to curb inflation, but also tends to reduce capital formation, which typically relies more heavily on credit.[26] A lower rate of inflation, if brought about through orthodox policies, may thus have an adverse impact on the share of capital formation in national income, and this may not be completely offset by whatever expansion of the real financial sector might accompany these orthodox policies. In this case, the link between inflation and capital formation may be ambiguous, unlike the link between real financial growth and capital formation.

ACKNOWLEDGMENTS

The authors wish to thank Kathleen Books, Francisco Chaves, and the Southern Illinois University computer center for assistance with data collection and computational work, and Susan Vogel for drawing the figures.

Appendix

When the ordering of risks assumed in the proofs of Theorems 1 through 5 is reversed such that $\sigma_H < \sigma_M$ (point A lies to the right of point B in Figure 1a), the efficient frontier is an envelope of curves that can no longer be identified with a single mix of nonmonetary assets. Accordingly, movements of point D along BC no longer have significance, and the graphical form of the proofs for Theorems 1 through 5 breaks down. However, the failure of the form of the proofs does not imply that the theorems themselves are invalid; in fact, a secondary line of proof indicates that the relationships between variables predicted by the complementarity hypothesis hold under reasonable cases of repression even when $\sigma_H < \sigma_M$.

For a change in a particular parameter, the response of the position and

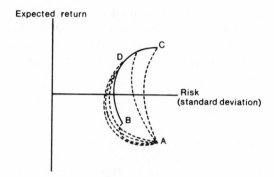

FIGURE 1a

slope of the efficient frontier is independent of the ordering of risks. The impact of such a change in the efficient frontier on the optimal point E can be decomposed into income and substitution effects analogous to the Slutzky decomposition in traditional consumer theory. The sign of the substitution effect is independent of the investor's preferences and is the same as the sign of the change in capital's share determined in the corresponding proof in Section 1. However, the sign of the income effect depends on the preferences of the investor and need not be the same as the substitution effect. If strong enough, a perverse income effect could reverse any of the relationships expressed in Theorems 1 through 5. However, the original proofs demonstrate that reversals of the complementarity relationships cannot occur when $\sigma_M < \sigma_H$, and even when $\sigma_H < \sigma_M$, the reversals can only occur when the income effect is both perverse and strong. Thus, regardless of the ordering of risks, the relationships between variables predicted by the complementarity hypothesis may typically be expected to hold under conditions of repression. While the reversal of the assumed ordering of risks remains interesting from the standpoint of theoretical completeness, the following informal analysis suggests that, as a practical matter, it is unlikely to occur except in rare instances.

When repression reaches the extreme that money is dominated by inflation hedges to such an extent that both $\gamma < \theta$ and $\sigma_H < \sigma_M$, it is only the possible gain from diversification that would cause investors to hold money at all in efficient portfolios. Moreover, even when money is present in some efficient portfolios, the corresponding section of the efficient frontier AD is very steep, and thus only the most conservative investors would include money in their asset portfolios beyond the absolute minimum required to meet transactions and precautionary needs. With the possible exception of the German experience and perhaps a few other cases, it is unlikely that the extent of financial repression has reached this extreme. On the basis of the lack of widespread exclusion of money from asset portfolios, one might reasonably infer that the inverted ordering of risks very rarely occurs. However, as Clark Reynolds has noted in commenting on an earlier version of the chapter, the ultimate resolution of this issue awaits further empirical analysis.

NOTES

1. See also the studies of inflation in Latin America by Despres [7], Harberger [8], and Shaw [9] that emphasize the importance of these evils and suggest some of the problems associated with financial repression.

2. This result is analogous to the theorem in consumer theory that it is not possible for all goods to be complements.

3. See, for example, the models of Tobin [3], Johnson [4], and Levhari and Patinkin [5].

4. The term inflation hedge reflects the view that the real rates of return on these nonproductive investments are independent of the rate of inflation. The real rates of return on inflation hedges are typically negative, as in the case of harvested crops withheld from the market and deteriorating in storage; but for high rates of inflation, these real rates of return may compare favorably with the real rate of return on money.

5. The assumed ordering of the expected real rates of return ($\gamma < \theta < r$) is clearly consistent with the condition of financial repression. However, it is conceivable that an extreme form of repression, as extended in this chapter to include increased variability of the real rate of return on money, could reverse the assumed ordering of risks, so that $\sigma_H < \sigma_M$. The authors are indebted to Clark Reynolds for raising the issue of the existence of such a case and for indicating its potential difficulty for the theorems presented. An analysis of this case in conducted in the appendix; and the conclusion is reached that, while the form of the proofs for Theorems 1 through 5 presented in the body of the chapter does indeed break down when $\sigma_H < \sigma_M$, the theorems themselves retain their validity in most cases.

6. The restriction that at least some money must be held in the portfolio can be relaxed if symmetric borrowing and lending opportunities exist. For the case where money is riskless, see Sharpe [12] and Lintner [11].

7. For evidence of significant empirical differences among the forms of money in a different context, see Peltzman's extension [13] of Friedman and Meiselman's work.

8. The concept of reserves can also be extended to include the secondary reserves of government securities that central banks in many less developed countries require commercial banks to hold at less than market rates of interest.

9. See, for example, Campbell [14] on Brazil, Deaver [15] on Chile, Diz [16] on Argentina, Dutton [17] on Argentina, Hynes [18] on Chile, Silveira [19] on Brazil, and Koot [20] on Argentina, Brazil, Chile, and Uruguay.

10. Complete explanations of these definitions can be found in *International Financial Statistics.* The International Monetary Fund also includes private-sector deposits at central banks and official entity deposits at central banks in its definition of money, and quasi-monetary deposits at central banks in its definition of quasi-money. Narrower definitions for the monetary variables are used in the present study because they appear more appropriate for the hypotheses being examined and are more likely to be comparable among countries. Regressions have also been run using the more inclusive definitions, but these results are not reported because they do not differ appreciably from the results using the narrower definitions.

11. Panama has been omitted because of its lack of an independent money supply, and British Honduras and the Guyanas because of political dependence and lack of data. The Caribbean island nations have also been excluded. Although the present study covers the period 1950 through 1971, complete data for all years are not available for each of the 16 countries, and the two initial observations for each country are lost in calculating percentage changes and introducing lagged variables.

12. For each of the countries where the rate of inflation has clearly changed from one period to another (i.e., Bolivia, Brazil, Paraguay, and Uruguay), similar relationships can be observed between the rate of inflation and the behavior of financial variables.

13. Individual time-series regressions for the countries that have data on central bank discount rates confirm this ambiguity. For some countries increases in the discount rate significantly increase real balances, while for others increases in the discount rate significantly decrease real balances. In still other cases there is no significant effect.

14. See, for example Griliches, [21] classic survey of distributed lags.

15. Previous studies of the demand for money in Latin America (see, for example, those cited in the foregoing notes) indicate that significant lags do not generally extend beyond two years. Where multicolinearity does present a problem, averages of each independent variable for the current and preceding year have been used; such averages have also been used in the individual country regressions where loss in degrees of freedom is a problem. Since these procedures are likely to underestimate the impact of inflation on the real size of the financial sector and on capital formation, one direction for further research is to use more sophisticated techniques (see, for example, Maddala [22]) to estimate more precisely the lags due to adjustment and expectations.

16. See, for example, Kuh [23] and Hanson and Vogel [24].

17. Real gross domestic product is introduced as an independent variable, as well as in the ratios that form the dependent variables, because the demands for currency, demand deposits, and time and savings deposits are not necessarily unit elastic with respect to real income.

18. As noted above, such averages have been used because of the presence of multicolinearity in some instances. For example, the correlation between current and lagged real gross domestic product is .99, as compared with a correlation of .75 between the current and lagged rate of inflation.

19. In comments on an earlier version of this chapter, Jacob Frankel suggested that an alternative specification of inflationary expectations might improve these results. In particular, he suggested that expected changes in a unit of purchasing power, the reciprocal of the price level, might be more appropriate than expected changes in the price level itself. However, regressions embodying this suggestion did not improve explanatory power or appreciably change the elasticities. Two related points are also worth emphasizing: (1) these elasticities embody not only the impact of the expected rate of inflation but also the impact of the uncertainty, and hence the risk, associated with the expected rate of inflation, because of the correlation between the rate of inflation and its variability; and (2) no simple model of expectations, based only on the rate of inflation over a two-year period, can fully represent the behavior of inflationary expectations. With regard to the second point, it should be noted that in all the regressions in Table 2 (with one insignificant exception) the rate of inflation in the current year has, as expected, a larger coefficient than the rate of inflation in the preceding year.

20. The study by Hanson and Vogel, which covers the same 16 Latin American countries for the period 1950 through 1969, is based on essentially the same data as the present study, but uses ratios of monetary assets to gross national product (velocity), rather than ratios of monetary assets to gross domestic product, as the dependent variables. Two other differences, however, might be more important in explaining the different results. The study by Hanson and Vogel does not use logarithmic transformations, and the various measures of velocity do not involve the separation of demand deposits and time and savings deposits from currency.

21. Some of the methods that have been used in Brazil to circumvent controls over nominal rates of interest are described in Silveira [26] and Simonsen [27]. Such controls may also create incentives that lead to the development of new varieties of financial assets; see, for example, Porter [28] on the development of a bill market in Colombia.

22. Jacob Frenkel's comments on an earlier version of this chapter led to a fuller recognition of this problem.

23. For the reasons previously discussed, interest rates have not been included in the following pooled regressions. Individual time-series regressions

for the countries with data on central bank discount rates (not reported here) reveal the same ambiguous impact of changes in central bank discount rates already noted.

24. The source of these data is *International Financial Statistics* [35], which also gives the definition of commercial bank reserves. A proxy for secondary reserve requirements (the ratio of commercial bank claims on the government and official entities to demand deposits plus time and savings deposits) was also introduced as an independent variable in several regressions, but proved to be insignificant.

25. There are other factors besides financial repression and liberalization that might affect capital formation in Latin America. It might be argued that any relationship between the financial sector and capital formation is due to reverse causation or to excluded variables that are correlated with both the dependent and the independent variables. However, it is not clear what impact capital formation might have on the financial sector, nor what the excluded variables might be.

26. Morley [30] on Brazil and Maynard and van Rijckeghem [31] on Argentina also emphasize the adverse impact of credit restraint on aggregate supply. For the traditional view of why orthodox policies have an adverse effect on aggregate demand, see Selowsky [32] on Chile and Thorp [33] for a summary. The dismal performance of stock markets in various inflationary Latin America countries (see Basch and Kybal [34]) when stocks are generally thought to provide a hedge against inflation, may also be attributable to the fears of orthodox stabilization policies involving undesirable credit restraint.

REFERENCES

1. Ronald I. McKinnon, *Money and Capital in Economic Development,* Brookings Institution, Washington, D. C., 1973.

2. Edward S. Shaw, *Financial Deepening in Economic Development,* Oxford, New York, 1973.

3. James Tobin, "Money and Economic Growth, " *Econometrica,* October 1965, pp. 671-684.

4. Harry Johnson, "Money in a Neo-Classical Growth Model," in *Essays in Monetary Economics,* Harvard University Press, Cambridge, Mass., 1967, pp. 143-178.

5. David Levhari and Don Patinkin, "The Role of Money in a Simple Growth Model," *American Economic Review,* September 1968, pp. 713-753.

6. Harry Johnson, "Is Inflation the Inevitable Price of Rapid Development or a Retarding Factor in Economic Growth?" in *Essays in Monetary Economics*, Harvard University Press, Cambridge, Mass., 1967, pp. 281-291.

7. Emile Despres, "Stabilization and Monetary Policy in Less Developed Countries," in Jesse W. Markham and Gustav F. Papanek (eds.), *Industrial Organization and Economic Development*, Houghton Mifflin, Boston, 1970, pp. 396-413.

8. Arnold Harberger, "Some Notes on Inflation," in Werner Baer and Isaac Kerstenetzky, eds., *Inflation and Growth in Latin America*, Richard D. Irwin, Homewood, Illinois, 1964, pp. 319-351.

9. Edward S. Shaw, "Comment [On Brazilian Inflation and Its Effects on Growth]," *Journal of Political Economy*, Supplement: August 1967, pp. 631-634.

10. James Tobin, "Liquidity Preference as Behavior Towards Risk," *Review of Economic Studies*, February 1958, pp. 65-86.

11. John Lintner, "The Valuation of Risk Assets and the Selection of Risky Investments in Stock Portfolios and Capital Budgets," *Review of Economics and Statistics*, February 1965, pp. 13-37.

12. William F. Sharpe, "Capital Asset Prices: A Theory of Market Equilibrium Under Conditions of Risk," *Journal of Finance*, September 1964, pp. 425-442.

13. Sam Peltzman, "Expenditures and the Composition of the Money Supply," *The Review of Economics and Statistics*, May 1970, pp. 208-211.

14. Colin D. Campbell, "The Velocity of Money and the Rate of Inflation: Recent Experiences in South Korea and Brazil," in David Meiselman, ed., *Varieties of Monetary Experience*, University of Chicago Press, Chicago, 1970, pp. 339-386.

15. John V. Deaver, "The Chilean Inflation and the Demand for Money," in David Meiselman, ed., *Varieties of Monetary Experience*, University of Chicago Press, Chicago, 1970, pp. 7-67.

16. Adolfo Cesar Diz, "Money and Prices in Argentina, 1935-1962," in David Meiselman, ed., *Varieties of Monetary Experience*, University of Chicago Press, Chicago, 1970, pp. 69-162.

17. Dean S. Dutton, "A Model of Self-Generating Inflation: The Argentine Case," *Journal of Money, Credit and Banking*, May 1971, pp. 245-262.

18. A. Hynes, "The Demand for Money and Monetary Adjustments in Chile," *Review of Economic Studies*, July 1967, pp. 285-293.

19. Antonio M. Silveira, "The Demand for Money: The Evidence from the

Brazilian Economy," *Journal of Money, Credit and Banking,* February 1973, pp. 113-140.

20. Ronald Koot, "Price Expectations and Monetary Adjustments in Latin America," *Schweizerische Zeitschrift für Volkswirtschaft und Statistik,* July 1973, pp. 223-232.

21. Zvi Griliches, "Distributed Lags: A Survey," *Econometrica,* January 1967, pp. 16-49.

22. G. S. Maddala, "The Use of Variance Components Models in Pooling Cross Sections and Time Series Data," *Econometrica,* March 1971, pp. 341-358.

23. Edwin Kuh, *Capital Stock Growth: A Micro-Econometric Approach,* North-Holland, Amsterdam, 1963.

24. James S. Hanson and Robert C. Vogel, "Inflation and Monetary Velocity in Latin America," *The Review of Economics and Statistics,* August 1973, pp. 365-370.

25. Ronald I. McKinnon, "Money, Other Stores of Value, and Real Capital Accumulation: The Inflation Tax Reconsidered: Part One: Self Finance," Stanford University Center for Research in Economic Growth, Research Memorandum No. 159, January 1974.

26. Antonio M. Silveira, "Interest Rate and Rapid Inflation: The Evidence from The Brazilian Economy," *Journal of Money, Credit and Banking,* August 1973, pp. 794-805.

27. Mario Henrique Simonsen, "Inflation and the Money and Capital Markets in Brazil," in Howard Ellis, ed., *The Economy of Brazil,* University of California Press, Berkeley, 1969, pp. 133-161.

28. Richard C. Porter, "The Birth of a Bill Market," *The Journal of Development Studies,* April 1973, pp. 439-450.

29. Raymond Mikesell and James Zinser, "The Nature of the Savings Function in Developing Countries: A Survey of the Theoretical and Empirical Literature," *The Journal of Economic Literature,* March 1973, pp. 1-26.

30. Samuel A. Morley, "Inflation and Stagnation in Brazil," *Economic Development and Cultural Change,* January 1971, pp. 184-203.

31. Geoffrey Maynard and Willy van Rijckeghem, "Stabilization Policy in an Inflationary Economy—Argentina," in Gustav Papanek, ed., *Development Policy: Theory and Practice,* Harvard University Press, Cambridge, Mass., 1968, pp. 207-235.

32. Marcelo Selowsky, "Cost of Price Stabilization in an Inflationary Economy," *The Quarterly Journal of Economics,* February 1973, pp. 44-59.

33. Rosemary Thorp, "Inflation and the Financing of Economic Develop-
     ment," in Keith Griffin, ed., *Financing Development in Latin America,*
     Macmillan, London, 1971, pp. 182-224.

34. Antonin Basch and Milic Kybal, *Capital Markets in Latin America: A
     General Survey and Six Country Studies,* Praeger, New York, 1970,
     chap. 3.

35. International Monetary Fund, *International Financial Statistics*
     (Washington: monthly).

Comment

CLARK W. REYNOLDS

Food Research Institute
Stanford University
Stanford, California

The authors are to be congratulated on their application of the insights of
Edward Shaw to a model of financial intermediation and development that
introduces a Tobin-type analytical framework for examining portfolio
choice. This treatise expands the investigation of complementarity versus
competitiveness between the holding of real and financial assets to a multi-
asset model, in which both the level and fluctuation of yields are allowed to
vary. The conceptual model is presented diagramatically in terms of risk/
return characteristics of three major components of the portfolio of savers:
monetary financial assets, real capital goods, and inflation hedges. The authors
point out that where more than two assets are involved in the portfolio,
the possibility of complementarity exists among pairs. They then proceed
to suggest cases in which this situation may hold for developing countries
subject to rapid inflation.

   While the theoretical introduction does not offer many surprises to those
familiar with the behavior of financial markets in developing countries, the
formal presentation has considerable heuristic value. Its greatest interest lies
in the possible real growth implications of complementarity between monetary
financial assets and capital goods, where the variance of the real rate of return
on the former is less than that of inflation hedges. Nonmonetary financial
assets are missing from the model. One problem in their approach is that the
risk/return diagram assumes monetary financial assets to have a lower mean
and variance of yield than the inflation hedge, with the resulting effect that
an upward shift in the real rate of return on cash balances tends to favor a

shift from inflation hedges toward both money and capital goods. However the variance of the inflation hedge might well be less than that of financial assets, and under these circumstances the sensitivity of the portfolio of non-monetary assets to an increased yield on cash balances would be less obvious.*

The second part of the chapter provides an econometric analysis of the relationship between inflation and holdings of cash balances, demand, time, and savings deposits. The importance of dummy variables in the results suggests the need for more disaggregative analysis, but some interesting findings do appear. The elasticity of cash and demand deposits as a share of GNP with respect to price-level increases appears to be highly significant if low (−.1), tending to support the Shaw thesis, as has earlier work by Hanson and Vogel [1]. Nevertheless the low absolute elasticity makes the results of modest policy relevance, except for supporters of the in-flation tax in which case beauty is in the eye of the beholder. The findings also indicate a significant relationship between inflation and the ratio of time and savings deposits to GNP (unitary elasticity), but, paradoxically, little effect of the latter on the gross investment rate. Another anomaly is the failure of inflation to show a relationship with in-vestment as a share of GNP. This seems to be somewhat inconsistent with the positive relationship between investment and the ratio of demand deposits to GNP, since the Shaw-McKinnon models presume the latter to be negatively correlated with the rate of inflation. One possible explana-tion that the authors mention is that anti-inflationary policy does not necessarily imply financial liberalization, except perhaps in the case of Brazil since 1964.

Another possibility is that the price level variables might be misspecified. An earlier paper by Vogel [2] found little relationship between the actual rate

---

*In a subsequent communication the authors point out that the proof in the case where $\sigma_H > \sigma_M$ breaks down when $\sigma_H < \sigma_M$. "In this case the efficient frontier is an envelope of curves and can no longer be identified with a single mix of nonmonetary assets. Accordingly movements of the point D along BC no longer have significance."

They go on to note that it is felt that the actual occurrence of such a case is unlikely since when $\sigma_H < \sigma_M$ and $\Pi - \delta < \theta$ "It is only the diversification effect that would cause idle balances to be held in portfolios at all." I would argue that since the "diversification effect" includes preference for liquidity, it could be much more important than the authors indicate. They note that, "If the diversification effect is small, the efficient frontier might be the line BC." Clearly the resolution of such issues will depend upon subsequent empirical testing.

of inflation and his proxy for expected changes in the price level (first difference of the logs of lagged price-level changes). In the discussion period Professor Frenkel suggested that the proxy used for expected prive-level increases might be weak, arguing that $E(1/P)$ is more relevant than $E(\dot{P}/P)$ to express expected changes in a unit of purchasing power. Looking at the demand side Frenkel also wondered why the speed of the adjustment of desired to actual investment should be a function of the price level.

One might also qualify the quantity theoretical approach of this and related studies, when applied to regions such as Latin America, by a point made much earlier by Harberger. In a world of weak central banks and log-rolling finance ministries, the quantity of money may be as much an effect of wage and other structural adjustments as a cause [3].

In the subsequent discussion Professor Vogel expressed concern about the partial analytical approach to the estimation of the demand for financial assets, since the paper lacks any complete model of the economies involved, and he reported that owing to lack of information, interest rates were not explicitly introduced. In the case of an economy such as Brazil where monetary correction has been applied since the mid-1960s, permitting a significant upward shift in real rates of interest on savings deposits and on nonmonetary financial assets, this omission had a significant impact on portfolio composition. Professor Patrick noted that the heterogeneity of the results suggests a possible nonlinear relationship between inflation and other variables. He also wondered whether a "Latin America" exists and suggested that the analysis be spread over more countries, perhaps disaggregating them by low, medium, and high rates of inflation.

In summary the authors' introduction of the portfolio model to Shaw-McKinnon type analysis is a step forward. The level of aggregation implicitly assumes that as the pattern of inflation changes, and with it the mean and variance of yields on physical and financial assets, portfolios will adjust *ceteris paribus*. But the "optimal portfolio" of the model represents a weighted average of portfolios of numerous sectors of the economy. If inflation is associated with changing income distribution, it will also be associated with changes in the level and composition of portfolios among income groups. Shifts in the distribution of income among sectors (e.g., through inflation-related shifts in profit/wage shares) could produce significant changes in the supply and demand for both financial assets and financial liabilities among income groups, the results of which would be reflected in the model's aggregate portfolio, nullifying the *ceteris paribus* assumption. Indeed, financial intermediation itself may play an important role in income distribuiton as can be shown in the Mexican case [4].

For Brazil the recent rapid rate of growth of output and financial intermediation was associated with concentration of the size distribution of income among the highest income groups, as well as a shift in the functional distribution of income favoring profits, rents, and executive salaries over the general wage bill. This rapid growth of financial intermediation was not necessarily associated with increased investment finance, due to the proportional expansion of short-term financial liabilities that were also concentrated in the upper-income groups. A similar pattern has occurred in a number of Latin American countries in which absolute and relative increases in real income of wealthier households were associated with demand shifts favoring credit purchases of consumer durables such that the accumulation of financial assets of net savers was matched by increased financial liabilities of net borrowers. Hence the relationship between increased intermediation and capital formation is by no means as apparent as the Vogel-Buser model would suggest. The Mexican and Brazilian cases suggest that fuller financial intermediation may or may not be associated with growth of the investment share of output and that the fiscal and distributive corollaries of financial policy must be examined before the ultimate effect of financial intermediation on growth can be deduced.

REFERENCES

1. James S. Hanson and Robert C. Vogel, "Inflation and Monetary Velocity in Latin America," *The Review of Economics and Statistics,* August 1973.

2. Robert C. Vogel, "The Dynamics of Inflation in Latin America, 1950-69," *American Economic Review,* March 1974, pp. 102-114.

3. Werner Baer and Isaac Kerstenetsky, *Conference on Inflation and Economic Growth in Latin America* (Rio de Janeiro, 1963), Richard D. Irwin, Homewood, Illinois, 1964.

4. C. Reynolds and J. Corredor, "The Recent Evolution and Savings and the Financial System in Mexico in Relation to the Distribution of Income and Wealth," prepared for the U.S.-Mexican Financial Relations Conference, March 14-16, 1974, Stanford, California.

Chapter 4

Saving Propensities and the Korean Monetary Reform in Retrospect

RONALD I. McKINNON

Center for Research in Economic Growth
Stanford University
Stanford, California

Besides Edward Shaw's direct influence on theorizing about monetary and financial processes, [1] and [10], he has been an active financial adviser in such diverse economies as Ghana, Korea, Iran, and Afghanistan, as well as many in Latin America. Most development advisers fall into two camps: (1) those who adapt to political constraints outlined in the domestic "plan" and work for marginal improvements; or (2) those who simply write their technical reports in a disassociated manner and leave. Shaw falls into neither category. He doesn't accept the broad outlines of the domestic planning process if they conflict substantially with his ideas of what good monetary and fiscal policy should be. On the other hand, he pushes his views with tenacity. The results can be explosive. Shaw may become persona non grata, precipitate a coup d'etat, or succeed in introducing some significant economic transformation.

The Korean financial reforms of September of 1965 are in the last category. Prior to 1965, the Korean banking system was quite moribund as a financial intermediary. Nominal rates of interest on both deposits and loans had been pegged at low levels relative to the rates of price inflation experienced in 1963 and 1964. Real rates of interest had become highly negative—see Table 1. For example, the real return on a one-year time deposit was between −10 and −15 percent. A variety of lending rates (negative in real terms) proliferated, and the trickle of real bank finance not directly appropriated by the government was arbitrarily rationed in favor of a few not politically disinterested borrowers. Bank deposits reached their nadir of 9 percent as a proportion of GNP in 1964 (Table 2).

Over the summer of 1965, Shaw collaborated with John Gurley and Hugh Patrick to submit a report [2] recommending the freeing of deposit and lending interest rates while maintaining control over the monetary base. The Korean government responded strongly although inexactly by shifting interest rates from relatively low pegs to much higher ones. While not paying interest on demand deposits, the weighted average of nominal rates on time deposits rose to 24 percent; whereas the "standard" bank lending rate rose from 14 to 26 percent (nominal). A few borrowers continued to have access to funds at lower rates: For example, exporters could borrow at 6 percent nominal—but about two-thirds of bank lending at that time came under the higher rate. Shaw returned to Korea several times in the ensuing years to provide follow-up advice.

But higher nominal deposit and lending rates of interest in the organized banking system need not lead to higher real rates if inflation accelerates. Fortunately, improved fiscal policy allowed the government to rely less on the central bank for finance, and the banking reform itself increased the demand for money in Korea. Thus inflation lessened substantially after 1965 (Table 1). From 1964 to 1966, the real rate of return (deflated by movements in the wholesale price index) rose about 11 percentage points on demand deposits, and rose about 26 percentage points on time deposits of longer maturities (Table 2).

The response of savers was enthusiastic. By 1969 the real money stock (M_2/WPI) was seven times what it had been in 1964, and amounted to about 33 percent of GNP. The flow of private saving increased from virtually nothing to about 8 percent of GNP. This huge increase in the real stock of deposits was matched by increases in bank lending at rates of interest that were also very high in real terms. Large scale financing from "organized" sources became available to many Korean enterprises in industry and agriculture for the first time, and contributed to the extraordinary growth in Korean real output.

That the reform was highly successful there can be little doubt. With the benefit of hindsight, however, I would like to consider two related current (1974) financial problems facing the Korean authorities that were not obvious to most observers in the late 1960s.

1. In the early 1970s, Korea remained heavily dependent on foreign saving that amounted to about 11 percent of GNP despite the very rapid growth in the real size of the domestic financial sector. In contrast, Japan and Taiwan were self-sufficient in net saving at comparable levels of real GNP per capita. Without slackening the

annual rate of growth in real GNP of 9 to 10 percent per year, the Korean government wishes to phase out dependence on foreign saving altogether by 1980 or 1981.

2. In the early 1970s, the government again appeared to lose control over the monetary base with a resurgence in inflationary pressure. The wholesale price index increased 14 percent in 1972. The problem can be traced back to the 1965 reform, when the then tiny export sector was exempted from paying the high rates of interest prevailing in the domestic economy, and the commercial banks discontinued export paper freely with the central bank.

In this chapter, I shall argue that the monetary-control problem and the continued overdependence of the Korean economy on foreign saving are closely related issues, and that the 1965 monetary reform—while extraordinarily successful—is still "incomplete."

I. Private Saving and the Real Stock of Money

Arguing from the premise that the monetary system provides a means of payment and a precautionary store of liquidity to depositors, the demand for real cash balances is usually specified to be more-or-less proportional to real income—i.e., the income elasticity of demand for money is close to unity. However, if one grafts on a Shavian finance-intermediation view of the role of the monetary system, then the flow of aggregate saving and investment in the economy, and the shifting composition of saving among sectors, can have a first-order impact on the money/GNP ratio. The last effect seems to be particularly important in the Korean case.

The monetary reform of 1965 initiated an upward shift in the stock demand for money (time and saving deposits inclusive) and with it an upward increase in the *flow* of private saving as a proportion of GNP. Figure 1 portrays the discrete shift in the private saving propensity from say zero, in 1962-64 to about 8 percent of GNP from 1966 to 1972 inclusive. While not as stable as the graph portrays, there was no pronounced upward trend in this private-saving propensity in the 1966-72 interval.

Suppose this level of private saving as a proportion of GNP is maintained at 8 percent. What would one then predict for the path of the money/GNP ratio? It began to rise sharply after 1964, but one thinks intuitively that the ratio of the money stock to the income flow should level out at some point.

Let us relate saving to monetary growth within a simple Harrod-Domar model.

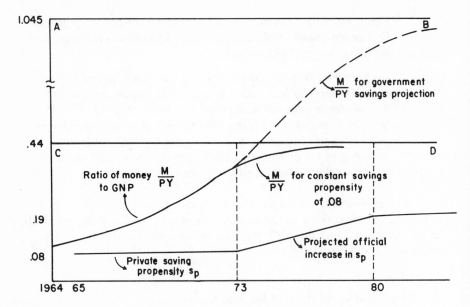

FIGURE 1. The money-income ratio and private saving propensities.

$$Y = \sigma K \tag{1}$$

where

Y = real GNP
K = capital stock
σ = output/capital ratio

$$I = S = sY = \dot{K} \tag{2}$$

where

I = investment
S = saving
s = propensity to save

$$\frac{\dot{K}}{K} = \frac{\dot{Y}}{Y} = \omega = \sigma s \tag{3}$$

where

$\dot{K}$ and $\dot{Y}$ = rates of change
in their respective variables.

The growth rate in Korean GNP has been about 10 percent per year, that is, $\omega = .10$. Gross investment financed from both foreign and domestic saving—official and private—has averaged about 25 percent of GNP per year, that is, $s = .25$. Hence, the output/capital ratio σ is about .4, a figure that is consistent with the Taiwanese and Japanese experience.

Let us divide the economy into three sources of gross saving for 1966-1972:

Sector	Saving as a proportion of GNP*
Government	$s_g \simeq 0.6$
Foreign	$s_f \simeq .11$
Private	$s_p \simeq .08$
Total	$s \simeq 0.25$

In order to calculate the equilibrium stock of money consistent with these saving propensities, assume that only domestic private savers utilize the banking system. That is, government saving takes place within the government budget to finance public investment or to purchase primary securities directly from government-controlled pension funds and the like. Foreign saving comes in the form of supplier credits, direct equity investment, or through the purchase of government-guaranteed bonds. Indeed, it is illegal for foreigners to hold time and saving deposits in Korean Won, and there are strict exchange controls. Hence the "money intensiveness" of both government saving and foreign saving is negligible.

With these considerable simplifications, the stock of monetary assets is determined jointly with private *domestic* saving s_p. The impact of maintaining a given level of s_p on the money/GNP ratio can then be calculated once the "money intensiveness" of the saving of households and firms is known.

In a developing economy like the Korean one, private savers still have relatively limited opportunities to acquire financial assets that are not direct claims on the monetary system. Open markets for stock, bonds, mortgages, etc. are still very limited. A vigorous curb market of pawnbroking, consumer loans, and business loans had existed in Korea until August 1972, but its extent is not easily measured. Otherwise, investing (saving) for individual households and firms boils down mainly to a choice of acquiring monetary claims or physical assets—consumer durable or producer goods. From household

---

*These numbers are roughly consistent with Woo H. Nam [8] and with the Korean Ministry of Finance [9].

surveys and flow-of-funds data, I have estimated [6] that between 50 and 60 percent of private saving flows into monetary assets. Let us define α_p to be this coefficient of the "money intensiveness" of private saving. That is, the change in the money stock in any one year can be defined as:

$$\frac{d(M/P)}{dt} = \alpha_p S_p \tag{4}$$

where S_p is the real flow of private saving: $S_p = s_p Y$.

II. The Equilibrium Money/Income Ratio

For given values of the parameters s_p, α_p, and ω as defined above, Eqs. (1) through (4) determine the money/income ratio in long-run equilibrium. For example, if the monetary reform of 1965 was associated with a discrete upward shift in all three flow parameters with no further changes, the money/income ratio would have risen sharply at first and then leveled off some years later. How can one calculate this equilibrium value?

On our equilibrium growth path for real output,

$$Y_t = Y_0 e^{\omega t} \tag{5}$$

where Y_0 is income in 1965.

The cumulative money *stock* at any one point in time can be described by summing all the increments to real cash balances through time:

$$\left(\frac{M}{P}\right)_t = \int_0^t \alpha_p S_p \, dt \tag{6}$$

Hence the ratio of the money stock to income is

$$\left(\frac{M}{PY}\right)_t = \frac{\int_0^t \alpha_p s_p Y_t \, dt}{Y_t} \tag{7}$$

Substituting for Y_t from (5), and then integrating (7), we have

$$\left(\frac{M}{PY}\right)_t = \frac{s_p \alpha_p}{\omega} + \frac{C}{e^{\omega t}} \tag{8}$$

where C is the constant of integration. C represents the "initial conditions" defined by the money/income ratio as it was back in 1964. However, as time passes, these initial conditions wash out, and

$$\lim_{t \to \infty} \left(\frac{M}{PY} \right)_t = \frac{s_p \alpha_p}{\omega} \tag{9}$$

This is a general expression for the equilibrium holdings of real cash balances as proportion of income. From 1965 to 1972, the numerical values of the relevant parameters as described above were:

s_p = .08

α_p = .55

ω = .10

Hence from (9), we have $M/PY \simeq .44$. That is, if domestic incentives to save remain unchanged, we would expect the money/income ratio to level out at 44 percent in the mid 1970s, having risen from just 9 percent in 1964. (This calculation implicitly assumes that the residual availability of foreign saving maintains the 10 percent rate of growth in income.) In Fig. 1, this 44 percent asymptote is represented by $\overline{CD}$. In 1972, the ratio of money to income had reached .375 (Table 2).

Obviously, this calculation is very crude from an empirical point of view, and it is only meant to illustrate the nexus between private saving and desired holdings of money, which is very strong but requires careful interpretation. Indeed some authors [4, 5] have interpreted the rising money/income ratio between 1965 and 1972 as evidence that the long-run income elasticity of demand for money in Korea is very high. The alternative interpretation given above is that a rising money/GNP ratio is a lagged response to an increase in the real return on holding money, but a response that won't continue indefinitely.

Using the same mode of analysis, one can trace out the monetary implications of the huge projected increase in private saving propensities from 8 percent in 1972-73 to about 19 percent in 1980-81, according to the Korean government's plan for domestic savings mobilization. The idea is to displace foreign saving completely so that the rate of growth, ω is still maintained at 10 percent per year. Thus we have a projected saving pattern for 1980-81:

Sector	Saving propensity
Government	s_g = .06
Foreign	s_f = 0
Private	s_p = .19
Total	s = .25

Under the heroic assumption that this wished for or induced higher level of private saving has the same money intensiveness that existed in the 1965-72 period, then α_p remains at .55. Again we can use Eq. (9) to calculate the long-run money/income ratio to be 104.5 percent! An extraordinarily large number that, however, has been approached in Japan in certain time periods. The line $\overline{AB}$ in Fig. 1 represents this higher asymptote, which the Korean money/income ratio might approach in the late 1980s if the saving projection was valid.

In Section III, the financial feasibility of inducing such an extraordinary spurt in private saving is investigated. Here it suffices to note that as the Korean financial system becomes more sophisticated in the sense of providing a wider variety of financial assets from which savers can choose, the money intensiveness of private saving α_p may well fall. Despite this, the large projected increase in the private propensity to save requires another sharp spurt of growth in the money/income ratio. The foreign saving being replaced does not utilize the domestic monetary system as a financial intermediary.

To test the validity of the government's projections of private saving, one cannot simply project money/income ratios based on statistical time-series analysis of Korean data from 1965 to 1972. The income elasticity of the demand for money, naively projected into the 1966-82 period, would look unduly high because of the lagged adjustment in the money/income ratio to the 1965 reforms.

Hence, the approach in this chapter toward financial policy will be less direct—perhaps less satisfactory—in terms of providing numerically precise projections. In some important senses, the Republic of China (Taiwan) has preceded the development phases experience by Korea, and in the last few years also eliminated its dependence on foreign saving as projected in Korea not to occur until 1980. An historical comparison of monetary policies in the two countries may give a rough idea of what financial policy in Korea should be in order to replicate Taiwanese patterns of saving.

III.   Real Rates of Return on Holding Money in Korea and Taiwan

Since private saving in monetary form has been critically important in both Taiwan and Korea, the reward or return on monetary assets is a policy variable of great importance in determining whether a high and rising private propensity to save can be maintained. What then is the best measure of this return that can be compared across countries?

We are concerned more with the banking system's role as a financial intermediary between savers and investors than with its provision of the convenience of chequing facilities for current transactions. Hence, the return associated with money's role as a *store of value* is of more direct concern than its convenience as a medium of exchange. For this purpose, the return on holding money can be approximated by the nominal deposit rate of interest minus the expected rate of price inflation, since the latter represents the rate of deterioration in the value of real cash balances through time. To simplify, it will be assumed that the expected and actual rates of price inflation are about the same. Moreover, it will also be assumed that the wholesale price index (WPI) is a preferred to the consumer price index and to the GNP deflator* as a measure of price changes.

Even with these simplifications, however, it seems advisable to make *two* rate-of-return calculations for each country. Since demand deposits and currency bear a zero nominal deposit rate of interest, the return to holding them is simply the *negative* of the rate of movement in the wholesale price index as shown in column 1 of Table 1. Since passbook saving accounts also bear low nominal rates of interest, column 1 would give some notion of changes in their attractiveness as well.

At the other end of the spectrum, one- and two-year time deposits are rather illiquid and it is administratively feasible to pay very high nominal rates of interest on them as was done in Korea after 1965 and in Taiwan during the 1950s. Hence our second measure of the real return on holding money is the nominal rate of interest on one-year time deposits minus the rate of increase in the WPI as shown in columns 5 and 6 of Table 1, which also approximate the returns on time deposits maturing in more or slightly less than one year.

A comparison of Korean and Taiwanese real rates of return on holding money shows that Taiwan has done consistently better in maintaining a higher rate of return on currency and demand deposits and, implicitly, a higher return on saving and passbook deposits of the shortest maturity. Remarkable stability in Taiwan's WPI, in contrast to continuing substantial inflation in Korea, makes Taiwan's real return higher by an average of about *eight percentage points* as shown in column 1, even after the favorable Korean financial reform of 1965.

Looking at our other dimension—the real return on holding a one-year time deposit as shown in columns 5 and 6, Korea has generally maintained a higher real return than has Taiwan since 1965. However, the gap has been narrowing and by 1972 it turned in Taiwan's favor. Unfortunately, the Korean real return on a one-year time deposit had become *negative* by the end of 1972 if the nominal deposit rate of interest is used, 12.6 percent, prevailing at the

---

*Some analytical justification for using changes in the WPI to measure the real return on money is provided in McKinnon [6], pp. 96-98.

TABLE 1

Rates of Return on Holding Money as a Store of Value:
Korea and Taiwan 1960-72

Year	Real return on currency and demand deposits (-percentage change in WPI)		Interest rate on one-year time deposits (%)[a]		Real return on holding one-year time deposits (%)[b]	
	(1) Korea	(2) Taiwan	(3) Korea	(4) Taiwan	(5) Korea	(6) Taiwan
1960	−10.7	−13.53	10.0	17.04	−0.7	+3.09
1961	−13.4	−3.97	12.1	14.40	−1.2	+10.03
1962	−9.2	−3.06	15.0	13.32	+5.3	+9.96
1963	−20.5	−5.93	15.0	12.00	−4.6	+5.73
1964	−34.6	−2.50	15.0	10.80	−14.6	+8.10
1965	−9.9	4.08	18.8	10.80	+8.1	+16.24
1966	−8.9	−1.54	30.0	10.08	+19.4	+8.41
1967	−6.5	−2.42	30.0	9.72	+22.1	+7.13
1968	−8.0	−1.97	27.6	9.72	+18.1	+7.60
1969	−6.7	0.29	24.0	9.72	+16.2	+10.04
1970	−9.1	−2.81	22.8	9.72	+12.6	+6.72
1971	−8.6	0	20.4	9.5	+10.9	+9.5
1972	−14.0	−4.7	12.6[c]	8.75	−1.2	+3.9
			(17.1)	(9.25)	(+4.0)	(4.3)

[a]Official ceilings on rates of interest. (Since these ceilings were subject to change within a calendar year, rough averages over the entire calendar year are presented in the table.) See Bank of Korea, Monthly Economic Statistics, and Taiwan Financial Statistics Monthly.

[b]$\frac{[(\text{col. 3}) + (\text{col. 1})] 100}{1 - (\text{col. 1})}$ yields column (5) for Korea. Column (6) for Taiwan would be calculated similarly from columns (2) and (4).

[c]12.6 percent was the nominal rate of interest after the financial reforms of Aug. 3, 1972. 17.1 percent was the rate preceding those reforms.

end of 1972. This nominal rate had been very substantially reduced from 17.1 percent by the policy changes occurring in August of 1972.

In very rough terms, what do these differences in real rates of return imply for the financial profiles of both countries through time? Substantial high growth in per capita income in Taiwan, accompanied by high domestic saving that significantly reduced dependence on inflows of foreign aid, began several years earlier in comparison with Korea. Also, the problems of economic dislocation caused by war and its aftermath occurred several years earlier in Taiwan than in Korea. Let us rather arbitrarily assume that Taiwan is approximately five years ahead of Korea in financial and general economic development. Hence, the relevant Taiwanese financial profile, comparable with Korea's experience since 1965, probably begins in 1960 or thereabout. This five-year difference should be kept in mind in interpreting Table 2.

Starting with a somewhat larger money/GNP ratio in 1960 (as compared to 1965 for Korea), Taiwan has managed to maintain steady real growth in this ratio to reach .53 in 1971, and .60 in 1972. Korea's money/GNP ratio for 1971 is .34, which is slightly smaller than Taiwan's 1966 ratio of .40. (Korea's money/GNP ratio for 1972 is not easily interpreted as part of a continuous historical series because the financial reform in August 1972 probably substantially increased the demand for monetary assets at the expense of the "unorganized" credit market.) The major question is: Can Korea maintain a rate of real monetary growth in the next five years that matches Taiwan's impressive performance for 1967-72?

One cannot help but worry about the recent significant fall in the real return on holding monetary assets in Korea compared with that return maintained by the central bank of Taiwan in 1967 and in succeeding years. This difference is particularly marked with respect to the real return on holding demand deposits and currency as determined by the negative of the rate of inflation in the wholesale price index. But even the Korean real return on time deposits slipped sharply in 1972. (It might be noted that in the pre-1960 period, the Taiwanese authorities were quite careful in keeping nominal deposit rates high in order to offset substantial and somewhat unpredictable bouts of price inflation.)

This analysis suggests that a more deliberate official commitment to maintain a higher real return to Korean holders of money is likely to be necessary for private saving to rise in Korea to a level comparable to that attained by Taiwan over the past few years, which in turn is consistent with the elimination of dependence on foreign sources of saving.

IV. Export Financing, Inflation, and Interest Rates

Within the last two years, what forces have operated on Korea's financial system to reduce real deposit and lending interest rates so sharply, possibly jeopardiz-

TABLE 2

The Financial Structures of Korea and Taiwan, 1960-1972[a]

Year	Money supply — Demand deposits plus currency (M_1) Korea	Taiwan	Time and savings deposits Korea[b]	Taiwan[c]	Total (M_2) Korea	Taiwan	Gross national product Korea	Taiwan	Ratio of M_2 to GNP Korea	Taiwan
1960	22.1	6.11	5.9	6.25	28.0	12.36	246.7	62.56	0.1135	0.1976
1961	32.5	7.34	8.9	10.24	41.4	17.58	296.8	69.79	0.1395	0.2519
1962	35.1	7.92	16.6	13.01	51.7	20.93	348.6	76.47	0.1483	0.2737
1963	37.6	10.20	17.5	17.18	55.1	27.38	488.0	87.34	0.1129	0.3135
1964	48.9	13.43	14.7	21.73	63.6	35.16	696.8	102.21	0.0913	0.3440
1965	65.6	14.84	31.5	25.50	97.1	40.34	805.8	112.87	0.1205	0.3574
1966	85.2	17.39	70.2	32.32	155.4	49.71	1,032.0	125.55	0.1506	0.3959
1967	122.0	22.10	130.8	38.92	252.8	61.02	1,242.4	143.04	0.2035	0.4266
1968	153.6	24.85	255.5	43.54	409.1	68.43	1,575.7	167.98	0.2596	0.4074
1969	218.2	28.92	452.5	53.07	670.7	81.99	2,047.1	190.81	0.3276	0.4297
1970	305.6	35.09	585.2	66.50	890.8	101.59	2,545.9	217.64	0.3499	0.4668
1971	357.4	45.68	716.2	85.56	1073.6	131.24	3,151.6	249.3	0.3407	0.5264
1972	521.5	60.81	918.4	122.62	1439.9	173.48	3,840.6	287.3	0.3749	0.6038

[a]Monetary and GNP data in billions of current won and New Taiwan dollars.

[b]Line 35 of IFS for Korea.

[c]Lines 35 plus 45 of IFS for Taiwan.

Source: International Financial Statistics of the International Monetary Fund.

ing future increases in the rate of private saving? The central bank's loss of control over the monetary base has yielded a high rate of price inflation, an overt 14.0 percent in 1972, and inflation in 1973 has had to be surpressed by new batteries of internal price controls. This problem is closely related to the way in which exports are being financed and subsidized.

Export financing is contributing to a loss of monetary control via two channels. First, bank finance extended to exporters for a variety of purposes—raw materials purchases, the extension of trade credit to customers, and so on—bears in 1973 the relatively low nominal rate of interest of 7 percent (a *negative* real rate of interest) in comparison to a "standard" nominal bank lending rate of 15.5 percent. (In 1965 these figures were 6 percent and 26 percent, respectively). Having thus created a heavy and highly subsidized demand for bank credit by exporters, the government makes the deposit banks willing and automatic lenders by having the Bank of Korea discount the export credit freely at a nominal rate of interest of 3.5 percent. The immediate prospect is that the demand for export credit will increase rather than diminish because exports have been growing relative to GNP and *relative to the monetary base.* For example, exports (on a national income accounts basis) have risen from 10.4 percent of GNP in 1966 to 21.0 percent of GNP in 1972. And exports are projected to rise until 1980 to eliminate the large current account deficit that now exists.

Insofar as credit subsidies to exporters create a balance of payments surplus, the resulting accumulation of exchange reserves also expands the monetary base. This accumulation of exchange reserves can be a more erratic and temporary phenomenon than the steady upward trend in the expansion of domestic credit to exporters, but also contributed to the central bank's loss of monetary control in 1973. Table 3 is a useful summary statement of the sources of growth in the monetary base for the six-month period from the end of December 1972.

The monetary reserve base consists of coin and currency held outside the banking system plus deposits by the commercial banks with the Bank of Korea. From Table 3, this base expanded by about 80 billion won from December 1972 to June 1973—a 19 percent increase over a six-month period. Of this total, discounting of credits to exporters accounted for 53.5 billion won, and the acquisition of foreign exchange accounted for about 37 billion more. These two channels "over explained" the increase in the monetary base so that there was a net contraction from all other sources—mainly other forms of private credit. This continuous heavy subsidy to exporters completely undermines monetary control by the Bank of Korea and virtually guarantees continued high price inflation in Korea as long as this preferential treatment of export financing is maintained.

TABLE 3

Central Bank Credits and the Reserve Base (in billion won)

	December 1972	June 1973
1. Government sector	102.1	126.7
2. Fertilizer sector	34.0	41.0
3. Foreign sector	112.5	149.7
4. Banking sector (private)	143.6	164.8
(export financing)	(99.9)	(153.4)
5. Others	35.3	25.2
Total reserve base	427.5	507.4

Source: Monthly Financial Statistics, Bank of Korea.

There are many arguments as to whether or not exports should be sub- sidized in a developing economy such as Korea. Much depends on whether the won is "correctly" valued in the foreign exchange markets. Since the won does not appear too much overvalued at the present time and exports are now quite high relative to GNP, the current rationale for an export subsidy is not strong. But this situation can change rapidly with the present infaltion.

What does seem clear is that providing exporters with cheap credit, backed with automatic rediscounting priviledges, is an *inappropriate* subsidy device. Not only is there a loss of monetary control by the Bank of Korea, but the subsidy is actually being financed by an implicit tax on private savers who hold monetary assets. On the one hand, the seven percent interest rate being charged to ex- porters by banks generates pressure to keep nominal rates of interest to bank depositors lower than would otherwise be the case. On the other hand, the re- sulting increase in price inflation further lowers the *real* return to depositors. In effect, depositors (holders of money generally) are paying for this export subsidy.

In view of the government's own desire to greatly increase the rate of private saving, one can only question whether this technique for subsidizing exporters is consistent with the ambitious target of eliminating dependence on foreign saving by 1980. Perhaps other techniques for subsidizing exporters should be found, and savers should be treated in a more even-handed manner.

In addition to financing subsidies to exporters, another reason for tolerating low nominal rates of interest to both depositors and certain classes of bank borrowers has been advanced. The term structure of finance in an inflationary economy is typically very short. Even if the government succeeds in raising short-term deposit and lending rates of interest to offset inflationary expectations (as the Korean government did successfully after 1965 and the Taiwanese government had done in the 1950s), it is not easy to channel the increased flow of saving to long-term finance for plant and equipment expenditures. Borrowers remain reluctant to lock themselves into a high nominal interest-rate costs with, say, a ten-year bond issue, because the rate of inflation may slow down and leave them with monetary commitments that they cannot meet. In contrast, savers (depositors) remain apprehensive lest accelerated inflation wipe them out.

The failure to reduce price inflation in Korea, and the need to offset this situation with high short-term nominal deposit and lending rates of interest, has meant that domestic sources of long-term finance have not developed commensurately with the high growth in the banking system's lending capacity; and the business sector remains quite vulnerable to short-term cyclical fluctuations. Hence, Korea continues to rely on foreign saving increasingly at the "long" end of the finance spectrum. Longer-term supplier credits for imported capital equipment and foreign equity investment can come in directly through the foreign exchange mechanism. Alternatively, the government sector can and does act as a financial intermediary in this process by running a surplus in its ordinary budget that is lent at long term to the Korean business sector perhaps through the banks, while government-owned enterprises borrow long abroad. Various development banks can perform a similar intermediation role.

Hence, the failure to develop *domestic* long-term sources of finance has left Korea unduly dependent on foreign financial resources. Indeed, if long-term debts are denominated in dollar terms, then continual exchange depreciation of the won, as occurred over the 1965-72 period, operates much like a system of indexed bonds. To some extent, this ameliorates the risk seen from uncertain price inflation as long as indexed bonds are not available for sale to domestic savers.

This pressure to provide long-term finance to domestic investors helps explain why the Korean government may have brought nominal rates of interest down too quickly (Table 1). There has been a whole series of interventions culminating in a draconian reform in August, 1972 to force longer-term borrowing rates down—both in the organized banking system and in the informal or traditional credit markets. But if banks are ordered to reduce their long-term nominal lending rates of interest, this procedure will of course force them to reduce short-term deposit rates to remain solvent. In an inflationary environment, the conflict between lengthening the term structure of business finance and raising the private propensity to save remains acute.

V.   Concluding Comments

The Korean financial system has grown rapidly since 1965 and has been a
leading force in Korea's highly successful economic development. The major
question asked in this chapter was whether current financial policy is adequate
to ensure the future sharp increases in the private saving propensity that are
necessary to maintain high growth while eliminating dependence on foreign
saving.

The present conjunction of policies is seen as high price inflation,
derived from inappropriate financial subsidies to exporters, coupled with a
desire to reduce nominal rates of interest in order to make it easier to lengthen
the term structure of business financing. This set of policies may well be inconsistent with the target of increased private saving. Indeed, the danger of
returning to a more repressed financial system, which existed prior to 1965, is
always present as long as savers are punished with low or negative returns on
monetary assets. A reduction in the willingness to hold monetary assets, and
bank lending based on it, may bind particularly sharply if the curb market
remains moribund. In the absence of a flexible fringe source of curb finance,
public policy toward the monetary-banking system becomes even more
critical.

The first-best solution is the conceptually simple one of ending suppressed
or overt price inflation (as measured by the wholesale price index) by gaining
strict control over the monetary base. This would require that savers holding
monetary assets be released from their onerous task of providing subsidies to
exporters. With stability in the WPI, nominal rates of interest might be kept
around the 10-percent level that Taiwan used successfully through the 1960s.

Rather less satisfactory second-best solutions abound if price inflation is
assumed to continue. One such solution is to introduce indexed bonds con-
taining a monetary correction factor that makes long-term borrowing more
attractive, and such indexed bonds may also seem attractive to some classes
of savers with a longer time perspective.

A second is to introduce more schemes of compulsory private saving
such as the newly mooted National Welfare Pension that would collect 4
percent of wages from workers and 4 percent from employers in most
"organized" industrial activities. Another partial solution is simply to keep
nominal rates of interest high to offset the continuing inflation and preserve
private saving propensities. One then has to scale down attempts to
lengthen the term structure of business financing. However, reducing
nominal rates of interest *before* inflation is brought under control seems
to be an unfortunate and unwise policy.

Nevertheless, one can't be too pessimistic about an economy like the
Korean one, that has enjoyed such remarkable success over the past ten years.

REFERENCES

1. J. G. Gurley, and E. S. Shaw, *Money in a Theory of Finance*, Brookings Institution, Washington, D.C., 1960.

2. J. G. Gurley, H. T. Patrick, and E. S. Shaw, "The Financial Structure of Korea," United States Operations Missions to Korea, July 1965 (processed).

3. International Monetary Fund, *International Financial Statistics*.

4. Kim Kwong Suk, "The Causes and Effects of Inflation in Korea," January 1973, Korean Development Institute (processed).

5. Kim Mahn Je, Song Heeyhm, and Kim Kwong Suk, "A Revised Note of Monetary Forecasts for 1973," January 1973, Korean Development Institute (processed).

6. R. I. McKinnon, "Saving Projections and the Money Supply," Korean Development Institute, July 1973 (processed).

7. R. I. McKinnon, *Money and Capital in Economic Development*, The Brookings Institution, Washington, D.C., 1973.

8. Woo H. Nam, "Domestic Savings: Projections and Feasibility," Korean Development Institute, August 31, 1972 (processed).

9. Republic of Korea, "Strategies for Domestic Saving Mobilization," Ministry of Finance, September 1973 (processed).

10. E. W. Shaw, *Financial Deepening in Economic Development*, Oxford, New York, 1973.

TIBOR SCITOVSKY

Department of Economics
Stanford University
Stanford, California

I despaired at first over having nothing to find fault with and so nothing to say on McKinnon's paper; but then I realized that I did not really understand his argument—the best reason for finding nothing to object to. If I am not alone in not fully grasping what he is saying, then my effort to spell out McKinnon's argument in my kind of language will not be useless.

In McKinnon's comparison of Korea with Taiwan, I was puzzled at first by his making two rate-of-return calculations for both countries; but then I realized that the rate of return on currency and demand deposits is merely an index of the rate of inflation with a negative sign. The argument then boils down to looking at the real return on savings as an index of the strength with which interest-rate policy is applied, and looking at the real return on currency as an index of the success of such policy—at least as far as its anti-inflationary impact is concerned. We then learn that although Korea applied stronger measures than Taiwan, in the sense of offering higher real returns on savings deposits, she was less successful in controlling inflation, presumably because the ravages of war were more recent in Korea, and also because Korea's high interest-rate policy was gradually eroding.

One reason for that erosion, more hinted at than stated, seems to have been the subsidization of exports in Korea through low-interest export credits and the success of that policy in expanding exports, and with them also the stock of export credit outstanding. That would naturally lower the average rate on loans outstanding and so presumably bring pressure to bear for lowering rates on savings deposits as well. McKinnon considers subsidizing exports but would rather rely on other means of doing it if done at all. His reason seems to be his fear that, quite apart from what export promotion through cheap export credits does to interest rates, it is inflationary also in a more direct way: It contributes too much to the expansion of the monetary base. I would feel happier with the chain of causality more explicitly laid out; but that may well be a very personal Keynesian unease, which others here may not share.

Let me concentrate therefore on just the more puzzling aspect of McKinnon's reasoning.

We are told that "exports are projected to rise to eliminate the large current account deficit that now exists" but in the very next sentence we are also told that "credit subsidies to exporters create a balance-of-payments surplus and the resulting accumulation of exchange reserves expands the money base." Put together, the two statements seem to say that the inflow of capital is excessive from a balance-of-payments point of view, though presumably not as a supplement to insufficient domestic capital formation.

The picture that emerges seems to be the following. Expanding domestic capital formation was and remains clearly desirable both as an anti-inflationary measure and also in order to make the country's growth less dependent on foreign capital; and if those aims were to be achieved, it would also be necessary to expand exports in order to maintain balance-of-payments equilibrium in the face of a diminishing inflow of foreign capital. However, whatever other policy mistakes the Koreans committed, they also chose the wrong method for encouraging exports. Not only did cheap export credits make it harder to pursue a high interest-rate policy as a means of encouraging saving; but the very success of that export policy added to the inflationary pressures and—paradoxically enough—encouraged a continued inflow of capital.

That brings me to a problem that McKinnon does not discuss explicitly, which bothers and has always bothered me, and which may well have to do with Korea's problems. I am an enthusiastic convert to Shaw's policy of encouraging financial intermediation and domestic capital formation through allowing the rate of return to small savers to approximate the rate of return on capital; but I have never understood how that policy can be coordinated with the requirement of making foreign capital available to less developed countries on the cheapest possible terms. How can you assure the efficient allocation of capital funds, the proper combination of labor and capital, and the proper degree of labor intensity, when you have pretty high real rates of interest on domestic capital and very much lower ones on foreign loans. I can think of some theoretically simple and politically unrealistic solutions to that problem but not of a practicable one. Yet, that problem may conceivably be another reason why Korea is increasingly straying from the straight Shavian path and falling back into its bad old ways.

Part II

**Alternatives to Domestic
Financial Intermediation**

Capital Markets in the Less Developed Countries: The Group Principle

NATHANIEL H. LEFF

Graduate School of Business
Columbia University
New York, New York

Students of economic development owe a large debt to Edward S. Shaw and his illuminating contributions on money and financial intermediation in economic development. His seminal 1960 work, with John G. Gurley, on *Money in a Theory of Finance,* taught us all a great deal, and provided as well a focus and stimulus for much high-quality research in this area.[1] The present paper attempts to continue in this line of analysis. However, it also introduces into the discussion some features of capital markets in the less-developed countries that have previously been neglected.

I. Introduction

The ideal type of efficient capital market performs two principal functions. First, it channels resources from savers to investors; and second, it allocates investment resources among different activities according to relative rates of return. A perfectly functioning capital market does not of course correct problems that may be associated with the initial distribution of wealth. Nor does it overcome some of the well known conditions of market failure, such as those caused by the existence of externalities and public goods. Nevertheless, the foregoing comments on the functions of a capital market suggest that an economy without an effective capital market would suffer the allocational losses involved in having no mechanism to ensure that capital is allocated where its marginal productivity is greatest. It would also fail to achieve an optimal intertemporal allocation of resources by equating marginal time preference with the marginal productivity of capital. Savings rates would be adversely affected because of the lower overall return to capital in the economy, as well as because of an unnecessarily large spread between the returns to savers and the returns to investors. Consequently, an economy without an effective capital market would suffer considerable efficiency losses, both static and dynamic.

Since less developed countries manifestly lack formal financial institutions that perform these tasks of a capital market, it has sometimes been suggested that they suffer from the losses just mentioned. The purpose of this chapter, however, is to suggest qualifications to this interpretation. The view, outlined above, of capital markets in terms of functions rather than formal institutions may seem self-evident. However, specifying it clearly, and adding some observations that have previously not been included in the literature on capital markets in the less developed countries avoids some misconceptions. In particular, this chapter draws attention to an institutional feature whose existence has not been widely noted, and analyzes its effects in mitigating the distortions that the weakness of a formal capital market would imply. Some of the implications for economic development, and for financial management and government policy in the less developed countries will also be considered.

The focus of this chapter is, however, limited. Throughout, it concentrates on the capital market activities related to saving and investment. It does not consider the full range of financial intermediation in less developed countries, nor does it deal with the special distortions introduced by such conditions as inflation and government regulations.

II.   The Groups

In many of the less developed countries, much of the modern, large-scale activity in the private sector is characterized by a special institutional feature. Following the Latin American term, we may call this structure the "Group," although this pattern of business organization is also common in Africa and Asia.[2] The Group is a multienterprise firm that draws its capital from sources extending beyond a single nuclear family; e.g., from people linked by communal, tribal, ethnic, or personal relations of trust and mutual confidence. In addition, somewhat like the *zaibatsu* in pre-World War II Japan, the Groups invest and produce in several product markets rather than in a single product line. For example, a Group's single decision-making center may encompass activities ranging as widely as textiles, cement, fabricated steel, zinc mining, and cattle ranching. The largest Groups also possess their own banks. Much of the private industrial sector, and particularly the activities that involve

large capital investments, are in practice Group operations. The Groups in fact
constitute a mechanism for mobilizing and pooling entrepreneurship and technical expertise as well as capital in large-scale, modern activities. Certain
negative aspects of the Groups' effects on economic development are discussed
elsewhere. What is important in the present context is that the Groups also
perform the principal functions of a capital market.[3]

Given their participation in the activities that are both capital intensive
and of large minimum scale, the Groups themselves own a large share of the
capital stock in the private industrial sector of the less developed countries.
Moreover, because of the Groups' quasi-rents and monopoly power in product
markets, their returns are likely to be above the economy-wide average.
Hence, the Groups account for a large share of corporate profits in the private
sector. In addition to this direct control of a pool of investable resources, the
Groups also have access to other savings in the less developed countries. As
is well known, the distribution of income in these countries is highly unequal,
and a large share of income goes to 5 percent of the population [20]. Because
of their high percentage in total income, even if their propensity to save is no
higher than that of the rest of the population, these people account for a large
portion of total household savings. The Groups' personal and family connections include relations with these monied elements outside of their immediate
circle of entrepreneur-managers. Consequently, taking account of their corporate profits, the Groups have access to a sizable share of total private savings in
the less developed countries. This conclusion is reinforced by the fact that, as
mentioned, the largest Groups also possess their own banks and insurance
companies, which can tap some of the savings of the nonrich.

Not only do the Groups provide a mechanism for channeling savings to
investors, but they also perform the interactivity allocational functions of a
capital market. Each Group allocates its overall resources among its various
activities according to (crude) criteria of their relative profitability. Because
of the Groups' interactivity capital flows, the concept of "self-finance" takes
on a special meaning: Cash flow generated in one activity can be used to increase the capital stock in other, widely diverse activities. The Groups'
diversified activities also facilitate the flow of information, and reduce the uncertainty that would otherwise raise the costs of investment throughout the
economy.

Furthermore, the various Groups overlap in their activities. That is,
Group A may be in activities x_1, x_2, x_5, x_{10}; Group B, in activities $x_2, x_6,$
x_9, x_{10}; Group C, in activities $x_2, x_3, x_4, x_7, x_8, x_9$, etc. The Groups' concentration of entrepreneurial and managerial resources also enables them to
enter a specific activity that is earning unusually high returns. Thus the Groups'
investment allocations channel capital to private-sector activities that are subject
to capital constraints, and exert a strong pressure for equalizing returns at the

margin in all private-sector activities. In effect, then, the Groups provide a
mechanism that arbitrages among investment opportunities and allocates capital
throughout the private sector according to marginal rates of return.[4]

III.   Some Apparent Limitations

The *de facto* capital market provided by the Groups is clearly subject to some
important limitations. However, even some of these deficiencies are more apparent than real. Also, in the interest of analytical clarity, it is essential to
distinguish between the distortions that arise because of other conditions in
the less developed countries (for example, inflation and government under-
pricing of capital) rather than because of capital-market distortions *per se.*

A.   Segmentation

First, such a "capital market" is notably lacking in financial intermediation, for
the Groups must create the real assets that enter their portfolios. Despite the
lack of financial intermediation, however, investors are able to include in their
portfolios assets with a large range of choice in their maturities and in their
risk-return profiles. Diversification is in fact a major feature of the Groups'
mode of operation, and their portfolios include assets ranging from short-term
commercial paper to urban real estate to widely diverse industrial activities.
        Another characteristic of this "capital market" is its high degree of
segmentation. That is, capital can flow only to those activities where the
Groups participate. Even this distortion is mitigated, however, because of the
Groups' capacity to marshal the entrepreneurial and technical resources
necessary to enter new activities that offer above-average returns. Entry into
new activities has in fact been a prominent feature of the Groups' pattern of
evolution, and has done much to reduce the potential negative effects of
capital-market segmentation. This willingness and capacity to enter new
activities has also been reflected in investments in the agricultural sector in
cases where (private) returns appeared to justify them.

B.   Portfolio Composition

One may also object to some aspects of the Groups' investment portfolios.
We should distinguish, however, between the allocation effects caused by
conditions that are intrinsic to the Groups' capital-market operations, and those
allocation effects that are due to other conditions of the less developed countries.
For example, the Groups' propensity to include urban real estate in their

portfolios is usually criticized in the less developed countries because of its alleged low social productivity. Such investments may, however, be justified for providing the relatively safe and liquid assets that are necessary, in terms of portfolio balance, to permit the Groups to make other investments in industrial activities that may be more risky and less liquid [4].[5] Moreover, in the conditions of rapid urbanization and growth of demand for urban facilities in the less developed countries, it is not even clear that investments in urban construction do have a low social productivity.

Similarly, the proclivity to invest in land near urban areas in less developed countries is often taken as evidence either of irrational preferences, or as reflecting a distortion created by the absence of an effective capital market. With rapid urban population growth and limited decentralization of infrastructure facilities, however, land offers profitable opportunities for capital appreciation. At the private level, wealth accumulation in land is as rational as asset growth in physical capital.[6] If a socially suboptimal allocation of resources results because of fiscal nonneutrality and the failure to tax pure rents, the cause lies with the pattern of taxation in less developed countries (which generally levy very low taxes on land) rather than with capital-market distortions [24].

Observers in the less developed countries have also criticized the banks controlled by the Groups for their allegedly irrational preference for short-term commercial paper. The considerations just cited concerning rates of return and portfolio balance also apply here. Moreover, a bank's assets cannot be considered in isolation from the pattern of its liabilities. Under the conditions in a less developed country, most bank liabilities consist of firms' working capital, which is held in the form of short-term balances.

It is also evident that the Groups do not channel a large volume of capital (directly) to peasant farmers and small-scale producers in the industrial sector. What is not always clear, however, is that this allocation pattern is due to imperfections in the capital market. Given the Groups' yield and risk alternatives, private returns (net of transactions costs to small-unit loans) may not justify a large volume of credit to small-scale producers. It is of course possible that the net social returns of such loans exceed the net private returns, and/or that social risk is less than private risk. Such a situation must be demonstrated rather than asserted, however. The experience of the U.S. government credit programs for small-scale and minority businessmen is not encouraging in this respect. In any case, failure to allocate credit in such instances is due to conditions leading to market failure in any (private) capital market rather than to the specific structure of the Groups.

Finally, another criticism levied against the Groups' capital-market operations is that they do not provide a market that voluntarily absorbs large quantities of government securities. This unwillingness is to some extent offset by government policies that oblige financial institutions to hold a large portion of their reserves in the form of public-sector securities. In any case, the reluctance to provide an active market in government paper is to be attributed not to intrinsic deficiencies in the capital market, but to government inflationary policies that lead to a very low or negative real rate of return on such securities.

C. Inflation

High and unstable rates of inflation in some less developed countries have also been the cause of other financial-market distortions. Apart from possible effects on portfolio composition, inflation has, in the absence of indexing provisions, adversely affected the market for debt instruments. This is especially unfortunate since in terms of their disclosure requirements, and their cultural proximity to locally familiar institutions, debt instruments may have a large potential market in less developed countries. Furthermore, inflation not compensated by other measures has also led to retrogression of formal stock exchanges.[7]

As discussed subsequently, the Groups may profit from inflation and add to its distortions. It would be too much, however, to ascribe to the Groups and to capital-market conditions a large role in causing inflation, even indirectly, in less developed countries. Rather, in relatively large less developed countries, which lack the discipline imposed by a large foreign-trade sector [26], political conditions may generate high rates of inflation.[8] This interpretation, which attributes high rates of inflation in some less developed countries to causes other than capital-market conditions, is supported by a comparative perspective. Although they also have Groups and weaknesses in their formal capital-market institutions, most less developed countries that do approximate the conditions of the small and open economy, have in fact had low rates of price inflation [28].

Finally, as we have seen, the Groups have available a large and varied range of investment opportunities. Consequently, it is not clear that in less developed countries where rapid inflation does occur, it leads to investment distortions any greater than would occur under inflationary conditions in countries with better-developed formal financial institutions. Inflation (and the usual government regulations associated with it) seem more relevant here than capital-market structure per se.

D. "Capital Flight"

Deficiencies in local capital markets have also been held responsible for "capital flight" from the less developed countries. Further analysis, however, suggests that this charge, too, may be excessive and misplaced. Political crises, mispricing of foreign exchange, and expectations of devaluation would of course lead to capital outflows regardless of financial institutional development in the less developed countries. More generally, acquisition of foreign-denominated instruments may be a normal part of the wealth-accumulation process in the less developed countries, to an extent that the very term "capital flight" is misleading.

As Professor Kindleberger has emphasized in his discussion of the European financial centers, there may well be economies of scale in the operation of capital markets [29]. Even under favorable economic and institutional conditions, the economies of the less developed countries are too small to achieve minimum-cost scale in the operation of capital markets. The phenomenon, cited by Kindleberger, of European investors buying European securities issued in Wall Street suggests that real cost savings may accrue through use of international capital markets.

Furthermore, as just mentioned, all less developed economies are relatively small—smaller, for example, than the economy of California. Because of systemic risk and the covariance in the yields of assets in a relatively small economy, portfolio balance requires holding external assets. Little is gained by labeling this diversification as capital flight. No one would expect Californian wealthholders to hold their assets exclusively in Californian instruments.

Inflation and the need for liquidity to achieve portfolio balance also account for another aspect of capital flight. In the more developed countries, short-term government securities provide a low-risk, highly liquid asset. As noted, however, these securities do not have the same properties in the less developed countries; and indeed no other domestic assets may have these attributes. In this capital market, private investors can invest only in assets that they create themselves, and private-sector capitalists cannot by themselves create the stable price level that would make the holding of money or government securities an attractive liquid asset. Indeed, as discussed subsequently, in terms of returns on their net asset position, a noninflationary environment may well not be in the Groups' overall interest. Consequently, to obtain low-risk, highly liquid assets, wealthholders in the less developed countries may have to hold foreign exchange or short-term instruments issued in the more developed countries. Assuming preferences that are unit wealth-elastic with respect to risk and liquidity, the magnitude of such capital exports will depend on the relative (private) returns available from investments in the less developed country. Under conditions of increasing income and wealth, unchanged risks, and nondeclining relative rates of return over time, such capital exports will proceed at a constant rate.[9] Even with such favorable assumptions, however, the absolute magnitude of the foreign assets held by domestic capitalists will, of course, increase.

Furthermore, because of portfolio-balance considerations and the need for liquidity and diversification away from local systemic risk, domestic capitalists may be expected to hold largely short-term, low-risk foreign assets. At the same time, for reasons of *their* portfolio balance, if they face the same menu of potential investments, foreign investors' portfolios should be heavily weighted toward longer-term investments in the less developed countries.[10] Such a differential composition of local and foreign investor international portfolios has often been attributed to differences in investors' preferences. However, the same pattern may be observed even if foreign investors are no more enterprising, and even if their time and risk preferences are identical with those of local capitalists.

More generally, the assets held in the Groups' portfolios reflect the need for portfolio balance as well as the risk and yield conditions present in the less developed countries. For example, in some cases, what may appear superficially as capital-market inefficiency in the persistence of differences in returns between activities should more correctly be ascribed to risks and uncertainties due to erratic relative price changes in a changing economic and policy environment [32]. Moreover, these risk and return conditions have themselves often been influenced by government policies. For reasons of private returns, the Groups have in fact generally responded to the incentives and disincentives created by government [18]. To the extent that the composition of the Groups' portfolios is judged unsatisfactory, the responsibility lies largely with other economic conditions and with the incentive structure created by government policies rather than with the deficiencies of the capital market.

IV. Some Distortions

Although the Groups perform some of the savings mobilization and investment allocation functions of a capital market, it is also clear that the Groups constitute a less than perfect private capital market. For example, both in the market for equity and in the market for debt capital, the Groups can often exert oligopsonist market power.

Furthermore, the proportion of total potential private savings that is channeled through the Group mechanism is surely less than unity. This limitation is to some extent relaxed by the activities of Groups with their own banks, which have an obvious interest in enlarging the domestic savings base. There is no intrinsic reason why Groups with financial institutions should not issue instruments that are attractive to small savers. In conditions where legislation, unit costs, and returns are favorable, as in Mexico, Groups have in fact followed such a policy. The magnitude of potential savings among the great mass of the population in less developed countries, however, may in any case be small because of demographic and economic conditions (including government regulation of deposit rates). But even among the monied elements of society, the "private placement" aspect of the Group structure may not mobilize the full volume of potential savings.

This limitation stems from an additional condition that must be satisfied for large volumes of capital to flow into the Group structure on "preferential" (undistorted) terms—social-personal connections that permit mutual trust. This condition is to some extent overcome by purposive actions in personal (and pseudopersonal) relations, for example, planned marriage. Some Groups have indeed expanded the volume of their resources by marriage policies resembling those of the Hapsburgs. Nevertheless, the addition of the personal constraint may limit the volume of individual Group activities below the level that might be obtained in a capital market where relations are limited to the cash nexus.

Not only is the volume of Group capital-market activities limited by personal conditions, but allocation patterns may be distorted as well. One feature of these capital markets is the relatively small number of large participants. Each of the major Groups is a relatively large fish, albeit in a small pool, with an ensuing sense of individual power and autonomy in decision making. Consequently, investment in projects that are beyond the capacity of an individual Group—given other portfolio commitments and the desire for diversification—and that would require joint action with other investors are difficult to arrange; for each Group is accustomed to complete control over its operations. The contrast is with capital markets such as those in the United States, where investment resources are available in smaller and more divisible units, and owners are too small individually to dominate the management of the enterprise. Consequently, a large project can be launched without the major investor's losing control.

In the less developed countries, however, this pool of resources from private investors, who are unable and do not expect to exercise close control, is not available. Hence, in the less developed countries, entry into some projects or activities would require an alliance with another Group. Control over such an enterprise, however, would reflect the instability implicit in bargaining between powerful Groups.[11] Consequently, unless a satisfactory fusion of Groups can be arranged, e.g., by marriage, investments in activities that, because of their capital intensity or large minimum scale, require especially large capital commitments, may not be undertaken by the private capital market. This situation may lead to suboptimal levels of investment in some activities. It has also been one of the factors accounting for the large role of state enterprises and foreign firms—which *can* mobilize the required resources and which do not face these potential intracompany political difficulties—in some activities in the less developed countries. In themselves, such investments by state and foreign enterprises do not, of course, constitute an economic distortion. The point is simply that partly because of the Group structure, private capital markets do not play as large a role in financing capital formation as they did historically in the more developed countries.

V. Aggregate Saving and Investment Rates

In addition to the activities of the Groups, which perform some of the functions of a capital market, two other institutions also mitigate the deficiencies of formal capital markets in the less developed countries. As mentioned above, direct foreign investment can often enter activities where returns are high in relation to those elsewhere in the economy, and thus align rates of return. Also, the government draws upon lower- and middle-class resources through its taxation, and accounts for a sizable share of total capital formation in a manner that often attempts to correct capital-market distortions. Much public-sector investment in less developed countries is directed to activities and regions where it is believed that the conditions of private-market failure—e.g., externalities, myopia, and uncertainty—lead to a socially suboptimal allocation of capital.[12]

Taking account of the activities of the Groups, direct foreign investors, and the government, then, it appears that institutions exist that greatly reduce potential distortions created by the weakness of formal capital markets organized on the American pattern in the less developed countries. These three investors account for a large percentage of aggregate investment in the less developed countries. Consequently, their capacity for new entry and interactivity capital flows reduces the variance in the economy-wide rate of return to capital.

Furthermore, Goldsmith's data show that despite the reputed deficiencies of their capital markets, the less developed countries have experienced a rate of growth of financial assets, in real terms, that is greater than the average rate experienced in the more developed countries during the postwar period [33]. This fact is especially noteworthy because some of the capital-market activities we have discussed—e.g., informal intra-Group placements, and government investments financed by taxation—took place without the issue of financial instruments that would be captured by Goldsmith's data.

In light of the de facto capital market present in the less developed countries, it is probably unrealistic to attribute much of the difference in aggregate rates of saving and investment between the more and the less developed countries to the difference in their levels of formal financial development. Some support for this suggestion is provided in Goldsmith's multivariate regressions [33]. These show no statistically significant relation between his measure of financial development—the ratio of the assets of financial institutions to GNP—and the share of fixed capital formation in GNP for a cross section of 18 more developed countries [33, p. 58]. Time-series estimates for six less developed countries showed a statistically insignificant relation for five countries, and a significant negative coefficient for one country [33, pp. 62-63]. It is also worth noting that most of the countries of Western Europe, the state of whose capital markets is also frequently lamented, have achieved aggregate saving and investment rates higher than those of the United States.[13]

More generally, ascribing much of the difference in rates of saving and investment between the more developed countries and the less developed countries to differences in their formal capital-market institutions misses some of the underlying real factors. For example, Goldsmith's data indicated that a major source of the disparity in financial development between the more developed and the less developed countries lies in the smaller contribution of insurance and pension organizations in the less developed countries.[14] A smaller demand for life insurance and pensions in the less developed countries is only to be expected, however. This is because a much smaller proportion of the population is in the prime age groups that normally purchase such instruments [35].

Furthermore, risk and rate-of-return conditions in the less developed countries may not be conducive to high rates of saving and investment. Not only may low overall rates-of-return to capital be low, [36] but uncertainty concerning future conditions in the economy may be high. The difficulties that private entrepreneurs face in anticipating the future in these environments is illustrated by the performance of public-sector agencies charged with this task. Despite their aggregate perspective and the superior information available to them, government planning offices in the less developed countries have not been able to avoid serious forecasting errors.

VI. Additional Financial and Monetary Effects of the Groups

Awareness of the Groups' structure and operations also helps clarify other aspects of the functioning of the less developed economies. As noted earlier, the Groups' pattern of expansion involves both entry into new activities financed from cash flow generated in earlier investments, and the channeling of investment resources among their diversified activities. Consequently, the growth of the capital stock in a given activity does not depend strictly on the magnitude of the corporate savings and reinvestment rate within that specific activity.[15] Furthermore, in cases where Groups have their own financial institutions, the supply-of-funds schedule that they face is less kinked between "internal" and "external" finance than might otherwise be imagined. Indeed, for Groups with their own banks, the distinctions between internal finance and external bank loans, or between long-term and short-term (but perpetually renewed) bank loans is not completely meaningful.

The Group structure and the capital-market conditions to which such structure leads also create a special environment for optimizing policy at the micro level. Noting some of these conditions is especially important because they sometimes differ from those assumed or posited in the corporate financial theory developed in the United States. Because of these different conditions, optimizing financial management in this environment may lead to decisions that might appear superficially as being irrational, or as indicating culturally different managerial preferences. For example, although corporate owner-managers might be expected to be especially concerned with the risk of bankruptcy, the situation is clearly different when they also own, or are in close relations with, the bank that is their creditor. At the same time, since profits accrue to the managers, they may optimize with higher debt-equity (gearing) ratios than would bureaucrat-managers. Equity is in any case less liquid than in the more developed countries, because of the thinness of securities markets, the cost of whose modification exceeds the gain to an individual firm. Also, because of the close relation between firms and their banks, "debt" may have some of the characteristics of equity. In particular, capital service on (non-debenture) debt may be adjusted or rescheduled if the firm comes on difficult times.

In fact, the Group structure does help to explain some features of financial management at the micro level in the less developed countries. The instability and uncertainty of the environment that confronts firms in the less developed countries might be expected to induce firms to hold relatively large cash balances. In fact, however, liquidity ratios for the private-industry sector in some less developed countries are low [37]. Three explanations related to the Group structure are relevant in explaining this apparent paradox. First, inventory-theoretic analysis of cash management indicates that optimal cash holdings increase less than proportionally with the size of a firm's operations [38]. Thus, the large scale of a Group's overall activities may reduce its demands for cash balances. Also, the flow of information among individual Group activities may reduce firm-specific (if not systemic) uncertainty, and hence reduce the need for precautionary balances [39]. Finally, an offsetting pattern for covariance in the demands for cash balances such as those between diverse Group operations may reduce the needs for overall liquidity.[16]

Low equity/debt ratios are another feature of firms in the less developed countries [37]. This financing pattern has usually been attributed to institutional distortions that limit the supply of equity capital. For example, the thinness of open primary-securities markets makes common stock relatively illiquid. As mentioned previously, however, in the case of the Groups, high gearing ratios may well reflect an optimizing policy of owner-managers who have a private incentive to assume the risks and potential gains of high leverage. This interpretation implies that the failure of many large firms in the less developed countries to "go public" and issue substantial equity to outsiders may derive largely from demand rather than from supply conditions in the capital market.

Finally, the phenomenon of the Groups helps explain the absence of real opposition on the part of bankers to the inflationary policies of many less developed countries [41]. This situation contrasts with that of the 19th-century United States, where the Eastern bankers constituted a distinct creditor class which, on income-distributional grounds, was strongly opposed to currency depreciation. With the Group structure, however, creditors and debtors (within the Group) are the same people. In the case of the Group with its own bank, in which bank liabilities to non-Group members are allocated to Group investments, the Group is in fact a net debtor.[17] Under these conditions, the Groups may not have a strong interest in the maintenance of price stability.

VII.   Policy Implications

A.   Some Specifics

An understanding of the role of the Groups in the functioning of the less developed economies also suggests some implications for government policy-makers. First, because of the Group structure, the supply of capital to individual activities is much more elastic than might be expected without taking account of intra-Group capital mobility. The need for government subsidies to increase the flow of capital to specific industries is correspondingly lessened. In fact, given the possibilities for capital mobility between Group activities, government subsidies to promote capital formation in specific activities may have ambiguous effects. As international aid agencies allocating capital to specific projects have learned, the marginal project that they are in fact financing can be very different from the project they have in mind. Similarly, because of intra-Group financial flows, government allocation of short-term credit to specific activities—a practice common in periods of overall monetary stringency such as those following a devaluation—also has unclear effects.

One can think of some obvious ways to improve the functioning of the capital markets described above. For example, a policy of granting more bank charters to permit greater entry would increase competition and reduce oligopsonist power in the capital (and product) markets. Since the object is to increase the number of decision-making centers in the banking sector, such a policy of permitting entry might also be extended to foreign-owned banks.

Similarly, policies permitting realistic deposit rates (and indexing of deposits in inflation-prone countries) may increase the volume of household saving that enters the capital market. The pre-World War I Japanese experience suggests that with appropriate deposit rates, savings accounts promoted through

the network of postal agencies can be used to mobilize savings even among
the broader population. Also, stricter accounting and disclosure regulation
might increase the willingness of people who are not immediate members of a
Group to participate in Group investments.[18] Finally, capital-market efficiency
might also be enhanced if government allocation criteria, which affect both
public- and private-sector investment decisions, were based to a greater extent
on explicit economic analysis rather than the implicit analysis contained in
economic ideology.

B. Capital-Market Reform and Aggregate Savings Rates

Perhaps the major implication of this discussion, however, is that changes in
formal capital market institutions per se should not be expected to yield
dramatic results, e.g., such as raising aggregate savings rates in the less developed
countries. Some of the functions of a capital market are already performed by
the institutions we have discussed. Also, improved formal financial institutions
would presumably have their greatest impact in increasing the opportunities
open to household savers. However, there appear to exist substantial substitution effects both between household and government savings [43], and between
household and corporate savings.[19] Hence, although household savings might
increase with improved financial institutions, aggregate savings would not rise
to the same extent.

    Furthermore, as noted earlier, unless real return-and-risk conditions in the
economy are favorable, transplanting capital-market institutions to the less
developed countries should not be expected to have significant effects. Although
the economic history of the developed countries indicates that capital-market
institutions played an important role in their development, objective economic
conditions are often very different in the present less developed countries. For
example, postal savings were able to mobilize the resources of small savers in
19th-century Japan. The institutions themselves, however would probably have
been insufficient if, as in many current less developed countries, inflation had
led to negative real returns on saving deposits. Similarly, pre-1914 Japan and
Russia used special banking institutions effectively to channel resources to high-
priority investors. As Rondo Cameron has pointed out, however, these resources
had already been mobilized in the real sector through a mechanism usually lacking in current less developed countries—a surplus in the public sector [1, p. 306].
Development of formal financial institutions in the less developed countries may
be a desirable goal for other reasons.[20] However, hopes that such institutional
changes will in themselves lead to significant increases in aggregate savings and
investment ratios appear exaggerated.

C.   Capital-Market Reform as a Goal for Policymakers

One can readily understand why "capital market reform" has been an attractive policy approach for policymakers in the less developed countries in recent years. Institutional improvement appears to be a relatively costless way to raise rate of savings and investment. Indeed, by narrowing the spread between the returns to savers and the returns to investors, institutional reform seems to be a policy solution with the very desirable properties of a nonzero game: Both savers and investors benefit, while national savings rates also rise. As suggested previously, however, the net benefits obtained by improving formal capital-market institution may have been overstated.[21] Hence, in a world in which the energies available for reform are always limited, policymakers' focus on improving capital-market institutions may itself have had net costs, by diverting attention from other, more fruitful approaches to raising saving rates and increasing allocative efficiency.

In any case, an approach that formulates problems of capital markets largely in terms of improving their institutions may suffer analytically from a serious identification problem. It is not clear whether the present situation stems largely from conditions on the supply side, or from the demand for financial services. The emphasis on formal institutional improvements seems to be based largely on a "supply" theory of institutional development. (A similar point was noted in ref. 49.) As such, the theory has neglected important "demand" conditions that have inhibited the development of some capital-market institutions along the American or European pattern. See the theory of institutional innovation presented in [50].

As noted earlier, the desire to maintain high leverage, taken together with the opportunities for obtaining capital from within the Group (or, on a debt basis, from government or foreign sources) help explain why many large firms in the less developed countries are not interested in issuing large blocks of equity on the stock exchange. It is also worth stressing that current less developed countries *have* adopted many banking and capital-market institutions that were innovated in developing countries during the 19th century. The list of institutional innovations that have been accepted includes: the use of nonspecie currency, demand deposits, discounting, country-wide bank networks, development banks, and central banking [1]. The major innovations that have not been implemented effectively are widespread markets for primary and secondary securities. The fact that these capital-market innovations have also been available, while less developed countries have adopted many new capital-market institutions for which local demand existed, suggests that demand rather than supply conditions may have inhibited development of these institutions.

VIII. Conclusions

Chapter 5 has pointed to the existence in the less developed countries of an institution, the Groups, which performs some of the functions of a capital market, by collecting private savings and allocating them according to relative rates of return. Taken together with the investment activities of the government and of foreign investors, the Groups' operations greatly reduce the allocation losses that would occur if capital markets in the less developed countries were, in fact, as deficient as is often alleged. The suggestion that, to a large extent, a different institutional framework can substitute for the "prerequisite" of a formal capital market in economic development is also supported by historical analysis. The Groups are clearly similar in some aspects to the large investment banks that played a prominent capital-market role in the industrialization of Japan and of "late-comer" countries in 19th-century Europe [51]. Similarly, "personal finance" along clique networks seems to have been important for modern large-scale industry in the United States, too, until the 20th century [31].[22]

Furthermore, as we have seen, some conditions that are sometimes attributed to the capital market in less developed countries—e.g., excessive rates of inflation, or "capital flight,"—stem from other causes. Also, many of the negative features that are ascribed to capital-market deficiencies in the less developed countries are in fact due to other conditions related to portfolio balance and to the level of risk and (private) returns. In cases where Group investment allocations do not coincide with optimal social criteria, a clear case exists, of course, for compensatory government incentives and disincentives in order to use the Groups more effectively as instruments of public policy. Finally, we have noted some distortions created by the Group structure itself.

In evaluating the allocative efficiency of the capital markets I have described, it is obviously important to specify the alternative against which a comparison is made. The Group system is surely better than having no capital markets at all. It is also inferior in efficiency to the capital market in, say, the United States.[23] Perhaps the most relevant standard for comparison, however, is with the capital markets that might be feasible within the conditions of the less developed countries themselves.[24]

In a general-equilibrium perspective, which takes account of the distribution of wealth, the skewed distribution of savings and entrepreneurship, small market size, and imperfect information—the conditions that give rise to the Group structure—the Group system is understandable. Nevertheless, it is clear that, even within these conditions, as discussed earlier, changed government policies could improve the functioning of these capital markets. Indeed, a general equilibrium framework suggests that the worst distortions engendered by these capital markets may not be those customarily listed. Rather, the most serious defects of the Group system may lie in the implications for monopoly power in the product market, and thence on the distribution of income. Also, by preempting the field, the Groups may foreclose the possibilities for future evolution toward a pattern of capital markets with broader public access.

Although we have noted the role of the Groups and their capital-market activities in the functioning of the less developed economies, both analytically and for policy purposes, more knowledge is needed on many aspects of Group operations within individual countries. The Groups' structure and activities may clearly vary in countries with different levels of development and with different development strategies. Further research is also necessary to quantify the volume of resources that passes through the Group allocative mechanism in different countries. Such resources may not always be an overwhelmingly large proportion of gross investment in the less developed countries, because of the large shares accounted for by the public sector and by foreign investors. However, capital formation by the Groups probably is a large portion of private investment in the modern, domestically-owned manufacturing sector. Before data on a phenomenon can be collected, however, it is essential to note its existence and delineate its basic structure. The present chapter is intended to fill this prior need.

Further empirical material is also necessary to facilitate analysis of the issues that the Groups' structure raise for corporate financial management in the less developed countries. For example, such management may be complicated by the joint costs and intra-Group externalities that affect analysis both of the cost of capital and of the returns for individual investment projects. These conditions may mean that managers in the less developed countries need technically more sophisticated tools of financial analysis than do managers in the more developed countries. More generally, specifying the special conditions and constraints present may facilitate development of corporate financial theory relevant for managers in this environment.

Furthermore, as our discussion of private-sector demands for cash balances indicates, such microeconomic analysis and decisions can have important macroeconomic consequences, for example, on the inflationary impact of a given increase in the money supply. Not least in importance, further research is needed to clarify the implications of the Groups' structure and financial-market activities for government monetary policy and overall development strategy. Finally, the Group structure involves an interaction between oligopoly power in the capital and in the product markets. Some of the less obvious implications of such interaction (e.g., in pricing decisions), and the effects of government intervention in such a context, remain to be worked out.

IX.   A Final Perspective

The recommendations often proposed to improve the functioning of capital
markets in less developed countries are fairly obvious. As in other cases
where apparently good ideas are ignored or contravened by policymakers, it
may be worth inquiring why this has been the case.

I suspect that part of the explanation relates to conditions cited earlier,
social externalities, and public goods, with which a private capital market
cannot deal. Also, as Marx and others have noted, the subject of capital
evokes much more than questions of allocative efficiency. On fundamental
moral and ideological grounds, policymakers in less developed countries
may be deeply distrustful of an economy based on the profit motive, and of
economic development based on private-sector interests. Such concerns
were also prevalent in the West before Bernard de Mandeville and Adam Smith.
Furthermore, for political reasons, policymakers may oppose, and desire to
bypass a pattern of development that fosters an economic and political base
for a (private) capitalist class.

Such concerns are understandable, but need not end the discussion.
Perhaps the real question is whether policymakers in the less developed
countries could achieve higher levels both of their own noneconomic (and
economic) goals *and* of capital-market allocative efficiency. For example,
might a reduction in capital-market distortions permit higher rates of economic
growth, and with increased rates of labor absorption, lessen inequality of income distribution? That is, have governments following policies of financial
repression located themselves on an interior point, *within* the tradeoff surface
relating allocative efficiency to other goals? In this context, Professor Shaw's
analysis of financial markets in economic development can be especially
illuminating.

ACKNOWLEDGMENTS

I am grateful to the Faculty Research Program of the Columbia Business School
for financial support of this research. An earlier draft of this chapter was
presented at the Finance Seminar of the Columbia Business School, and at the
Monetary Economics Seminar of Columbia University. I am grateful to participants at these seminars for their helpful suggestions. I am also indebted to
Michael Adler, Frank Child, Stanley Engerman, Michael Edelstein, David Felix,
Raymond Goldsmith, Ronald McKinnon, Kazuo Sato, and Julian Simon for
their useful suggestions on an earlier draft. I bear sole responsibility for any
deficiencies in the chapter.

NOTES

1. A partial list, which also indicates the diversity of the different foci in the research stimulated, includes refs. 1-6.

2. Documentation on operations of Groups in various less developed countries is sparse. This is not surprising, for collection of data on a phenomenon usually requires that its existence first be noted in the professional literature, and that a theoretical framework be developed to delineate its structure and operation. Such a framework has previously not been developed for the Group. However, for some observations (albeit formulated in different terms) on Groups in individual less developed countries, see [7-17]. Perhaps the most detailed and focused study now available on the Group phenomenon in a single country is Harry Strachan's "The Role of Business Groups in Economic Development: The Case of Nicaragua," (D.B.A. thesis, Harvard Business School, 1973). I have also been informed by Steven Resnick, K. Lee, and by José Buera that a similar pattern exists in the Philippines, South Korea, and the Dominican Republic, respectively. On the basis of his field experience in Asia and Africa, Richard C. Porter has also written to me that the Groups are also common in other countries of Asia and Africa.

3. A detailed analysis of the causes of the Group structure and its effects on economic development is presented in two papers by the author [18, 19]. As discussed there, the Group structure appears to emerge largely because of certain purely economic conditions present in the less developed countries. Government dispensation, e.g., of bank charters, import licenses, and tax privileges, which provide a nexus around which a Group can conveniently form to deal with the authorities seems to be a much less important causal factor, though the Groups undoubtedly benefit from such largesse. The second paper cited discusses policy options for dealing with negative aspects of Group activities, e.g., monopoly power. The similarities in some respects between the Groups and the American conglomerate are obvious. However, the Group is an institution that, for reasons discussed in [18 and 19], developed indigenously in the less developed countries, and considerably antedates the emergence of conglomerates as a general phenomenon in the United States. Finally, the Groups discussed here are, for reasons of comparative advantage and private returns, largely in the "modern" sector of the economy. Another kind of Group, often purely ethnic, sometimes forms to operate in informal credit markets in activities where "organized" sources of finances are limited.

4. Because of the neglect of the Groups in the professional literature, otherwise excellent theoretical discussions of capital markets in the less developed countries have often had to begin from premises of limited empirical validity. See, e.g., the statement by Ronald I. McKinnon at the beginning of [6, p. 11]: "There are few if any great indigenous agglomerations of capital under the control of organizatins with proven technical expertise." The Groups

are just such agglomerations, and the Group structure can be conceived of as an institutional innovation for reaping the gains that accrue from overcoming capital-market distortions, which are often assumed to exist in less developed countries. McKinnon's analysis does apply nicely to the small-scale sector of craftsmen, retailers, and farmers (with which most of his illustrations deal). As mentioned earlier, because of reasons of private returns, the Groups usually do not operate in those activities.

5. Similarly, Shaw [21] and McKinnon [6] have emphasized the complementarity of cash balances and physical capital for portfolio balance in less developed countries. Strong empirical evidence consistent with this suggestion is presented by K. Marwah [22a, 22b].

6. For a model analyzing physical capital accumulation under conditions of secular appreciation of land values, see [23].

7. In some countries, inflation generated by the public sector has reduced the liquidity of private-sector firms, and hence their capacity to pay cash dividends. Consequently, the value of equities expressed in constant prices has fallen sharply, reducing the attractiveness of equity purchases, and the ability of stock exchanges to mobilize savings. See the data [25].

8. A model of inflation based on political structure and process in less developed countries is presented in [27]. The analysis developed there indicates that in the absence of knowledge and experience on the costs associated with ultimately having to reduce inflation, high rates of inflation can be generated even if the government has been able to greatly expand its share in GNP by fiscal measures [27, pp. 36-37, 191-192].

9. A formal model of "capital flight" under economic growth in such conditions is presented in [30].

10. Such portfolio balance considerations may also be helpful in explaining the pattern of foreign investment in the 19th-century United States. For other approaches to this question, see [31].

11. Inter-Group rivalries, and/or particularistic preferences for cooperating only with individuals from within the same family, ethnic, or communal group may also play a role.

12. See, for example, the discussion of the implicit criteria in the ideology determining public-sector investments in Brazil, which is presented in [27, Ch. 8].

13. In a cross-section study of less developed countries, James W. Christian and Emilio Pagoulatos have demonstrated a statistically significant correlation between aggregate investment ratios and the fractions of demand deposits and time deposits in the total money supply [34]. However, they did not include an index of financial development like Goldsmith's financial issue

ratio. Also, since no standardizing variable such as the level of per-capita income was specified in their equations, the correlation they report may reflect only the direct relation between aggregate investment ratios and level of per-capita income.

14. As mentioned earlier, Goldsmith's principal indicator of the level of financial development is the ratio of assets of financial institutions to GNP. In 1967, this ratio averaged 154 for a sample of 20 more developed countries, and 111 for a sample of 26 less developed countries [33, pp. 44-45]. Almost a third of this disparity was due to the smaller contribution of insurance and pension organizations in the less developed countries [33].

15. Considerable concern on this point has been evinced by some writers because of their failure to note the existence and effects of the Groups. See, for example, [4, pp. 11].

16. Price inflation may clearly be another important factor in reducing demand for cash balances in less developed countries. However, Eshag [37] reports a low liquidity ratio for Mexico despite the low rates of inflation experienced there. Finally, a possibility that requires further research is that firms in the less developed countries substitute relatively low-cost labor for cash balances in their production functions. For some evidence on such substitution in the United States, see [40].

17. In inflationary conditions where (regulated) deposit and lending rates are low relative to the rate of inflation, Groups with bank charters are also able to appropriate seigniorage. This situation is not, however, due to the special features of the Group structure.

18. Excessive optimism on this routine recommendation, however, may require qualification. See George J. Benston's reexamination of this issue in the United States [42].

19. On the interdependence of household and corporate savings in less developed countries, see [44]. Similarly, in a sample of 22 more developed countries, Professor Franco Modigliani found that total "private" savings (the sum of household and corporate saving) were not affected by the magnitude of household saving. Modigliani's results and discussion are reported in [45].

20. For example, it has been sometimes suggested that capital-market development would facilitate the separation of ownership from control and management in the less developed countries; and that such a shift, in turn, would lead to increased efficiency. Some evidence from the United States, however, raises doubts concerning this last proposition [46]. Institutional improvements in capital markets might facilitate portfolio investment from abroad. In present conditions, this allocating function is performed, for nondirect foreign investment, by local planning agencies and by foreign institutions such as the World Bank Group.

21. On other grounds, other writers have also expressed reservations

concerning the magnitude of the net benefits to be expected from capital market reform in the less developed countries. See, e.g., the important work in [5 and 47]. Raymond Goldsmith has also stated doubts concerning the appropriateness of transplanting western-type capital markets to the less developed countries. This discussion is contained in [48].

22. These European and American experiences raise questions about the conditions which were associated with the subsequent shift from such personal finance to more formal institutions. One obvious hypothesis is that a rise in rates of return to investors and/or a fall in savers' rates of time preference increased the returns to financial intermediation.

23. Little but frustration would be gained, however, from over-idealizing the efficiency of the capital market in the United States. For some evidence on rigidities see [51]. Nerlove's data and analysis relate to corporations listed on the Stock Exchange. For a discussion of capital market imperfections affecting smaller firms in the United States, see [52].

24. If we choose to remain within the realm of the feasible rather than the optimal, some welfare questions that have been raised in the context of the conglomerate movement in the United States are not relevant for a discussion of the Groups' capital market efficiency. For example, in discussing the diversification advantages claimed for the conglomerate firm in the United States, Haim Levy and Marshall Sarnat have pointed out that there is no gain in having the firm do what investors can do for themselves [53]. However, in the Group context, this approach neglects the possibilities for appropriating externalities and gains due to improved information and resource allocation that stem from the Group structure. Also, in the absence of formal capital markets in the less developed countries, individual households can *not* acquire this diversified portfolio by themselves.

REFERENCES

1. Rondo Cameron et al., *Banking in the Early Stages of Industrialization,* Oxford University Press, New York, 1967.

2. Irma Adelman and Cynthia Taft Morris, "An Econometric Model of Socio-Economic and Political Change in Underdeveloped Countries," *American Economic Review,* December 1968, p. 1205.

3. Raymond Goldsmith, *Financial Structure and Development,* Yale University, New Haven, Conn., 1969.

4. Stephen Hymer and Stephen Resnick, "Capital and Wealth in the Development Process," Yale University, Economic Growth Center, New Haven, Conn., mimeo., 1969.

5. R. S. Eckaus, "Notes on Financial Intermediation, Savings, and Monetary Controls," Massachusetts Institute of Technology, mimeo, 1972.

6. Ronald I. McKinnon, *Money and Capital in Economic Development,* Brookings Institution, Washington, D.C., 1973.

7. W. Dean, *The Industrialization of Sao Paulo,* Part I, University of Texas Press, Austin, Texas, 1969.

8. A. Lauterbach, "Management Aims and Development Needs in Latin America," *Business History Review,* Winter 1965, pp. 558-559.

9. Marco Alcazar, "Las Agrupaciones Patronales en Mexico," El Colegio de Mexico, mimeo, 1966, pp. 33-53.

10. Robert T. Aubey, "Entrepreneurial Formation in El Salvador," *Explorations in Entrepreneurial History,* 6, 3, 1969, especially pp. 272-276.

11. D. W. Stammer, "Financial Development and Economic Growth in Underdeveloped Countries: Comment," *Economic Development and Cultural Change,* 20, January 2, 1972.

12. Andrew J. Brimmer, "The Setting of Entrepreneurship in India," *Quarterly Journal of Economics,* 1955.

13. G. Rosen, *Some Aspects of Industrial Finance in India,* Glencoe, 1962, Chapter 1.

14. R. K. Hazari, *Structure of the Corporate Private Sector,* Asia, Bombay, India, 1966.

15. Gustav Papanek, *Pakistan's Development,* Cambridge, Mass., 1967, pp. 67-68.

16. Lawrence J. White, *Industrial Concentration and Economic Power in Pakistan,* Princeton Univ. Press, Princeton, New Jersey, 1974.

17. E. W. Nafziger, "The Effect of the Nigerian Extended Family on Entrepreneurial Activity," *Economic Development and Cultural Change,* 17, October 1969.

18. Nathaniel H. Leff, "Entrepreneurship and Industrial Organization in Less-Developed Countries," Columbia Business School Working Paper, mimeo, 1974.

19. Nathaniel H. Leff, "Industrial Organization and Monopoly Capitalism in the Less Developed Countries," Columbia Business School Working Paper, mimeo, 1974.

20. Simon Kuznets, *Modern Economic Growth,* Yale University, New Haven, Conn., 1965, pp. 168-169, 422-425.

21. Edward S. Shaw, *Financial Deepening in Economic Development,* Oxford, New York, 1973, Chap. 3.

22a. K. Marwah, "Econometric Explorations in Growth," paper presented to the Econometric Society, December 1970.

22b. K. Marwah, "Measuring the Role of Liquid Assets in Consumption: A Cross-Section View of the World Economic Periphery," mimeo, 1969.

23.   D. A. Nichols, "Land and Economic Growth," *American Economic Review,* June 1970.

24.   R. W. Bahl, "A Representative Tax System Approach to Measuring Tax Effort in Developing Countries," *International Monetary Fund Staff Papers,* March 1972, especially Table 2.

25.   Felipe Pazos, *Chronic Inflation in Latin America,* Praeger Publishers, New York, 1969.

26.   Milton A. Iyoha, "Inflation and 'Openness' in Less-Developed Economies," *Economic Development and Cultural Change,* 22, October 1973, pp. 35-36.

27.   Nathaniel H. Leff, *Economic Policy-Making and Development in Brazil,* Wiley (Interscience), New York, 1968, Chap. 9.

28.   A. Kafka, "Adjustment Under the Bretton Woods Code with Special Reference to the Less-Developed Countries," in J. N. Bhagwati and Richard S. Eckaus, eds., *Planning and Development,* MIT Press, Cambridge, Massachusetts, p. 214.

29.   Charles P. Kindleberger, "The Formation of Financial Centers: A Study in Comparative Economic History," Massachusetts Institute of Technology, Working Paper No. 114, 1973.

30.   R. Komiya, "Economic Growth and the Balance of Payments: A Monetary Approach," *Journal of Political Economy,* January/February, 1969.

31.   Lance Davis et al., *American Economic Growth,* Harper and Row, New York, 1972, p. 327.

32.   Carlos F. Diaz-Alejandro, *Exchange-Rate Devaluation in Semi-Industrial Economies,* MIT Press, Cambridge, Mass., 1965, pp. 114-115.

33.   Raymond W. Goldsmith, "The Development of Financial Institutions in the Post-War Period," *Banca Nazionale del Lavora Quarterly Review,* 97, June 1971, p. 17, Table 3.

34.   James W. Christian and Emilio Pagoulatos, "Domestic Financial Markets in Developing Economies: An Econometric Analysis," *Kyklos,* 26, March 1973.

35.   Nathaniel H. Leff, "Dependency Rates and Saving Rates," *American Economic Review,* December 1969.

36.   Nathaniel H. Leff, "The Rate of Return to Capital in Developing Countries," *Kyklos,* 28, December, 1975.

37. E. Eshag, "The Relative Efficacy of Monetary Policy in Developed and Less-Developed Countries," *The Economic Journal,* September 1971.

38. William J. Baumol, "The Transactions Demand for Cash: An Inventory Theoretic Approach," *Quarterly Journal of Economics,* November 1952. Also J. H. G. Olivera, "The Square-Root Law of Precautionary Reserves," *Journal of Political Economy,* 79, September 1967.

39. Ernest Baltensperger, "The Precautionary Demand for Reserves," *American Economic Review,* March 1974.

40. Allen Sinai and Houston Stokes, "Real Money Balances: An Omitted Variable from Production Functions?", *The Review of Economics and Statistics,* 54, August 1972.

41. Tom E. Davis, "Eight Decades of Inflation in Chile," *Journal of Political Economy,* August 1963.

42. George J. Benston, "Required Disclosure and the Stock Market; An Evaluation of the Securities Exchange Act of 1934," *American Economic Review,* March 1973.

43. S. K. Singh, "The Determinants of Aggregate Savings," *Development Economics,* Lexington Books, Indianapolis, Indiana, 1976.

44. J. G. Williamson, "Personal Savings in Developing Countries," *Economic Record,* June 1968, pp. 198-209.

45. Franco Modigliani, "The Life Cycle Hypothesis of Saving and Intercountry Difference in the Savings Ratio," in W. Eltis et al., *Trade, Growth, and Induction: Essays in Honour of Sir Roy Harrod,* Oxford University Press, London, 1970, especially pp. 219-222.

46. R. J. Monsen, J. S. Chiu, and D. E. Cooley, "The Effect of Separation of Ownership and Control on the Performance of the Large Firm," *The Quarterly Journal of Economics,* August 1968.

47. Richard C. Porter, "The Promotion of the 'Banking Habit' and Economic Development," *Journal of Development Studies,* 2, July 1966.

48. Raymond Goldsmith, "A Century of Financial Development in Latin America," *Memória de la Reunión de Técnicos de Bancos Centrales del Continente Americano,* Caracas, 1972.

49. E. Jucker-Fleetwood, *Money and Finance in Africa,* New York, 1964, p. 118.

50. Lances E. Davis and Douglass C. North, *Institutional Change and American Economic Growth,* Cambridge Univ. Press, Cambridge, Mass., 1971, Chapters 1-4.

51. Marc Nerlov, "Factors Affecting Rates of Return in Individual Common Stocks," *The Review of Economics and Statistics,* August 1968.

52. R. Averitt, *The Dual Economy*, Norman C. Norton, New York, 1969.

53. Haim Levy and Marshall Sarnat, "Diversification, Portfolio Analysis, and
     the Uneasy Case for Conglomerate Mergers," *Journal of Finance*,
     September 1970.

Comment

FRANK C. CHILD

Department of Economics
University of California at Davis
Davis, California

Like capital itself, organized capital markets are scarce in less developed countries. This trite observation has intrigued development planners and their advisers, leading some of them to seek development by creation of capital-market institutions in the image of those of highly developed, mature economies. The practice has proved nugatory. The securities markets of lower Manhatten or old London Town moved from the curb to fancy buildings and acquired rules of behavior and disclosure when it served the interests of the traders, when the number of traders and the volume of transactions made organization convenient if not essential. Until there is a similar need, sophisticated money markets are not likely to be much used in Lusaka or Luanda; they will be of minor consequence in Delhi or Dacca. Meantime, the multienterprise "Groups" of certain less developed countries may serve as mobilizers and allocators of capital.

Leff has brought these Groups to our attention and notes the need for study of their structure, behavior, and their implications for public policy. He suggests, quite rightly, that Groups may reduce the cost of intermediation, may increase available saving, and may reduce distortions. His preliminary analysis abstracts from distortions or inefficiencies attendant to government regulation; he recognizes but does not treat problems of monopolistic distortions or of distributional inequities associated with Groups. I suggest that these omissions leave serious gaps; fruitful research on the subject of Groups requires explicit recognition of their monopolistic or oligopolistic quality as well as their interaction with government. Indeed, government approbation

of their monopoly power is essential if Groups are to play their socially designated role in the development process.

My remarks, then, are extensions rather than critiques Chapter 5. Along
the way I will have a couple of minor quibbles about Leff's description of
Groups.

Groups certainly exist in virtually all the developing countries of South
and Southeast Asia, in many Latin American countries, and in parts of Africa.
Groups flourish in countries that have chosen to pursue economic growth
within the framework of a private but not necessarily free or competitive
enterprise system. They are associated with extremely skewed distributions
of income, wealth, and economic power. Leff says (Sec. VIII) that this
characteristic may be a defect. I suggest the contrary: in many developing
countries, concentration of economic power is considered an essential virtue.

> The theory underlying this system is (briefly) that diversion of
> income to an elite group mobilizes society's "economic surplus."
> Incomes beyond the ability or desire of the recipients to consume
> will be saved and invested and hence will generate growth. The
> entrepreneurial skills of this group, something in scarce supply in
> an underdeveloped country, is another critical ingredient of the
> system. Government has responsibility for political stability and
> for social (unprofitable but necessary) investment. Society's
> economic surplus is mobilized by diverting a disproportionate share
> of the income into the hands of those with the ability to save and
> the talent to invest and whose social function is to generate growth.
> All benefit from income levels which rise more rapidly than would
> otherwise be possible.*

Groups can become an integral part, the "chosen instrument" of a country's
development strategy. Groups and governments may enter into a symbiotic relationship of mutually reinforcing status, power, and wealth. Monopoly power
can be reinforced by subsidies, tax holidays, investment licensing, tariff protection,
and discriminatory rationing of raw materials or foreign exchange. The opportunities for political influence and outright corruption are numerous. Saving from
the rest of the economy may be tapped as well. For example, the Groups' banks
and insurance companies provide an outlet for some savings of the middle class.
The possibility of investment in the Groups' mutual fund(s) may encourage
saving, especially if the government offers investors the incentive of a tax credit.
Not the least of the motives behind establishment of government-sponsored,
compulsory pension plans is creation of a market for the Groups' securities. Mixed

---

*Frank C. Child, "Reform of a Trade and Payments Control System,"
Economic Development and Cultural Change, 1968, **16**, 4, p. 547.

enterprise, which combines government capital with a Group's capital, organization, and entrepreneurial input, is a "reform" that may increase the effective use of public saving from the development budget. Compulsory mixtures of foreign and domestic capital might increase the total resources available for development projects.

The system is hardly foolproof. Examples of failure are at least as numerous as success stories. There may be more equitable systems. But if Groups and the government play their roles well, capital formation and economic growth will be enhanced. One may hypothesize that saving and investment will be greater, but at the cost of some allocative efficiency. There will be further discussion of that. Here, let me note that if the economies involved manage to take off rather than suffer continued stagnation along with chronic exploitation, we may confidently predict that some future economic historian will look back and describe this era as "the age of the 20th-century robber barons."

Leff neglects to mention one type of firm that has joined the Groups' cast of characters only recently, a management services enterprise. Such an enterprise might increase the effective supply of high-level managerial resources. Also, a management contract contributes to improved cash flow and investment protection in the case of a mixed (with government or foreign capital) enterprise. If the venture succeeds, the Group shares in profits after "reward for management"; if it does poorly or fails, the Group still has a prior claim on the venture's revenue and assets. Either way, the Group can take its return off the top.

While Group-government interaction can be mutually beneficial, very close identification with government is risky. Governments change; change may be accompanied by reform; reform may mean withdrawal of subsidies, (re)imposition of taxes, expropriation, or criminal penalties. I suggest that such possibilities, more than the lack of a domestic securities market, explain the chronic export of capital by Groups. (See Leff, Sec. III-D). The records of group functionaires in Uganda or Pakistan during 1972 or 1973 attest to the high real rate of return on a store of external assets.

The Groups' need for protective, paternalistic government increases over time, and not just because the Groups or the politicians become greedy. There is a limited number of investment opportunities in modern, large-scale, capital-intensive development projects, the type favored by the Groups, by development planners, and by their foreign advisers. A continued high volume of such investment requires constantly increasing incentives: larger tax concessions, lower interest ceilings, higher levels of protection to go with an import substitution strategy, remission of import duties and/or concessional exchange rates on imported capital goods and raw materials. Similar concessions are not extended to other sectors of the economy. In the process, development planners, in concert with the Groups, create a factor proportions problem. The price of capital is reduced by a variety of subsidies. Any excess demand for capital by other users, in agriculture, small-scale industry, or traditional enterprise, is cut off by discriminatory pricing or direct rationing. (Of course, black markets may appear.) The price structure is distorted, capital is misallocated, labor is unemployed. Depending on how far the policy is pushed, allocative inefficiency can become severe, even monumental.

Confirmation or refutation of this story requires, as Leff says, empirical research. Study of Groups themselves or of their relationship with government is not always feasible. Neither Groups nor governments will be sympathetic toward a researcher's poking around in their politically sensitive affairs. Even a new regime, after a changing of the political guard, will hesitate to open a Pandora's Box. More feasible is examination of the other side of the coin, analysis of other sectors of the economy that have been affected by public policy toward the groups: agriculture, small-scale industry, traditional or intermediate sectors.

A substantial start has already been made. For example, Pakistan relied heavily on some 16-20 Groups to implement major development programs during the 1960s. A series of studies emanating from the Pakistan Institute of Development Economics has revealed that a satisfactory (5.5 percent per annum) growth rate was accompanied by substantial inefficiencies. Heavily subsidized capital created unemployment but did not increase output per acre in agriculture; despite low capital/output and capital/labor ratios in small-scale enterprise, expansion has been inhibited by discriminatory licensing and rationing; modern, large-scale industries dominated by the Groups exhibit substantial, chronic excess capacity. Similar conclusions are to be found in work published in the late sixties and early seventies under the ILO's program of research into the relationship between employment and growth. Preliminary results from my own current work show that reallocation of investment away from the Group- and foreign-dominated modern sector in Kenya, toward the very small-scale enterprise of the "intermediate" sector, would raise both the growth rate and the level of employment.

While a pattern of static inefficiency is emerging, the evidence is not sufficient to conclude that the growth rate would be higher in a more atomistic or egalitarian economic system. We need to know much more about the relationship between concentration of income and wealth, the aggregate rate of saving and capital formation, and allocative efficiency. But the mere existence of distortions or inefficiencies in Group-dominated developing countries suggests that they could do better. Surely economists can recommend (persuade the use of?) better, more appropriate public policies that will permit both rapid accumulation of capital and greater efficiency in allocation. One important case comes to mind, Korea, where a group of economic advisers under the leadership of Edward S. Shaw did just that.

Chapter 6

International Financial Intermediation
for Developing Countries

CHARLES P. KINDLEBERGER

Department of Economics
Massachusetts Institute of Technology
Cambridge, Massachusetts

I am delighted to take part in this effort to pay notional interest on the intellectual debt that we as economists all owe to Edward Shaw. Perhaps more than most, I am obliged to acknowledge that debt since I took part some years ago, with others, in attempting to apply the Gurley and Shaw concept of financial intermediation to the international monetary scene and the balance-of-payments experience of the United States. The others were Walter Salant, and a colleague of Edward Shaw, whom we deeply miss, the late Emile Despres.

The discovery of national capital markets in developing countries, and the need for monetary deepening recognized by Shaw, or for raising the return on monetary assets relative to that on real assets, as McKinnon puts it, have of course, an international dimension [1].* It is not enough to emphasize the improvement of domestic money and capital markets. In a well functioning developed or developing economy, domestic money and capital are connected to international markets. There is a correct proportion of international money to domestic money, and an appropriate structure of connections, producing an appropriate set of flows, between internal and external monetary and capital markets.

These statements sound banal, but it must be borne in mind that the adherents of flexible exchange rates typically include among the benefits of

---

*Throughout this chapter, the Shaw work and the McKinnon work referred to are given in [1], unless otherwise noted.

exchange-rate flexibility, its effect in disconnecting domestic from international money and capital markets. With flexible exchange rates, in the usual view, it is possible to have what was thought to be highly desirable: an independent monetary policy and a differing set of interest rates. With fixed exchange rates, the public determines the money supply; with flexible rates, government makes that determination.

Or this used to be the position. More recently, leading adherents of flexible exchange rates have modified this judgement so far as developing countries are concerned. Harry Johnson's reasons for withdrawing credence in flexible exchange rates for small developing countries—"banana republics" is the term— is that it is entirely clear to the country and its citizens that the only relevant price of bananas is that in foreign exchange [2]. The domestic price is irrelevant. A similar view is adopted, with little if any need to articulate it, in the oil crisis [3]. No flexible-exchange-rate adherent to my knowledge has suggested that oil-producing countries should balance exports and imports through appreciation of the riyal and similar currencies. In bananas, the case against exchange-rate flexibility would appear to be the absence of exchange illusion, which McKinnon [4] has noted is a requirement of an optimum currency area that the republics fall short of. In oil, it would seem to be a combination of absence of exchange illusion and presence of elasticity pessimism. No conceivable exchange appreciation would sufficiently reduce the value of oil exports and/or reduce the cost of imports of consumers goods and capital equipment. The oil countries must balance their accounts by accumulating international money or other claims on the world.

For Milton Friedman and Allan Meltzer, however, the objection to flexible exchange rates is that they provide an opportunity for an independent monetary policy, and the developing countries tend to have worse monetary policies than their major trading partners [5]. It is not clear whether this is only a second-best policy, however. If developing countries were to have their monetary and capital structures improved by McKinnon and operated by Shaw, so that their policies were better than the developed countries, the argument for floating would dominate. In his testimony to the Joint Economic Committee, Friedman cited Panama, in which the U.S. dollar circulates as domestic money. In this instance, the only "policy" that Panama has is that it expands its money supply as a result of surpluses, and contracts it through deficits. Fortunately, the Panamanian capital market is closely integrated with the American so that current account deficits may be easily covered by short-term capital inflows. With no capital movements except the changes in money brought about by departures from zero in the current account, however, a country has a simple and possibly brutal adjustment mechanism of the sort described by David Hume.

Shortly after World War II, there was considerable discussion of this issue, insofar as British Commonwealth currency boards were concerned (see, for example, Greaves [6]). One line of argument was that in requiring colonial currency boards to hold 100 percent reserves of sterling against issues of local currency—which amounts practically to the same as having British pounds sterling actually circulate—the British were exploiting the colonies by making them lend to her. The matter could have been put in the language used in the subsequent discussion of the dollar standard, as one of the mother country extracting seigniorage from the children. If money and capital markets are ig-nored, as they were in early discussion, the colonies had to earn increases in money in circulation by export surpluses—giving up real resources to acquire money. In the absence of capital movements, Panama exchanged goods for money, and so did the Gold Coast, Malaya, the Strait Settlements, etc. (using their designations prior to independence).

But of course it was not accurate to describe the system as one without money flows or capital movements. Colonial currency boards were free to borrow from London banks and through the London bond market, and they did so. They borrowed long to acquire pounds sterling, which they loaned back to Britain short. This was international financial intermediation. Since long-term rates were usually higher than short, the colonies on balance paid for the liquidity thus obtained. The discounted value of the difference between long- and the short-term yields, however, was far short of the capital value of the gross holdings of sterling, which had been regarded as the appropriate measure of seigniorage. Whether colonies or mother country should have appropriately paid for the cost of the public good of money is a political quesiton that we ignore. It is worth noting that the cost would be reduced if the currency board held long-term instead of short securities, as was the practice of Puerto Rican banks noted by Ingram and considered by him to be a practice capable of generalization to the international monetary system [7].

At an early stage in economic development, international financial inter-mediation is likely to be developed much further than internal intermediation. Domestic money and capital markets may be so primitive that a dollar of credit creation directly results in a dollar of imports or of capital outflow, a finding that John Exter seems to have developed when he was the head of the central bank of Ceylon, which he later applied to the larger U. S. money and capital market (see, for example, [8]). A 1952 IMF (International Monetary Fund) mission to India led by E. M. Bernstein suggested more cogently that the extent to which domestic money creation resulted in capital outflows (or increases in imports) is a function of the development of the country, and more generally, its level of income and specifically, the sophistica-tion of its money and capital markets [9].

These relations between the domestic and the international money and capital markets add a dimension, which has perhaps been inadequately stressed, to the Shaw-McKinnon system. Financial deepening within the country,—i.e., more money per unit of annual income (an increase in Goldsmith's Financial Interrelations Ratio [10]), or increasing the market interest rate and improving the flows among segments of the money and capital markets to tne point where the return on money equals the return on real assets plus the imputed yield of liquidity—has an external counterpart. It is not enough to improve internal money and capital markets. Connections between them and external markets must be regulated. There is a temptation to suggest that these connections must either function effectively on a fixed-rate system, with some banks and substantial borrowers and lenders—including the treasury, central bank, or currency board—having access to both markets for loans and deposits, or that they must be cut. Such alternatives are probably too extreme, and a number of intermediate limping positions are doubtless possible: The central bank or currency board may hold foreign reserves, and the government may be in position to borrow abroad, when no other borrower is creditworthy and no other depositor is permitted to hold foreign currencies. In first-best circumstances, however, domestic and foreign money and currency markets will be integrated through a number of connections, and internal monetary deepening will proceed *pari passu* with deepening externally through international financial intermediation.

It is useful to reiterate that an international financial intermediation system modifies the oversimplified monetary model of the balance of payments in which increased demand for money leads to export surplus, and reduced demand for money to deficits in current account. With intermediation it is possible to expand the domestic money supply by increasing gross liabilities, and not solely by giving up real assets; and the money supply can be contracted through international financial disintermediation.

International, like domestic, liquidity provides utility. McKinnon's contention that developing countries pay too little heed to the benefits conferred by domestic liquidity can be extended to the external sector. In the literature on the optimum amount of liquidity for a country, recently reviewed by John Williamson [11], attention has been directed to developed countries, which are concerned lest they have to deflate in a period of export shortfall and thus suffer unemployment, rather than to developing countries with fluctuating export proceeds and the need for reserves to maintain a steady inflow of materials and capital equipment to support development. Recent increase in reserves of oil countries, and of those limited number of countries that are experiencing higher export prices for sugar, coffee, copper, etc. underlines the function of reserves in increasing welfare by redistributing expenditure through time when export receipts follow an uneven path. The flexible-exchange-rate system, which would balance exports and imports in each period, is intertemporally inefficient. If liquidity provides utility, it is worth paying for. One means, as noted, is to give up real assets; another, for creditworthy borrowers, is international financial intermediation, which costs the difference between the long- and short-term international interest rates. Creditworthiness is crucial. Domestic preoccupation with real assets to the neglect of the benefits of internal liquidity (emphasized by McKinnon) has its counterpart in developing countries that neglect the benefits conferred by international liquidity, convert foreign exchange into imports at a reckless pace, and lose their creditworthiness in the process. These are the countries that subvert the United Nations Conferences on Trade and Development (UNCTAD) case for the issuance of Special Drawing Rights (SDRs) to the developing countries because the world is persuaded by their past behavior that they fail to appreciate the benefits of liquidity, and want SDRs for the sake of the additional real assets into which they can be converted.

In a recent discussion of financial integration, Mundell detected a paradox: "If we start off with a world currency there will be a tendency for it to break down into currency areas as countries try to exploit the gains from reserve saving. When two members pool their reserves they no longer need as many reserves jointly as they needed singly . . . [They thus drop out of the world system to form a currency union]. The optimum currency area is the world, but a currency area is unsustainable" [12]. Balassa found the fallacy in this reasoning [13]. If one starts with national currencies and no central banks, individuals will need reserves of foreign exchange as well as domestic reserves to protect themselves against liquidity requirements. With reserves concentrated in central banks, the need for the individual to carry reserves in foreign exchange declines, under the insurance principle; domestic liquid assets, possibly somewhat enlarged, cover both domestic and foreign liquidity needs. When two countries form a currency union, the insurance principle works further, and each central bank needs smaller reserves. When a world currency and world central bank is achieved, there is no need for foreign reserves, since the world currency is domestic. National central banks may or may not need reserves of domestic currency, depending on the clearing mechanism.

However, the paradox is a real one in a scheme with 100 percent reserve money and international financial intermediation. Under the 100 percent scheme with intermediation, an integrated community of one developed and one developing country in effect has one money. Firms and individuals in the developing country hold domestic liquid assets that are equivalent to foreign liquidity through the 100 percent reserves of the central bank, currency board, or foreign banks. But 100 percent is high, given the insurance principle. Not all domestic money will be converted into foreign money at the same time. It may be desirable to maintain 100 percent money at the margin, so that export surpluses will expand the money supply and import surpluses contract it in sufficient degree to set the adjustment mechanism fully into motion. There is, however, some inframarginal amount that is not needed, and can be repaid, in the case of intermediation, or spent on real assets, in the event of a money supply built on past export surpluses. Like the fiduciary circulation in the Bank of England after the Napoleonic War, and its subsequent enlargement by incorporation of the "Bradburys" of World War I, gold conversion can be maintained one for one at the margin, with the inframarginal backing of the national money represented by government debt. When currency boards were converted to central banks upon colonial independence, the opportunity was seized to economize on reserves, as 100 percent was excessive. Some countries, particularly in Africa, overdid it, and failed properly to gauge the risk of running out of reserves. Introduction of domestic monetary policies was more at fault than mistaken judgement of the possibility of saving through withdrawing reserves off the bottom. The correct proportion of the domestic fiduciary issue and foreign reserves to the money supply will vary from case to case and from one set of institutions determining the extent of international financial intermediation to another. 100 percent money at the margin and no domestic monetary policy except to encourage or discourage foreign borrowing, is a recipe for effective monetary development.

The Panama case of the use of U.S. dollars in circulation has been cited by Friedman. Better known and understood by the writer is the precentral bank (1935) system in Cuba where the U.S. dollar and the Cuban peso circulated side by side. The money supply could be expanded through an export surplus or through borrowing from U.S. or Canadian banks operating in the island. Gresham's law was contained by a fixed or only slowly growing supply of pesos and the ready flow of U.S. currency into and out of the country. Financial intermediation took place through New York or Canadian banks lending to Cuban borrowers in the form of U.S. bank notes, which entered into domestic circulation, and which, to the extent that they were not spent on imports and withdrawn from circulation, represented the countervailing demand loan by Cuba to the United States. A particularly interesting case arose where a Canadian bank made loans to Cuban borrowers in U.S. bank notes, which remained in circulation. In this instance, Canada is in effect making a loan to the United States by means of Cuba, a complex case of international financial intermediation.

Canadian financial history offers a case of international financial intermediation that shifted from one market to another, and was followed after development, by the evolution of a domestic money and capital market that made it possible to lessen dependence on international financial intermediation. A rapid sketch of the position is interesting in considering the question of whether Shaw and McKinnon are right in focusing on domestic money and capital market integration, and regarding international integration as a separate issue. More properly, the two processes are linked in a functional manner and international financial integration might typically precede domestic integration.

Early in the 19th centry, the leading financial center in Canada was Halifax, which was closely linked abroad to London. With the westward settlement of the country, two rival centers were established: Montreal and later Toronto. After the eclipse of the wooden ship in the 1870s, Halifax subsided into a regional rather than a national center. Montreal and Toronto, moreover, shifted their external dependence to New York, a financial center that emerged as the leader in the United States beginning in 1818, but was conclusively established by the time of the failure of the Second Bank of the United States in Philadelphia. Toronto and Montreal were linked in a state of tension with each other and with New York. As Viner's classic work made clear, triangular intermediation led to Montreal's borrowing in London between 1898 and 1913, and holding a liquid portion of the proceeds on deposit in New York. Loans were sought to acquire real assets but a significant proportion of them served as a fractional reserve for the expansion of the Canadian money supply on a permanent, and not merely transitional, basis.

In due course, the Canadian money and capital market developed with its own central bank, money market instruments, and monetary policy. The need for international financial intermediation with the United States, and especially New York, diminished but was not extinguished. The Bank of Canada remained in Ottawa, aloof from the struggle between Toronto and Montreal, which seemed unduly prolonged by comparative standards [14]. In the last few years, still another money and capital market appears to be developing in Vancouver, but it is by no means completely disintegrated with respect to Toronto and Montreal. Vancouver has established new external connections of the sort that permit some intermediation with San Francisco, Portland, and Seattle, that in their turn are linked back to New York. The Canadian case is of great interest as one in which international integration precedes domestic, rather than the other way about, and one that is followed by some international financial disintegration as a national money and capital market rises to assert a measure of independence for Canadian policies suited to Canadian requirements. The order may well have been determined by the history of settlement of Canada, from east to west, closely along the southern boundary, and filling up and out only gradually. Canadian history may thus not serve as a guide to problems of less developed countries that were always independent, and its history may differ from that of former colonies that achieve independence. In the last instance, especially, independence may introduce discontinuities into the evolutionary process of building more and more sophisticated monetary and capital institutions.

The need of Canada to be free of the United States, and of Vancouver to develop rival banking and financial institutions to those of Toronto and Montreal, underlines an important conflict of principles. There are economies

of scale in the larger market, owing to greater specialization in instruments
and techniques, and the spread of risks through the insurance principle. At
the same time there is an important diseconomy of scale: the lack in the
large financial center of local knowledge. Where the remote region is primitive, local knowledge may be insufficient to compensate for the benefits
of the more advanced financial center in specialized instruments, the insurance
principle, etc. Banks and bankers having an understanding of the differences
in creditworthiness of various borrowers are never dispensable when the less
developed region or country begins banking. As banking develops local
institutions gain in sophistication and acquire the techniques developed in the
center.

A possible pattern, therefore, is international financial integration that
precedes national, followed by financial integration of the less developed area—
whether national or regional. Subsequently, financial development may follow
two paths. On the one hand, a hierarchical pattern of local money and capital
markets may be linked to regional money and capital markets, and then to
national and international resources, in a structure that ties the local lender
and borrower into the total structure through a series of ascending links. On
the other hand, a short circuiting of the hierarchical locality-to-region-to-
nation-to-international ordering may occur when some substantial borrowers
and lenders skip one or more stages because of their knowledge of the
facilities of higher stages, and because of the knowledge of the higher stages
of their credit standing. In the normal course, Ashtabula would be related to
the euro-dollar market through Cleveland and then New York. However,
there are many banks, commercial and industrial enterprises, and individuals
in Ashtabula having accounts and borrowing facilities in Cleveland, a few of
which deal in New York, and perhaps one or two of which operate in euro-
dollars directly.

Cheaper transportation and communication, and more effective information storage and retrieval reduce the advantages of local knowledge and
increase direct connections between the locality and centers at higher stages.
Moreover, direct connections can be established, possibly with international
financial intermediation (though this is unlikely), laterally across the vertical
structure. The point was put to me recently that Scottish banks have no
need to learn the techniques of financing oil exploration and development
in the North Sea from Texas via London and New York because they have
established direct connections with banks in Dallas.

For developing countries, however, integration with the world financial
system is likely to lie through one center, with lateral connections growing up
only at an advanced stage of sophistication.

Friedman and Meltzer, who view developing countries to be better off
with a fixed exchange rate, no monetary policy of their own, and dependence

on the monetary policy of the country with which they trade mainly
(Friedman), or that of the United States (according to Meltzer who advocates
a world dollar standard) omit mention of the disadvantage of integration.
Financial integration is helpful when mistakes of policy or other disturbances
are likely to originate at home. In a liquidity crisis, the smaller entity is
assisted by financial intermediation, i.e., by discounting at a higher level in
the financial structure. But when the trouble originates abroad, financial
integration communicates it to the local level. The fear of the locality without independence of monetary policy is that its interests will be neglected in
time of stress. The counterpart of lack of knowledge of local conditions at
the center is lack of interest in them. Financial integration helps when the
difficulty is at home and help comes from abroad; it hurts when the trouble
is abroad and the links of international financial intermediation communicate
trouble inward through disintermediation. Israel should give up independent
monetary policy and adopt a fixed exchange rate on, say, the dollar, if one
has mainly in mind the domestic inflation. But in periods of "crunch" in
which mortgage difficulties in Los Angeles are communicated to New York
and to the euro-dollar market, these same ties of dependence will ensure that
Israel shares the hurt.

If monetary disorder occurred with increasing frequency as one descended
in the scale of development, there would be a strong argument in favor of
world financial integration. If such disorders are skewed the other way, increasing with development, or are distributed randomly, there is likely to be
some optimum degree of integration that takes into account economies of
scale in the more developed markets, the need for local knowledge, and the
risk of infection by pathological monetary conditions in another market to
which one's own is attached. Even where local money and capital markets
have been operated by Shaw or his students, and function in a perfectly
competitive way with much deepening, there is advantage in connections with
more advanced money and capital markets to achieve the economies of scale,
i.e., more sophisticated credit instruments, and pooling of risks. Since credit
risks are higher in the local money and capital market and local reserves of
savings smaller, there are normally higher interest rates on the periphery and
lower rates in the center.

Where the local credit market functions perfectly but is cut off from
the center, there will normally be a departure from Pareto-optimality with
interest rates too high, and financial assets acquired by savers insufficiently
liquid. Long-term borrowing from abroad is insufficient to bring the structure
of interest rates down to the appropriate position in relation to the world
level; and the level of international liquid assets is too small, to the extent that
it can be raised by international financial intermediation. In a few cases, i.e.,
Switzerland, perfect markets cut off from the world may depart from

Pareto-optimality in the other direction by having too low a level of interest rates, and too much liquidity. The Swiss case raises the issue of restricting foreign borrowing in order to exercise market power and reduce borrowing rates of interest. This issue lies outside the scope of Chapter 6.

With less than perfect markets, as McKinnon emphasizes, some parts of the market in developing countries may have interest rates too low and others too high in relation to the outside world. To the extent that the capital-control system is permeable, savers in the low interest-rate sector will seek to export capital to earn a higher return, while stranded would-be borrowers in the neglected portions of the market lack the creditworthiness to borrow abroad.

In summary, financial deepening, perfecting the capital market, and raising financial intermediation ratios, all have an international dimension that should be subject to economic analysis and made the object of policy formation. The much greater attention given to domestic money and capital markets in the process of economic development is probably warranted by imperfections in these markets. Banking enclaves, at least prior to colonial independence, have meant that poorly integrated domestic money markets have been perfectly connected internationally. But these strong historical connections lie in total disarray.

The first step toward healthy monetary and capital-market conditions, is surely the restoration or new development of effectively functioning domestic markets. Such necessity explains and justifies Shaw's emphasis of domestic financial deepening. In the long run, however, both for adjustment and for optimal (competitive) international lending, it is desirable to deal with international connections. The pendulum may have swung too far from the international to the domestic.

REFERENCES

1.   Edward S. Shaw, *Financial Deepening in Economic Development,* London, Oxford University Press, 1973; Ronald I. McKinnon, *Money and Capital in Economic Development,* The Brookings Institution, Washington, D.C., 1973.

2.   Harry G. Johnson, "The Case for Flexible Exchange Rates," Federal Reserve Bank of St. Louis, *Review,* **51**, 6, June 1969, pp. 12-24.

3.   Morgan Guaranty Trust Company of New York, *World Financial Markets,* January 22, 1974.

4.   Ronald I. McKinnon, "Optimum Currency Areas," *American Economic Review,* **53**, 4, September 1963, pp. 717-724.

5.   Testimony of Milton Friedman and Allan Meltzer before the Subcommittee on International Economics of the Joint Economic Committee, Congress of the United States, "How Well are Fluctuating Exchange Rates Working?" June 20, 21, 26, and 27, 1973, pp. 126ff.

6.   Ida Greaves, "The Colonial Sterling Balances," *Essays in International Finance,* No. 20, September 1954; also, the discussion in the *Economic Journal* for 1953-55 among Greaves, Hazlewood, Niculescu, King.

7.   James E. Ingram, *Regional Payments Mechanism: The Case of Puerto Rico,* University of North Carolina Press, Chapel Hill, 1962.

8.   John Exter, "Gold Losses and the Domestic Economy," a talk presented at the First National City Bank *Insurance Forum,* November 14, 1963.

9.   E. M. Bernstein et al., "Economic Development with Stability," IMF, *Staff Papers,* **3**, 3, February 1954, pp. 354-355.

10.   Raymond W. Goldsmith, *Financial Structure and Development,* Yale University Press, New Haven, Conn., 1969.

11.   John Williamson, "International Liquidity, A Survey," *Economic Journal,* **83**, 331, September 1973, pp. 685-746.

12.   Robert A. Mundell, "Uncommon Arguments for Common Currencies," in Harry G. Johnson and Alexander K. Swoboda, eds., *The Economics of Common Currencies,* Harvard University Press, Cambridge, Mass., 1973, p. 127.

13.   Bela Balassa, "Comment," in Harry G. Johnson and Alexander K. Swoboda (eds.), *The Economics of Common Currencies,* Harvard University Press, Cambridge, Mass., 1973, pp. 44-45.

14.   C. P, Kindleberger, "The Formation of Single Financial Centers," Princeton *Studies in International Finance,* **36**, November, 1974.

Comment

HUGH T. PATRICK

Department of Economics
Yale University
New Haven, Connecticut

This is a stimulating chapter, with a potpourri of insights and ideas provocative of further thought. Kindleberger's main point is that we should not exclude international financial intermediation in our analysis of domestic financial reform and development, since domestic financial markets in developing countries are and should be linked to international financial markets to some degree.

This last phrase—"to some degree"—is important, since it seems to me to be what the paper is all about: determination of the optimal degree of integration of a developing country with much larger foreign markets for goods and finance. In the first-best conditions of a neoclassical world, integration would be complete, and any deviation would be an aberration. I find such an extremely rigid use of the neoclassical approach, even as a norm, essentially uninteresting and even misleading. In that reference world, there is no such thing as a developing country or any problem of development. In the real world the interesting issues are how extensive and pervasive are the degree of linkage, how large are the flows, and what are the actual and desired barriers, as was brought out in the general discussion of Chapter 6.

Kindleberger moves away from that extreme. In various parts of the chapter he suggests criteria for determining the optimal degree of integration of domestic and international financial markets. He discusses three criteria: the economies of scale in the more developed market—London or New York can handle finance better; need for local knowledge—only someone in, say, Bogota can evaluate a local loan request; and the chance of unpleasant exogenous shocks emanating from the foreign markets to which the LDC (less developed country) is attached.

He also considers briefly the pros and cons of flexible versus fixed exchange-rate systems, a topic also treated in other chapters in this volume. Clearly, as he indicates, it depends on the country; we all too often tend to characterize all LDCs as small, open, lagging. We need a typology of cases for determining the optimal degree of integration. Fixed exchange rates make sense for such small and open countries like Panama. Certain oil countries— Saudi Arabia and, Kuwait, for example—are special cases of extreme trade price inelasticities, since export prices are fixed by OPEC, and import demand is limited, i.e., domestic investment opportunities are limited. I regard the oil country problem as one of asset portfolio selection between one domestic asset (oil) and a wide range of foreign assets.

It is not quite clear how domestic financial markets in LDCs fit into Kindleberger's analysis. On the one hand the Canadian historical experience is held up as an example of international financial internationalization preceding domestic financial development. On the other hand, Kindleberger eventually seems to reject this case as not relevant for independent LDCs today: Domestic financial reform and development must come first. I strongly agree, for most countries at least.

The Canadian case provides an illustration both of the evolutionary process of development and the importance of spatial considerations—the linkage of local, regional, national, and international financial markets in an ever-rising hierarchy. We need to view the development process in a much broader, dynamic, evolutionary context in which markets and relative prices play an important role, but are far from perfect because of the basic characteristics of LDCs—lack of human skills, knowledge, sophistication, institutions, and technology, as well as real capital. How can an LDC cope with the superiority of the economically advanced countries in these respects? There is an inequality in the international distribution of perceived economic opportunities. The exchange rate helps, but does not fully solve the problem, especially for flows of information and knowledge. Infant industry arguments apply to finance as well as to manufacturing. Such issues become a further criterion, or consideration, in determining an LDC's optimal degree of international interdependence.

By international financial intermediation, I assume Kindleberger means portfolio capital flows. He presumes that the flow is from international capital markets to LDCs. I wish he had separately considered short-term and long-term capital flows more explicitly. Given LDC ignorance, lack of sophistication, and short time horizons, should foreign intermediaries have open, even preferred access to LDC domestic financial markets? For example, should they be allowed to purchase blue-chip equities at very low price-earnings ratios in a LDC nascent stock market with privileges of repatriating gains in foreign currency—something local nationals typically cannot do? On the other hand, lack of local knowledge seriously impedes foreign financing of private local firms. Intermediation may most effectively work, as Kindleberger notes, through the government as foreign borrower and domestic lender—or preferably a more market-oriented development bank or similar institution that uses interest rates and prices for allocating finance.

A more real problem is that the saving flows may be perverse—from LDC to international capital market. This certainly is true of repressed LDC financial systems, where domestic controls give all the wrong signals: The after-tax yield net of economic risk may be higher abroad. The inevitable consequences of such domestic controls, as Shaw stresses in *Financial Deepening in Economic Development,* are controls over the foreign-exchange markets and capital outflows. Inevitably such controls are both expensive and less than fully effective; some degree of linkage with international capital markets always occurs through black markets. The obvious solution, as Shaw preaches, is that both domestic financial markets and their linkage with international financial markets must be reformed and liberalized.

But this may not be enough. LDCs in many cases present their own asset-holding nationals with higher risks, both economic and political, and perhaps greater variance of riskiness than do most economically advanced countries for their residents. Moreover the range of alternative asset choices is probably smaller in a LDC. This raises a basic question: Should a wealthy citizen of a LDC have the right to diversify his risks by holding a large part of his assets abroad? To do so reduces the amount of real capital domestically available to the LDC.

This has positive as well as normative aspects, as Nathaniel Leff pointed out in the discussion. If foreign assets are complementary to domestic assets— as a means of persuading rich persons or families in LDCs to engage in productive domestic investment that would not otherwise occur—then international diversification is appropriate, it was argued. This seems to me a very expensive way to purchase domestic entrepreneurship and investment; surely superior alternatives can be found. A related political economic argument is that wealthy persons might fear domestic expropriation less if they had a higher proportion of assets abroad, and hence might have less need for exercising control over government, while being more amenable to social change. These hypothetical points were not pursued in the time-constrained discussion, nor was any empirical evidence adduced.

To the extent that domestic and foreign assets are substitutes, then the criterion involves a normative weighting of conflicting value judgments concerning individual freedom-of-choice in selection of assets and the socially optimal distribution of wealth (and income). A neoclassical view might take the wealth distribution as given (an implicit value judgment that it is also desirable), and optimize individual portfolios accordingly between domestic and foreign assets.

In the second-best real world, society (i.e., whoever determines policy) may judge the wealth distribution to be inequitably unequal but may not have the instruments to redistribute wealth. Controls on capital outflow are a second-best attempt to prevent a decline in the domestic capital stock and to reduce the benefits accruing to great wealthholders. Thus, distributional criteria are an important component in determining the optimal degree of integration between LDCs and international financial markets.

I, like Kindleberger and all other participants in the conference, in principle support policies leading to financial deepening—to use Shaw's short-hand phrase for the freeing of administratively frozen, repressed domestic financial markets. From this follows support of policies that make foreign portfolio capital inflow to LDCs more attractive. Yet, I here have recorded a cautionary note. International financial intermediation should be predicated upon relatively strong, at least unrepressed, domestic financial markets in LDCs. Elaboration of additional criteria for determining the optimal degree of international financial integration suggests the following policy moral: Make haste, slowly.

Chapter 7

Concepts, Causes, and Cures of Instability
in Less Developed Countries

DAVID C. COLE

Harvard Institute for International Development
Harvard University
Cambridge, Massachusetts

Edward Shaw, in his recent book *Financial Deepening in Economic Development,* has put forward the thesis that instability is a more serious problem in the lagging or less developed countries than in the developed ones; that the main cause of instability in LDCs (less developed countries) is not the external trading relations or excessive specialization and inflexibility of production, but internal policy errors that generate an episodic cycle; that the cycle follows the sequence of an initial increase in saving that causes increased investment that soon exceeds voluntary savings, which leads to inflation, a stabilization crisis, and a recession that takes the economy back to its original low growth path; and that the main means for achieving greater stability are freeing up interest and exchange rates and doing something to improve fiscal performance. Since I disagree with a number of these propositions, I cannot resist the opportunity afforded by this conference to join the debate in the interest of providing better policy guidance for those dealing with instability in developing countries.

The basic disagreement that I have with the approach to stabilization that Shaw, the IMF (International Monetary Fund), and many others have followed is that in my judgement the stabilization objective is misspecified and the policies employed to achieve the wrong objective result in other forms of instability that are harmful to orderly and rapid economic development. In developed countries the stabilization targets have generally been defined in terms of the growth of output, the level of unemployment, the rate of inflation, and the balance of payments. In most developing countries, on the other hand, the output and employment statistics are not accurate enough to serve as meaningful indicators; the balance of payments objective is difficult to define or measure with any precision, so the rate of inflation and the central bank's foreign exchange reserves have moved, by default, to the center of the stage. But the question that then has to be answered is: What rate or pattern of price change and what level of foreign exchange reserves should serve as targets for stabilization?

On the price side, the tendency has been to look at the rate of inflation and to suggest that increases in the rate of inflation are bad, reductions are good, and the closer to zero rate of inflation the better. Since practically all countries have exhibited a trend rate of inflation greater than zero in recent decades, these criteria call for continuing efforts to press that trend down. This compulsion to reduce the rate of inflation and accept zero price increase (ZPI) as an ultimate standard has led most countries to stick with such arrangements as fixed exchange rates and interest-rate ceilings in the vain hope that eventually the millennium will arrive and inflation will disappear. Pursuit of ZPI has also provided the impetus for repeated stabilization efforts that may have slowed down the inflation for a brief period, but such efforts have frequently foundered for many reasons and prices have resumed their upward movement. These stabilization drives have, in some cases, probably resulted in greater instability and disruption than would have occurred if the inflation had been allowed to continue.

The question that I wish to pose is whether the rate of inflation, or the degree of variation in the rate of inflation, is the more significant measure of price instability and focal point for stabilization policy. It seems to me that the main disadvantage of instability is that it increases uncertainty. All the participants in economic activity have to make assumptions about future developments; the greater the uncertainty about the future movements in key economic variables, the more difficult it is to formulate assumptions in which one can have much confidence. If a country has been experiencing a relatively constant rate of inflation, it is reasonable to expect that the average inflation rate of the recent past will be taken as the expected rate for the future unless there is some good reason to anticipate a change. On the other hand if the rate and direction of price change have been erratic in the past, there is likely to be much greater uncertainty about what will happen to prices in the next year or two.

Such uncertainty in turn causes individuals to try to protect themselves in ways that interfere with efficient development. The best way to avoid uncertainty about the future is to live for today. If the time horizon is somewhat more extended, it still pays to invest in those commodities or skills that will be readily saleable within the relevant time frame. Long-term investment in highly specialized fixed capital or skills is irrational in a world of uncertainty, but essential for achieving higher levels of economic development. This is the fundamental conflict between instability and growth, and the primary justification for seeking a reasonable degree of stability.

In the following discussion I will endeavor to assess whether the rate of inflation or variations in the rate of inflation give a better measure of instability. The statistical series used for this analysis are the consumer price indices as reported in the International Financial Statistics of the IMF. I realize that the weights and coverage of consumer price indexes in many LDCs are not very representative and that some governments consciously distort their numbers from time to time, but they are the best we have and, from my experience in Indonesia, which probably has one of the least adequate consumer price indexes, I believe they give a reasonably accurate measure of broad price movements.

The other major concern of stabilization policy in developing countries is the balance of payments. There are a number of possible measures of deficit or surplus in the balance of payments and no single unambiguous measure of a good, or desirable, condition. The best indicator that I have found to use in evaluating stability is the ratio of foreign reserves to imports as published in the International Financial Statistics. There are clearly many deficiencies in this measure in that it combines, and covers over, changes in imports, exports, and capital movements. A shift out of current into long-term assets will lower the ratio, as will an increase in imports—but these have quite different implications. Still, the ratio gives some indication of the countries' ability to finance imports, and variations in the ratio over time indicate instability in the trade and balance of payments situations that are likely to generate problems for the smooth functioning of the economy.

After dealing with the concepts and measures of instability of prices and the balance of payments, I will review the major causes of instability in developing countries, and then take up the various policy instruments that can be used to achieve greater stability in ways that are also conducive to economic growth.

I. Comparative Rates of Inflation

There is a common impression that most less developed countries are highly inflation prone. Chronic inflation, which imposes a tax on the holding of money, is cited by Shaw as the principal cause of the financial repression that he finds in most developing countries. Many books have been written about chronic inflation in Latin America, conveying the impression that it is ubiquitous.

The evidence for the period 1960-72 indicates that these impressions are misleading. While there have been a few less developed countries that have experienced high rates of inflation, there are many more that have had inflation rates no greater than those in the developed countries.

TABLE 1

Trend Rates of Inflation for Developed
and Developing Countries, 1960-72

	Country	Trend rate of inflation (%)
I.	Developed countries	
	1. Germany	2.90
	2. United States	2.97
	3. Canada	2.98
	4. Italy	3.94
	5. France	4.07
	6. Sweden	4.31
	7. Great Britain	4.39
	8. Norway	4.58
	9. Japan	5.59
	10. Denmark	5.87
II.	Developing countries	
	Low inflation	
	1. Guatemala	0.74
	2. El Salvador	0.86
	3. Malaysia	1.12
	4. Singapore	1.26
	5. Venezuela	1.45
	6. Cyprus	1.51
	7. Ethiopia	1.91 (1966-72)
	8. Iran	1.94
	9. Kenya	2.03 (1960-71)
	10. Lebanon	2.03 (1960-70)
	11. Dominican Republic	2.14
	12. Nicaragua	2.17 (1960-69)
	13. Thailand	2.18
	14. Morocco	2.19
	15. Iraq	2.22
	16. Syria	2.27
	17. Greece	2.29
	18. Honduras	2.31
	19. Guyana	2.31
	20. Costa Rica	2.32
	21. Paraguay	2.66
	22. Mexico	2.76 (1960-71)
	23. China (Taiwan)	2.91

TABLE 1 (continued)

	Country	Trend rate of inflation (%)
II.	Developing countries (cont'd)	
	Moderate inflation	
1.	Ceylon	3.05
2.	Ivory Coast	3.06 (1961-72)
3.	Tunisia	3.16
4.	Cameroon	3.23 (1962-72)
5.	Trinidad and Tobago	3.34
6.	Sierra Leone	3.82
7.	Pakistan	4.08
8.	Jamaica	4.08
9.	Nigeria	4.39 (1960-71)
10.	Uganda	4.4
11.	Ecuador	4.57
	Relatively high inflation	
1.	Portugal	5.27
2.	Libya	5.33 (1964-72)
3.	Bolivia	5.34
4.	Jordan	5.44 (1967-72)
5.	Israel	5.72
6.	Philippines	5.91
7.	India	6.59
8.	Turkey	7.11
9.	Ghana	7.18 (1960-71)
10.	Peru	9.48
11.	Colombia	10.78
12.	Korea	12.64
	Very high inflation	
1.	Argentina	21.28
2.	Vietnam	21.62
3.	Chile	25.40
4.	Brazil	34.86
5.	Uruguay	40.20
6.	Indonesia	77.67 (1963-72)

Source: Based on logarithmic trends fitted to annual values of the Consumer Price Index as reported in the International Financial Statistics of the IMF.

The ten major developed countries included in Table 1 had average and median trend rates of inflation of slightly over 4 percent per year. Comparing this with the experience of 52 less developed countries, we find that 31, or three-fifths, had trend inflation rates below the average for the developed countries. Of the 21 LDCs with rates of inflation higher than the average of the developed countries, nine were in the range 4.2 to 5.9 percent, six in the range from 6 to 13 percent, and six more above 20 percent. It is these latter six countries, and especially the Latin American foursome—Argentina, Brazil, Chile, and Uruguay—that are responsible for the misconception about the inflationary tendencies of LDCs. Inflation in Vietnam has been a consequence of the war, while in Indonesia it was due to the economic policies of President Sukarno, which have since been reversed.

At the other end of the spectrum, there are eight countries with trend rates of price increase of less than 2 percent per annum, and fifteen more in the 2.0 to 2.9 percent range. Ten of the twenty Latin American countries fall in these two groups, i.e., having inflation rates below 3 percent. Thus Latin America is less inflation prone than we often assume.* And the same is true for the majority of LDCs.

II.   Comparative Variability of Inflation

Whereas the developing countries appear to be no less stable than the developed countries on the basis of the rate of inflation, the picture changes when fluctuations in the rate of inflation are used as the criteria of stability. To make such a comparison I have used the average deviations from the trend rate of inflation for the period 1960-72 as shown in Table 2. Because a number of countries, upon inspection, appeared to have experienced an accelerating or decelerating rate of inflation during this period, both T (time) and T^2 have been used as independent variables for those countries. Thus the deviations are measured from a curved trend line in the cases marked with an asterisk.

The developed countries as a group have very low deviations, averaging 1.16 percentage points. Among the LDCs there is a much wider range and higher average. I have separated the LDCs into three groups according to this index of instability: Those below 3 percent, which are labeled relatively stable; those from 3 to 10 (actually, only 7) percent, which are called relatively unstable; and those above 20 percent—the very unstable.

It is interesting to compare the deviation measure of instability with the trend rate of inflation for these four groups of countries. Table 2 shows the

---

*R. C. Vogel, "The Dynamics of Inflation in Latin America, 1950-1969," *American Economic Review,* March 1974.

TABLE 2

Comparative Measures of Instability of Prices, Exports, and Exchange Reserves for Developed and Developing Countries, 1960-72

Country	Average deviation of prices from trend (1)	Trend rate of inflation (2)	Standard error of export ratio (3)	Standard error of exchange reserve to import ratio (4)
I. Developed countries				
1. Canada	.72 *	2.98	.578	5.44
2. Denmark	1.13 *	5.87	.766	4.43
3. France	1.22 *	4.07	.910	12.69
4. Germany	1.01 *	2.90	.765	8.09
5. Italy	1.73 *	3.94	.539	6.84
6. Japan	.90 *	5.59	.62	16.73
7. Norway	1.34 *	4.58	.91	1.91
8. Sweden	1.39 *	4.31	.82	3.53
9. Great Britain	1.39 *	4.39	.92	7.65
10. United States	.81 *	2.98	.143	5.99
Average	1.16	4.16	.697	7.33
Median	1.18	4.19	.765	6.42
II. Developing countries Relatively stable				
1. Cyprus	.66 *	1.51	5.84	7.12
2. Singapore	.66	1.26	-	2.91
3. Mexico	.71 *	2.76	1.08	3.57

(continued on next page)

TABLE 2 (continued)

Country	Average deviation of prices from trend (1)	Trend rate of inflation (2)	Standard error of export ratio (3)	Standard error of exchange reserve to import ratio (4)
II. Developing countries (cont'd)				
4. Portugal	.76 *	5.27	2.5	10.63
5. Venezuela	.77 *	1.45	2.07	7.27
6. Guyana	.85	2.31	4.75	3.22
7. Thailand	.97	2.18	1.53	10.25
8. Malaysia	1.01	1.12	3.14	4.31
9. El Salvador	1.04	0.86	3.94	2.64
10. Libya	1.07	5.33	7.94	68.96
11. Honduras	1.08 *	2.31	2.74	2.79
12. Guatemala	1.10	0.74	1.71	4.50
13. Ecuador	1.15 *	4.57	0.88	5.49
14. Kenya	1.20	2.03	1.01	-
15. Greece	1.29	2.29	0.80	4.63
16. Nicaragua	1.33	2.16	2.64	6.42
17. Ceylon	1.53 *	3.05	0.85	4.2
18. Jordan	1.65	5.44	1.41	28.59
19. Iran	1.71	1.94	1.04	7.43
20. Iraq	1.75 *	2.22	5.04	16.72
21. China	1.80 *	2.91	2.55	11.61
22. Costa Rica	1.81	2.32	2.18	2.53
23. Jamaica	1.83 *	4.08	2.17	3.69
24. Tunisia	1.85	3.16	1.61	-
25. Trinidad-Tobago	2.	3.34	3.79	1.6
26. Lebanon	2.03	2.03	-	4.66

27.	Cameroon	2.14	3.23	1.39	5.5
28.	Syria	2.23	2.27	–	5.49
29.	Bolivia	2.4	5.34	3.76	5.49
30.	Morocco	2.46	2.19	6.81	9.44
31.	Sierra Leone	2.68	3.82	–	–
32.	Paraguay	2.86 *	2.66	2.06	3.66
33.	Turkey	2.93	7.11	0.82	14.64
34.	Dominican Republic	2.94	2.19	1.88	11.19
	Average	1.60	2.80	2.82	9.06
	Median	1.59	2.31	2.12	5.49
	Relatively unstable				
1.	Ivory Coast	3.0	3.06	1.8	–
2.	Pakistan	3.44	4.08	0.3	6.85
3.	Philippines	3.46 *	5.91	1.75	5.58
4.	Ethiopia	3.74	1.91	0.54	–
5.	Israel	3.82	5.72	2.03	20.18
6.	Nigeria	3.92 *	4.39	–	9.05
7.	Korea	3.94 *	12.64	1.29	9.09
8.	Ghana	4.68 *	7.18	3.33	9.30
9.	Peru	4.92	9.48	1.98	9.61
10.	India	5.32	6.59	0.33	8.7
11.	Colombia	6.78	10.78	2.13	7.32
12.	Uganda	7.06	4.4	–	–
	Average	4.51	6.35	1.55	9.52
	Median	3.93	5.81	1.77	9.05

(continued on next page)

TABLE 2 (continued)

Country	Average deviation of prices from trend (1)	Trend rate of inflation (2)	Standard error of export ratio (3)	Standard error of exchange reserve to import ratio (4)
II. Developing countries (cont'd)				
Very unstable				
1. Brazil	24.59 *	34.86	1.35	12.03
2. Argentina	26.36	21.28	1.71	19.27
3. Vietnam	35.58 *	21.62	2.73	–
4. Chile	36.89	25.40	1.13	6.29
5. Indonesia	55.6 *	77.67	–	12.52
6. Uruguay	155.17	40.20	2.57	12.71
Average	55.70	36.84	1.90	12.56
Median	36.3	29.7	1.71	12.52

Notes: Column 1. The average deviation of prices from trend is the average of the absolute value of the positive and negative deviations from either a straight-line logarithmic trend of the form $\log P = a + bT$ or of a curved logarithmic trend of the form $\log P = a + bT + cT^2$, which was used for those countries, indicated by an asterisk (*), where observation indicated a curved trend would give a better fit.

Column 2. The trend rate of inflation is the value of b from the straight-line logarithmic trend $\log P = a + bT$.

Column 3. The standard error of estimate of the export ratio is derived from fitting a least squares time trend to the ratio of exports to GDP in current prices. (I assume they are current prices.)

Column 4. The standard error of estimate of the exchange reserve to import ratio is derived from the least squares time trend of the foreign exchange reserve to annual import ratio.

Source: All the basic statistics are from the International Financial Statistics.

medians as well as the means, because some groups have several extreme cases. The deviation measure is well below the inflation rate for most countries except those in the very unstable category, which consists of all the high-inflation countries. For the relatively unstable group of LDCs the deviation measure is about two-thirds of the inflation rate; while for the relatively stable group it is about three-fifths. In the developed countries the ratio is about one-fourth. There are several countries that have had what might be called "stable inflation," consisting of moderately high rates of inflation and low deviations. These are:

	Inflation Rate (P_t)	Deviation (P_d)
Portugal	5.27	.76
Libya	5.33	1.07
Ecuador	4.57	1.15
Jordan	5.44	1.65
Bolivia	5.34	2.4
Turkey	7.11	2.9

At the other extreme are Ethiopia and Uganda where the deviations are significantly greater than the inflation rate.

There is clearly some correlation between the rate of inflation and the average deviation of prices, but it is found mainly in the unstable countries. For the whole group of LDCs, the R^2 for the regression of price deviations on price trend is .51. For the relatively stable countries it is .12, whereas for the relatively and very unstable countries it is .81. Values for P_d (price deviation) are (where P_t is price trend and numbers in parentheses are standard errors):

For all countries ($N = 50$)

$$P_d = -1.369 + 1.295\,P_t \qquad R^2 = .507 \tag{1}$$
$$\;\;(2.72)\quad\;\,(.182)$$

For relatively stable countries ($N = 34$)

$$P_d = \;\;1.135 + .16\,P_t \qquad R^2 = .118 \tag{2}$$
$$\;(.250)\quad(.078)$$

For relatively and very unstable countries ($N = 16$)

$$P_d = \;\;1.851 + .778\,P_t \qquad R^2 = .810 \tag{3}$$
$$\;(2.44)\quad(.101)$$

Using the relation in Eq. (3) between the actual P_d and the estimated P_d based on regression for the unstable countries suggests that Korea should be included in the "stable inflation" group, (its ratio of P_d to P_t is 3.94/12.64, relatively low), while Argentina, Vietnam, Chile, and Uruguay have relatively high ratios of P_d to P_t. Their instability exceeds that which might be expected, given their rate of inflation.

　　　One test of whether the price deviation measure is a better indicator of instability than the price trend is provided by comparing the relation between these two instability indicators and the trend rate of real growth of GDP during the 1960s, on the assumption that instability has a negative influence on growth. The following regressions for 32 LDCs suggest that the deviation measure P_d is better than the inflationary trend P_t and that the ratio P_d/P_t is most closely associated (negatively) with the growth rate G. While the R^2 is not high, even for the third regression, it is still significant at the 99 percent level.

$$G = 6.28 - .072\ P_d \qquad R^2 = .156 \tag{4}$$
$$(.35)\quad\ (.031)$$

$$G = 6.28 - .064\ P_t \qquad R^2 = .082 \tag{5}$$
$$(.40)\quad\ (.039)$$

$$G = 7.45 - 2.10\ \frac{P_d}{P_t} \qquad R^2 = .20 \tag{6}$$
$$(.65)\quad\ (.77)$$

(Numbers in parentheses are standard errors.)

There have been numerous statistical studies of the relation between inflation and growth, which have given conflicting conclusions. I am not aware of any that have tried to use a measure similar to P_d or P_d/P_t, but my preliminary findings suggest this may be a fruitful relation to explore.

III.　Variability of Exchange Reserves

The measure of stability or instability of the balance of payments that I have used is the deviations in the ratio of exchange reserves to imports for the years 1960-72. In column 4 of Table 2, the standard error of estimate (SEE) of this variable around a least squares trend against time is shown. The median values for the four groups of countries are more appropriate than the averages because of the exceptionally high values for a few countries. Crude comparisons for the four groups show that this measure of exchange reserve instability is much the same in the developed and the relatively stable developing countries, but it rises significantly in moving from the relatively stable to the very unstable countries. More formal attempts at correlation analysis were unrewarding. There is no significant correlation between the SEE of the reserve/import ratio and P_d for all the LDCs or for the relatively stable and unstable groupings of Table 2. The only evidence of positive association was between the reserve measure and the trend rate of inflation for the relatively stable countries.[2]

Another approach to measuring instability affecting the balance of payments is to look at the instability of exports, on the assumption that large variations in the ratio of exports to GNP will not only cause instability for the economy as a whole, but also have destabilizing effects on the balance of payments and foreign exchange position. I therefore calculated the SEE for the time trend of the export to GNP ratio (See Table 2, column 3). The most interesting features of this measure are:

1. It is much lower in the developed than it is in the developing countries.

2. The variability of exports is not very different for the three groups of LDCs.

3. It appears to be somewhat higher in the relatively stable than in the unstable countries.

This last observation is somewhat surprising, but it may be due primarily to the tendency for the relatively stable group to be smaller countries that have higher average ratios of exports to GNP. Some of these countries, such as Cyprus, Guyana, Iraq, and Morocco, have managed to maintain a surprising degree of price stability in the face of sizeable fluctuations in their export ratio.

There is no significant correlation between the instability of the export share and either the instability of prices or the rate of inflation.

As indicated previously, the measures for instability in the balance of payments are not very satisfactory. More work is needed in defining and compiling statistics on such indicators. Then we may find more meaningful relations with the other indicators of instability.

IV. The Causes of Instability

Although there can be many different factors that generate instability, most of them can be encompassed in three broad categories: events of nature such as floods, typhoons, and drought that affect agricultural output and destroy economic infrastructure; external economic developments that affect the demand for exports, the supply of imports, or the flow of foreign capital; and shifts in domestic economic policies or performance that affect mainly internal demand conditions.

The significance of natural events is due to the relatively large share of agricultural production in GNP. As shown in Table 3 the standard error of estimate of the time trend for the agricultural share of GDP for 26 developing countries in the 1960s was, on average, more than twice the standard error for the manufacturing share (columns 1 and 2). But the agricultural share was nearly double the manufacturing share (columns 3 and 4), so the average ratio of the standard error to the share of GDP (columns 5 and 6) was very similar for agriculture and manufacturing. For several countries such as Korea and Morocco the agricultural sector is both large and unstable, contributing significant instability to output. In Uruguay, agricultural output is quite unstable, but it is a small share of GDP and therefore has limited overall impact. Tunisia's agricultural output is the most unstable of the group, but the share of GDP is relatively low so that the effect is moderated somewhat.

These overall measures do not adequately reflect the impact of agricultural instability on the price level and the general welfare. If a country experiences adverse weather conditions for one year, they are likely to drive up food prices, draw down food stocks, and force a sizeable shift in foreign trade patterns. When such calamities occur in two successive years, as in Korea in 1962-63 and in India in the late 1960s, the country can scarcely avoid serious instability. Emergency supplies of food from abroad may alleviate some of the suffering that results from such disasters, but such suppliers are generally too late to prevent major changes in relative prices and the price level and/or pressures on the exchange rate. The response of government to the problem arising from natural disasters may either mitigate or aggravate the destabilizing forces, depending on whether the government adds to or restrains aggregate demand in the face of reduced food supplies. Under such circumstances a government may decide that greater instability is a necessary price to pay in the interests of redistributing the reduced supplies of essential commodities. Favorable natural events are less likely to generate serious instability because it is generally easier to absorb increased output into inventories or adjustments in exports or imports without precipitating major price changes. Also, subsequent production decisions are likely to be influenced by prevailing prices and inventories, so that the price effects of high production in one year will be compensated for in subsequent periods. It is generally easier to cut back than to expand production of particular crops in the short run. The adjustment to surpluses is basically easier unless the government injects policies that curtail or eliminate the market effects of the surpluses.

External developments have been a common source of instability in the LDCs. Many countries experienced the Korean War boom when demand for,

TABLE 3

Comparative Measures of the Instability of Agricultural and
Manufacturing Output, 1960s

Country	Standard error of agricultural share (1)	Standard error of manufacturing share (2)	Average agricultural share (3)	Average manufacturing share (4)	Col. 1 Col. 3	Col. 2 Col. 4
Argentina	.65	.82	14.42	30.08	4.51	2.73
Bolivia	.7	.34	28.22	14.67	2.48	2.32
Ceylon	.48	.26	36.83	8.68	1.3	3.0
Chile	.36	.49	10.52	24.95	3.42	1.96
Columbia	.45	.13	30.83	18.52	1.46	.70
Dominican Republic	1.14	.69	26.03	16.54	4.38	4.17
El Salvador	1.52	.34	28.85	16.56	5.27	2.05
Greece	.96	.27	20.34	15.71	4.72	1.72
Guatemala	.66	.33	28.88	14.26	2.29	2.31
Honduras	1.37	.36	37.98	12.79	3.61	2.81
Iran	.32	.57	22.69	31.82	1.41	1.79
Kenya	1.32	.34	34.31	9.46	3.85	3.59
Korea	2.44	1.21	37.78	18.08	6.46	6.69
Mexico	.32	.23	17.7	27.76	1.81	.83
Morocco	1.89	.47	31.62	13.83	5.98	3.39
Nicaragua	1.14	.26	29.75	10.92	3.83	2.38
Paraguay	.69	.21	34.4	16.14	2.01	1.30
Philippines	.81	.35	26.59	15.14	3.05	2.31
Portugal	.54	.62	18.61	30.22	2.90	2.05
Sierra Leone	1.03	.23	29.87	5.40	3.45	4.26
Syria	1.81	1.27	27.05	16.79	6.69	7.56
Tunisia	1.79	.59	18.11	12.09	9.88	4.88
Venezuela	.20	.11	6.81	12.79	2.94	.86
Uruguay	1.09	.53	13.63	20.56	8.0	2.58
Thailand	1.04	.238	35.63	14.58	2.92	1.63
Pakistan	.87	.40	48.46	10.84	1.80	3.69
Average	.984	.44	26.77	16.89	3.95	2.83
Median	.81	.34	28.22	15.14	3.05	2.32

Notes: Column 1. The standard error of estimate of agricultural share is derived from fitting a least squares time trend to the ratio of agricultural output to GDP. Column 2. The standard error of estimate of manufacturing share is derived from fitting a least squares time trend to the ratio of manufactured output to GDP. *Sources:* All the basic statistics except for Pakistan are from *Yearbook of National Accounts Statistics 1970* (in constant prices). Statistics for Pakistan are from *Bulletin State Bank of Pakistan* (in current prices).

and prices of, raw material exports shot up. The subsequent inflow of foreign-
exchange earnings caused internal monetary expansion and demand inflation in
numerous cases. There were fewer such disturbances in the 1960s, as both the
developed and less developed countries took steps to prevent or mitigate them.
Still, the variability of the ratio of exports to GNP (Table 2, column 3) in the
LDCs has been significantly higher than in the developed countries, and also
higher than the variability of either the agricultural or the manufacturing share
of GDP in the LDCs shown in Table 3. In recent years accelerating inflation
in developed countries, the frequent realignment of major currencies and the
current oil crisis have had severe destabilizing effects on many LDCs as they
experience changing prices of major imports or exports and the need to choose
which major currencies to follow at the time of exchange-rate adjustments.
For some countries these events have resulted in overvalued or undervalued exchange rates with consequent effects on the balance of payments, aggregate
demand, and prices. For others they have necessitated imposition of strict
import controls, sharp changes in relative prices, and great uncertainty about
the future course of development.

The third major cause of instability in most LDCs is, as Shaw has suggested, shifts in government policies in response to political pressures or various
other influences. One such example that is consistent with Shaw's hypothesis
is the four-year inflation-deflation cycle in the Philippines, which was directly
related to the election cycle. From Independence in 1946 to the discontinu-
ance of normal electoral procedures in 1973, the Philippines experienced a
pattern of financial profligacy at election time, which spilled over into inflation
and foreign-exchange crisis the following year. The next two years then encompassed a period of constraint and contraction to prepare the way and
build up the financial resources for another election spree.

Other countries have experienced less regular shifts in policy reflecting
changes in government leadership or in the influence of key policy advisors,
or even in the existing leadership's assessment of what is politically expedient
or necessary. I know of no systematic study of the relation of such political
changes to shifts in economic policy that generate instability, but personal
observation in a number of countries and reports on others suggest that there
is a frequent association. New political leadership arrives on the scene committed to rapid development and initiates expenditure programs before
additional financial resources have been provided for. Or, a country that has
been living beyond its means runs out of foreign-exchange resources and a
new finance minister or central bank governor is installed with a mandate to
deal with the crisis and restore economic balance.

Frequently these changes in policy direction are not fully worked out
to take account of all their consequences. A need is perceived for some
corrective action, or a new initiative, and the policy instruments are applied
to deal with that need; but if a partial analytical framework is used that

ignores the full ramifications of the new policy, it is likely that some unexpected and undesired consequences will also arise. Also, in many cases the potential effect of the policy instrument in meeting the perceived need or objective is not well known, and it proves either too weak or too potent. Time is required to perceive the error, to take corrective action, and for the action to have effect. Also, there may be so much political capital invested in the initial policy change that it is very difficult to alter or reverse that policy.

The combination of partial or inaccurate policy analyses, the erratic nature of new policy initiatives, and the sluggishness of applying correctives all contribute to instability. When these varieties of policy-generated instability are coincident with either the natural or externally-generated disturbances, very severe fluctuations in the main stability measures are likely to occur. For example, South Korea in 1962-63 initiated a very ambitious new development program calling for a rapid increase in investment. The inflationary consequences of this program were greatly exacerbated by drought and poor harvests in the same years. As a result, the rate of inflation rose sharply and foreign-exchange reserves dropped precipitously. In the next two years, the development program was curtailed and replaced by a stabilization program. The effectiveness of the latter was greatly enhanced by very favorable weather conditions and harvests, so that by 1966 it was possible to resume the development efforts.

One conclusion that might be drawn from this example and the discussion so far is that the best way to avoid policy-generated instability is to curtail new economic initiatives and concentrate on counteracting the natural and external disturbances. This policy might be appropriate if stability were the only, or the overriding, economic objective, but it clearly isn't, and shouldn't be. The basic concern of less developed countries is to develop as efficiently as possible, and stability is important primarily because it appears to be conducive to development. The question then becomes: how to maintain reasonable stability in a developmental context.

V.   The Instruments of Stabilization

One obvious requisite of effective stabilization policy is to have an appropriate analytical framework. There is no single or simple model that is suitable for all situations. A good model must reflect the likely sources of instability and those policy instruments that are both realistically available and effective in dealing with the problems. Also, such a model should, to the extent possible, give quantitative estimates of the potential effects of the instruments on the targets and also the probable side effects on the other important variables of the economy.

A major defect of many stabilization policy models for LDCs, especially those devised and applied by the IMF, is that they are too simple. They reflect what I term the one-problem one-instrument syndrome. Tinbergen has demonstrated that efficient approaches to economic policymaking require at least one instrument for each target. Since stabilization, as I have already indicated, involves several targets—the price level, exchange rate or exchange reserves, and output levels—it is to be expected that several instruments must be used. Before considering possible models for analyzing stabilization policies, it is, therefore, useful to take up the main types of instruments that can be used to reach the stabilization targets. I shall not attempt to discuss these in great detail, as there are many possible variations that can have differing degrees and types of effectiveness in different settings. Instead, I shall deal with the broad types of instruments in terms of their major effects and limitations and highlight some instruments that have been neglected.

A.   Monetary Instruments

There are two basic categories of monetary instruments: those that regulate the supply of liquidity, and those that influence the demand for liquidity.[3] Unquestionably, the supply-regulating instruments have received the most attention over time and there are many economists and policymakers who ignore the demand-influencing instruments completely, probably because they are considered ineffective. Recently, however, this one-sided approach has been questioned, as some experiments with the demand-influencing instruments in LDCs have demonstrated their efficacy.

The supply-regulating instruments include reserve requirements, central bank credit, rediscount rates, ceilings on commercial bank lending, and many variations of these patterns.[4] There is no need to deal with them in any detail in this paper, as they are discussed extensively in all monetary economics texts, but I would note several points of special relevance to the developing countries. Many of these countries have utilized a number of these instruments concurrently and redundantly, so that it has been difficult to determine which instruments were actually operative at any given point in time. Shaw has argued on numerous occasions for simplifying the supply-regulating instruments and he, together with Gurley and Patrick, designed one of the simplest approaches for Korea. Their proposal was to establish an account at the central bank, sometimes referred to lightly (but with impressive clairvoyance) as the President Park Glorification Account, which would either be credited or debited with blocked reserves transferred from or to the reserve accounts of the commercial banks. The mopping up or dispensing of reserves could be by formula or at the discretion of the monetary authorities and interest could be paid on the blocked balances or charged on the transfers to the commercial bank's reserve accounts. This mechanism has been used in several forms in

Korea over the past decade and has given the monetary authorities flexible, discretionary, and sometimes discriminatory control over the reserve base.

Rediscount rates have not been a significant instrument for controlling the money supply in most developing countries because they are usually well below bank lending rates, which in turn are below prevailing open-market interest rates. It is the actual supply rather than the price of central bank credit that provides a meaningful constraint on liquidity supply. Some central banks have used low or differential rediscount rates to subsidize either selected banks or certain categories of loans in an effort to assist the growth of the favored banks or to influence the allocation of credit. In such circumstances there is much resistance to varying rediscount rates in response to stabilization needs because such a policy is likely to have more influence over the composition of credit or the relative rates of expansion of different institutions than over the total growth of credit.

While the instruments for control of the supply of liquidity are well known, they are not always effectively utilized. The major difficulties that arise are either the overriding demands for accommodation from the government or foreign capital flows. Even if the monetary authorities have the means to make the offsetting adjustments, they are often unwilling to implement them because of the severe pressure these may put on other sectors or groups in the economy. A partial solution to this dilemma is to be found by moving away from a single-minded concentration on the supply of liquidity and giving greater attention to the demand side.

The main instruments for influencing the demand for liquidity are the interest rates paid on liquid assets. One of the essential features of less developed countries is that the money and capital markets are highly unintegrated and imperfect. Consequently, there is no single interest rate, and the different interest rates on many types of financial instruments are unresponsive to change in the general availability of credit. Also, in many cases interest rates are set by law, custom, or collusion, and are either fixed or slow to change. For these reasons it is appropriate to make the distinction, in the context of LDCs, between policy instruments affecting the level and structure of interest rates on loans and those that affect the rates on deposits. As countries develop and financial markets become better integrated and more responsive to changing conditions, or as restraints on the flexibility of interest rates are removed, the distinction becomes less relevant.

I presume that there is no longer much need to argue that real interest rates influence the demand for liquid assets. A number of the individuals involved in this conference have participated in the experiments in Korea and Indonesia that demonstrated this proposition, and both Shaw and McKinnon have described these and other experiences in their recent books. Still, there seems to be considerable difference of opinion over which categories of liquid assets are more important and how to go about changing real interest rates.

As I interpret their arguments, Shaw emphasizes the demand for narrow money, currency, and demand deposits, while McKinnon points up the importance of time deposits—quasi-money in the IMF lexicon. My own inclination is to try to work on all three: currency, demand, and time deposits. Shaw will probably say that I have misinterpreted his position; that he is really concerned with the demand for all types of liquid assets, but that he would not like to see widely divergent real rates of interest on different types of liquid assets, which would distort demand, reduce the real benefits, and increase the costs of financial intermediation.

Because he believes that banks are unwilling to pay a positive nominal interest rate on demand deposits (he doesn't mention currency), Shaw concludes that the only means to reduce the negative real rate of interest on money is to maintain a low (zero?) rate of inflation. He also argues for low variance in the rate of inflation to minimize the risk of holding financial assets (*Financial Deepening in Economic Development*, p. 118). The main instrument for controlling the rate of inflation, according to Shaw, is control of the growth of the nominal money supply to keep it in pace with the growth of real demand for money at some target rate of inflation.

McKinnon, while agreeing with Shaw on the desirability of low inflation is, on the other hand, willing to tolerate moderate inflation because high interest rates on time and savings deposits can be used to offset such inflation and achieve real growth in the banking system.

It seems to me that these prescriptions for influencing the demand for liquid assets are less than optimal. Shaw is counting on control of the money supply to achieve a low rate of inflation and, thereby, sufficiently attractive real interest rates on all liquid assets. McKinnon is more willing to see discontinuities in the interest-rate structure to stimulate the demand for time deposits. I am concerned about the exogenous forces, that Shaw discounts, that may generate instability in the short run and which I believe cannot be offset by changes in the supply of nominal money as Shaw suggests. But I share Shaw's concern about the distortions in asset holdings that may result from very different interest rates on liquid assets that are normally close substitutes.

The solution that I would propose to this dilemma lies in the direction of doing something about interest rates on demand deposits and currency in order to compensate for the inflation tax, and maintain whatever real interest rate is desired on these assets in the interest of financial growth. There is no real reason, other than convention, for not paying interest on demand deposits. Many commercial banks compute monthly service charges on demand-deposit accounts and there would be little difficulty in adding an interest calculation based on the average balance. This was done in Indonesia during the period of high time-deposit rates (1968-70) to reduce the incentive for shifting funds from demand to time accounts. As a result, demand deposits maintained a roughly constant proportion of M_2 in Indonesia, whereas in Korea, where no interest was paid on demand deposits, they declined as a portion of M_2. There are various possible criteria for setting such an interest rate, such as the recent rate of inflation or prevailing rates in the money market, and the choice would depend on what is most appropriate for the particular country. But, it is my conviction that such a system of interest rates on demand deposits could be introduced fairly easily with a little encouragement from the central bank and ministry of finance. It is probably not needed in those countries where inflation is low and stable, but in all other countries it could provide both an incentive for long-term growth of the financial system and an instrument for offsetting perverse movements in the demand for liquid assets in the short run and even inducing movements that would contribute to stability.

Doing something about the inflation tax on currency has commonly been ignored or dismissed as impractical; but I find this position difficult to understand. I have not scoured the literature for what I am sure must be a number of crackpot schemes to do this, but instead have come up with one of my own which seems eminently practical and simple. It would involve annual dating of all notes and then redeeming them any time after a full year after issue at a premium based upon the rate of inflation (in the consumer price index) between the year of issue and the most recent year. Thus notes issued in 1970 could be exchanged for new notes plus a premium anytime after January 1, 1972. The premium paid during 1972 would be equal to the increase in the average price level between 1970 and 1971. (If inflation is very rapid it might be better to adjust premiums on a monthly or quarterly rather than annual basis.) In subsequent years the premium on 1970 currency would rise with the price index up to some terminal year (e.g., 1975) after which the premium would be constant. There may be objections to the fact that currency of different years would not have the same value, but the relative values could be widely publicized and easily known. Undoubtedly currency dealers would emerge who would anticipate future premium changes (based on actual or expected price increases) and help to establish current values of the outstanding currency that would smooth out the effects of the discontinuous adjustments in the official premium. (Anyone who has visited Hong Kong, or even passed through an international airport, knows that the existence of many currencies of differing value is not an impediment to commerce.) There would probably be some tendency to hold increased currency balances in the months preceding the change in the official premium, especially by those who did not have ready access to dealers, but such hoarding of currency is a desirable outcome.

As has been suggested to me by Millard Long, the effect of this measure would be to make the price index, rather than money, the numeraire, but I don't consider that a defect. Undoubtedly, it would be appropriate to relate most types of financial instruments to the price index or have some form of flexible interest rate that reflected recent price changes. I am sure that central banks and ministries of finance would be unenthusiastic about paying premiums on the note issue, but if they felt badly enough about it they might be more diligent in applying the necessary measures to hold down the rate of inflation to a level that would not warrant use of a currency premium, which I would think might be less than 10 percent per annum.

I was somewhat distressed to read in the *New York Times,* April 30, 1974, that Milton Friedman, after a visit to Brazil, has also concluded that the way to deal with inflation is to tie everything to the price index. However, it did not appear from the article that he would include money as one of the items to be indexed. The article mentions wages, interest rates on time deposits, government and corporate debt, income tax brackets, and business accounting for fixed assets. If everything but money were indexed, money illusion would disappear and the negative effects on the demand for money would be severe. I am confident that, if he stops to think about it, Friedman will want to include money in the package of indexed items.

B.   *Fiscal Instruments*

Frequently the main fiscal instrument that is proposed for coping with instability is varying the rate of development or investment spending. Current expenditures are considered essential, revenues are inflexible or respond perversely to inflation, so the only area in which there is any give to reduce excess demand is in the development expenditures. A desirable alternative would be to build some elasticity into the revenue system, but this is often thought to be tied to personal and corporate income taxes, which have a limited role in the tax systems of developing countries.

One of the most controversial areas of adjustment in the fiscal domain is the real wages of government employees. In Latin America, and particularly in the inflation-prone countries of Latin America, it is claimed that wage rates must keep pace with inflation, and there is no possibility of reducing government spending by squeezing real wages of civil servants. In many Asian countries, on the other hand, civil servants' nominal wages are consistently below comparable private-sector wages, and there are various means for supplementing income of the government employees. The Asian pattern gives much more room for flexibility in the real wage payments of government. In times of accelerated price increases, if wage adjustments lag behind, the government employees may pursue their supplementary sources of income more aggressively. This may take the form of higher side payments for government permits or services, or increased time spent on alternative jobs. In Indonesia during the period of hyperinflation, when the nominal salaries of cabinet ministers were about $20 per month and for janitors about $2, the government continued to function, but at a very low level of efficiency, and a major portion of the income of the government employees was collected and distributed outside the normal fiscal channels. While some may object to such practices on moral or efficiency grounds, the deferral of wage adjustments is one way of reducing budget deficits and resulting inflationary pressures.

An alternative is to try to achieve greater flexibility on the revenue side. Many national tax systems are inelastic in response to changes in the rate of inflation, which means that revenues decline in real terms when inflation accelerates and vice versa. One obvious improvement in this regard is to replace all specific or unit taxes with *ad valorem* taxes. Another is to reduce the lag between time of incurring and paying tax liabilities. A less widely recognized technique is inherent in the sizeable degree of administrative discretion found in the tax system of many LDCs. It is my impression, based on numerous discussions with tax administrators and taxpayers in developing countries, that a significant portion of the tax assessments is arrived at through negotiation, which bears little or no relation to the original tax declaration or other financial statement. This practice is an outgrowth of the traditional system of "tax farming" where it was up to the private tax collector to negotiate as large payments as he could from prospective taxpayers, subject to a few general ground rules and the mediation of local officials.

In the context of the "semi-modern" tax systems of the LDCs, the amount of revenues actually collected through this negotiation process is very much dependent on the amount of pressure that can be and is applied through the tax administration apparatus. Clearly there are upper limits of potential revenue that are constrained by the nature of the taxes, the level of economic activity, and the capability of the tax-enforcing agencies, but I am suggesting that the relation between actual and potential revenues is influenced to a significant degree by the combination of incentives and threats that the policymakers can apply.

In Korea the ratio of government revenues to GNP was raised from 6.5 percent in 1964 to 12 percent in 1967 without any significant change in the tax laws. The administrative apparatus was reorganized, however, in 1965 and a very tough administrator was put in charge with a clear mandate from the president to raise revenues. Similarly, in Indonesia the ratio of revenues to GNP went from 4.2 percent in 1966 to 10 percent in 1967, mainly because of increased pressure on the administration, although a decline in the inflation rate also helped.

It is widely recognized that tax officials in LDCs put forward very

conservative estimates of potential revenue which, if accepted, would make
their lives very easy. There follows a negotiating process in which the economic
policymakers try to balance the spending demands, the revenue estimates, and
the potential destabilizing effects of varying deficits or surpluses. What I am
suggesting is that, in the interest of improved stability, the policymakers should
be aware of the administrative flexibility of the revenue system, that they
should not be unduly cowed by the firm upper limits of estimated tax revenues
presented by the tax authorities, and that even in the short run (e.g., on a
quarterly basis), they should be prepared to make adjustments in tax targets in
response to changing economic conditions and stability needs.

One other technique for applying temporary restraint to demand, which
is often discussed in theoretical terms but seldom applied in practice, is the
imposition of temporary taxes, where it is clearly specified that the tax will
be removed by some date or when certain conditions have been satisfied. One
example of this, in a developed country, was the 10 percent import surcharge
used by the United States in 1971 to restrain imports and force a realignment
of major world currencies. LDCs could use similar taxes, with less traumatic
effects on world finance, to curtail demand for all or selected imports, or
certain commodities that were both exported and domestically consumed.
Temporary subsidies could also be used to shift demand or production to
close substitutes.

Clearly there are limitations to the use of such an instrument. If the
administrative requirements or the excess burden of distortion of consumption
or production are substantial, then these disadvantages are likely to outweigh
the gains. But, I believe there are circumstances in which a temporary tax or
subsidy can be implemented simply with beneficial effects on overall stability.

C.   Balance of Payments Instruments

The move away from fixed exchange rates, which is now being led by the
developed countries and should in time become a legitimate practice for the
developing countries, will reduce one of the major sources of stabilization
crisis. I concur with Shaw's and McKinnon's advocacy of flexible exchange
rates as means of guiding both trade and capital flows. The main advantage
for stabilization purposes of flexible rates is that both the trauma of major
exchange-rate adjustments and the preceding speculation are avoided. On
the other hand, it needs to be remembered that exchange-rate depreciation
tends to raise aggregate demand relative to aggregate supply, which contributes to rising prices. If these adjustments come in small doses rather than
big discontinuous leaps, they should be easier to cope with.

The other major area of stabilization instruments relating to the balance
of payments is foreign debt. Many countries handle their foreign debt in the

same manner as the exchange rate: They wait for a crisis before they try to
do anything. It is my impression, based on both limited and casual observation, that more aggressive approaches to the management of foreign debt
would help in stabilizing the balance of payments. A number of countries
have practically sold their souls for very limited amounts of standby money
from the IMF. Usually, in the process, they commit themselves to restrict
borrowing from other sources, even on terms that may be more favorable
than the IMF offers. (It's interesting to note that suppliers credits of 5 to 10
years are considered by the IMF to be more burdensome than 3-year money
from the Fund.)

Faced with short-run payment problems, many countries would be well
advised to borrow short-to-median-term money, even at relatively high rates,
if they would subsequently refinance those loans on more favorable terms
when their own problems or world credit conditions have eased. There may
be more of this type of refinancing than I am aware of, but I know of no
country that has consciously sought to rearrange its own debt, except through
very complicated rescheduling negotiations like those for Indonesia and Ghana,
or that has encouraged and assisted private borrowers in refinancing their
obligations on more favorable terms. This is an area where both developed
and less developed countries could strive for greater flexibility and thereby
reduce the likelihood of countries being caught in a payments crisis. Perhaps
the increasing involvement of the LDCs in the Euro and Asian dollar markets
is an indication that this is already occurring.

I am fully aware of the problems of distinguishing between a fluctuation
and a trend and that some countries might use short-term borrowings to dig
themselves into deeper holes. But, what I am suggesting is more aggressive
action during periods of favorable borrowing conditions to free up the constraints for the future, and also more flexible borrowing policies combined
with other stabilization moves in the monetary and fiscal areas if crises do
occur. "Toughing it out" (to use a popular phrase) with only a standby loan
from the IMF is not likely to be an optimal solution.

D. Commodity Supply Instruments

In those countries where food grains are a major element in both production
and consumption, changes in internal or world market supply conditions can
be important sources of instability. The monsoon climate in Asia imparts a
strict seasonal pattern to agricultural production, and periodic failures of the
monsoon not only affect production within each of the countries, but also
cause world market shortages that can result in a doubling or tripling or the
world market price. Because rice is such an important part of total consumption, wage rates and other prices tend to follow the rice price. Also,

speculators are very alert to climatic conditions so that price movements in unconstrained markets tend to anticipate emerging shortages and surpluses. Those who are responsible for stabilization policy should be as well informed about climatic and crop conditions as the speculators, and should be prepared to take action when danger signals appear.

If the governments in such countries want to reduce the instability of the overall price level, they generally need to find some means of dampening but not eliminating both the seasonal and cyclical swings in grain prices. This is a complicated process if it is to be done efficiently, without creating excessive demands for internal or external financing and managerial capability. Without going into a detailed discussion of alternative arrangements for such activities, I believe the major elements that might be incorporated in the design of a reasonable approach are:

1. The government should generally try to supplement rather than eliminate the private-sector operations in the commodity market. This requires a sufficient spread between the buying and selling price, seasonal movement of both prices and, where necessary, regional differentials to give reasonable returns to the private dealers. On the other hand, greater stability or regularity of price movements will reduce the risk of the private dealers and the margins required to keep them in business.

2. The average or trend prices need to be maintained at levels that give adequate production incentives while avoiding unwanted surpluses.

3. Revolving stockpiles should be maintained at levels consistent with the known fluctuations of domestic and world market supplies and some politically determined acceptable degree of risk of being caught short.

The actual system appropriate for each country will depend on these and other factors, among which are the potential for regional buffer stocks and the terms and ease of access to supplies from developed countries. Failure to implement some system of basic commodity price stabilization in countries that need it is likely to place an unreasonable burden on the other stabilizing instruments. It is my judgment that the Indonesian inflation could have been reduced from 600 percent to 20-30 percent in one year instead of two if there had been adequate supplies of grain in 1967, either from a favorable domestic crop or from imports. Grain shortages in 1967, spilling over into 1968, kept the inflation rate up near 100 percent in 1967.

E. Wage Adjustments

Another dimesion of stabilization that is important in some countries is that of wage adjustments, which are always trying to catch up with previous price increases, and, in turn, causing continuing cost-push inflation. This pattern seems to be particularly acute in the Latin American countries that have experienced continuous high rates of inflation and whose labor unions are relatively powerful.*

So long as the inflation runs at a fairly constant rate, there is no serious problem, but when the attempt is made to reduce the rate of inflation, some means must be found to reduce wage increases *pari passu* rather than with a lag.

Pazos discusses several techniques that have been tried at various times in the high-inflation countries of Latin America, pointing out their advantages and disadvantages. I have little to add to his discussion and have had no practical experience with this type of problem. I would simply indicate my agreement that, in certain countries, it is probably necessary to deal with this problem.

F. Jawboning

There are situations in which the government, through publicity and direct negotiations with key economic groups, can exert some pressure for stability (or instability). The effectiveness of such measures depends on the political system, the relative power and receptivity of different major groups in the economy, and the skill of the government in implementing such measures. Exhortation cannot succeed alone. Other supporting and persistent pressures are needed so that the government's efforts to influence private decisions can serve to reinforce basic policies.

The Korean government announced in the summer of 1972 that it was going to reduce the trend rate of inflation from 10 percent to 3.5 percent. It advised businesses to act accordingly—to hold down price increases, to curtail high-cost borrowing, and generally to prepare for a lower rate of inflation. These measures were proving quite successful until the fuel and raw material prices skyrocketed in 1973, thus bringing back the old rate of inflation. In countries with less authoritarian governments, it may be very difficult to initiate such actions.

---

*Felipe Pazos, *Chronic Inflation in Latin America,* New York, Praeger, 1972.

VI.   The Design of Stabilization Policies

The discussion so far has given ample indication of, and I hope some support for, my thesis that inflation and instability are not synonymous and that it is difficult to generalize about the causes and cures of instability. The design of stabilization policy must be tailored to the needs of the particular country and time if it is to be efficient. While it is possible to reduce the rate of in-flation and the amplitude of price fluctuations by using a limited set of instruments in conventional ways, the costs of doing so in terms of retarded growth, reduced output, distortions of income distribution, and so forth, are likely to be very high.

Rather than trying to spell out alternative models of stabilization policy, which I will hope to do in a subsequent paper, let me suggest some general propositions that will serve both to summarize the previous discussion and give some guidance to the formulation of policy models.

1. The first requirement is to decide what it is that is to be stabilized, for example, the price level, price fluctuations, imports, foreign-exchange reserves, etc.

2. The various potential sources of instability need to be identified and evaluated in terms of their severity and frequency.

3. Generally, policy instruments should be sought that will deal most directly and effectively with the potential source of instability, which will tend to reduce the disruptions of the rest of the economy.

4. In developing economies that are relatively unintegrated, changes in some markets or regions may be slow to spread throughout the economy. This may accentuate the instability within the affected market or region, but it also means that the policy instruments may be more narrowly focused, and that relatively harsh policy measures may be applied to particular markets without severe spread effects. (This is clearly not true for all markets or for long time periods.)

5. The policy instruments should be readied for action during times when they aren't needed so they can be studied carefully and the way cleared to implement them when needed.

6. The problems of stabilizing movements around a trend are likely to be easier than trying to change a trend, because in the former case, some success will reduce uncertainty while in the latter, success will generally increase uncertainty. Also, reduced fluctuations around the trend may make it easier subsequently to change the trend if that is desired.

7. As is well known from economic theory, but often forgotten in practice, very short-run adjustments to changes in policies or prices mainly take the form of changing (reservation) prices for stocks of existing assets. Flows only become significant over time, and changing the rate of flow of either outputs or inputs is even slower for most types of commodities. Exogenous causes of instability such as adverse weather or an export boom lead to changes in expectations and current prices. If policy instruments are intended to have a quick effect in counteracting such disturbances, they should be directed toward changing the demands for existing assets which, because their quantity is relatively fixed in the short run, will result mainly in the change of the price of those assets.

NOTES

1. Uruguay is included in the first regression for all countries but is omitted in the third regression because its unusual pattern of very high P_d seems to distort the relation.

2. The regression equation was:

$$\text{Reserve/import deviation} = 2.337 + .057\,P \quad R^2 = .208$$
$$(.312) \quad (.021)$$

for the 34 relatively stable countries.

3. The term liquidity is here used as synonymous with liquid assets, or money plus near money (such as time deposits), that can be readily converted into liquid assets.

4. The IMF has debated whether it is better to try to control central bank credit or total bank credit, and their preferences have shifted back and forth over the years. One of the factors influencing their position appears to be the desire for a clearly defined magnitude over which the monetary authorities can be presumed to have sufficient control so that they can be held accountable for staying within certain agreed ceilings. A central bank credit ceiling is obviously preferable on these grounds. On the other hand, some countries, once they have agreed to a ceiling on central bank credit, have devised many ingenious ways for breaking the normally stable relationship between central bank credit and total bank credit, so that total liquidity can rise more rapidly than the IMF deemed appropriate. See Manual Guitian, "Credit Versus Money as an Instrument of Control" *IMF Staff Papers,* **20**, 3, November 1973.

CHARLES R. BLITZER

*International Bank for
Reconstruction and Development
Development Research Center
Washington, D.C.*

I must start by saying that it is a real pleasure to comment on such an interesting and thought-provoking chapter. Not only is it relevant to the academic economist, but it carries a clear message to policymakers as well. The basic themes can be easily stated:

1. Instability is a complex, multifaceted economic problem.

2. The parameters and divisions of instability are, by their very nature, country specific.

3. Being a vector-valued phenomenon, instability problems should be dealt with using a variety of flexible policy instruments.

In particular, Cole warns about the dangers of rigidly adhering to what he refers to as the IMF approach to stabilization—namely, identifying instability with inflation and changes in reserves of foreign exchange. Although Cole does not provide specific evidence on this point, he believes that when stabilization policy is geared solely towards these two problems the result is often "harmful to orderly and rapid economic development."

In a very interesting section, Cole outlines the principal causes of economic instabilities. Three broad categories of causes are discussed. First, natural events (particularly the weather) have a very significant impact on agricultural production. Since agriculture is a relatively large sector in the developing countries, variations in yields not only directly affect rural incomes, but also have important feedback effects on the rest of the economy, both in real and monetary terms. The second cause of instability arises from external sources, in particular shifting demand levels for a country's export products. Finally, government policy itself is often a prime destabilizing element. Not only may governments pursue "bad" policies, but frequent changes in policy also increase instability.

The problem is that all of this discussion is too general. Most of the chapter is devoted to trying to pry deeper, to define measures of instability and to devise appropriate policies to deal with stabilization problems. In these attempts, I think Cole's analysis is not quite satisfactory.

Although he emphasizes that instability is vector valued in the general discussion, Cole specifically talks in terms of foreign-exchange reserves and inflation. In doing so, and in seeking a satisfactory "measure of instability," he slips into the IMF trap that he warns about. He presents little justification for focusing on inflation and the balance of payments, other than pointing out that this is the common practice in developing countries.

Cole suggests using an average deviation from the trend rate of inflation as the measure of price instability, rather than using the rate of inflation itself. In Table 2, he shows that when measuring price stability this way, that on the average developing countries appear more unstable then developed countries. While apparently true, there seems to be little evidence that this is an important distinction.

In the first place, his regression Eqs. (1) through (3) indicate that the trend rate of inflation (P_t) is a major explanatory variable for the deviation of prices from the trend (P_d). Indeed, the fit is especially good for the more "unstable" countries. Second, neither the rate of inflation nor the deviations from it appear to have much impact on overall real economic growth. Comparing regression Eqs. (4) through (6), we see that P_t, P_d, and P_d/P_t all have about the same, rather minimal, power for explaining variations in the growth rate. Thus, if the appropriate test of a measure of instability is how well it accounts for changes in the growth rate (implying a scaler measure for instability), both measures appear somewhat less than satisfactory.

As a measure of instability in the balance of payments, Cole suggests two alternatives: (1) the deviation around a time trend of the ratio of foreign-exchange reserves to imports; (2) variation in the ratio of exports to GNP. It is hardly surprising that he finds that countries relatively unstable in terms of P_d are also relatively unstable in terms of the reserves/imports ratio. After all, both rapid inflation and variations in the rate of inflation tend to work havoc on relative prices, including the exchange rate, and through it, on foreign reserves and trade in general.

In discussing these two measures, Cole says that neither is very satisfactory, without really telling us why. He seems to say that one of the problems is that neither measure correlates well with his measure of price stability P_d. Once again, he seems to be falling into the trap of defining stability in terms of inflation.

Leaving aside the still unanswered questions regarding the definition of and the appropriate measures for instability in prices, growth, balance of payments, income, etc., Cole emphasizes the need for a set of policies to insure "reasonable" stability in conjunction with other economic goals. In this spirit, he discusses a number of short-run instruments, most of which can be applied for reasons other than just stabilization.

Cole focuses special attention, most appropriately for this conference, on monetary instruments that can be used to manage the supply and demand for financial assets (M_2). Noting the past attention paid to supply instruments and the political limits to their usage, he emphasizes the use of various instruments for demand management. In particular, the Shavian technique of increasing interest rates on deposits is recommended as a way of increasing the flow of real financial resources through the banking system. Cole moves beyond standard Shavianism in recommending that a positive nominal interest rate be placed not only on demand deposits, but on currency as well. Several participants characterized this proposal as "funny money" and thought that its implementation would not only be extremely complicated (dated currency, etc.), but would permanently institutionalize a high rate of inflation. The same aims could be achieved more efficiently through increasing the proportion of demand deposits in the money supply by paying interest on them only.

A number of other short-run policy instruments are discussed. On the fiscal side, taxes, expenditures, and the budget deficit are mentioned. To deal with balance of payments problems, Cole recommends flexible exchange rates, debt refinancing, and aggressive short-run borrowing from foreign money markets. Finally, he briefly discusses wage adjustment policy, jawboning, and community stock management. There is little I have to add to his straightforward presentation.

In conclusion, Cole's paper probably raises more questions than it answers. Keeping in mind the three general dicta mentioned earlier, we are left not yet knowing either the welfare losses of instability of various kinds, or appropriate measures to counteract such losses. Perhaps the most important lesson is that in designing effective public policies, there is no replacement for "wise" teachers and practitioners such as Edward S. Shaw.

Part III

Inflation and Deflation: The Short-Run Dynamics

Some Dynamic Aspects of the Welfare Cost of Inflationary Finance

JACOB A. FRENKEL

Department of Economics
University of Chicago
Chicago, Illinois

and

Department of Economics
Tel-Aviv University
Tel-Aviv, Israel

A government can live for a long time, even the German government or the Russian government, by printing money . . . It is the form of taxation which the public finds hardest to evade and even the weakest government can enforce, when it can enforce nothing else. (John M. Keynes, *A Tract on Monetary Reform* [1])

[D]epreciation of currency is a tax on the community and a fraud on creditors. (John Stuart Mill, *Principles of Political Economy*)

The notion that the right to issue non-interest-bearing money entails monopoly rents is fundamental to the understanding of the concept of seigniorage embodies in money creation. It is the basis for Edward Shaw's observation that:

> Ministers of finance have been known to regard fresh printing of
> nominal money as perfect substitute for real tax revenue . . .
> Their revealed preference is to keep the inflation tax under their
> own jurisdiction [2, p. 96]

This property right provides governments with incentives to use inflation as an instrument of public finance. The purpose of this paper is to elaborate on some aspects of the welfare cost of inflation in a dynamic context. Section I contains a brief summary of the steady-state analysis of the welfare cost and government revenue from inflationary finance. The discussion in that section is confined to the situation prevailing in the long run when anticipations are realized. The concept of the "lagging economy" as viewed by the debt-intermediation view (DIV) of money and finance is one of the numerous contributions of Shaw to monetary theory and policy. This concept along with

---

*This is a revised version of a paper also presented at the Conference on Inflation in the World Economy, University of Manchester, Manchester, England, July 17-19, 1974.

the contributions of his colleagues John Gurley and Ronald McKinnon came to be known as the Stanford View. In contrast to the case where all anticipations are realized, the "lagging economy"–discussed in Shaw's *Financial Deepening in Economic Development* is characterized by:

> A continuous, imperfect adjustment . . . of expected prices and rates of return to unforseen experience with changes in prices and yield. On the market for money, rates of inflation . . . do diverge from expected rates . . . The result is that assets bearing unescalated nominal yields, and money in particular, are subject to imperfectly forseen changes in real value [2, p. 49].

The analysis of the steady state is extended in Section II to the "lagging economy" by introducing some dynamic considerations relevant to the transition period during which not all anticipations are realized. The dynamic analysis depends on the process by which expectations are formed. These considerations are then applied in Section III to the dynamic analysis of the welfare cost. One of the questions discussed in that section concerns the appropriate evaluation of the welfare effects of disequilibrium positions. Section IV contains some concluding remarks.

I.   The Steady State

A.   The Conceptual Framework

Much of the recent analysis of the welfare cost and government revenue from inflationary finance is confined to the steady state in which expectations are realized [3-11].

The welfare cost of anticipated inflation stems from substituting real resources for money services. The cost arises from reasons involving excessive time spent on increased frequency of purchases; adaptation of barter transactions; and increased frequency of payments that involve substituting accounting services for those of money and the like.

The height of the demand curve for real cash balances at any point measures the marginal flow of services per unit of time rendered by the unit of real cash balances. These services can take the form of either a direct utility yield, or an indirect yield provided by the additional resources made possible by the replacement of barter by money and by economizing on the cost of producing a flow of utility derived from the consumption of real goods and services. Thus, the area under the demand curve over a given segment of the horizontal axis measures the flow of services from the indicated quantity of real balances. The equilibrium holdings of real cash balances provided (at the margin) liquidity services at a (percentage) rate that is equal to the nominal rate of interest.

Figure 1 describes the demand for real cash balances M/P as a function of the nominal rate of interest i where $i = r + \pi^*$, r_0 is the real rate of interest (assumed constant), and π^* the anticipated rate of inflation. When the anticipated rate of inflation is zero, desired holdings of real cash balances are $(M/P)_0$; and when the anticipated rate of inflation is π_0^*, desired holdings are $(M/P)_1$. Assuming that the utility yield can be measured by the area under the demand curve, the welfare cost of (anticipated) inflation at the rate π_0^* is represented by areas A and B. Notice that the welfare cost is described by the areas of a conventional triangle A plus a rectangle B in contrast with Bailey's computations. The presence of the rectangular area is due to the fact that the initial holdings of real balances $M/P(r_0)$ have been suboptimal. The initial distortion stems from not paying interest on money—a distortion that results in a welfare loss measured by area C [12].

The rate of government (real) revenue from the creation of cash balances (abstracting from the banking system) is $\dot{M}/P$ where $\dot{M}$ denotes the time derivative of the nominal value of cash balances and P the price level. Thus, when holdings of real cash balances have adjusted to an inflation rate π_0^*, government revenue is $\mu_0 (M/P)_1$ where μ_0 denotes the percentage rate of monetary expansion $(\dot{M}/M)$. In a nongrowing economy, in equilibrium, the (percentage) rate of monetary expansion equals the rate of inflation and the flow demand for real cash balances equals the rate at which the existing (equilibrium) stock depreciates. Thus, the rate of government revenue from inflationary finance is represented by area G in Fig. 1. The above analysis of government revenue assumes that the decline of the stock of real balances

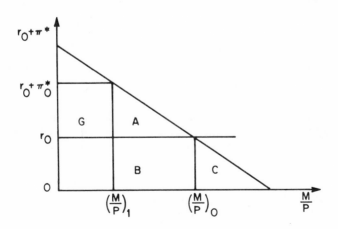

FIGURE 1

from $(M/P)_0$ to $(M/P)_1$ is attained through changes in the price level. Such transitory changes need not occur if the government accompanies the change in the rate of monetary expansion with a once and for all adjustment of the nominal stock of money. This possibility, which is not pursued further in this chapter, is analyzed by Phelps [13], Auernheimer [3], and Sjaastad [14].[1]

B.   A Special Case

Many of the illustrative computations of the welfare cost and government revenue from inflationary finance involve the assumption that the demand for real cash balances is some variant of the function introduced by Cagan [16]. (See [3, 4, 6-11]. Barro [5], however, introduces an alternative demand function.)

Earlier analyses differ with respect to the various assumptions concerning the real rate of interest r and the rate of growth of output λ. Consequently, some of the formulas and conclusions pertaining to the welfare cost and government revenue are different in the various analyses.

The following describes the basic formulas for the steady state. Assume the following variant of Cagan's demand for real cash balances:

$$\frac{M}{P} = y_0 e^{-\epsilon-\alpha(r_0+\pi^*)+\lambda t} \tag{1}$$

where ϵ and α are two parameters (α denotes the slope of the semilogarithmic demand function). Output y is assumed to be growing at a constant exponential rate λ:

$$y_t = y_0 e^{\lambda t} \tag{2}$$

Let $k(0)$ denote the desired ratio of money to income when the anticipated rate of inflation is zero:

$$k(0) = \frac{y_0 e^{-\epsilon-\alpha r_0+\lambda t}}{y_0 e^{\lambda t}} = e^{-\epsilon-\alpha r_0} \tag{3}$$

Since income grows at the rate λ, the demand curve in Fig. 1 is shifted continuously to the right. At any given point in time (for which the schedule is drawn), the welfare cost of positive inflation is the sum of areas A and B where:

$$\text{Area } A = \int_0^{\pi^*_0} \left[\frac{M}{P}(r_0 + \pi^*) - \frac{M}{P}(r_0 + \pi^*_0) \right] d\pi^* \tag{4}$$

$$\text{Area } B = r_0 \left[\frac{M}{P}(r_0) - \frac{M}{P}(r_0 + \pi_0^*) \right] \tag{4a}$$

When the income elasticity of the demand for money is unity, it is convenient to normalize the various quantities by the value of income. Diagrammatically, this normalization is done by dividing the abscissa in Fig. 1 by the value of income. Consequently, the demand curve describes the desired money/income ratio as a function of the nominal rate of interest, and the various areas describe percentages of income.

Using (1), the welfare cost of inflation as a percentage of income is:

$$WC = \frac{k(0)}{\alpha} \left\{ 1 + \alpha r_0 - e^{-\alpha \pi^*} [l + \alpha(r_0 + \pi^*)] \right\} \tag{5}$$

Similarly, the welfare cost (as a percentage of income) arising from the nonpayment of interest on money is area C (normalized by income):

$$C = \frac{k(0)}{\alpha} [e^{\alpha r_0} - (1 + \alpha r_0)] \tag{6}$$

and the sum of (5) and (6) is the welfare cost of suboptimal money holdings.

Government revenue GR as a percentage of income is area G (normalized by income)

$$GR = \mu_0 k(0) e^{-\alpha \pi^*} \tag{7}$$

Since in the steady state, the anticipated rate of inflation equals the rate of monetary expansion minus the rate of growth (when the income elasticity of the demand for money is unity), it follows that in the steady state:

$$\mu_0 - \lambda = \pi^* \tag{8}$$

Substituting (8) into (5) and (7) yields the *steady state* welfare cost w^* and government revenue g^* as a percentage of income.

$$w^* = \frac{k(0)}{\alpha} \left\{ 1 + \alpha r_0 - e^{-\alpha(\mu_0 - \lambda)} [1 + \alpha(\mu_0 - \lambda + r_0)] \right\} \tag{5'}$$

$$g^* = \mu_0 k(0) e^{-\alpha(\mu_0 - \lambda)} \tag{7'}$$

The welfare cost can be viewed as the cost of collecting government revenue from money creation.

The steady-state marginal cost of collection as a function of the rate of monetary expansion is obtained from (5') and (7'):

$$\frac{dw^*}{dg^*} = \frac{dw^*/d\mu}{dg^*/d\mu} = \frac{\alpha(\mu_0 - \lambda + r_0)}{1 - \alpha\mu_0} \tag{9}$$

From $(7')$ it is clear that the revenue maximizing rate of monetary expansion is $1/\alpha$, which is independent of the rate of growth, i.e., revenue is maximized at the point where the elasticity of the demand for real balances, with respect to the rate of monetary expansion, is unity. Since $\mu - \lambda = \pi^*$, the revenue maximizing rate of inflation is $(1/\alpha) - \lambda$ [6]. This revenue maximizing rate of inflation is reached when the elasticity of the demand for real cash balances with respect to the nominal rate of interest equals $-(r + \pi^*)/(\lambda + \pi^*)$ which exceeds unity (in absolute value) when $r > \lambda$.[2] Equation (9) reveals that, in general, the marginal cost of collection can be written as the ratio $\eta_i/(1 - \eta_\mu)$ where η_i and η_μ denote, respectively, the elasticity of the demand for money with respect to the nominal rate of interest and the rate of monetary expansion [10]. It is also seen that the marginal cost (9) is declining monotonically with the rate of growth.

In the steady state, government revenue and the welfare cost grow at the rate λ, the rate of growth of income, and thus the ratios of the welfare cost and government revenue to income are independent of time. Consequently, the expressions for C, w^*, and g^* pertain also to the ratios of the capitalized values of the costs and the revenue to the capitalized value of income.

Table 1 presents the results of illustrative steady-state computations for alternative value of annual μ, r, λ, and α with $k(0) = .25$; the values of α are based on [6].

TABLE 1

Percentage of Welfare Cost and Government Revenue From Steady-State Inflation

μ	r	λ	w^*		g^*		C		$100(w^*/g^*)$	
			$\alpha = 5$	$\alpha = 10$	$\alpha = 5$	$\alpha = 10$	$\alpha = 5$	$\alpha = 10$	$\alpha = 5$	$\alpha = 10$
.1	.05	.0	.94	1.45	1.52	.92	.17	.37	62.2	157.7
		.03	.61	1.02	1.76	1.24	.17	.37	34.8	82.1
	.1	0	1.43	2.24	1.52	92	.74	1.80	94.6	243.7
		.03	.98	1.65	1.76	1.24	.74	1.80	55.7	132.8
.2	.05	0	2.11	2.57	1.84	.68	.17	.37	114.8	379.2
		.03	1.76	2.29	2.14	.91	.17	.37	82.5	250.5
	.1	0	2.90	3.65	1.84	.68	.74	1.80	157.7	538.9
		.03	2.48	3.31	2.14	.91	.74	1.80	116.0	362.4

II.   An Extension to a Dynamic Framework

The formulas developed in Section II [Eqs. $(5')$ and $(7')$] apply only to the steady state when $\mu - \lambda = \pi^*$. In the transition toward the steady state, the anticipated rate of inflation differs from the excess of the rate of monetary expansion over the rate of growth. Consequently, the effects of raising the rate of monetary expansion from μ_0 to μ_1 cannot be ascertained by substituting the value of μ_1 for μ_0 in the above formulas. The rates of the welfare cost and government revenue during the transition to the steady state do not change at the same percentage rate as income. Consequently, their ratio to income changes through time in contrast with steady-state computations in Table 1. Since the various flows change through time at different rates, an appropriate measure should be their present values where the discounting factor is the social rate of discount (ρ).

Consider the effects of raising the rate of monetary expansion (at $t = t_0$) from μ_0 to μ_1. The present value of income is $y_0/(\rho - \lambda)$; thus the ratio (w) of the present value of the rates of welfare cost to the present value of income is:

$$w = (\rho - \lambda) \frac{k(0)}{\alpha} \int_{t_0}^{\infty} \left\{ 1 + \alpha r_0 - e^{-\alpha \pi^*} [1 + \alpha(r_0 + \pi^*)] \right\} e^{-(\rho - \lambda)(t - t)} \, dt \quad (10)$$

where the anticipated rate of inflation π^* depends on time.

By similar reasoning, the ratio g of the discounted flows of government revenue to the discounted flows of income is:

$$g = (\rho - \lambda)\mu_1 k(0) \int_{t_0}^{\infty} e^{-\alpha \pi^*} e^{-(\rho - \lambda)(t - t_0)} \, dt \quad (11)$$

The significant difference between these equations and their steady-state counterparts $(5')$ and $(7')$ is the explicit dependence of (10) and (11) on the time path of the anticipated rate of inflation $\pi^*(t)$.

To realize the implications of the transition period, it is sufficient to observe that as long as the anticipated rate of inflation is below the steady-state rate of inflation $(\mu_1 - \lambda)$ the welfare loss w along the path computed from (10) must be smaller than the value w^* computed from the steady-state formula. Moreover, the steady-state formula $(5')$ (and the computation in Table 1) imply that the welfare cost is an increasing function of the rate of monetary expansion, that is, $w^*(\mu_1) > w^*(\mu_0)$. Such a presumption does not hold when the entire path is considered; depending on the path of $\pi^*(t)$ following the acceleration of the rate of monetary expansion from μ_0 to μ_1, the welfare cost w may be larger or smaller than $w^*(\mu_0)$. In other words,

since during the transition period the path of anticipated inflation may include
a transitional increase in the (desired) holdings of real cash balances, it is quite
possible that the welfare cost of the entire path, corresponding to the *higher*
rate of monetary expansion, might be smaller than the steady-state loss $w^*(\mu_0)$
corresponding to a lower rate of monetary expansion.

By a similar reasoning, consideration of the transitional period implies
that, in general, the constant rate of monetary expansion that maximizes (the
present value of) government revenue exceeds $1/\alpha$.

Indeed, there is ample evidence that a rise in the rate of monetary expansion induces initially a *rise* in the real quantity of money. Such short-
run effects are documented for the United States (e.g., [17]) as well as for
many Latin American experiences (e.g., [18]). Figure 2 describes a typical
path corresponding to the stylized facts on the effects of the acceleration of
the monetary growth rate on real money holdings. As is shown, the real stock
rises initially (until $t = t_1$) and then declines toward its (lower) steady-state
value. However, for the time interval between t_0 and t_2, real holdings of cash
balances exceed their intial level. A possible explanation for the observed
short-run increase in the real monetary stock is that during the initial phase of
the inflationary process, expectations are that the process will reverse itself,
resulting, thereby, in a transitory decline in desired velocity. It is only in the
later phases of the inflationary process that expectations catch up and desired
real balances fall. This process, in which the regressive component dominates
the short run, will be denoted as the Keynes-Cassel explanation. It is well
described in Keynes [1, pp. 40-41], and in Cassel [19, p. 8].

Clearly, the comparisons of $w^*(\mu_0)$ and $g^*(\mu_0)$ with w and g (where w
and g are the present values computed from the paths following the acceleration of μ from μ_0 to μ_1) depend on the social rate of discount and on the

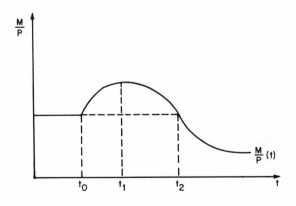

FIGURE 2

entire path of the anticipated rate of inflation $\pi^*(t)$. This path depends in turn on the process by which expectations are formed. Since during the transition period individuals revise their expectations and alter their desired holdings of real balances as new information becomes available, a relevant analytical question is whether it is appropriate to evaluate the welfare cost over the transition period by employing a similar method that is used for evaluating steady-state positions. A detailed discussion of this question is postponed to Section III. It is sufficient to indicate here that as long as individuals are "on" their demand for cash balances, the usual evaluation procedure can also be applied to the period of transition.

III. An Application of the Expectations Function to the Dynamic Framework

A. The Analytical Aspect

The discussion in Section II implied that when the adjustment period is taken into account, the welfare effects of changes in the rate of monetary expansion are not clear cut. The ambiguity arises from the fact that initially, following the acceleration of the rate of monetary expansion, individuals increase their desired holdings of real cash balances and thereby reduce (for a while) the dead-weight loss of the distortion.

   The issue involved is described by means of Fig. 3 in which, to simplify the exposition, it is assumed that the growth rate is zero.

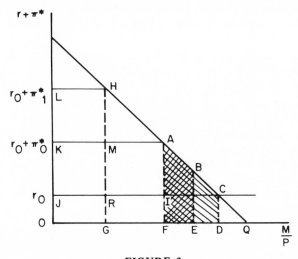

FIGURE 3

Consider an initial steady state with $\mu = \mu_0 = \pi_0^* = \pi_0$. At this steady state, desired holdings of real cash balances are OF, the rate of welfare cost (due to the inflation) is the area $ACDF$, and the rate of government revenue is the area $KAIJ = \mu_0 (M/P)_0$. The welfare cost exceeds the triangle AIC since money (which is produced costlessly), is a non-interest-bearing asset. At a higher rate of monetary expansion μ_1, the new steady state is reached when $\mu_1 = \pi_1^* = \pi_1$, desired holdings of real cash balances fall to OG, the welfare cost increases by the area $HAFG$, and government revenue becomes $LHRJ$. The revenue rises or falls depending on the interest elasticity of the demand. However, the process of reaching the steady state takes time. Since, for a time, desired holdings increase (e.g., up to OE), the initial phases appear to reduce the excess burden. At the time when desired holdings are OE, the dead-weight loss declines by the area $ABEF$ while government revenue must rise. In fact, as long as money holdings exceed the initial level (OF), the excess burden is lower and government revenue is higher. In a later phase of the process, as expectations start catching up, desired holdings decline and the excess burden increases. Since the benefits accrue during the early phase of the process while the costs accrue later, there exists some rate of discount for which the net present value of the entire "project" might not indicate a net loss.

While the implications of the analysis are straightforward for the case of government revenue, the analytical aspects involved in analyzing the welfare cost are more complex. A relevant question is whether it is appropriate to evaluate the welfare effects of a disequilibrium situation using the same method used to evaluate equilibrium positions. The key to this question lies in the assumption that individuals are *on* their demand schedule. For any given expectation on the future course of prices, individuals hold exactly the desired quantity, i.e., if expectations were to be realized, desired holdings would not change. Therefore, at any given nominal rate of interest, "market price" is equated to the "demand price," which measures the perceived yield on the marginal unit of real balances.[4]

The use of the concept of equilibrium might be questioned, however, on the grounds that since individuals alter their behavior as new information becomes available they reveal that their previous position was not an equilibrium one. However, the welfare gain from the social viewpoint stems precisely from the fact that individuals move to the "wrong direction" when faced with a distortion. Since initial holdings of cash balances are suboptimal due to the distortion of money being a non-interest-bearing asset, a policy that induces larger holdings reduces the cost of the distortion. The evaluation of the rate of welfare cost at each point in time should be independent of later flows resulting from altered behavior. Those later flows are represented in the capitalized value of the entire path, but should not affect the evaluation of the instantaneous rate at each point along the path.

Although it is difficult to construct a complete analogy to this case, the following example from the theory of tariffs captures some of its main features. Consider a tariff-ridden economy whose optimal tariff is zero. The welfare cost of the tariff arises from distorting consumption and production. Consumption of the distorted activity is lowered below the socially optimal level, while production is raised above the socially optimal level. Suppose that the government announces a plan to raise the tariff rate at a specified future date. Assume that following the announcement, consumers decide to alter their inter-temporal consumption plan so as to substitute present consumption for future consumption of the protected goods that is expected to rise in price. Similarly, assume that producers decide to substitute future production (at the higher anticipated protection rate) for present production. Thus, both consumers and producers alter their behavior so as to reduce the distortive effect of the prevailing tariff. Suppose now that at the specified date the government announces that the original plan was changed and that the tariff rate was to remain unchanged. Producers and consumers would restore the initial production and consumption patterns, but the welfare cost of the tariff over the entire period has been reduced. The misleading announcement "inflicted" gains on the society by reducing the distortive effects of the initial distortion. The fact that individuals regret their past decisions induces them to restore the higher rate of the excess burden, but should not affect the social gain in the intervening period.

Similar considerations are also relevant for stabilization programs. In that case, when the rate of monetary expansion is reduced, a movement in the "wrong direction" reduces welfare and might outweigh the long-run gains. The short-run losses can be viewed as elements of the set-up cost of the stabilization program.

B.   The Formation of Expectations and Some
   Illustrative Computations

As was indicated before, the computation of the present values of the welfare cost and government revenue associated with changes in the rate of monetary expansion depends on the process by which expectations are formed. One possible theory of the formation of expectations, which is consistent with the early phases of the inflationary process along the Keynes-Cassel explanation, is developed by Frenkel [20]. To illustrate the implications of considering the dynamic aspects of the welfare cost and government revenue from inflation, we have used the path of $\pi^*(t)$ that was derived in [20]. Without describing that theory in great detail, one can state that its key elements lie in the distinction between the long-term (normal) and the short-term expected rates of inflation and can be summarized as follows: Individuals are assumed to possess expectations with regard to the entire path of the *price level*. Implicit in the expectations is an expectation on the long-term average rate of inflation π_n. These expectations are assumed to adjust in response to observed differences between the actual rate of inflation $\pi = \dot{P}/P$ and π_n:

$$\dot{\pi}_n = \gamma(\pi - \pi_n); \gamma > 0 \tag{12}$$

The second central variable is the short-term expected rate of inflation π^*, which is assumed to determine the demand for money. It is hypothesized that these short-term expectations are influenced by two elements: (1) the relationship between the actual rate of inflation π and the expected average rate π_n and (2) the relationship between the actual rate of inflation and the expected short-term rate π^*. The rule by which π^* is adjusted is:

$$\dot{\pi}^* = \delta(\pi_n - \pi) + \beta(\pi - \pi^*) \quad \delta > \beta > 0 \tag{13}$$

The first term in (13) states that if the actual inflation rate were above the expected rate in the immediate past, then the actual rate in the immediate future must be lower to maintain the long-run average rate and thereby conform with the anticipations about the trend of the price level. This is the regressive component in the determination of π^*. The second term is an extrapolative component that states that if the actual rate were above the short-term expected rate, the short-term rate would be revised upwards. The assumption that $\delta > \beta$ is required to insure that the model produces behavior consistent with the empirical evidence of the short-run effects of changes in the monetary growth rate. Finally, the assumption that the demand function is always satisfied implies (upon differentiating Eq. (1) with respect to time) that

$$\dot{\pi}^* = \frac{\pi - (\mu - \lambda)}{\alpha} \tag{14}$$

The complete model of expectation formation is given by Eq. (12) through (14). A steady state for expectations occurs with $\pi^* = \pi_n = 0$. Given the rate of monetary expansion, it is easily established that the only steady state occurs when $\pi = \pi^* = \pi_n = \mu - \lambda$. The explicit solutions are derived in [20], where it is shown that the solution for the path of π^* (in the non-oscillatory case) is:

$$\pi^*(t) = \mu_1 - \lambda + c_1 e^{-\eta_1(t-t_0)} + c_2 e^{-\eta_2(t-t_0)} \tag{15}$$

where the constants c_1 and c_2 are determined by the initial conditions and where η_1 and η_2 are the (absolute values of the) roots of the characteristic equation of the system. A typical path that is generated by (15) is described in Fig. 2. The illustrative computations presented below derive the values of w and g from (10) and (11) by using the path of $\pi^*(t)$ from (15).

TABLE 2

Percentage Welfare Cost and Government Revenue
from increasing inflation: $r_0 = \rho = 10\%$; $\mu_0 = 10\%$; $\mu_1 = 20\%$

α (1)	γ (2)	β (3)	δ (4)	λ (5)	w (6)	w − w* (7)	g (8)	g − g* (9)	100(w/g) (10)	$\frac{100(w-w*)}{g-g*}$ (11)
5										
	.02	.8	1.8	0	.61	−.83	4.05	2.53	15.0	−32.7
				.03	.21	.78	4.70	2.94	4.4	−26.4
	.02	2.8	3.8	0	1.25	−.18	3.23	1.71	38.8	−10.5
				.03	.91	−.08	3.64	1.88	24.9	− 4.1
	.04	1.5	2.5	0	1.19	−.25	3.32	1.81	35.7	−13.7
				.03	.90	−.08	3.68	1.92	24.6	− 4.0
	.04	2.5	3.5	0	1.43	.00	3.06	1.55	46.8	.0
				.03	1.15	.17	3.39	1.63	34.0	10.4
10	.02	1.4	2.4	0	1.67	−.58	2.48	1.56	67.2	−36.9
				.03	1.05	−.60	3.29	2.05	32.0	−29.1
	.02	3.4	4.4	0	2.10	−.14	2.00	1.08	104.9	−13.4
				.03	1.61	−.04	2.55	1.31	63.1	− 2.8
	.04	6	7	0	2.54	.30	1.58	.66	160.6	45.1
				.03	2.20	.55	1.94	.70	113.2	75.5
	.04	10	11	0	2.66	.42	1.47	.55	181.2	76.5
				.03	2.32	.68	1.80	.56	128.9	120.4

Table 2 presents the results of some numerical computations of the effects of raising the rate of monetary expansion from $\mu_0 = 10$ percent per year to $\mu_1 = 20$ percent per year for alternative values of the parameters with $k(0) = .25$ and $\rho = 10$ percent. The values of the parameters were chosen in order to generate a stable and nonoscillatory path.[4] Columns 6, 8, and 10 present the welfare cost w, government revenue g, and the average cost of collection w/g, respectively, along the path. The more interesting computations are contained in columns 7 and 9. These columns provide the comparison between the welfare cost and government revenue along the path (when $\mu_1 = 20$ percent) with their steady-state counterparts (when $\mu_0 = 10$ percent). The values of $w*$ and $g*$ (corresponding to the steady state with $\mu = \mu_0$) are taken from Table 1.

As shown, in many of the cases the welfare loss of the higher rate of monetary expansion is lower than the steady-state loss of the lower rate of monetary expansion, that is, $w - w^*$ is negative. Moreover, in all cases $g - g^*$ > 0, that is, government revenue is increased with the rate of monetary expansion. In particular, it is noteworthy that when $\alpha = 10$ and $\mu_0 = 1/\alpha$ (the steady-state revenue maximizing rate), an acceleration of the monetary growth rate raises government revenue. As seen in column 11, the marginal cost of collection in these cases is negative. Obviously, since the parameters where not estimated from actual data, the magnitudes in Table 2 should be interpreted only as illustrative.

IV.   Concluding Remarks

Before this chapter is concluded, it must be emphasized that the foregoing analysis focuses on an extremely narrow aspect of the inflationary problem. The assumptions that the paths of output (employment) and the real rate of interest are exogenously given are especially restrictive. It should be noted, however, that although transitional variations in employment have not been considered, the second-best framework can also be applied to the labor market if the initial situation is distorted. Thus if, for example, labor unions reduce employment below the nondistorted level, then the transition toward a higher steady rate of inflation may induce welfare gains if the short-run Phillips curve is not vertical. Similar welfare gains are implied if the transition period induces an expansion of output of monopolized industries. The assumption that the real rate of interest is fixed is based on the implicit assumption that the capital stock remains fixed during the transitional period. Thus, the assumption that the supply of capital is perfectly inelastic assures that the dynamics of inflation do not introduce new distortions associated with misallocation.[5] The analysis is further limited in that it abstracts from possible welfare costs associated with the inflation-induced changes in the distribution of income. Even if there were systematic changes in the distribution of income, a significant part of the welfare loss would be private and should not be attributed to the welfare cost from the social viewpoint. It should be noted, however, that this, of course, does not imply that systematic income redistribution among social groups may not induce social cost associated with different saving behavior as well as social turmoil.[6]

To avoid any misunderstanding, it must be emphasized that the foregoing analysis should not be interpreted as "the case for inflation." Rather, the purpose of the discussion has been to emphasize the limitiation of using steady-state analysis for issues that involve the dynamics toward the steady state. From the analytical viewpoint, the conventional measures of the instantaneous rates of excess burden and government revenue are basically static. The discussion in this chapter suggests that a more appropriate measure should be the present discounted values of these (time dependent) rates.[7]

The application of these concepts to the analysis of inflation reveals the second-best nature of the problem. Since the initial situation is characterized by the presence of distortions, changes in policies (that do not instantaneously eliminate all of the distortions) cannot be evaluated independently of the size of the parameters.

To illustrate the relevance of the dynamic framework to the inflationary problem, the analysis employed a specific form of an expectations function that is consistent with empirical data (Cagan [17]). It should be emphasized, however, that the main issue under consideration does not depend on the details of the expectations function. Any expectation-formation process that generates path-of-money holdings similar to that of Fig. 2, raises the analytical issues discussed in the present chapter.[8] Similarly, to conform with previous discussions of the welfare cost of inflation, the analysis was conducted in terms of the well known "triangles" approach. Consequently, the use of demand curves implicitly assumed the pursuit of compensating variations. The same principles could alternatively be presented directly in terms of the utility function.

Finally, in performing the numerical computations, it was assumed that the policy change amounts to a once-and-for-all change in the rate of monetary expansion. A more elaborate analysis should compute the welfare cost and government revenue along the optimal path of the monetary growth rate.

ACKNOWLEDGMENTS

I am indebted to R. J. Barro, R. Dornbusch, B. Eden, S. Fischer, H. G. Johnson, E. Karni, A. Marty, M. Mussa, and C. A. Rodrigues for helpful comments on an earlier draft of this chapter.

NOTES

1. An additional source of government revenue stems from the non-indexed progressive tax system that results in pushing taxpayers into higher tax brackets as nominal income rises. This important source of government revenue is not pursued further here. For a further analysis of the inflation tax within the framework of the optimal tax structure see [15].

2. The optimal policy of fiscal management should equate with marginal cost of collecting revenue from inflationary finance with the marginal cost of collecting revenue from other tax sources. Although the relevant concept of comparison is the marginal cost of collection, earlier authors have also computed

the average cost of collection as a benchmark for the comparison with cost of collection of other forms of taxes [4, 8, 9]. The steady-state *average* cost of collection is obtained by dividing Eq. (5') by Eq. (7'):

$$\frac{w^*}{g^*} = \frac{(1 + \alpha r_0)\, e^{\alpha(\mu_0 - \lambda)} - [1 + \alpha(\mu_0 - \lambda + r_0)]}{\alpha \mu_0}$$

The average cost of collection depends on the rate of growth and reaches a minimum when

$$\lambda \cong \frac{1}{\alpha}\left[1 + \alpha r\left(\frac{1 - \alpha r}{2}\right)\right]$$

When the government maximizes revenue and the growth rate is zero, the average cost of collection is $(e - 2) + \alpha r(e - 1)$, which is significantly larger than the cost computed by Bailey and Marty [9, p. 1140].

3. For expositional and computational purposes, no distinction has been made between the long-run and the short-run demand functions. It could alternatively be assumed that the short-run demand function differs from the long-run function, in which case the statement that at each moment individuals are *on* their demand schedule refers to the relevant short-run schedule. Although this distinction complicates considerably the computation of the welfare loss, it does not affect the analytical issues involved in the evaluation of welfare.

4. Given that $\delta > \beta$, the stability condition is: $\beta + \gamma(1 - \alpha\beta) > 0$. The condition for a nonoscillatory path is: $[\beta - \gamma(1 - \alpha\beta)]^2 > 4\alpha\beta\gamma\delta$; these conditions are derived in [20].

5. The fixity of the real rate of interest is consistent with the steady-state results of many of the optimizing models (see, e.g., Sidrauski [21], Dornbusch and Frenkel [22], and Mussa [23]). The dynamics of adjustment, however, is typically associated with half a cycle of the capital stock.

6. Note, however, that Kessel and Alchian [24] and Bach and Stephenson [25] have not found evidence that inflation induces systematic redistribution along the stylized facts.

7. For a development of a dynamic concept of the excess burden of a tax, see Levhari and Sheshinski [26]. Cathcart [27] has also considered the present value of the entire paths. This chapter differs from [27] in the formulation of the expectations function as well as in its emphasis on the analytical questions concerning the evaluation of welfare when expectations are not realized and the implications of the second-best framework resulting from an initial distortion.

8. The specific form of the expectations function that was employed in

the simulations is consistent with some evidence on the mixture of regressive and extrapolative components. A relevant question would be whether, as time passes, individuals learn to know the structure of the system so that the monetary authority could not repeat similar operations in the future. It seems likely to assume that individuals do learn and raise the speed of adjustment. However, it also seems that much of the learning is done within the time span of a political cycle, while less is done between political cycles. This interpretation provides a rationale for governments to pursue credible stabilization policies at the start of their political term, and inflationary policies toward the end of their term. For an analysis along these lines see Sjaastad [14].

REFERENCES

1. John M. Keynes, *A Tract on Monetary Reform*, 1st ed., 1923. (Volume IV of *The Collected Writings of J. M. Keynes,* Macmillan, New York; 1971.

2. Edward S. Shaw, *Financial Deepening in Economic Development,* Oxford, New York, 1973.

3. Leonardo Auernheimer, "The Honest Government's Guide to the Revenue From the Creation of Money," *Journal of Political Economy,* **82**, 3, May/June, 1974, pp. 598-606.

4. Martin J. Bailey, "The Welfare Cost of Inflationary Finance," *Journal of Political Economy,* **64**, April 1956, pp. 93-110.

5. Robert J. Barro, "Inflationary Finance and the Welfare Cost of Inflation," *Journal of Political Economy,* **80**, 5, September/October 1972, pp. 978-1001.

6. Milton Friedman, "Government Revenue from Inflation," *Journal of Political Economy,* **79**, July/August 1971, pp. 846-856.

7. Harry G. Johnson, *Essays in Monetary Economics,* Harvard University Press, Cambridge, Mass., 1967.

8. Alvin L. Marty, "Growth and the Welfare Cost of Inflationary Finance," *Journal of Political Economy,* **75**, 1, February 1967, pp. 71-76.

9. Alvin L. Marty, "Growth, Satiety, and the Tax Revenue from Money Creation," *Journal of Political Economy,* **81**, 5, September/October, 1973, pp. 1136-1152.

10. Alvin L. Marty, "A Note on the Welfare Cost of Money Creation," unpublished manuscript, University of Manchester 1974.

10a. Robert Mundell, *Monetary Theory,* Goodyear Publishing Co., Pacific Palisades, 1971.

11. Edward Tower, "More on the Welfare Cost of Inflationary Finance," *Journal of Money Credit and Banking,* 3, November 1971, pp. 850-860.

12. Harry G. Johnson, "Inside Money, Outside Money, Income, Wealth, and Welfare in Monetary Theory," *Journal of Money Credit and Banking,* 1, 1, February 1969, pp. 30-45, reprinted in his *Further Essays in Monetary Economics,* Allen and Unwin, London, 1972.

13. Edmund S. Phelps, "Inflation in the Theory of Public Finance," *Swedish Journal of Economics,* 75, 1973, pp. 67-82.

14. Larry A. Sjaastad, "Why Stable Inflations Fail: An Essay in Political Economy," in Michael Parkin and Genge Zis (Eds.), *Inflation in the World Economy,* University of Toronto Press, Toronto, 1976, pp. 73-86.

15. Jeremy J. Siegel, "Is There An Optimal Rate of Inflation," Report No. 7449, Center for Mathematical Studies in Business and Economics, University of Chicago, Chicago, November, 1974.

16. P. Cagan, "The Monetary Dynamics of Hyperinflation," in M. Friedman, ed., *Studies in the Quantity Theory of Money,* University of Chicago Press, Chicago, 1956.

17. P. Cagan, *The Channels of Monetary Effects on Interest Rates,* National Bureau of Economic Research, No. 97, New York, 1972.

18. David Meiselman (ed.,) *Varieties of Monetary Experience,* University of Chicago Press, Chicago, 1971.

19. Gustav Cassel, *Post-War Monetary Stabilization,* Columbia University Press, New York, 1928.

20. Jacob A. Frenkel, "Inflation and the Formation of Expectations," Journal of Monetary Economics, 1, No. 4, October 1975, pp. 403-421.

21. Miguel Sidrauski, "Rational Choice and Patterns of Growth in a Monetary Economy," *American Economic Review,* 57, May 1967, pp. 534-544.

22. Rudiger Dornbusch and Jacob A. Frenkel, "Inflation and Economic Growth: Alternative Approaches," *Journal of Money and Credit Banking,* 5, 1, Part 1, February 1973, pp. 141-156.

23. Michael Mussa, "A Study in Macro-Economics: A Metzleric Model of Macro-Economic Dynamics," unpublished manuscript, University of Rochester, 1973.

24. Reuben A. Kessel and Armen A. Alchian, "The Meaning and Validity of the Inflation-Induced Lag of Wages behind Prices," *American Economic Review,* 50, 1, March 1960, pp. 43-66.

25. G. L. Bach and James B. Stephenson, "Inflation and the Redistribution of Wealth," *Review of Economics and Statistics,* **56**, 1, February 1974, pp. 1-13.

26. David Levhari and Eytan Sheshinski, "Lifetime Excess Burden of a Tax," *Journal of Political Economy,* **80**, 1, January/February 1972, pp. 139-147.

27. Charles D. Cathcart, "Monetary Dynamics, Growth, and the Efficiency of Inflationary Finance," *Journal of Money and Credit Banking,* **6**, 2, May 1974, pp. 169-190.

Comment

JOHN L. SCADDING

Council of Economic Advisors
Washington, D.C.

The inflation tax is one of the oldest, continually used taxes that we know of. Despite its age, it remains in good health; indeed it has been thriving of late. Such vigor has always disturbed economists—or some of us anyway—because of the suspicion that inflation must be a relatively inefficient way to raises revenue. In 1956 Martin Bailey calculated explicitly the tax's ratio of excess burden to revenue yield. His calculations confirmed one's worst suspicions: Even at fairly low inflation rates the welfare loss per dollar of revenue was substantial [1].

Subsequent attempts to soften this verdict failed. Neither allowing for growth in money demand [2] nor assuming that the inflation tax proceeds are invested to raise the rate of growth [3, 4] helped. And recent contributions to this literature suggest that even Bailey's classic indictment of the inflation tax is too charitable—that it both understates the excess burden [5] and overstates the revenue potential [6].

Frenkel's chapter (along with a recent article by Cathcart [7]) represents yet another attempt to scale down Bailey's verdict against the inflation tax, and to rehabilitate it using the same welfare criterion that once convicted it. I suspect that what motivates these continuing attempts to make a better case for the inflation tax is a desire to explain why the tax is so popular in the face of economists' misgivings about it. If so, it seems to me that such efforts are misguided. I expect that governments resort to inflation out of necessity—or at least out of necessity as they perceive it. In those circumstances, I doubt that they attach much importance to the tax's efficiency. Economists' attempts to rehabilitate it on that ground therefore are essentially self-serving: They make economists feel better if they succeed, but that is about the extent of their impact.

Frenkel's argument rests on a comparison of the present values of the inflation tax's welfare cost and revenue yield during transition periods with their present values in the stationary state. One can think of the comparison as being between two different states of the world: one in which full adjustment is made instantaneously to a new rate of monetary expansion (the steady-state case); the other in which real money balances are adjusted with a lag to the new money rate of growth.

Suppose then that we calculate the present values for each of the two states of the world after there has been an increase in the rate of monetary expansion.* In the incomplete adjustment case real balances are never smaller than they are in the perfect foresight, instantaneous adjustment case. Consequently, the present value of the tax yield must be higher, and the loss in consumer's or producer's surplus less, then when there is incomplete adjustment. Hence it would appear that allowing for incomplete adjustment in the short run makes a stronger case for the inflation tax than does the conventional analysis, which assumes perfect anticipations and complete adjustment.

But is that really true? The long-run static solution of the conventional analysis is surely the individual's preferred solution in the sense that he would choose, were it not for adjustment costs, costs of information gathering and the like. If he is observed to hold more real balances during the transition it must be because of those sorts of costs. But that in turn must mean that the individual is worse off: Besides the direct income loss from the tax he must shoulder the expenses and inconveniences of learning about the tax and adjusting to it.

The trouble with Frenkel's transition states is that they are of this second-best variety. Frenkel's explanation for incomplete adjustment is that individuals initially underestimate changes in the inflation rate. But that only makes sense if accurate prediction is too costly. Otherwise, there would be some gain from improving one's forecasting: Underestimating the inflation rate means underestimating the tax rate, holding too much of the taxed commodity, and consequently paying too much tax.† Hence individuals pay more tax in the short

---

*Frenkel puts the comparison between the transition state and the stationary state at the *old* rate of monetary expansion. It seems to me however that the relevant comparison is the one in the text—that it better expresses the core of Frenkel's argument.

†Expectations are certainly not rational in Frenkel's model. A rise in the rate of inflation today leads to predictions of a *lower* rate in the future. Translated into a statement about tax rates, that says that individuals expect a lower tax rate in the future for a higher tax rate today—a touching belief in the benevolence of government for which there is no empirical evidence.

run because of the costs of avoidance are even higher. But Frenkel's welfare calculations do not take those costs into account. It is not at all clear, therefore, that allowing for partial adjustment makes a stronger case for the inflation tax. In fact, I would think the presumption is just the opposite. How can we meaningfully say that welfare is in any sense improved when people are misled? That seems to me to contradict our basic notions of what economic welfare is.

REFERENCES

1. Martin J. Bailey, "The Welfare Cost of Inflationary Finance," *Journal of Political Economy*, **64**, April 1956, pp. 93-110.

2. Alvin L. Marty, "Growth, Satiety, and the Tax Revenue from Money Creation," *Journal of Political Economy*, **81**, September/October 1973, pp. 1136-1152.

3. R. A. Mundell, "Growth, Stability and Inflationary Finance," *Journal of Political Economy*, **73**, April 1965, pp. 97-109.

4. Alvin L. Marty, "Growth and the Welfare Cost of Inflationary Finance," *Journal of Political Economy*, **75**, February 1967, pp. 71-76.

5. Edward Tower, "More on the Welfare Cost of Inflationary Finance," *Journal of Money, Credit and Banking*, **3**, November 1971, pp. 850-860.

6. Leonardo Auernheimer, "The Honest Government's Guide to the Revenue from the Creation of Money," *Journal of Political Economy*, **82**, May/June 1974, pp. 598-606.

7. Charles D. Cathcart, "Monetary Dynamics, Growth, and the Efficiency of Inflationary Finance," *Journal of Money, Credit and Banking*, **6**, May 1974, pp. 169-190.

Chapter 9

Two Approaches to Ending Inflation

BASANT K. KAPUR

Department of Economics
University of Singapore
Republic of Singapore

Perhaps the most exciting and potentially fruitful financial approach to economic development that has originated in recent years is that pioneered by E. S. Shaw and R. I. McKinnon. Although this approach has been crystallized in two recent works by Shaw and McKinnon ([11], [8]), its antecedents stretch back to the early sixties. Its primary proposition is that policies that repress and distort the functioning of financial and capital markets in less developed countries—policies such as the maintenance of high inflation rates and of low, disequilibrium loan and deposit rates on financial instruments—can and do, in Shaw's words, "intercept and destroy impulses to development."

    This chapter will not present a detailed discussion of arguments supporting this proposition. Instead, its focus is more short-run in character. Assuming that it is considered desirable to liberalize the functioning of financial and capital markets in less developed economies, the question we seek to answer is, how the transition from a financially repressed to a financially liberalized economic condition can best be achieved. To narrow the discussion even further, we propose to examine here the short-run, macroeconomic implications of alternative policies designed to lower the "steady-state" rate of inflation in a "typical" underdeveloped economy.

    The basic monetarist position is adopted here to the effect that high rates of inflation are caused by growth in the nominal supply of money significantly in excess of the growth in the real quantity of money that would have been demanded had the price level remained stable. From this point of view, the solution to the price stabilization problem appears obvious: Reduce the rate at which the nominal supply of money is expanded. The defect of this prescription, as is well known, is that a discrete reduction in the rate of monetary expansion frequently precipitates an immediate, though temporary, fall in the level of real output of the economy, which is clearly undesirable on social grounds. With this taken into consideration, the plan of this chapter is as follows. First, we shall briefly discuss three alternative explanations of the mechanism that generates this initial fall in real output. Secondly, we shall summarize an alternative stabilization policy proposed by McKinnon [8], which, it is contended, need not entail any fall in real output in the process of reducing the inflation rate. Finally, we shall specify a simple, structural macroeconomic model of a less developed economy in the context of which a rigorous examination of some of the issues raised will be conducted.

I. The Fall in Output During a Monetary Contraction

The first approach to the problem of explaining why a reduction in the rate of monetary expansion frequently induces a temporary fall in real output may be termed the "demand-constrained" view, which tends to be espoused by economists engaged in the study of Latin American economies.[1] Logarithmically differentiating the identity $MV = PY$ with respect to time, where M = nominal money supply, V = income velocity of circulation of money, P = the average price level of final output, and Y = final real output, we have:

$$\frac{\dot{M}}{M} + \frac{\dot{V}}{V} = \frac{\dot{P}}{P} + \frac{\dot{Y}}{Y} \tag{1}$$

where dots denote time derivatives. Let $\dot{M}/M = \mu$, $\dot{P}/P = \pi$ (the actual rate of inflation), $\dot{Y}/Y = \gamma$, and let π^* = the expected rate of inflation. The demand-constrained view may then be elucidated as follows. Suppose the economy is in a highly inflationary state initially, with high values of μ and π (the latter being equal to π^* in steady-state equilibrium), and the government suddenly reduces μ to a lower, but still positive, number. At some time in the stabilization process, π^* will begin to decline, whereupon $\dot{V}/V$ becomes negative (the demand for money as a proportion of income starts increasing). If $\dot{V}/V$ becomes sufficiently negative, $\mu + \dot{V}/V$ also turns negative: In economic terms, aggregate demand in nominal terms has declined because the increase in the supply of nominal money is not sufficient to meet the increased demand for money at the prevailing instantaneous price level.

Since $\mu + \dot{V}/V$ is negative, $\pi + \gamma$ must also be negative. However, it is then argued that in the short run, prices are "sticky" downward, so that π is bounded from below by zero. Once π approaches this lower bound, the remaining adjustment must be borne by γ, which therefore has to turn negative:

Real income has to decline in the face of a reduction in aggregate demand in nominal terms, and downward rigidity of the price level. Eventually, however, π^* declines to its new equilibrium (possibly in a cyclical manner), so that $\dot{V}/V$ stabilizes at zero (assuming that the demand for real money balances is homogeneous of degree one in real income): $\mu + \dot{V}/V$ is now positive, so that both π and γ can turn positive, and growth in real income resumes.

This view appears to be fairly plausible, if indeed it is correct that $\mu + \dot{V}/V$ turns negative during the stabilization process. This clearly is an empirical matter: We shall discuss subsequently the extent to which it is possible to distinguish empirically between this explanation and an alternative view that is developed in the following.

The second approach may be termed the "supply-constrained" view, and has been developed by McKinnon [8, Chap. 7]. A strategic element in this approach is the role played by commercial banks as a source of financing for the holding of working capital by productive enterprises, where the term *working capital* has been defined by McKinnon to include "inventories of goods in process, trade credit, and advances to workers prior to the actual sales." To quote McKinnon: "In the process of deflation over the short run, the key component of investment that is influenced most by monetary policy is working capital . . . . In moderately wealthy LDCs, such as Brazil and Chile, the real supply of bank credit to some manufacturing and commercial concerns has become large enough to be vital to their operation." [8, p. 87.]

Suppose, once again, the monetary authorities abruptly reduce μ. One could then plausibly argue that some time must necessarily elapse before this step induces an appreciable decline in π^*. In the meantime, the reduction in μ will, through a mechanism that will be described more precisely, have the effect of reducing the flow of real bank credit below what it would otherwise be. This reduction constricts the capacity of productive enterprises to hold working capital, and an immediate reduction in real output may result. It is thus the linkage between bank financing and aggregate supply through the working capital nexus that is employed to explain the initial downturn in real output, as well as its subsequent expansion once π^* converges to its new, lower, steady-state value. Notice that this argument assumes, legitimately for most less developed countries, that the commercial banking system is the most important source of external financing for productive enterprises.

The third approach is based essentially on "Phillips-Curve" type reasoning. Certain elements of the approach may be found in a recent article by Selowsky [10], although he develops his complete argument along somewhat different lines. Let us assume, following the classic analysis of Lewis [7], that producers are faced with an infinitely elastic supply of labor from the "subsistence sector" of the economy at a fixed real wage rate. In the initial steady-state equilibrium, therefore, nominal wages are rising at the same rate as the price level. Assume also, as Selowsky does, that even in the short run, there exists smooth neoclassical substitutability between the (fixed) capital stock and the labor input, so that the demand for labor is based on the condition that its marginal physical product equal the real wage rate. Finally, suppose the rate of increase of nominal wages is equated to the *expected* rate of inflation, which simply implies that workers seek to maintain unchanged their expected real wage rate. If now μ is reduced, and the decline in π^* lags behind the decline in π, the realized or ex post facto real wage rate will rise, since nominal wages increase at a rate equal to π^*. The employment of labor is then reduced until its marginal product rises to equality with the higher real wage rate, and since the capital stock is fixed, the lower level of employment necessarily implies a reduction in real output.

A deficiency with this argument lies precisely in its assumption that there exists smooth substitutability between capital and labor even in the short run: With a fixed capital stock and technology one might well expect fixed proportions between the utilized capital stock and labor to prevail instead. If that were the case, a transitory rise in real wages would not induce employers to reduce the volume of employment they offer if they were able to earn nonnegative "quasi-rents" on the fixed capital stock despite the transitionally higher real wage rate.

It is, however, possible to effect a reconciliation between this approach and the supply-constrained view outlined in the foregoing. Suppose that, as already mentioned, one component of working capital consists of advances to workers prior to actual sales, and that entrepreneurs are heavily dependent on bank credit to meet these advances. If a reduction in μ initially reduced the flow of real bank credit, while nominal wages continued at first to rise at the same rate as before, then entrepreneurs may be constrained to reduce their employment level to the amount that could be financed out of the temporarily reduced "wage fund." Notice that this argument does not require the assumption of smooth substitutability between capital and labor. We shall, in fact, adopt an analog of this argument in the model presented here; however, there is a subtle difference between our treatment and the above-mentioned third approach.

Consistent with his supply-constrained view of the stabilization problem, McKinnon has proposed the use of an alternative monetary policy instrument in the initial stages of the stabilization program: Rather than reduce μ (the rate of growth of the nominal supply of money), the monetary authorities should initially raise the average deposit rate d on money holdings, thereby reducing the excess supply of money by raising the demand for real money balances. Concomitant with this increase in M/P there will, as shown below, occur an immediate increase in the flow of real bank credit. Subsequently, the monetary authorities can proceed to gradually reduce μ as π^* falls, so that the flow of real bank credit need not decline at any time during the stabilization process, and the short-run squeeze on working capital and real output is completely avoided.

II.   The Basic Model

We proceed now to construct a short-run dynamic model that seeks to incorporate formally the considerations just adduced. It turns out that the model does substantially bear out the validity of McKinnon's analysis. It is hoped, however, that the model serves the useful purpose of "screening" the precise assumptions required for the analysis to go through, as well as of permitting a more detailed determination of the relationships involved. In addition, it enables us to derive explicit analytical expressions for the time paths of the endogenous variables resulting from the use of the alternative control variables μ and d. Finally, the model is of use in enabling us to discriminate, in some instances, between the demand-constrained and the supply-constrained explanations of the short-run reduction in real output that typically results from an abrupt reduction in μ.

Let the total flow of *fixed* capital services that is available at time t be denoted by $\hat{G}(t)$. Suppose, however, that there exists a technical complementarity between each hour of use of fixed capital and the associated requirement of working capital. If the economy is financially repressed, the capacity of entrepreneurs to finance the holding of working capital will be severely limited: this will reduce the actual usage of working capital, and hence, as a result of the abovementioned technical complementarity, the flow of fixed capital services that is actually utilized, denoted by $G(t)$, will be less than the total availability $\hat{G}(t)$. Such a situation of persistent excess capacity is perfectly compatible with a steady-state equilibrium if we make the further assumptions that (1) technological indivisibilities in the size of each unit of fixed capital render it impossible for each entrepreneur to exactly "tailor" the size of his machines to the availability of working capital; (2) the rate of profit that is yielded from the operation of the capital stock is deemed an adequate return for entrepreneurial effort despite the fact that the capital stock is not fully utilized; and (3) owing to transactions and information costs, it is not feasible for entrepreneurs economy-wide to associate and decide to restrain further increases in $\hat{G}$ until the growth in the availability of working capital is sufficient to fully utilize all currently available fixed-capital equipment.

Let the total utilized flow of capital services per unit time, both fixed and working, be denoted as $K(t)$, consisting of $G(t)$ plus the usage of working capital. Let $G/K = \alpha$, which we have assumed to be fixed by technical factors: thus, the ratio of working capital to the total utilized capital flow is simply $(1 - \alpha)$. For simplicity, we shall assume that the aggregate production function of our one-sector economy is of the Harrod-Domar variety:

$$Y = \sigma K \tag{2}$$

It is, of course, not necessary to account separately for the labor input, since it is treated as part of the flow of working capital.

The nominal stock of money M is divided into two components:

$$M = C + L \tag{3}$$

C is defined as "high-powered" money, assumed to be issued by the government as transfer payments: Part of it is held as currency in active circulation, and the remainder deposited with commercial banks. L is equal to the total outstanding volume of loans made by the commercial banking system: The proceeds of these loans are in part withdrawn as currency, and in part redeposited as "secondary" bank deposits, which justifies Eq. (3). For simplicity, we shall assume that the public's desired and actual currency/deposit ratio and the banks' desired and actual reserve/deposit ratio are stable through time, so that L/M and C/M are constant: Let $L/M = q$, so that $C/M = 1 - q$. One of the monetary policy parameters is thus the rate at which the monetary base C is expanded: if $\dot{C}/C = \mu$, the constancy of q implies that $\dot{L}/L = \dot{M}/M = \mu$ also.

It is necessary next to specify the sources of finance for the holding of working capital. These are assumed to be threefold: (1) replacement of worn-out working capital that is financed out of the internal resources of productive enterprises; (2) replacement of worn-out working capital that is financed by borrowing from commercial banks; and (3) net investment in working capital that is financed by bank borrowing. For simplicity, it is assumed that fixed capital assets do not depreciate, and that net investment in working capital is financed solely out of bank borrowing: however, once the stock of working capital has been so augmented, its subsequent maintenance is financed partly as in item (1), and partly as in item (2). It is further assumed that bank credit is used entirely to finance the holding of working capital.

Since the total flow of capital services at time t is $K(t)$, the total usage of working capital at that time is $(1 - \alpha)K(t)$. Again for simplicity, we shall assume that a fixed fraction θ of this usage is replaced through bank finance, while $(1 - \theta)$ of it is replaced through internal finance. θ is constrained to lie in the open interval $(0,1)$, as also is α. Clearly, entrepreneurs have first of all to repay to the commercial banks the loans they had previously incurred in order to purchase the fraction θ of the working capital that they have since used up. These repayments are now available for relending by the commercial banks. Thus the *extra* amount that the banks have to lend in order to maintain the stock of working capital intact is in nominal terms simply equal to $\dot{P}\theta(1 - \alpha)K$, which represents the increased cost of replacement as a result of a rise in the price level (since ours is a one-sector model, the price of working capital is the same as the price of final output, provided, as we shall assume, that the real wage rate is always fixed). The rate of capital accumulation in our model is then given by Eq. (4).

$$\dot{K} = \frac{1}{(1 - \alpha)} \left[\frac{\dot{L} - \dot{P}\theta(1 - \alpha)K}{P} \right] \tag{4a}$$

$$= \frac{1}{(1 - \alpha)} \left[\frac{\dot{L}}{P} - \pi\theta(1 - \alpha)K \right] \tag{4b}$$

$$= \frac{1}{(1 - \alpha)} \left[\mu q \frac{M}{P} - \pi\theta(1 - \alpha)K \right] \tag{4c}$$

The numerator of the square-bracketed expression of (4a) is the excess of the increase in nominal bank lending over the increase in the nominal cost of replacing the bank-financed component of worn-out working capital: this excess is available to finance net investment in working capital. Dividing this excess by P, the square-bracketed expression is seen to be equal to real net investment in working capital. This net increase is then multiplied by $1/(1 - \alpha)$ to obtain the net increase in the utilized flow of total capital services, both fixed and working. For example, if working capital is one-quarter of K (so that $(1 - \alpha)$ equals ¼), then a unit net increase in the availability of working capital is capable of sustaining a fourfold increase in the total utilization of capital, given the presence of excess capacity in the economy.[2,3]

A convenient money demand function with which to work is that originated by Cagan [2] assuming that money is the sole financial asset available to savers:

$$\frac{\hat{M}}{P} = Ye^{-a(\pi^* - d)} \tag{5}$$

where a is a positive parameter, d is the average nominal interest rate paid on money holdings, and $\hat{M}/P$ denotes desired holdings of real money balances (M/P should then be taken to refer to actual holdings of real money balances).

Dividing (4) by K, noting from (2) that $Y/K = \sigma$, and hence that $\dot{K}/K = \dot{Y}/Y = \gamma$, we have:

$$\gamma = \mu \frac{\sigma q}{(1 - \alpha)} \frac{M}{PY} - \pi\theta \tag{6}$$

Before turning to the analysis of short-run dynamics, let us first examine the steady-state properties of the system corresponding to given initial values of the policy parameters μ and d. The steady state in our model is defined by the conditions (1) that actual holdings of real cash balances are equal to desired holdings, the latter being given by Eq. (5) (outside the steady state we shall allow for the possibility of a discrepancy between these two variables); and (2) that the expected rate of inflation π^* is equal to the actual rate π, and that both of these are constant. The latter implies that velocity is constant, so that Eq. (1) specializes to: $\mu = \pi + \gamma$. From this, we have $\pi^* = \pi = \mu - \gamma$: Substituting this into Eq. (5), and then substituting (5) into (6) we have, in the steady state:

$$\gamma = \mu \frac{\sigma q}{(1 - \alpha)} e^{-a(\mu - \gamma - d)} - \mu\theta + \gamma\theta \tag{7}$$

This is an implicit equation in the single unknown γ. We shall assume that there exists at least one differentiable solution to this equation. Let us denote all points satisfying the left-hand side of this equation as $z = \gamma$, and all points satisfying the right-hand side as $z = \mu[\sigma q/(1 - \alpha)]e^{-a(\mu - \gamma - d)} - \mu\theta + \gamma\theta$. The slope of this latter curve with respect to γ is denoted by Δ, which is equal to:

$$\Delta = a\mu \frac{\sigma q}{(1 - \alpha)} e^{-a(\mu - \gamma - d)} + \theta \tag{8}$$

This is an increasing function of γ, so that the curve $z = \mu[\sigma q/(1 - \alpha)]e^{-a(\mu - \gamma - d)} - \mu\theta + \gamma\theta$ slopes increasingly steeply upward. We shall, however, assume that the following two restrictions hold. First, that the values of the parameters of the model are such that this curve has a nonnegative intercept with the vertical axis (i.e., at the point $\gamma = 0$); second, that at this intercept Δ is strictly less than unity. (Notice that the slope of the line $z = \gamma$ is simply unity.) We then have the two possibilities shown in Fig. 1a and 1b, depending on whether the intercept is zero or strictly positive. In each case, therefore, we have two solutions, given by the intersections of the two curves, to Eq. (7). (Notice that in case (b) of Fig. 1, tangency between the two curves is ruled out by our requiring that at least one solution be differentiable.) However, we demonstrate in the following that, given the dynamic adjustment mechanisms that we shall postulate, solutions at which the curve $z = \mu[\sigma q/(1 - \alpha)]e^{-a(\mu - \gamma - d)} - \mu\theta + \gamma\theta$ cuts the line $z = \gamma$ from below (in other words, solutions at which $\Delta > 1$) are locally unstable, while solutions at which $\Delta < 1$ are locally stable. We shall, therefore, in this chapter confine ourselves to an examination of the properties of solutions at which $\Delta < 1$. Implicitly differentiating Eq. (7) with respect to μ, rearranging terms, and assuming that $\Delta < 1$ at the solution, we have:

$$\frac{d\gamma}{d\mu} = \frac{1}{(1 - \Delta)} \left\{ \frac{\sigma q}{(1 - \alpha)} e^{-a(\mu - \gamma - d)} [1 - a\mu] - \theta \right\} \tag{9}$$

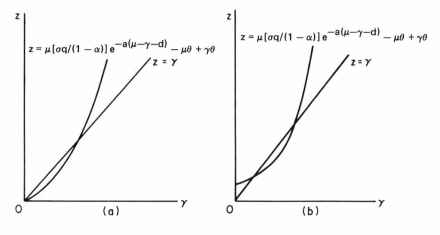

FIGURE 1

Suppose, hypothetically, that μ were equal to zero: in that case, from (7), we see that $\gamma = 0$. Moreover, at this point, assuming that $[\sigma q/(1 - \alpha)]e^{ad}$ exceeds θ, $d\gamma/d\mu$ is positive. On the other hand, if $\mu = 1/a$, $d\gamma/d\mu$ is negative. Thus, there exists an intermediate value of μ at which $d\gamma/d\mu$ equals zero, since $d\gamma/d\mu$ is continuous in μ and a continuous function defined over a connected domain has a connected range. Moreover, at the point at which $d\gamma/d\mu$ is equal to zero, $d^2\gamma/d\mu^2$ can easily be shown to be negative, so that it represents a maximum of γ with respect to μ. Finally, this point is unique: If there existed two local maxima, they would have to be separated by a local minimum, whereas $d^2\gamma/d\mu^2$ is negative when $d\gamma/d\mu$ is equal to zero. Thus, the steady-state value of γ, as a function of μ, may be graphed as in Fig. 2 (for the time being the points μ_0 and μ_1 should be ignored).

We turn now to the analysis of short-run dynamics. First of all, as regards the evolution of π^* through time, we shall simply adopt Cagan's adaptive expectations formulation:

$$\frac{d\pi^*}{dt} = \beta(\pi - \pi^*) \tag{10}$$

where β is a positive parameter.

Secondly, consider the most important specification in the model relating actual to expected inflation. To "set the stage" for it, let us consider the following interpretation by McKinnon of the Brazilian stabilization experience of the mid-1960s:

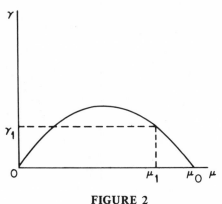

FIGURE 2

"The industrial recession in Brazil over the 1964-67 period was due as much or more to the reduction in the *real* size of the banking system (the money/GNP ratio declined to its historical nadir of 21 percent in 1966) as to the forced switch in the granting of credit from industry to agriculture. This contraction in the real stock of money—and real bank credit—was due primarily to the extraordinary inflationary expectations built up in the early 1960s, when inflation accelerated from 54 percent in 1962 to 73 percent in 1963 to 91 percent in 1964. The real return to holders of money declined sharply. Thereafter, an "orthodox" policy of deflation was implemented, which slowed inflation to 51 percent in 1965, 37 percent in 1966, and 25 percent in 1967. It was during the latter period, however, when rates of inflation were declining, that the industrial recession bit most sharply." [8, pp. 84-85]

For our present purposes, two features of this analysis are noteworthy. In the first place, it is contended that an "orthodox" deflationary policy— by which McKinnon essentially means a reduction in μ—has the effect of initially reducing the money/GNP ratio, or, equivalently, of increasing V, the velocity of circulation of money. In the second place, this initial rise in velocity is attributed to the fact that inflationary expectations are slow to adjust downward in the face of an orthodox deflationary policy.

McKinnon does not, however, precisely identify the nature of the mechanism linking variations in μ, π^*, and V. Indeed, such a mechanism is more elusive than it may appear to be at first sight: I have demonstrated elsewhere [5], in the context of a static model in which the level of real output is assumed to be constant throughout the stabilization process, that if we merely assume that π^* adjusts to π with a lag, and that the actual level of velocity adjusts to its desired level with a lag, then it is *not* the case that a reduction in μ will induce an initial phase of rising velocity, as had been erroneously claimed by Mundell [9]. Instead, velocity will initially commence to decline.

Suppose, however, that we were to adopt the following notion: namely, the assumption that the *actual* rate of inflation is a function, *inter alia*, of the *expected* rate of inflation. (This possibility was originally suggested to me by McKinnon in a private communication.) Such an assumption would be justified if sellers in the economy were to raise prices in part because they expected that prices would rise in the near future. (Readers may recall that Arrow, in a well-known paper [1], had in fact argued that even under perfect competition sellers do have some freedom to set prices in disequilibrium situations.) It would be desirable to provide a detailed microeconomic rationale for this assumption, although it is not attempted in this chapter. In my earlier paper I have demonstrated that incorporation of this assumption, suitably formulated, into a static model does indeed generate the result that an abrupt reduction in μ would induce an initial phase of rising velocity.

Models that assume π to be a function of π^* and of "demand pressure" have been proposed by Hadjimichalakis [4] and by Goldman [3]. Analogously to Goldman, we may write:

$$\pi = f\left(\frac{\text{excess demand for goods}}{\text{goods supply}}\right) + \pi^* \tag{11}$$

where f is an increasing and sign-preserving function of demand pressure. By Walras' Law, however, excess demand for goods must equal the excess supply of money, since these are the only two markets in the model. Thus, we can change (11) to:

$$\pi = h\left(\frac{M}{PY} - \frac{\hat{M}}{PY}\right) + \pi^* \tag{12}$$

where for simplicity we shall take h to be a positive constant, and where M/P and $\hat{M}/P$ denote actual and desired holdings of real cash balances, respectively.[4]

Our specification of the model is now complete. To facilitate the mathematical analysis, it is convenient to introduce some additional notations. Let V equal the actual level of velocity, which in turn is equal to PY/M, and let $\hat{V}$ be the desired level of velocity or $PY/\hat{M}$. Moreover, let $W = \log V$ and $\hat{W} = \log \hat{V}$ (all logarithms are to base e). Equation (1) then becomes:

$$\mu + \dot{W} = \pi + \gamma \tag{1a}$$

Moreover, $M/PY = 1/V = e^{-W}$, since $\log(1/V) = -W$. Equation (6) can therefore be written as:

$$\gamma = \mu \, \frac{\sigma q}{(1 - \alpha)} \, e^{-W} - \pi \theta \qquad (6a)$$

Similarly, $\hat{M}/PY = e^{-\hat{W}}$, and Eq. (12) becomes:

$$\pi = h(e^{-W} - e^{-\hat{W}}) + \pi^* \qquad (12a)$$

$$= h(e^{-W} - e^{-a(\pi^* - d)}) + \pi^*$$

since, from Eq. (5), $\hat{W} = \log PY/M = a(\pi^* - d)$.

Substituting from Eqs. (6a) and (12a) into (1a) we can express $\dot{W}$ as a function of W and π^*. Similarly, substituting from (12a) into the adaptive expectations function, which is (10) above, we can express $d\pi^*/dt$ as a function of these same variables. The model is thereby reduced to the following self-contained dynamic system:

$$W = -\mu(1 - \frac{\sigma q}{1 - \alpha} e^{-W}) + (1 - \theta)\pi^* + (1 - \theta)h(e^{-W} - e^{-a(\pi^* - d)}) \qquad (13)$$

$$\frac{d\pi^*}{dt} = \beta h(e^{-W} - e^{-a(\pi^* - d)}) \qquad (14)$$

The steady state in this model is defined by the conditions that $\dot{W} = 0 = d\pi^*/dt$: These can be easily shown to imply that $\pi = \pi^*$ and $W = \hat{W} = a(\pi^* - d)$. Linearizing (13) and (14) about the steady-state equilibrium, the resulting matrix is:

$$\begin{bmatrix} -\mu \dfrac{\sigma q}{1 - \alpha} e^{-W} - (1 - \theta)he^{-W} & (1 - \theta) + (1 - \theta)hae^{-a(\pi^* - d)} \\ \\ -\beta he^{-W} & \beta hae^{-a(\pi^* - d)} \end{bmatrix}$$

A necessary and sufficient condition for the local stability of this dynamic system is that the trace of this matrix be negative and its determinant positive, where both of these are to be evaluated at the point $W = a(\pi^* - d)$. The trace is equal to $[-\mu(\sigma q)/(1 - \alpha) - (1 - \theta - a\beta)h]e^{-W}$: We shall assume that this entire expression is negative. The determinant is equal to $\beta he^{-W}[1 - \theta - a\mu(\sigma q)e^{-W}/(1 - \alpha)]$: Since this is to be evaluated at the point of steady-state equilibrium, the entire expression within square brackets is seen to be equal to $[1 - \Delta]$, where Δ is defined in Eq. (8). For stability, this expression has to be positive, thereby establishing our earlier assertion that only the steady-state equilibrium at which $\Delta < 1$ is locally stable.

A diagrammatic representation of this system is illuminating. For this purpose, we require some further derivations:

$$\frac{dW}{d\pi^*}\bigg|_{\dot{W} = 0} = \frac{(1 - \theta) + a(1 - \theta)he^{-a(\pi^* - d)}}{\mu[\sigma q/(1 - \alpha)]e^{-W} + (1 - \theta)he^{-W}} \qquad (15)$$

and

$$\left. \frac{dW}{d\pi*} \right|_{d\pi*/dt\,=\,0} = a \qquad\qquad (16)$$

Evaluating these two derivatives (both of which are positive) at the point of steady-state equilibrium, it is easy to show that at that point the condition $1 - \Delta > 0$ is precisely equivalent to the condition

$$\left. \left(\frac{dW}{d\pi*} \right) \right|_{\dot W\,=\,0} > \left. \left(\frac{dW}{d\pi*} \right) \right|_{d\pi*/dt\,=\,0}$$

and we have the phase diagram of Fig. 3, in $W - \pi*$ space.

It is not difficult to verify from Eqs. (13) and (14) that the arrows in Fig. 3 have the directions indicated. Starting from any arbitrary initial position, such as B, the system will, as drawn, converge to the steady-state equilibrium point A (at which $\Delta < 1$). In the figure, the convergence is depicted as being cyclical in character; this need not always be the case. If we extend the broken segment of the locus $\dot W = 0$ further back, it will again intersect the locus $d\pi*/dt = 0$, and this intersection would constitute a steady-state equilibrium at which $\Delta > 1$. (We know that this second equilibrium occurs to the left of point A because, as indicated in Fig. 1, the equilibrium at which $\Delta > 1$ always exhibits a higher steady-state growth rate than the equilibrium at which $\Delta < 1$, and therefore a lower steady-state value of $\pi*$.)

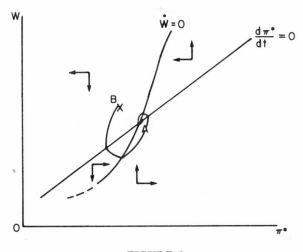

FIGURE 3

Since the equilibrium at which $\Delta > 1$ is unstable (in fact, it can be shown to be a saddle point), we shall not consider it in any detail.

III.   Deflating by Reducing the Supply of Money

We can now employ the apparatus just developed to examine the short-run implications of alternative stabilization policies. The first policy to be discussed is a sudden reduction by the monetary authorities of the rate of monetary expansion: Suppose μ is initially equal to μ_0 in Fig. 2, so that γ is initially zero, as in Fig. 1a,[5] and that the monetary authorities reduce μ to μ_1, as a result of which the steady-state growth rate of the economy is raised to γ_1 in Fig. 2. What about the transitional response of W, π^*, π, and γ? From Eq. (14), it is seen that the reduction in μ has no effect on the locus $d\pi^*/dt = 0$ in Fig. 3. As regards the effect on the locus $\dot{W} = 0$ we have, from Eq. (13):

$$\left. \frac{\partial W}{\partial \mu} \right|_{\dot{W}\,=\,0} = -\frac{1 - [\sigma q/(1 - \alpha)]\,e^{-W}}{\left\{ \mu[\sigma q/(1 - \alpha)] + (1 - \theta)h \right\} e^{-W}} \tag{17}$$

The denominator of the expression on the right-hand side of (17) is positive. As regards the numerator, using Eq. (6a) and the fact that, in the steady state, $\pi = \mu - \gamma$, it is easily shown that $1 - [\sigma q/(1 - \alpha)]\,e^{-W}$, evaluated at Point A. in Fig. 3, will be positive as long as the steady-state value of π is positive (as indeed it is at Point A). Thus, $\partial W/\partial \mu|_{\dot{W}\,=\,0}$ is, at that point, negative: by continuity of the locus $\dot{W} = 0$ it follows that a reduction in μ will cause this locus to shift upward in at least some open neighborhood of the Point A. The transition to the new steady-state equilibrium may therefore be depicted as in Fig. 4.

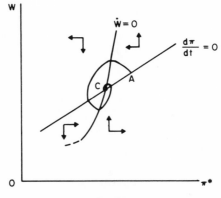

FIGURE 4

Clearly, the arrows in Fig. 4 have to be oriented toward the new steady-state equilibrium, which is Point C, rather than the previous equilibrium, Point A. Thus, starting at, say, time 0 at Point A, the effect of reducing μ will be to induce first of all a phase of rising W (and hence rising velocity) and falling π^*, followed by a phase of falling W and falling π^*, followed by a possibly cyclical convergence to the new equilibrium point: Once again, however, the convergence need not necessarily be cyclical in character.

Before explaining the economic rationale for these time paths, let us consider the impact of a reduction in μ on the other two variables of interest, π and γ. From Eq. (12a) we see that, since W and π^* are continuous functions of time, the downward shift in μ does not generate any instantaneous movement or jump in π: In other words, at time 0, π is completely unaffected by the reduction in μ. Immediately thereafter, however, the rise in W (which implies a reduction in the real supply of money relative to output) and fall in π^* (which increases the real demand for money relative to output) jointly generate an excess demand for money, which causes π to fall (this effect is additional to the fact that a falling π^* itself causes π to fall). Thus, in the first phase delineated above, π is unambiguously falling. In the second phase, π^* is still falling, which would tend to cause π to continue falling; however, in this phase W is also falling, implying an augmentation in the real supply of money relative to output, which could very well offset the effect of a falling π^* and cause π to rise instead.

The effect on γ is given by Eq. (6a). At time 0, neither W nor π jump in response to the reduction in μ; therefore, the reduction in μ causes an instantaneous downward jump in γ, and since γ was assumed to initially equal zero, this implies that γ initially turns negative, so that real output commences declining. The economic rationale for this result is that the reduction in μ instantaneously reduces the *net* flow of real bank credit (in other words, the flow of bank credit in excess of the lending out of repaid loans): However, the demand for bank credit to finance replacement investment in working capital is growing at rate π, which has yet to adjust downward. Thus, the flow of bank credit is insufficient to meet the replacement demand, leading to negative net investment in working capital and a fall in real output.

After time 0, γ is subject to opposing influences. On the one hand, in the first phase, π is falling, which would tend to cause γ to rise. On the other hand, W is rising, which further reduces the net flow of bank credit (this time, owing to "disintermediation"—a reduction in the real size of the banking system relative to output), which would tend to cause γ to fall further. A priori, it cannot be ascertained which of these effects dominates. In the second phase, W is falling, so that the real size of the banking system relative to output, and hence the net flow of real bank credit, is rising; however, as mentioned earlier, in this phase π may be rising, which might offset the increasing net flow of real bank credit.

The situation is therefore as follows. We know that a reduction in μ precipitates an instantaneous fall in γ. We also know that eventually γ will converge to a new, higher, steady-state equilibrium level. However, we cannot unambiguously trace out the complete time path followed by γ in the interim in the absence of numerical simulations.[6] However, the analytical discussion of this section is perhaps useful in precisely isolating the various influences on the short-run behavior of γ.

Let us now temporarily retrace our steps to examine why velocity initially rises in our model—while recognizing that any such explanation must necessarily be somewhat heuristic in character, since velocity is both influenced by and influences the other variables of the model. Fundamentally, the rise in velocity is attributable to the fact that π does not adjust downward as rapidly as μ. That is to say, velocity V is equal to PY/M; initially, P/M must rise as P rises as fast as in the previous equilibrium, while M rises at a slower rate. It is true that this effect is somewhat offset by the falling Y; however, from Eqs. (1a) and (6a), it is easily shown that since, as pointed out earlier, $[\sigma q/(1 - \alpha)]e^{-w} < 1$ at time 0,[7] Y will not fall fast enough to offset completely the rising P/M. It is only subsequently, once π has fallen sufficiently (under the influences of falling expectations and increasing excess demand for money), that velocity will cease rising and commence falling.[8]

IV. Deflating by Increasing the Demand for Money

We turn next to a consideration of the second stabilization policy instrument, the nominal deposit rate d. Let ℓ be the nominal interest rate charged on bank loans. If we assume that (1) banks are in competitive equilibrium with zero excess profits, (2) the government pays no interest on bank reserves or on currency in circulation, and (3) the costs of the monetary system are a constant fraction z of the real money supply M/P, then it is easily shown that $d = q\ell - z$. Hence, barring governmental subsidies to the banking system, a change in d requires a concomitant change in ℓ. Although we shall henceforth be referring to changes in d, the corresponding changes in ℓ will always be assumed to have been effected.

At this point, a slight digression is perhaps in order. In many neo-classical monetary growth models (although not in the model of this chapter), the assumption is generally made that instantaneous adjustments of the price level serve to continuously equilibrate the demand for and supply of real money balances (or instead, the desired and actual levels of velocity). Whatever its merits for other purposes, this assumption can be seriously misleading when we are considering the effects of a shift in d. Suppose that at time 0, there is a once-and-for-all upward shift in d, and that no other policy changes are initiated either then or subsequently. Consider now the identity $MV = PY$: At that instant of time, M is unchanged, as also is π^* (since π^* is generally specified to be an everywhere differentiable function of time, as in the case of the adaptive expectations function). However, the expected real return to holding money, $d - \pi^*$, is instantaneously increased by the rise in d. Thus, if the actual level of velocity is assumed to adjust instantaneously to the desired level, V must jump downward, and hence so also must MV.

At this point, exponents of the standard neoclassical approach would have to assume that P also jumps downward, in order to maintain the identity $MV = PY$. However, we had earlier argued that in the short run, prices are likely to be rigid downward. If P cannot fall, then the reduction in V will precipitate an instantaneous fall in Y. Thus, the standard neoclassical approach would predict that even a rise in d would create a temporary "stabilization problem." Empirically, on the other hand, it is known that increases in d have not induced a temporary fall in real output. In discussing the Korean financial reforms of September 1965, for example, which involved significant increases in bank lending and deposit rates, McKinnon points out [8, p. 110]: "The rise in output and employment growing out of the increase in investment and exports began right after the reforms took hold, so that the economy did not suffer temporary losses from the price stabilization program." This outcome clearly suggests that the assumption that the actual level of velocity adjusts instantaneously to the desired level is inappropriate. (It should be added that, as Table 8-8 of [8] indicates, prices continued to rise in Korea after the reforms were instituted, although at a slower rate than previously.)

We have here what may, therefore, be termed a "methodological precept": In seeking to examine the economic effects of a shift in d, it is analytically imperative that one allow for a lag between actual and desired levels of velocity. The model of this chapter, which, through Eqs. (12a) and (1a), does incorporate such a lag, may among other things be viewed as an illustration of this precept.

Returning to the main thread of our analysis, by implicitly differentiating Eq. (7) with respect to d, it is readily verified that an upward shift in d raises the steady-state value of γ, which is what we would expect, since it raises the real size of the banking system and hence the net flow of bank credit to finance investment in working capital. This shift raises the question of whether there is any upper bound to the feasible range of values that d may assume, a question that is taken up in the following section. As regards short-run dynamics, an upward shift in d will, at least in some open neighborhood of the Point A in Fig. 3, cause both of the loci in that figure to shift downward: however, from Eqs. (13) and (14), it can be easily shown that the locus $d\pi^*/dt = 0$ will definitely shift down by more, so that the new steady-state value of π^* is lower (which is consistent with the fact that the new steady-state value of γ is higher, while μ is unchanged). The dynamic evolution of the system to its new equilibrium is thus as in Fig. 5.

The new steady-state equilibrium is given by Point C' in Fig. 5. We thus see that, unlike the case of a reduction in μ, an upward shift in d generates an initial phase of *falling* W (and hence falling velocity) and falling π^*, both of which then proceed to converge in a possibly cyclical manner to C'.

Before providing an intuitive explanation for this result, let us examine the time paths of π and γ. At time 0 itself, there is no jump in either W or π^*. Thus, from Eq. (12a) we see that the upward shift in d produces an instantaneous downward shift in π at time 0. This is attributable to the fact that the increase in d immediately increases the desired level of real money holdings (although the actual level does not change at that instant), and thereby creates an instantaneous excess demand for money. An increase in d therefore exerts a more rapid deflationary effect than a reduction in μ (since, as pointed out earlier, the latter has no effect on the value of π at time 0). As McKinnon has suggested to the author, this effect is due to the fact than an increase in d directly increases the expected real return to money perceived by moneyholders, whereas a reduction in μ can only increase the expected real return after it has worked through the entire system to produce a fall in π^*.

After time 0, π is subject to opposing influences. On the one hand, π^* commences declining, which would tend to cause π to fall further. On the other hand, W also declines, thereby augmenting the real supply of money relative to output, which would tend to cause π to rise. Which effect dominates cannot be ascertained a priori.[9]

As regards the time path of γ, from Eq. (6a) it is seen that, since at time 0, π registers an instantaneous downward jump, γ registers an instantaneous upward jump. This occurs because the increase in d has no instantaneous

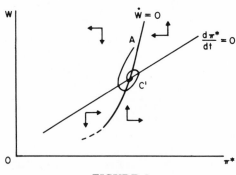

FIGURE 5

effect on the net flow of real bank credit; however when π is reduced, the rate of increase in the cost of replacing worn-out working capital is reduced. Some portion of the net flow of real bank credit is thus released to finance net as opposed to replacement investment in working capital, thereby generating an upward shift in γ. After time 0, W commences falling, which implies an increase in the real size of the banking system relative to output, and hence an increase in the net flow of real bank credit and a further increase in γ. However, this tendency may be offset partly or wholly by the fact that, as pointed out earlier, π may also be rising after time 0, and so the resultant time path for γ cannot be predicted a priori.

From the adaptive expectations function given in Eq. (10), it is clear that since π registers a downward jump, π^* must commence falling for at least some time after time 0. The rationale for the fall in velocity is slightly more subtle. V is equal to PY/M. Since M grows at the same rate as before, while P grows at a lower rate, P/M must commence falling. This effect is to some extent offset by the rise of Y; however, from Eq. (6a) it is seen that, since $\theta < 1$, the upward shift in γ is lower than the downward shift in π, so that on balance velocity must commence falling.[10]

The reader may at this point be tempted to inquire into the "robustness" of our results, given that we have found it necessary to resort to numerical simulations to resolve certain indeterminacies in the analysis. Analytically, however, it is possible to definitely establish two conclusions. Firstly, since at time $0, \gamma$ registers an instantaneous upward jump when d is raised and an instantaneous downward jump when μ is reduced, and since the time path of γ is a continuous function of time after time 0, both at time 0 and for at least some time thereafter, the time path of γ resulting from an increase in d will dominate (be higher than) the time path of γ resulting from a reduction in μ. Secondly, by similar reasoning, the time path of π resulting from an increase in d must, at least in the early time periods, be *lower* than that resulting from a reduction in μ. These considerations do establish a presumption in favor of stabilization through an initial increase in d.

There is, however, one important constraint that this system must satisfy as mentioned briefly above. At all points along the transition path, as well as at the final equilibrium, care must be taken to ensure that the nominal loan rate ℓ never exceeds the expected nominal rate of profit on working capital (the latter depending on the production function and on output and expected input prices), since otherwise business borrowing from commercial banks for the purpose of investing in working capital will fall to zero. Since, as pointed out earlier, increases in d have to be "financed" out of corresponding increases in ℓ, this fact will set an upper bound on the permissible values of d, and so the validity of the foregoing derivations is predicated upon a choice of d that does not violate this upper bound.

It is possible also to consider various combinations of the two "pure" policies that we have just discussed. For example, the authorities could initially raise d and then, as inflationary expectations start to taper off (π^* commences declining), they could delicately lower μ and/or d in such a way as not to precipitate a fall in the economy's growth rate. Ideally, it would be desirable to specify a loss function and to choose the values of d and μ over time in such a manner as to minimize the integral of the loss function over a finite or infinite time horizon. Such an optimization exercise is not attempted here: however, it is hoped that the analysis contained in this chapter provides most of the ingredients required for such an exercise.

ACKNOWLEDGMENT

This work is taken from a chapter of the author's doctoral dissertation [6]. I would like to acknowledge my deep indebtedness to my principal adviser, Professor R. I. McKinnon, for most valuable guidance at all stages of the dissertation research. I am, however, solely responsible for all the views expressed herein.

NOTES

1. I am indebted to Frederick Berger of the Organization of American States for outlining this view to me.

2. The reader will undoubtedly have noticed that no allowance is made in Eq. (4) for the repayment of loans incurred in previous periods to finance net (as opposed to replacement) investment in those periods. The implicit asasumption here is that such loans are viewed by productive enterprises as part of their "set-up" costs for new projects, and are never amortized (repaid). This assumption vastly simplifies the non-steady-state analysis conducted subsequently without, in my opinion, biasing the qualitative results of this chapter.

3. Some readers may at first glance consider implausible the assumption that commercial banks finance the whole of net investment in working capital, and only a fraction θ of replacement investment in working capital. This, however, is entirely consistent with the notion of "financial repression," whereby producers do not have access to external nonbank financing to initiate new projects involving net investment in working capital; they are, however, in a position to undertake some replacement investment out of the

sales proceeds from on-going projects. Implicitly, it is assumed that if entrepreneurs did have some additional funds of their own, these are either invested in fixed capital accumulation, or have already been "stretched to the limit" in investment projects undertaken in past periods. Clearly, the "story" we are telling would not be very consistent if entrepreneurs had significant uninvested funds of their own which, despite the presence of underutilized fixed capacity, they were holding back from net investment in perfectly divisible working capital until an adequate volume of accompanying bank financing were made available.

Nevertheless, it should be pointed out that our analysis can be generalized somewhat to allow for this possibility. Let us assume that a fraction θ_1 of all net investment in working capital, and a fraction θ_2 of all replacement investment, are financed through bank loans. In that case, Eq. (4) becomes:

$$\dot{K} = \frac{1}{\theta_1(1 - \alpha)} [\mu q \frac{M}{P} - \pi \theta_2(1 - \alpha)K] \qquad (4')$$

since the term within square brackets now represents only bank-financed net investment, and not total investment in working capital. If θ_1 is sufficiently close to unity, then use of Eq. (4') in place of (4) would not change any of our results: to simplify the notation, however, we shall continue to work with (4). If θ_1 is significantly less than unity, then the results in this chapter would certainly be altered. However, for the reasons just indicated, the notion of "financial repression," which we are seeking to model, would become quite nebulous were producers not significantly dependent on bank financing to initiate new projects.

4. As Duncan Foley has pointed out to the author, there is a dimensionality problem in going from Eq. (11) to Eq. (12), since an excess demand for goods constitutes a flow disequilibrium in the commodities market, whereas an excess supply of money constitutes a stock disequilibrium in the asset market. One technique for reconciling the two would be to assume that at any given time moneyholders act to eliminate some fraction k of the discrepancy between actual and desired money holdings. Multiplying the excess supply of money by k would convert it into an expression of flow disequilibrium. In Eq. (12), we have implicitly subsumed the fraction k under the constant h (h may reflect other influences as well, such as the speed with which sellers raise prices in response to an excess demand for their goods). Given this interpretation, (11) and (12) are mutually consistent.

5. In economic terms, a zero value of γ simply implies that financial repression has become so pronounced that the entire increase in nominal bank credit is always used for replacement purposes.

6. A summary of the empirical results from one possible simulation model is provided in Kapur [6a].

7. This inequality states that the real volume of bank loans in the original steady-state equilibrium is strictly less than the real stock of working capital, since we had assumed that a fraction $(1 - \theta)$ of replacement investment in working capital is financed out of the internal resources of productive enterprises. Intuitively, it is precisely because businesses are not totally dependent on bank credit to finance their holdings of working capital that γ at time 0 does not jump downward by as much as μ (the fall in μ being in absolute value equal to the percentage rate of increase of P/M at time 0).

8. It is seen that a reduction in μ is capable of generating a period of negative γ despite the fact that π remains significantly positive not only at time 0 but also throughout the stabilization process. This fact furnishes us with a test between the supply-constrained and the demand-constrained explanations of the initial fall in the level of real income. If the rate of inflation were to remain significantly positive despite this fall in real income, it is likely that the supply-constrained explanation is correct. On the other hand, if the inflation rate were to fall to a level that is close to zero, then both explanations could be valid, and a more careful empirical examination would be required in order to disentangle their relative importance. In his discussion of the stabilization program in Chile from 1955 to 1958, McKinnon quotes Albert Hirschman as pointing out that the rate of inflation did not fall below 17 percent, despite the fact that Chile experienced a severe industrial recession at this time: This phenomenon suggests that supply rather than demand constraints were primarily operative during this period.

9. Again the reader is referred to the simulation results summarized in Kapur [6a].

10. Once again, the fact that $\theta < 1$ implies that not all holdings of working capital are financed through bank loans. Thus, a one percent increase in the volume of bank-financed holdings of working capital implies a less than one percent increase in the volume of total holdings of working capital, and hence a less than one percentage point increase in the economy's growth rate.

REFERENCES

1. K. J. Arrow, "Toward a General Theory of Price Adjustment," in M. Abramovitz et al (eds.), *The Allocation of Economics Resources,* Stanford University Press, 1959.

2. P. Cagan, "The Monetary Dynamics of Hyper-inflation," in M. Friedman (ed.), *Studies in the Quantity Theory of Money,* University of Chicago Press, 1956.

3. S. M. Goldman, "Hyperinflation and the Rate of Growth of the Money Supply," *Journal of Economic Theory,* October 1972.

4. M. G. Hadjimichalakis, "Equilibrium and Disequilibrium Growth with Money—the Tobin Models," *Review of Economic Studies,* October 1971.

5. B. K. Kapur, "A Note on Mundell's 'Growth Stability and Inflationary Finance'," unpublished paper, June 1974.

6. B. K. Kapur, "Monetary Growth Models of Less Developed Countries," Ph.D. Dissertation, Stanford University, August 1974.

6a. B. K. Kapur, "Alternative Stabilization Policies for Less Developed Countries," *Journal of Political Economy* (Forthcoming).

7. W. A. Lewis, "Economic Development with Unlimited Supplies of Labour," *Manchester School of Economic and Social Studies,* May 1954.

8. R. I. McKinnon, *Money and Capital in Economic Development,* The Brookings Institution, 1973.

9. R. A. Mundell, "Growth, Stability and Inflationary Finance," *Journal of Political Economy,* April 1965.

10. M. Selowsky, "Cost of Price Stabilization in an Inflationary Economy," *Quarterly Journal of Economics,* February 1973.

11. E. S. Shaw, *Financial Deepening in Economic Development,* Oxford University Press, 1973.

JOSEPH J. BISIGNANO

Federal Reserve Bank of San Francisco
San Francisco, California

Mr. Kapur has quite neatly put the cake batter of his chapter, that is, the McKinnon-Shaw supply-constrained view of development, into a standard Mundellian inflationary dynamics cake mold—where most of the analysis is spent proving the uniqueness and stability of equilibrium. His mathematical analysis appears to the point and technically correct. If one judiciously "massages" (raises) the deposit rate one can reduce the expected holding cost of money and by this mechanism gradually reduce price inflation through a reduction in the rate of growth of nominal money balances, while increasing real money demand. This reduction in price inflation can come about without a decline in real output. Well, on the face of it, this procedure certainly seems reasonable.

If we free one of the previously fixed prices in a market economy, goods get allocated more efficiently. Here one of the "prices" is institutionally determined, the deposit rate, and this price must be jiggled so that people want to hold real money balances. Fine. But, while we are told that raising the deposit rate on nominal money balances will increase the demand for real money balances, thereby lowering the anticipated rate of inflation and raising the steady-state value of real income growth, we are left hanging over our less developed country asking what rate we ought to deflate to. What is the optimum rate of growth in the money supply and the optimum rate of inflation? Implicit in the analysis, I think, is the assumption that government investment is nonproductive, so we ought to deflate to a very low number. This would leave little room for government revenue collection

222

through the inflationary process, which the prevailing view seems to think is a good thing. But I wonder if this is not being a bit too cavalier.

At the end of Mr. Kapur's chapter I was hoping to see some optimizing scheme that would lead me to the selection of some target terminal value for the rate of money growth and the rate of inflation. Given the Cagan money-demand function used, the government can maximize revenue by setting the rate of growth of money to one over the slope parameter. With a more general demand function, the revenue maximizing rate of inflation is dependent on not only the sensitivity of real money demand with respect to the rate of price increase, but also to the income elasticity, population growth, and real income growth. Does Mr. Kapur's analysis suggest that the government raise no revenue through price inflation?*

The policy world is filled with reasonable propositions. Increasing the return on nominal money balances in order to increase the demand for real money is among them. However, I don't think it is enough of a long-run guide to finance ministers, who if they are not raising revenue through inflation are raising it through other means, perhaps less efficient. To repeat, there seems to be the presumption in this type of analysis that government investment is less productive than private investment, so that the government is best that inflates least. The appeal to steady-state solutions for growth rates in prices and income provides no answer to whether these rates are optimal, given some meaningful objective function of a finance minister. Maybe I am really expecting another analysis, but I don't think it is unreasonable, if one is listening to the advice of a consulting economist who is recommending deflation, to ask what is the optimal rate of inflation and money growth.

Lastly, some appeal to real numbers would have been awfully nice. For example, what is the quantitative impact of a rise in the deposit rate (a decrease in the cost of holding money) on velocity in cases where these policy suggestions have been put into place? Mr. Kapur's chapter has very strong policy implications for less developed economies. Hiding these policy recommendations in a maze of useful, but attention-diverting Mundellian mathematics without strong appeal to some real numbers and illustrations detracts from the strong policy appeal this type of analysis contains.

Let me add that Mr. Kapur has offered us an excellent, vigorous treatment of the effect of loosening financial constraints on real output and prices. It remains for the rest of us, as well as for him, to add as well thought out empirical substance to his theoretical framework.

---

*Mr. Kapur's paper is exclusively concerned with deflating efficiently in the short run. For those readers interested in the issues Mr. Bisignano raises, such as the optimal long-run rate of inflation in poor economies where the banking system is also the principal intermediary between savers and investors, these are covered in other chapters of Mr. Kapur's Ph.D. dissertation: *Monetary Growth Models of Less Developed Economies,* Stanford University, 1974.–ED.

Part IV

**Aspects of International
Economic Integration**

Some Policy Implications of Foreign Capital Flows in Certain Developing Countries

RICHARD T. STILLSON

International Monetary Fund
Washington, D.C.

The objective of this chapter is to examine the policy implications of some
types of foreign capital flows to certain less developed countries (LDCs); the
discussion emphasizes the need for policies to counter some of the domestic
effects of these inflows. It is shown that there is a relationship between
various stabilization policies and development policy, which, if not properly
understood, could lead to policy inconsistencies. The chapter concentrates
attention on budget policy and develops the concepts of domestic and foreign
budgets to better explain the monetary effects of the budget.

Section I reviews the theory of the adjustment mechanism relating
monetary expansions or contractions to prices and the balance of payments.[1]
Foreign capital inflows frequently result in monetary expansion and it is the
adjustments of the economy to the expansion that can cause some policy
problems. Section II outlines the impact of the budget on the money market;
it is shown that some modifications are needed in the analysis of the monetary
impact of the budget in situations in which the budget receives substantial
inflows of foreign exchange. These modifications are outlined by using the
concepts of the domestic and foreign budgets. In Section III various policy
considerations relevant to certain types of foreign capital inflows are discussed.
Finally, in Section IV some case studies of the budgets and balance of payments of certain LDCs are presented to illustrate the relevance of this analysis.

I.   The Effects of Monetary Disturbances in an Open Economy

The analysis presents a fully open economy with four markets; those for
export goods, import goods, nontraded goods, and money. We assume that

all goods are substitutable in consumption and that the price of both traded goods is exogenous to the domestic economy. Domestic resources, especially incremental resources, will move among the production of import-competing goods, exports, and nontraded goods in response to shifts in the structure of internal relative prices. Therefore, the price of currently nontraded goods is primarily determined by domestic factors subject to a ceiling which is the domestic price at which the goods will be imported. The only financial asset considered is money. This simplification allows the adjustment mechanism to be described relatively easily, but it is not crucial for the results. The demand for the stock of money is dependent on current nominal income; whereas the supply of money is dependent on the balance of payments, the government budget, direct credit from the central bank, and other policy instruments such as the reserve requirements on commercial bank liabilities.

The adjustment to a monetary disturbance can be described as follows. Consider a disturbance to equilibrium that creates an excess demand for money (such as a sudden reduction in domestic credit by the central bank); individuals and firms will attempt to increase their money holdings through increased sales and decreased purchases of goods. This will release goods for export and reduce the demand for imports, import-competing goods, and nontraded goods so as to improve the trade balance and depress the price of nontraded goods relative to traded goods. The change in relative prices will create an incentive to move resources, at the margin, out of nontraded goods and into exports and import-competing goods. Each of these adjustments may occur after some lag. The two main lags are a portfolio lag (the time it takes for the shortage of domestic credit to cause decreased demand for imports, import-competing goods, and nontraded goods) and a resource-flow lag (the time it takes for resources to respond to the changed pattern of domestic demand).

If an excess supply of money is created (either by a domestic credit expansion or an inflow of foreign capital) individuals and firms will attempt to increase their purchases of goods. This will increase imports relative to exports and increase the relative prices of nontraded goods; the relative price change will shift resources, at the margin, out of the production of exports and import-competing goods into the production of nontraded goods. As in the case of excess demand for money, the effect on relative prices and the domestic production structure is dependent on the resource-flow lag and the extent of foreign capital flows that respond to domestic credit policy.

Equilibrium in the model will be reestablished when the stock of

money equals the demand for that stock and the changes in money supply
equals changes in money demand. Changes in money supply are a function
of endogenous changes in the balance of payments because the exchange rate
is fixed. Adjustments in money supply through the balance of payments
will continue until equilibrium in the money market is reestablished. The
nature of the equilibrium can best be described by considering a stationary
economy that adjusts to a continuous expansion of domestic credit at a
higher level than its previous equilibrium. In the first period, depending on
the various lags, this expansion will cause an excess supply of money resulting in a trade deficit and an increase in the relative price of nontraded
goods. The higher prices of nontraded goods would increase the demand for
money balances to some extent, but probably not to the full extent of the
increased domestic credit creation. In the second period, a larger part of
the adjustment to the excess money supply will be borne by the trade
balance because of the new, higher price of nontraded goods. Equilibrium
will be reestablished when the relative price of nontraded goods is
sufficiently high to cause adjustments in demand and supply in the
goods markets and in the demand for money so that the excess supply of
money at each period generated by the domestic credit expansion will flow
out through the trade balance.[2]   When that occurs, the stock of money
will be constant, as required for equilibrium in a stationary economy,
although the balance of payments will not be in equilibrium. This adjustment process could continue if the balance of trade deficit is financed
by foreign capital inflows or a reduction in international reserves. If
there is a one-period increase in domestic credit creation, the first period's
adjustment would be the same as that described; but, in subsequent
periods, the economy would adjust back to its previous equilibrium save
for a lower level of international reserves. If there is growing excess
domestic credit creation, there will be continual adjustment in prices of
nontraded goods and the trade balance.

For a growing economy, the demand for money will increase as the
economy grows. Money market equilibrium in this situation requires that
the money stock grow at the rate of growth in income. Hence the effect
of increasing domestic credit creation will be partly absorbed by the
growth in money demand.

The effects of excess demand or supply of money on relative prices
depend on the assumption of a fixed exchange rate, since an exchange-
rate change may offset the effects of an excess credit expansion on
relative prices. A depreciation of the exchange rate immediately increases
the price, in domestic currency, of imports and increases the return in
domestic currency to the production of exports and import-competing

goods. This increase will counter the effects on relative prices of continuous excess credit expansion, and diminish or eliminate the shift of resources from traded to nontraded goods.

II. Foreign Capital Inflows and Tax Receipts:
   The Government Budget

An implication of the foregoing analysis is that the adjustment to a monetary disequilibrium at a fixed exchange rate may induce a shift of resources between traded and nontraded goods through a change in the relative prices of these goods. In particular, in cases of persistent monetary expansion the competitive position of the country is eroded and exports become increasingly concentrated in goods in which the country has the greatest comparative advantage. Since achieving particular distributions of production, including increased diversification, is frequently a goal of development policy, this analysis indicates that excessive monetary expansion might be inconsistent with these policies. In these cases, the relative production effects of monetary disequilibrium should therefore be countered by various policies including domestic credit policy, budget policy, or appropriate exchange rate policies.

The analysis given above applies equally well to any monetary disequilibrium. However, policy alternatives are different when a monetary disequilibrium is caused by a temporary balance-of-payments surplus, a foreign capital inflow through the banking system, or foreign cash loans to the government. The reason is that in these situations, the monetary, price and production effects described are the same, but international reserves will not decrease. This may make the evaluation of the appropriateness of the exchange rate more difficult. A further complication arises if substantial foreign capital inflows accrue to the government budget. In that situation even a balanced budget will be substantially expansionary and the analysis of the effects of budget policy is quite different from when the budget receives no foreign revenues, as is demonstrated below.

Various items in the government budget have an immediate impact on aggregate demand, and on the demand and supply of money. (An earlier analysis, in which many of the problems mentioned are discussed, is given in [7].) The magnitude of these effects depends primarily on the extent to which the budget item affects domestic or foreign income. Revenues derived from foreign sources such as net receipts from oil exports, foreign cash loans, etc., do not affect the domestic aggregate demand of the private sector or the supply of money, since they represent withdrawals from foreign income streams.   Expenditures that are made abroad, such as direct government imports, embassy expenses, amortizations of foreign debts, etc., do not affect private-sector domestic demand or the supply of money since they accrue to nonresidents. Conversely, domestic revenues and direct borrowing from the private sector decrease both the supply of money and aggregate demand of the private sector, since they are withdrawn from domestic income; domestic expenditures increase both the supply of money and private-sector aggregate demand. These observations suggest that budget items can be disaggregated into domestic and foreign components in order to assess the monetary and balance-of-payments effects of budget policy on the rest of the economy.

A "domestic budget" is defined as the difference between domestic receipts and expenditures; and a "foreign budget" is defined as the difference between foreign receipts and expenditures. These are distinguished from the "cash budget," which includes all receipts and payments during the same period.[3] A hypothetical cash budget, in which important budget items are disaggregated into foreign and domestic components, is given in Table 1. Some comments on the difficulties of classifying particular items are contained in the footnotes to that table.

Domestic receipts and expenditures are defined as those subtracting from or adding to domestic income, which is defined as income accruing to economic agents within the country. This definition is such that, if the domestic budget is balanced, then there will be no supply of liquid assets from the budget to the private sector. If, however, the domestic budget balance changes, and there is no borrowing or debt repayments vis-à-vis the private sector, there will be an immediate impact on the supply of liquid assets. A few examples can illustrate this point. Starting from balance in all budgets, consider the effect of a deficit in the foreign budget, which is matched by an equal surplus in the domestic budget. In this case, the cash budget is still balanced although there will be a net contractionary effect (equal to the surplus in the domestic budget), because the government is collecting domestically more money than it spends. The level of foreign-exchange reserves will decrease to the extent that the proportion of foreign exchange of private-sector expenditures at the margin is less than unity. If there is a foreign-budget deficit while the domestic budget is in balance, there will be a decrease in the level of official foreign-exchange reserves, but there will be no direct impact on the stock of money held by the private sector.

TABLE 1

Hypothetical Government Budget

I. Government expenditures

   1. Domestic

      Current expenditures on wages and salaries
Current expenditures on domestically-produced goods[a]
Transfer payments to residents
Capital expenditures on domestically-produced goods
Acquisition of land

   2. Foreign

      Current expenditures abroad (embassy expenses, etc.)
Imported materials
Transfers abroad
Net foreign lending
Imported component of purchases of domestic goods

II. Government revenues

   1. Domestic

      Taxes paid by residents
Rents, interest, and dividends received from residents
Profits received from the central bank[b]
Profits received from the domestic operations of state enterprises
Net sale of physical assets to residents
Domestic counterpart of program aid[c]

   2. Foreign

      Taxes paid by nonresidents
Taxes on foreign trade[d]
Taxes of resident foreign corporations[e]
Profits received from the foreign operation of state enterprises[f]
Local currency counterpart of grants and untied aid from abroad[c]
Sale of assets abroad
Net foreign borrowing

        Cash budget balance: II   minus I
Domestic budget balance: II.1 minus I.1
Foreign budget balance: II.2 minus I.2

---

[a]Only the domestic component of materials expenditures should be included.
[b]Revenues received from the foreign operations of the central bank, such as interest earnings on foreign securities, should be considered as foreign revenues.

These examples illustrate the point that the monetary impact of the budget on the domestic economy can best be measured through the domestic budget deficit. The effects of a monetary expansion through domestic budget deficits are similar regardless of how the deficits are financed; e.g., the monetary effects of domestically spending tax receipts from an oil sector or from cash loans is equivalent to central bank credit to the government. However, measuring the direct and indirect foreign-exchange content of the government expenditures in most countries is quite difficult since the appropriate data are often not available. (See Section IV for some illustrations.)

III. Policy Responses

In periods during which there are substantial receipts from foreign cash loans or other equivalent foreign-exchange inflows (whether to the private or public

---

cShould be included only when funds are directly related to specific import purchases of the private sector; if the counterpart funds are obtained by a sale of the aid exchange to the central bank, not related to specific import purchases, the revenues should be classified in the foreign budget.

dIncludes tariff revenues, export tax revenues, import licensing fees, etc. The incidence of these taxes in terms of foreign or domestic revenues depends on assumptions about supply and demand elasticities for exports and imports. Consistent with the "small country assumption" we assume that the supply elasticity of imports and the demand elasticity of exports is infinite, which implies that export taxes are completely shifted back onto domestic producers and that export taxes should be considered domestic revenues. (A major exception might be export taxes borne by foreign corporations in lieu of, or in addition to, income or profits tax of foreign corporations). The incidence of various taxes on imports, however, will depend on the elasticity of demand for those imports. For a more complete discussion of these effects, see [1], pp. 363-365.

eOnly that proportion of tax that would have been repatriated by the foreign corporation should be included in the foreign budget. However, this calculation becomes complicated by the fact that the proportion of earnings that would be repatriated may be affected by the tax.

fThe profits of the foreign operations of state enterprises should be considered foreign receipts unless they are indirectly derived from local operations. Thus, if a state-owned marketing board made profits as an intermediary between private-resident producers and foreign purchasers, this profit derives from the local producers.

sectors), the appropriate policies may be somewhat different from policies during periods of no foreign inflows; the appropriate policies may also be different for various types of inflows. The resources from a foreign capital inflow are of primary importance to the recipient country; it is also important that policies encourage the use of these resources in such a way that undesirable domestic effects do not occur and that debt problems do not arise in the future. The appropriate policies will depend on the nature of the capital inflow (in terms of the length of time it is likely to continue, whether or not it has to be paid back, and the interest cost) and the policy instruments available to the authorities. In this section we will examine some of the considerations relevant for policy with regard to three classes of capital inflow common to some LDCs: short-term cash loans that cannot be rolled over, longer-term cash loans or equivalent foreign exchange receipts, and foreign exchange receipts from depletable natural resources.

Consider a capital inflow through short-term cash loans that cannot be rolled over. If these loans are used to finance expected balance-of-payments deficits and their maturity falls within the period of reversibility of the balance of payments, then they economize on the use of reserves of the country. However, if this inflow leads to additional domestic expenditures by the government or the private sector, it will cause pressures for an increase in the prices of nontraded goods and a greater balance-of-trade deficit. Thus, the immediate impact of the short-term capital inflow in this situation would be a pressure on resources causing a domestic price increase. A foreign-debt problem would be created when the cash loans have to be paid back. At that time, domestic policies must more than reverse the monetary effects of the foreign inflow, so that a balance-of-trade surplus is created to repay the loans. Thus, it may be desirable to offset these domestic effects by various combinations of budget and credit policies.

The analysis of the domestic effects of longer-term cash loans primarily differs from that of short-term cash loans in that there is more time for adjustment and reallocation of resources. If the foreign resources are used to supplement domestic investment and are profitably invested, the longer-term and possible low-interest cost of these loans may allow the development of a balance-of-trade surplus from which the loans can be paid back. However, the specific policies used to facilitate the desired reallocation of resources are important. For instance, if foreign capital is allowed to lead to an excess monetary expansion and ultimately a reallocation of domestic resources from traded goods to nontraded goods, the economy and the balance of trade will be adjusting to the inflow in such a way as to be less able to pay back the loans. When the loans must be repaid, a reverse reallocation of resources must occur from nontraded goods to traded goods to create the surplus that will allow repayment. Of course, if the present value of the increased profitably of the nontraded-goods sectors over the period of the loan is greater than the cost of the initial and subsequent reverse reallocation of resources, it would still be efficient to allow these transfers. However, since planners can have little knowledge of these costs, it would seem prudent to implement some combination of fiscal, credit, and exchange policies that does not cause an excessive monetary expansion, but creates a set of relative prices consistent with long-run efficient resource allocation and a long-run improvement in the balance of trade.

Foreign-exchange receipts from depletable natural resources have some characteristics of foreign capital inflows; the period of time that they will continue is uncertain and they frequently use few domestic resources and are thus relatively unresponsive to domestic policies. In the case of oil, the foreign-exchange receipts from the exports frequently accrue directly to the government and can finance significant domestic budget deficits. In this situation, it is important that budget policy be coordinated with monetary policy to avoid an undue monetary expansion, which may ultimately cause a shift in the internal terms of trade in favor of nontraded goods, and an increased specialization of exports. In many cases, the economy's dependence on oil will be increased, and that may be inconsistent with various development policies that attempt to achieve a balance-of-payments structure that can be sustained when these foreign-exchange receipts are reduced or eliminated.

With longer term cash loans or oil tax receipts from abroad, therefore, the deficit in the domestic budget might well be kept significantly lower than the surplus in the foreign budget. The resulting accumulation of financial claims on foreigners could be saved for a rainy day while, at the same time, domestic distortions are mitigated.

IV. Case Studies

In the following, an attempt is made to estimate the domestic budgets and compare the surpluses or deficits with the cash budgets of three countries: Indonesia, Jordan, and Oman. The monetary effects of the balance of payments are also shown by dividing the overall balance of payments into a government sector (equal to the foreign budget balance) and the private sector. The private-sector balance of payments is defined as the algebraic sum of nongovernmental foreign receipts and expenditures. Other things being equal, a private-sector balance-of-payments deficit will decrease the stock of money by the amount of the deficit, and a private-sector balance-of-payments surplus will increase the stock of money by the amount of the surplus. The sum of the domestic-budget balance and the private-sector balance of payments, along with changes in the credit of the central bank to the private sector, should identify the primary sources of changes in high-powered money in these countries.

In the countries surveyed the government receives a substantial amount of foreign revenue, a part of which is used for domestic expenditures. In each country the government budget is relatively large in relation to the monetized sector, there is no significant borrowing by the government directly from the private sector, there is a large sector that produces nontraded goods, and the countries are relatively small in relation to the world markets for their imports and exports. In constructing the tables, judgments had to be made concerning the inclusion of various items in the domestic budget or the foreign budget. Therefore, the tables should be regarded as approximations to the quantitative impact on the domestic budget and private-sector trade balance. It was not possible to account for all changes in high-powered money because of the imprecision of the estimates. Also, a comparison of the domestic-budget balances and private-sector balance of payments with changes in nontraded-goods prices or changes in specialization in production was not possible because of lack of disaggregated price data. The purpose of these exercises is simply to illustrate the usefulness of the concepts used in assessing the domestic effects of the government budget. No comments will be made concerning the appropriateness of the policies described.

A.   Indonesia

Since 1966, the Indonesian economy, under new fiscal, monetary, agricultural, industrial, and trade policies has maintained a rapid rate of growth with relative price stability [8]. An important development in the last seven years has been the substantial growth in the extractive industries, particularly oil and timber. Net oil and timber earnings as recorded in the balance of payments increased from $78 million in 1968 to $546 million in 1972; and with the recent oil price rises, the foreign exchange earnings from oil and timber are expected to exceed $3.1 billion in 1974. However, Indonesia has a fairly large and diversified economy with forestry, mining (including oil), and quarrying accounting for only about 7 percent of estimated GDP in 1970 [9]. At present, the main benefits to the economy from timber, mining, and oil are the taxes, royalties, and license fees collected by the government on these operations and the foreign-exchange earnings from these sectors. Thus, one would expect that the impact of these sectors on the budget and the balance of payments would be much greater than the proportion of total output that they represent.

The domestic and cash budgets for fiscal year 1971-72, and estimates for 1972-73, are given in Table 2; the assumptions implicit in the table are explained in the footnotes. The table shows that the Indonesian budget had a small cash-budget surplus in 1971-72 and 1972-73. However, the effect of their budget policy has been expansionary. This is demonstrated by the domestic budget that had a deficit equal to Rp 30.4 billion, or about 6 percent of total expenditures, in 1971-72 and Rp 88.8 billion, or about 12 percent of total expenditures, in 1972-73.

Table 3 shows the balance of payments disaggregated into private and government sectors. The rupiah equivalent of the private-sector balance-of-payments balance (Rp −13.6 billion in 1971-72 and Rp 81.0 billion in 1972-73) gives an indication of the monetary effects of the private-sector balance of payments. By combining the private-sector balance of payments with the domestic budget surplus or deficit and any changes in central-bank-direct credit or other monetary control variables, one should get a good explanation of changes in the money supply.

In 1971-72 the estimated domestic budget deficit was Rp 30.4 billion and the private-sector trade deficit was Rp 13.6 billion, implying a net expansion from these sources of Rp 16.7 billion. During that period, net credit of Bank Indonesia to the private sector and state enterprises expanded by Rp 29.8 billion; this expansion and an additional Rp 12.7 billion from other increases in net credit of the central bank, would have expanded the money supply through the credit multiplier. The actual stock of money expanded by about Rp 81 billion during the period.

The 1972-73 estimates show a large generation of liquid assets due to the increased domestic budget deficit (Rp 88.8 billion) and a private-sector balance of payments surplus (Rp 81.0 billion), implying an expansion of high-powered money of Rp 169.8 billion from these sources. During this period the central bank increased its credit, not including its credit to the government, by Rp 33.6 billion and the money supply and quasi-money expanded by about Rp 230 billion.

It is not possible to isolate the effects of the monetary expansion on prices and the structure of production. However, this survey of the recent data for Indonesia shows that the domestic budget deficit has been an important factor in monetary growth in the years surveyed. This deficit, along with the inflow of private foreign capital dominated monetary developments over the period.

B.   Jordan

The Jordanian economy experienced a high rate of growth for a number of years prior to June 1967; at the same time the balance of payments was in surplus, and dependence on external aid was being gradually reduced. The interruption of these favorable trends following the June 1967 war resulted in a sharp increase in the need for foreign financial assistance. This came mainly from certain Arab countries in the form of cash grants to the budget and resulted in a substantial increase in public expenditures and an expansion

TABLE 2

Indonesia: Government Budget (in billions of rupiahs)

	1971-72 (actual)	1972-73 (estimated)
Government expenditures		
Domestic	423.8	561.2
Routine budget		
Personnel expenditures	154.8	191.6
Material expenditures	62.9	83.9
Subsidies to regions[a]	67.9	83.9
Debt service payments	5.8	7.4
Other	5.0	8.0
Development budget		
General[b]	106.6	156.5
Regional government	20.8	20.8
IPEDA[c]	-	9.1
External	116.8	165.0
Routine budget		
Personnel expenditures	5.2	6.9
Material expenditures	11.2	10.4
Debt service	41.0	46.0
Development budget		
Project aid	40.6	62.3
General development expenditures[b]	18.8	39.4
IPEDA[c]	-	6.1
total	540.6	732.3
Government receipts		
Domestic	393.4	472.4
Income taxes[d]	68.4	86.2
IPEDA	-	15.2
Other	1.1	4.1
Consumption taxes[e]	101.5	121.5
Taxes on trade[f]	117.7	133.7
Nontax receipts	12.0	14.2
Aid counterpart funds[g]	92.7	97.5
External	155.3	260.2
Corporate tax, foreign oil companies	112.7	197.9
Project aid	40.6	62.3
total	546.7	732.6
Cash budget balance	6.1	0.3
Domestic budget balance	-30.4	-88.8

in domestic liquidity. However, in 1967 and 1968 there were no apparent effects on prices or the balance of payments because of an increase in cash holdings. In 1970, financial policies were also expansionary due to the unrest starting in June and culminating in the outbreak of civil war in September of that year. The following discussion and the tables cover the years 1971 and 1972 during which the economy grew rapidly,[4] but with some pressure on prices.[5]

The domestic cash budgets for the years 1971 and 1972 are given in Table 4. As in Table 2, the assumptions made to classify various items such as domestic or foreign revenues and expenditures are contained in the footnotes to the table. Foreign receipts of the government, along with smaller amounts of other external revenues, increased from JD 55.3 million (or 61

---

[a] It is assumed that none of the central government's subsidy to regions is directly spent on imports.

[b] These expenditures are primarily domestic expenditures related to development projects financed by project aid, total expenditures of other development projects, and some subsidies for the imports of cotton, fertilizer, and sugar. It was estimated that 15 percent of these expenditures was used for imported materials of nonproject aid development projects and this amount was allocated to the foreign budget; import subsidies included in this budget item amounted to Rp 10.0 billion in the 1972-73 budget and these were also allocated to the foreign budget.

[c] This is the land tax that is earmarked for regional development programs. It is estimated that 40 percent of these expenditures consisted of imported materials. In 1971-72, IPEDA expenditures amounted to Rp 11.9 billion but were not included in the budget of the central government.

[d] Includes personal income tax, corporation tax, and withholding tax. Some of the corporation tax is paid by foreign corporations and hence should be classified as external receipts; however, it is not possible to determine exactly how much.

[e] Includes sales taxes, excises, revenue from domestic sales of oil products, and miscellaneous.

[f] Includes import duties (assumed totally shifted to consumers), sales tax, and export tax.

[g] These funds are related to specific private-sector imports and are only credited to the budget upon receipt of the rupiah payment for the imports. The figures are less than the amounts listed in the balance of payments because of various government subsidies paid for by selling foreign exchange directly to the subsidized importer at an exchange rate that is lower than the official exchange rate. These foreign-exchange receipts do not enter the budget and they have no monetary impact since they are used to pay for imports directly.

Source: Data received from Indonesian authorities and Fund staff estimates.

TABLE 3

Indonesia: Balance-of-Payments Summary (in billions of rupiahs)[a]

	1971-72 (actual)	1972-73 (estimated)
Private sector		
Goods and services	−74.7	−177.6
Nonoil exports	(325.4)	(402.6)
Imports[b]	(−276.4)	(−410.9)
Services (nonoil)[c]	(−123.7)	(−169.3)
Miscellaneous capital	78.9	229.5[d]
Errors and omissions	−17.8	29.1
Government sector		
Taxes on foreign oil companies	112.9	198.0
Foreign expenditure[e]	−75.9	−119.1
Debt service payments[f]	−72.6	−89.6
Official transfers on capital	174.3	215.0
Imports paid for with program aid[g]	−127.0	−152.7
Private-sector balance	−13.6	81.0
Overall balance	−1.9	132.6
Allocation of SDRs	12.5	–
Monetary movements (increase in assets −)	−10.6	−132.6

[a] Indonesian rupiahs were converted on the basis of Rp 415 = US $1.
[b] Equals total imports minus government foreign expenditures and imports paid for with program aid.
[c] Total of services in the overall balance of payments. Thus, it is assumed in Tables 2 and 3 that the government imports only goods.
[d] Includes an inflow of short-term and medium-term foreign capital primarily through direct foreign borrowing of enterprises and increased foreign deposits in local banks.
[e] Personnel and material expenditures shown in Table 2 plus external expenditures made under the development budget.
[f] Include debt service payments of state enterprises.
[g] Utilizations of program loans and grants for the period; they are listed in the government since they have no monetary impact.
Source: Data received from Indonesia authorities and Fund staff estimates.

percent of total revenues) in 1972. Thus, while the overall fiscal position has shown relatively small cash deficits, the domestic deficit has amounted to JD 41.0 million in 1971 and JD 49.9 million in 1972.

Following the 1967 war, the previously favorable trends in the balance of payments on the goods and services account were reversed although there were overall balance-of-payments surpluses in 1967 and 1968 due to large cash grants from other Arab countries. From 1969 to 1971, Jordan incurred balance-of-payments deficits due to increased deficits on the goods and services account and a decline in external grants. Table 5 gives a summary of the balance of payments for Jordan for 1971 and 1972. The overall balance of payments shows a deficit of JD 12.7 million in 1971 and a surplus of JD 5.8 million in 1972. In these years, budget support in foreign exchange was the largest source of foreign-exchange earnings and the private sector balance-of-payments was substantially in deficit in each year (JD 37.9 million in 1971 and JD 36.9 million in 1972).

The monetary effects of the budget and the balance of payments in 1971 amounted to an expansion of high-powered money equal to JD 3.1 million since the domestic budget deficit was that much larger than the private-sector payments deficit; the money supply increased by JD 6 million during the year. During 1972 the domestic budget and the private-sector balance of payments contributed JD 13.0 million to monetary expansion and the actual monetary expansion was JD 11.4 million. This seeming contradiction is possibly due to the effects of some military spending which were not counted in the budget. Unfortunately, it was not possible to assess the impact of the monetary expansion on prices and the structure of production. There were price increases in 1972 but they were at least partly due to increases in import prices; trends in production and exports have also been greatly affected by the recovery from the war of 1967 and the civil disturbances of 1970. However, this survey of the recent data from Jordan indicates the relevance of the domestic budget and private-sector balance of payments in explaining the source of monetary expansion when a government receives substantial amounts of revenue from foreign sources.

C. Oman

The oil sector is crucially important for the Omani economy since it contributes about two-thirds of GDP, 95 percent of budgetary revenue, and almost all foreign-exchange receipts. The only oil company currently producing in Oman (The Petroleum Development, Oman, PDO) is completely foreign owned and accounts for only about 1 percent of total employment. In the nonoil sectors, the primary industries are agriculture, fisheries, and various services. In 1971, services accounted for about two-thirds of total value-added and are the fastest

TABLE 4

Jordan: Government Budget (in millions of dinars)

	1971 (actual)	1972 (actual)[a]
Government expenditures		
Domestic	73.3	85.2
Administration	9.1	9.0
Defense and police[b]	33.7	37.4
Social services[c]	10.1	10.4
Economic services[d]	3.5	4.8
Extraordinary expenditures[e]	9.8	9.1
Interest on public debt	1.8	2.3
Development expenditures[f]	5.3	12.2
External	10.9	12.3
Current defense and police[b]	6.0	6.6
Other development[f]	4.9	5.7
Total expenditures	84.2	97.5
Government receipts		
Domestic	32.3	35.3
Taxes[g]	18.9	22.3
Nontax receipts[h]	13.4	13.0
External	37.8	55.3
Budget grants[i]	29.5	46.2
Economic and technical assistance	0.5	1.6
Oil transit dues	3.5	2.6
Net external borrowing[j]	4.3	4.9
Total receipts	70.1	90.6
Cash budget balance	−14.1	−6.9
Domestic budget balance	−41.0	−49.9

[a] Preliminary.

[b] Include only current defense expenditures; it is assumed that 85 percent of current defense and police expenditures are domestic, primarily wages and salaries.

[c] Include current expenditures on health, education, and other. It is assumed that they are totally domestic, primarily wages and salaries.

[d] Include current expenditures on agriculture, transportation, communications, and other.

[e] Include relief and compensation payments to persons suffering property damage from the events of 1967 and subsequent civil disturbances plus financial investment in business enterprises experiencing financial difficulties due to these events.

growing components of DGP [10].[6] Imports accounted for about 36 percent
of GNP in 1971 and since total imports grew by about 53 percent during 1972
they would undoubtedly represent a larger proportion of GNP in the latter
year. Thus, the economy of Oman may be characterized as a small, open
economy with an important oil enclave sector.

The case of Oman is particularly interesting because oil exports began
relatively recently and one can observe the impact of the oil revenue on the
economy. Oil production and exports began in 1967, before which Oman was
largely a subsistence economy. Oil production rose very rapidly from 1967
through 1969 and then leveled off. Production increased slightly in 1970 and
actually declined in 1971 and 1972, although oil receipts and government
revenue from oil continued to rise due to rising prices. Substantial growth in
construction, public administration, and wholesale and retail trade began in
1970; also, it is estimated that from the beginning of 1970 to the beginning of
1972 rents increased threefold and wages and salaries doubled. Beginning in
1970 there was a substantial monetary expansion; from end-1969 to end-1971
the stock of money increased by RO 10.0 million, or 287 percent; beginning
from a much larger base, the stock of quasi-money increased by RO 6.6
million, or 26 percent. Prices of basic food items increased substantially from
1970 to 1972, but by much less than did wages, salaries, and rents [10, Table
9.1].[7] During this period of expansion in oil production and services, the
agriculture and fishing industries, previously the principal economic activities,
registered only insignificant growth.[8]

---

[f] Nonextraordinary development expenditures are divided into external and internal components in the following manner: 80 percent of external loans are
   subtracted from total nonextraordinary development expenditures to obtain
   the external component; the remainder is the internal component. The reason
   for this procedure is that all foreign loans are allocated to the development
   budget and that it is estimated that about 80 percent of the foreign loans are
   required for external expenditure on development projects.
[g] Include taxes on income, profits, property, domestic production, consumption,
   transactions, exports, imports, and other.
[h] Include primarily revenues from licenses, fees, and profits of state enterprises.
[i] Does not include various classifications of military aid such as military aid in
   kind and a special military grant of JD 12.5 million (see also footnote d of
   Table 5.
[j] Military loans excluded except for JD 2.2 million of loan repayment estimated
   for 1973.
Source: Data supplied by the Jordanian authorities and Fund staff estimates.

TABLE 5

Jordan: Balance-of-Payments Summary (in millions of Jordanian dinars)[a]

	1971	1972[b]
Private sector		
Goods and services	−40.9	−39.3
Exports, f.o.b.	(11.4)	(17.0)
Imports, c.i.f.[c]	(−4.6)	(−5.0)
Investment income (net)	(4.8)	(3.3)
Receipts from Jordanians abroad	(4.9)	(7.4)
Other services (net)	(−3.0)	(−1.8)
Private transfers	1.1	2.3
Capital transactions	−1.3	−0.4
Errors and omissions	3.2	0.5
Government sector		
Imports[c]	−21.8	−34.7[d]
Budget grants[e]	35.5	66.0[d]
Oil transit dues	3.4	3.2
Borrowing[f]	8.1	8.2
Private-sector balance	−37.9	−36.9
Overall balance of payments	−12.7	5.8
Allocation of SDRs	0.9	0.9
Monetary movements (increase −)	11.8	−6.7

[a] Jordan dinars were converted on the basis of JD 1 = SDR 2.80 in 1971 and of JD 1 = SDR 2.58 in 1972.

[b] Preliminary.

[c] Equals total imports minus external government expenditures listed in Table 4, plus purchases of civilian aircraft and parts by state-owned airlines minus estimated military imports not included in the budget.

[d] Includes a special grant of JD 12.5 million for military assistance which is not included in the budget. It is assumed that this is entirely spend on imported equipment and the figure for government imports and budget grants from Table 4 has been increased by that amount. Other discrepancies between this figure and the corresponding figure in Table 4 are due to other military aid not included in the budget (including all military aid in kind) and other smaller grants such as United Nations aid to Palestinian refugees.

[e] Includes economic and technical assistance. It also includes various classes of military assistance not included in the budget (see footnote d).

[f] Includes some loans to the military that are not included in Table 4.

Source: Data supplied by the Jordanian authorities and Fund staff estimates.

TABLE 6

Oman: Government Budget (in millions of rials)

	1971 (actual)	1972 (actual)
Government expenditures		
Domestic	19.6	28.7
Defense[a]	1.7	2.3
Other general service[b]	5.9	8.3
Social services[c]	1.9	3.2
Economic services[d]	1.0	1.4
Other	1.1	1.5
Development budget[e]	8.0	12.0
External	26.4	42.9
Development budget[e]	12.0	17.9
Defense imports[f]	14.4	25.0
Total expenditures	46.0	71.6
Government revenues		
Domestic	2.2	3.4
Customs	1.1	1.6
Corporate income tax	0.3	0.5
Other income[g]	0.8	1.3
External	47.9	49.6
Oil royalties	12.1	12.1
Income tax	35.8	37.2
Oil installation port dues	–	0.3
Total revenues	50.1	53.0
Cash budget balance	4.1	−18.6
Domestic budget balance	−17.4	−25.3

[a] Includes the current and domestic capital expenses of the defense department. For other categories, domestic capital expenses are listed under the domestic development budget.

[b] Includes current expenditures of the Privy Purse, Office of the Secretary for Financial Affairs, Local and Regional Governments, Police, Foreign Affairs, and Dhofar province.

[c] Includes current expenditures in health and education as well as payments to shaikhs.

[d] Includes the current expenditures of the Public Works Department and in agriculture and transportation.

[e] Domestic development expenditures are estimated to be 40 percent of total expenditures on development projects: the remainder is classified as governmental imports.

[f] Defense imports as recorded in budgetary accounts.

[g] Consists of Zakath, a traditional religious tax and various items of nontax income.

Source: Fund staff estimates based on data received from Omani authorities.

TABLE 7

Oman: Balance-of-Payments Summary (in millions of rials)[a]

	1970 (actual)	1971 (actual)	1972 (actual)
Private sector			
Goods and services			
Oil exports	4.4	5.9	6.1
Nonoil exports	0.4	0.4	0.4
Imports	−7.6	−13.8	−18.7
Private transfers[b]	n.a.	n.a.	−7.0
Errors and omissions	−6.7	−0.5	−10.8[c]
Government sector			
Payments from oil companies[d]	44.4	47.7	49.6
Imports[e]	−4.4	−26.4	−42.9
Private balance	30.5	13.3	−23.3
Overall balance	30.5	13.3	−23.3
Allocation of SDRs	−	−	0.3
Government short-term borrowing	−	−	7.2[f]
Monetary movements (increase −)	−30.5	−13.3	−15.8

[a] The exchange rate for Omani rials is RO 1 = SDR 2.4.
[b] Primarily remittances of 5,000-6,000 foreign workers in Oman. Separate data on private transfers were collected for the first time in 1972; in previous years private transfers would be included in errors and omissions.
[c] This large residual is primarily due to an underestimation of imports and unidentified capital flows.
[d] These figures correspond to external government revenues listed in Table 6.
[e] These figures correspond to external government expenditures listed in Table 6.
[f] The purpose of this borrowing was to partially finance the balance-of-payments deficit; it was not included in the government budget.
Source: Data supplied by the Omani authorites and Fund staff estimates.

The domestic and cash budgets for 1971 and 1972 are given in Table 6. The table shows that the cash budget in 1971 was in surplus although the domestic budget recorded a deficit of RO 17.4 million (equal to about 38 percent of total expenditures). In 1972, expenditures increased very rapidly and the cash budget recorded a deficit and the domestic budget deficit increased to RO 25.3 million. Table 7 shows the balance of payments from 1970 through 1972 disaggregated by private sector and government. The year 1970 is included even though there is no comparable budget data to show the trend in the balances. There were large, though declining, overall balance-of-payments surpluses in 1970 and 1971 with moderate private balance-of-payments deficits. In 1972, the private-sector balance-of-payments deficit increased substantially and the overall balance of payments sustained a deficit. The primary reason for these trends was the large increase in both private and government imports during 1971 and 1972.

Tables 6 and 7 indicate an expansionary monetary effect of the budget on the balance of payments of RO 9.4 million in 1971; this compares to an increase in the stock of money plus quasi-money of RO 10.2 million. In 1972 the monetary effect of the budget on the balance of payments was slightly contractionary and the stock of money and quasi-money decreased by RO 4.7 million in that year.

This brief review of the recent data from Oman again illustrates the importance of the domestic budget and the private-sector balance of payments in assessing monetary developments. The Omani case provides better insight into the impact that large scale foreign inflows have on a small, open economy than the cases of Indonesia or Jordan because of the relatively small size of the Omani economy and the magnitude of the impact over relatively few years. The first effect was a large increase in the money supply through large domestic budget deficits. This increase helped stimulate large increases in the prices of nontraded goods (particularly construction and local commerce) and greatly increased their production. Meanwhile the production of previous exports and import-competing goods stagnated. After a lag of about two years (between 1969 and 1971) both private and government imports increased substantially until the drain of liquid assets through the private-sector balance of payments completely absorbed the increase in liquid assets created by the domestic budget deficit. The Omani economy in 1972, was considerably more special-ized than in 1969 and during the period a substantial shift in relative prices in favor of nontraded goods had occurred. This sequence of events is identical to that in the analysis contained in this chapter and suggests that the time lags involved in the adjustment process in a country as small and open as Oman are relatively short.

ACKNOWLEDGMENTS

I wish to thank Walter Salant of the Brookings Institution for his many helpful comments on the chapter. In addition to the comments published here, he made suggestions that resulted in revisions to the paper, particularly in Section III. Of course, errors that remain are my responsibility.

NOTES

1. The analysis presented here follows closely what has been called the monetary theory of the balance of payments, and elaborates that theory slightly by developing the implications for the relative production of internationally traded and nontraded goods. The analysis stems from that in ref. 1. A paper in which a similar analysis is developed is ref. 2. Recent surveys of this theory are given in refs. 3 and 4. See also, J. M. Parkin and D. Laidler [5, 6].

2. Similar results are demonstrated mathematically in an unpublished paper by Manuel Guitian, "The Effects of Changes in the Exchange Rate on Output, Prices and the Balance of Payments," International Monetary Fund, (May 3, 1973). The argument in Mr. Guitian's paper is expressed in terms of the effects on the commodities markets rather than the effects on the money market. It is shown that the degree to which adjustment takes place through prices is primarily dependent on the income elasticities and price elasticities of demand for traded and nontraded goods, as well as the marginal rates of substitution between the two types of goods. See pp. 7-12 of the paper by Guitian and the Appendix.

3. The cash-budget balance CB is the difference between total receipts (domestic DR plus foreign FR) and total expenditures (domestic DE plus foreign FE). Symbolically:

$$CB = FR + DR - FE - DE \tag{1}$$

I have rearranged this definition in the following way:

$$CB = (FR - FE) + (DR - DE) \tag{2}$$

where $(FR - FE)$ is defined as the government's foreign balance FB and $(DR - DE)$ is defined as the domestic budget balance DB.

Since only domestic receipts and expenditures affect domestic income, the direct effect of the government budget on aggregate demand and the supply of money is measured through the domestic budget balance, which can be shown in the following way. Assuming no other domestic borrowing is possible from the private sector, any cash budget deficit is ultimately financed by increasing high-powered money (currency plus bank reserves) or by reducing the stock of official foreign exchange reserves. The overall budget constraint of the government can be written:

$$CB = FB + DB = \Delta H + \Delta R \tag{3}$$

where ΔH is the change in high-powered money and ΔR is the change in the stock of official foreign-exchange reserves. The foreign budget imbalances change reserves by the amount of the foreign imbalance. Therefore, $FB = \Delta R$ and, substituting into (3), we have:

$$DB = \Delta H \tag{4}$$

The direct effect of the government budget on high-powered money, and hence the money supply, is determined by the domestic budget balance. The above would not hold if there is substantial borrowing directly from the private sector since this borrowing would decrease the stock of money. In these cases, an additional term would have to be inserted in (3) and (4); however, the result that it is only the domestic budget that affects the money supply would be unaltered.

4. There are no adequate statistics on gross national product after 1966 due to lack of information on economic developments in the West Bank. However, agricultural output, industrial production, mining, and construction achieved substantial growth in these years.

5. Prices rose by 4.2 percent in 1971 and 8.2 percent in 1972.

6. The primary service industries are construction, wholesale and retail trade, public administration, and defense. These four service sectors accounted for about 55 percent of nonoil income in 1970 and increased in nominal terms by about 44 percent from end-1970 to end-1971. This compares to a growth of about 14 percent of the oil sector and of about 25 percent in nominal GDP.

7. Examples of price rises from first-quarter 1970 to first-quarter 1972 are: wheat 25 percent, rice 14 percent, fresh fish 100 percent (although there is evidently a wide variability in fresh fish prices), tea no increase, dates 60 percent, and milk 33 percent.

8. The value of agriculture and fishing grew from RO 16 million in 1969 (about 20 percent of GNP) to RO 16.8 million in 1971 (about 15 percent of GNP). This represents a growth of only about 2 percent per year.

REFERENCES

1. J. J. Polak, "Monetary Analysis of Income Formation and Payments Problems," IMF *Staff Papers,* November 1957.

2. R. McKinnon, "Portfolio Balance and International Adjustment," in R. Mundell and A. Swoboda, (eds.), *Monetary Problems of the International Economy,* 1969.

3. H. G. Johnson, "The Monetary Approach to Balance of Payments Theory," lecture delivered to the Graduate Institute of International Studies, Geneva, Switzerland, February 1971.

4. H. G. Johnson, "Inflation and the Monetarist Controversy," de Vries lectures, Amsterdam, 1971.

5. J. M. Parkin, "Inflation, the Balance of Payments, Domestic Credit Expansion and Exchange Rate Adjustments," in R. Aliber, ed., *National Monetary Policies and the International Financial System,* University of Chicago Press, 1974.

6.   D. Laidler, "Price and Output Fluctuations in an Open Economy," mimeo, December 1973.

7.   William F. White, "Measuring the Inflationary Significance of a Government Budget," IMF Staff Papers, April 1951.

8.   IBRD, *The Main Report,* "Development Issues for Indonesia," 1, pp. 1-8.

9.   IBRD, *The Main Report,* 1, Table 1, p. 2.

10. IBRD, *The Economy of Oman,* August 22, 1971.

Comment

WALTER S. SALANT

The Brookings Institution
Washington, D.C.

Richard Stillson's chapter contains a number of suggestions that are useful in empirical work and raises interesting questions of analysis and policy. I shall concentrate on a few analytical and policy points.

I. Relative Price Changes of Tradeable and Nontradeable Goods under Fixed and Flexible Exchange Rates

First, I want to clarify an analytical point that could lead to confusion if one does not read Stillson's statements about it with sufficient care. In his review of the effects of monetary disequilibrium, Stillson compares the relative movements of the prices of traded and nontraded goods (presumably, tradeable and nontradeable goods) under fixed and flexible exchange rates. He points out that under fixed exchange rates an excess supply of money raises the relative prices of nontraded goods, shifting resources at the margin out of the production of exports and import-competing goods into that of nontraded goods and shifting demand to imports and exportable goods. However, he then goes on to say, "The effects of excess demand or supply of money on relative prices depend on the assumption of a fixed exchange rate." Under flexible rates, an excess supply of money causes a depreciation of the currency in question, and this "immediately increases the price in domestic currency" of traded goods; in other words, it *lowers* the relative prices of nontraded goods. These statements are perfectly correct, but taken together, they may give the impression that an excess supply of money has effects on the relation between prices of traded and nontraded goods under fixed exchange rates opposite to the effects it has under flexible rates. Such a conclusion would certainly be anomalous, implying as it does opposite real effects of the same monetary disequilibrium on two models in which prices are flexible in both directions. The apparent anomaly arises from possible confusion between the introduction of the disequilibrium itself (i.e., the excess supply of money) and the adjustment process that restores equilibrium (i.e., elimination of the excess supply of money through reduction in its supply or increase in the demand for it or both).

It is obvious that if an excess supply of money affects the relative prices of nontraded and traded goods in a way that causes a trade deficit (the form a payments deficit must take in a model that, like Stillson's, has no capital account but only a current account and reserve changes), that effect must be to make prices of nontraded goods too high relative to traded goods. Correspondingly, insofar as the disequilibrium is to be remedied through changes in these relative prices, the remedy must *lower* the prices of traded goods relative to nontraded goods, for this is the direction of change required to shift domestic demand from imports and exportable goods to nontraded goods and to shift domestic resources from production of nontraded goods to that of export and import-competing goods. The point that needs to be made clear is that the appearance of an excess money supply tends to raise the relative prices of nontraded goods under *both* exchange-rate regimes. The lowering of their relative prices under flexible rates is not part of the disease (i.e., the disequilibrium itself) but part of the cure (the restoration of equilibrium). As such, its counterpart in the fixed-rate case is not the appearance of the excess supply of money, but the loss of reserves and the presumed resulting deflation. Thus, the appearance of anomaly arises from not distinguishing clearly between the disease and the cure. It is easy to confuse them when one refers merely to "effects" of a disturbance in all systems that are self-correcting, because in such systems both the disequilibrium and the negative feedback that eliminates it are effects of the original disturbance.

I agree with the emphasis that Stillson puts on changes in the relative prices of tradeable and nontradeable goods in accomplishing adjustment. In fact, I have stressed that in the real world such changes in relative prices are an important part of the adjustment process [1]. It is worth noting, however, that in theory such changes are not necessary for adjustment to occur. As has been persuasively argued by Rudiger Dornbusch, the adjustment can occur in a model with only traded goods and money as a result of the efforts of moneyholders to eliminate their excess holdings [2]. The interesting question is the importance of such changes in practice. That is an empirical question that is not easy to answer, because it is difficult to develop a category of approximately nontradeable goods, all goods being potentially tradeable if the difference in price is great enough to cover the transportation cost from the country with the lower price. My guess is that if the question could be answered for many cases, it would be found that the role of these relative price changes differed greatly among them, and in general would be smaller, the more open the economy.

II. Some Technical-Analytical Problems

The shifts of resources to the production of nontraded goods that occur when there is persistent monetary expansion give rise to the main policy problems that Stillson's chapter addresses. Such expansion always erodes the competitive position of the country's exports. Stillson then goes on to argue that this effect may be inconsistent with other objectives. Before pursuing this point, he develops a useful technical point that is something of a diversion. I shall follow him in this diversion by commenting on the technical point first. He points out that the private sector's income and money supply is not affected by transactions between the government and foreigners. While this may seem obvious enough when stated in that way, it is less obvious when stated in an alternative way, viz: the *total* government budget and the *total* balance of payments are irrelevant or misleading indicators of changes exogenous to the private sector; one should look only at the government's domestic transactions and the portion of the balance of payments involving domestic private residents.

I thought, on the first reading, that the chapter implied that changes in the total government surplus or deficit that leave the domestic budget balance unchanged do not affect the private sector's income. The balanced-budget-multiplier literature tells us that such changes do affect the combined total output and income of the private sector and the government, provided that the change in the government's domestic expenditure is on goods and services rather than transfers. If this increase in expenditure takes the form of purchases from the private sector rather than increases in the government's own output, the change of income occurs in the private sector, although the consumption or investment affected is that of the government.[1]

I would note, also, that even changes in GNP that leave the private sector's income unchanged should not be neglected. They affect demand for resources, prices, and other variables.

III. Policy Responses to Certain Capital Inflows

I return now to the more substantive part of Stillson's chapter, Section III,
which deals with policy problems resulting from monetary expansion caused
by capital inflows from abroad. It considers three kinds of inflow, two in the
form of cash loans and the third, the export oil, in the form of liquidation of
a depletable tangible asset.

The first inflow Stillson considers is short-term cash borrowing that
cannot be renewed or replaced when it matures. He sees no problem if these
loans are used to finance expected balance-of-payments deficits and if they
mature within "the period of reversibility" of the balance of payments. (I
presume he means if they mature when or *after* the deficit is converted into a
surplus.) However, even then if the loan leads to additional domestic expenditures, either governmental or private, the prices of nontraded goods will
be raised, the payments deficit will be greater than expected, and the borrowing country will not only have to reverse the loan-induced change, but go
beyond that. The point is, I take it, that even if the expected deficit would
have been followed by an equal surplus, permitting repayment of the loan
had it been sterilized, the failure to sterilize it makes for a larger deficit and
therefore makes a larger surplus necessary later. Stillson concludes that a
sterilization policy may be desirable, presumably because both the initial
reallocation of resources and the subsequent reversal are costly and un-
necessary, and could be avoided by sterilizing both the borrowing and the
repayment.

I have no quarrel with his analytical conclusion in this case. I wonder,
however, under what circumstances any positive policy action is required to
sterilize such a loan. If it is a private loan induced by a rise of interest rates
in the borrowing country, perhaps positive action would be required, but if
the government does the borrowing specifically to finance a deficit that is
both expected and expected to be temporary, it is not economically sensible
to increase its expenditure or to allow an increase in the income or money
supply of the private sector. The activation of a swap line would fall into
this category of short-term loan.

The second case—that of longer-term cash loans—gives me more serious
pause. Stillson accepts the conclusion (standard for at least a century in the
literature analyzing capital imports in the development process) that if the
foreign resources are used to supplement domestic investment and are
profitably invested, they may allow a trade surplus to develop from which
the loans can be repaid. But he then goes on to say, "However, the specific
policies used to facilitate the desired reallocation of resources are important.
For instance, if foreign capital is allowed to lead to an excess monetary
expansion and ultimately a reallocation of domestic resources from traded

to nontraded goods, the economy and the balance of trade will be adjusting to the inflow in such a way as to be less able to pay back the loan."

I believe that a reallocation of resources from traded to nontraded goods is in some cases, a desired effect of a long-term capital inflow. The very economic purpose of borrowing real resources from abroad is to permit an increase in domestic absorption of a productive kind. That increase in absorption may take the form of an increase in imports that releases domestic resources from import-competing uses or of a decrease in exports that releases resources in industries producing exportable goods, with the released resources moving into the most productive potential investment demand that was unrealized prior to the borrowing. Although this most productive unrealized potential investment might be in industries producing tradeable goods, there is no presumption that it is; it might equally well be in industries producing nontradeable goods—for example, in the education "industry." If so, the shift of domestic resources from tradeable to nontradeable goods is desirable. Of course when the time for repayment comes, which in a continuing process of development may be several decades later, an export surplus must be developed, and this will require reallocating domestic resources back to tradeable goods again. Nevertheless, a shift of resources from tradeable to nontradeable goods is desirable if the most productive incremental investment is in the industries producing nontradeable output. This conclusion should be subject only to the qualification (perhaps a novel one) that the inflow of capital must last long enough to permit the present value of the future increments in productivity resulting from the reallocation to offset the sum of the cost of the initial reallocation and the present value of the cost of the subsequent reverse reallocation required to repay the capital. The transfer process may be effectuated indirectly in such cases, but the reallocations are desirable if the increment to investment in the nontradeable-goods industries is the most productive and is large enough to meet the condition I have stated. It should then generate enough increase in the excess of output over absorption to permit the development of a surplus and repayment of the loans. All that policy need do in such cases is prevent absorption from rising above its initial level by *more* than the excess of the rise in output over the amounts to be repaid.

The same general argument applies to the third case discussed in the chapter, that of foreign-exchange receipts from export of a depletable resource. In discussing this case, Stillson notes that a monetary expansion that he calls "undue" (which I take to mean one that raises the relative prices of nontradeable goods) causes an increased specialization of exports. That increased specialization may make the economy dependent on exports of a shrinking number of commodities, and that result may conflict with a developing country's desire to diversify its exports. Viewed analytically, that possible conflict need not mean that the specialization should be prevented. What is at issue in such cases is a choice between the goals of maximizing the productivity of the economy as a whole and of diversifying exports, goals that may be in conflict. Adjustment to a higher price of oil, for example, may indeed take the form of monetary expansion that raises internal costs so high that all output other than oil ceases to be exportable. But if the most costly barrel of oil that is then exported yields a higher net return to the country than the last pound of nonoil squeezed out of the export trade, the country's real income is higher if it exports that last barrel of oil and not the last pound of nonoil.

A policy of achieving a structure of exports that can be sustained when foreign receipts from oil are reduced or eliminated may be sensible if the date when these receipts will be reduced cannot be foreseen. This situation involves a policy decision requiring assessment of risk. But the mere fact that a more concentrated structure of exports cannot be sustained forever is not necessarily an objection to it. A concentrated structure that can be sustained for an assured and long time may be acceptable and, indeed, preferable to one that is more diversified but less productive, so long as one can adjust back to the more diversified structure after the concentrated one can no longer be sustained. A country in such a situation must choose between conflicting goals of productivity and diversification to avoid risk. These objectives are not entirely mutually exclusive; they involve a tradeoff between degrees of productivity and of diversification.

More generally, the economic purpose of importing capital is to get real resources from abroad, and that implies importing more or exporting less or both. In general, I should think that the sensible policy is to take temporary inflows in the form of reserves and avoid reallocation of resources in otherwise undesired directions, and to take assuredly continued borrowing in the form of a net import surplus, delaying efforts to diversify exports if the net import surplus would involve a cut in exports. But note that market forces may permit a country to maintain exports and take the increase in real resources entirely in the form of greater imports. If market forces do not yield that result but a country still wants it, the government can permit the monetary expansion that Stillson warns against and subsidize exports.

NOTES

1. Another question that might be raised about the treatment of government arises from the fact that the purchase and sale of foreign exchange by the central bank is an open market operation and, like other open market operations, affects the domestic monetary base. If such operations are regarded as transactions with foreigners, this effect may appear to conflict with Stillson's conclusion that the only government transactions affecting that base are those with the domestic private sector. But there is no conflict. If in that case the monetary

base is nevertheless affected, there must be another transaction between the foreigner and the domestic private sector. This example brings out the fact that no accounting error results from leaving transactions between the government and the rest of the world in both the government budget and the balance-of-payments accounts, because the two entires offset each other. However, errors of interpretation may occur if one looks only at one of the two accounts. Stillson's suggestion eliminates that risk.

REFERENCES

1. Randall Hinshaw, ed., *The Economics of International Adjustment,* The Johns Hopkins Press, Baltimore, 1971, p. 100.

2. Rudiger Dornbusch, "Real and Monetary Aspects of the Effects of Exchange Rate Changes," in Robert Z. Aliber, ed., *National Monetary Policies and the International Financial System,* University of Chicago, Chicago, 1974, pp. 64-81.

Chapter 11

Trade Credit and Other Forms of Inside Money

ARTHUR B. LAFFER

Graduate School of Business
University of Chicago
Chicago, Illinois

In the analysis of the markets for most commodities, it is unusual to find economists unanimously assuming that (1) the number of units supplied is determined by the government; (2) the price of the commodity tends to rise more easily than fall; and (3) the rental rate paid for that commodity is arbitrarily below competitive equilibrium and unresponsive to changes in market conditions. Yet these three assumptions are the basis of monetary economics' analysis of money. According to this traditional theory (1) the supply of nominal money is generally assumed to be exogenous to the private sector, i.e., under the primary influence of the monetary authorites; (2) except in the long run, the aggregate price level is assumed to respond slowly to any disequilibrium between the goods and money markets (this response in the extreme becomes almost negligible when pressures are for a fall in the price level); and (3) money is assumed not to earn a competitive market rate of return.*

Because prices are assumed to rise more easily than they fall, traditional economic theory postulates that at some point increases in the growth rate of the money supply will result in an increase in the rate of inflation. The level of nominal interest rates, again perhaps with a long lag, would rise to reflect this more rapid inflation.

---

*Either by law (Banking Acts of 1933 and 1935) or by custom (bank deposits at the Federal Reserve do not earn interest), money supposedly does not earn any pecuniary yield.

As long as money is not paid interest, nominal interest rates represent the real costs of holding money. Thus the higher pecuniary yields are in the marketplace, the more costly it becomes to hold money balances. Higher interest rates will result in smaller holdings of money balances. In effect this means that control over the nominal supply of money is tantamount to control over the equilibrium real supply of money. The anomalous observation—referred to as the Wicksell effect—is that the faster nominal money grows, the more real money is reduced. However, the government itself can maintain this control only so long as money does not earn interest.

These three assumptions are responsible for many of the modern propositions in monetary theory. And while they may turn out to be fully appropriate for gauging reality, it is interesting how little analysis has proceeded along lines other than those dictated by these assumptions. Economists have rarely examined models where one, two, or all three of these assumptions are absent. Nor have many economists investigated the implications of these assumptions to see if they are even consistent with actual behavior or microeconomic theory. Part of the reason there has been so little analysis of the validity of the theories themselves is due to the fact that tests of their predictions are difficult and/or yield inconclusive results.

In *Money in a Theory of Finance* [1], Gurley and Shaw begin analyzing monetary models in which these traditional assumptions are relaxed. They used the concept of *inside money*—money issued by the "banking bureau" backed by private securities—in a world where there is only a demand for net money (i.e., money is demanded solely as a net item in a wealth portfolio). Gurley and Shaw's approach raises many questions concerning the existence and uniqueness of a price level. These same questions are raised whenever the supply of money is not assumed to be controlled by the government. Gurley and Shaw's attempt to reconcile a pure inside-money world with a determinate price level rests on the introduction of portfolio balance considerations. They conclude that an economy has an explicit, well defined demand for real money as a function of real interest even when the money demanded is not a net asset. When money is a net asset it means that the consolidated balance sheet of the private sector contains money on the asset side. When money is not a net asset it means that all money assets in the private sector are offset by an equivalent amount of private liabilities.

Whether Gurley and Shaw adequately answer the questions they pose remains an open issue. But there isn't any doubt that the questions they pose materially altered the course of monetary theory. However, the sharp distinction they draw between inside and outside money is blurred by the uncertainty in the way people conceive of the assets and liabilities of the government. Only when people do not fully incorporate the discounted present value of all future taxes as a liability item in their portfolios, i.e., they have "bond illusion," can there be net "outside money" [2, 3]. In the case where the private sector includes as a liability the discounted present value of all future taxes and as an asset the discounted present value of all future expenditures, then all money is truly inside. In the inside-money case the consolidated balance sheet does not contain any money items. Aware of this, and to show some of the frustration associated with the implications of the logic, Gurley and Shaw write:

> If there are to be financial markets, somebody must escape the consolidation process. All financial assets and debt cancel out in complete consolidation, leaving nothing in the financial sphere to analyze [1, pp. 136-137].

Gurley and Shaw analyze the implications of distinctions between inside and outside money as net and gross money. The purpose of this chapter, by contrast, is to look at some of the means by which the supply of money may be outside the government's control. Since many of the same questions are raised in the analyses of private control over money as are raised by the existence of pure inside money, the issue of private control follows the tradition of the Gurley-Shaw work.

The remainder of this chapter will examine several ways in which nominal as well as real money balances can be endogenous. Specifically, the analysis will include the use of unutilized trade credit available, foreign deposits of domestic transactors outside domestic regulations, reserve movements via the balance of payments, and changes in the so-called "money multiplier" outside the monetary authority's direct control. Price flexibility is another way in which the real money supply is made endogenous, but it does not affect the endogeneity of nominal money. In the last section of the chapter, we will take a cursory look at some of the implications generated in a world where the real money supply is endogenous.

For the purposes of this chapter, I do not use an empirical definition of money, but appeal to the reader to consider what the appropriate money stock would be for domestic transactions purposes. To the extent that money is considered relevant in the context of the U.S. economy, it affects or is affected by U.S. transactions and U.S. GNP. Ultimately, the concern over money is a derived concern emanating entirely from our concern over domestic output.

I.   Non-U.S. Deposits as Money

One way in which private demanders of money can avoid the domestic monetary authority's power to regulate the relevant quantity of money is to hold their money balances outside the area of the authority's controls. Deposits held and used outside the country, even when used to facilitate domestic transactions, are practically, if not legally, beyond the control of the central bank.

These foreign-located money balances may be denominated in either foreign or domestic currency units. And when they are denominated in foreign currency units, they may or may not include forward contracts to cover potential exchange risks. In the same sense that foreign-located deposits of U.S. citizens may evade domestic monetary controls, domestic deposits owned by foreigners and used for foreign transactions also reduce the Federal Reserve's power.

By transferring U.S. deposits to and from U.S. transactors, foreigners are able to alter the relevant money supply for income-stabilization purposes, that is, the amount of money held by U.S. domestic transactors in domestic banks. When foreign transactors transfer their dollar balances to U.S. domestic transactors, the relevant domestic money supply has expanded even though the officially defined money supply has not changed. Precisely the reverse result occurs when foreign transactors increase their dollar deposits held in the United States. In this case, the money supply supporting U.S. transactions has declined, although the officially reported figure has not. Likewise, U.S. domestic transactors are able to evade some of the U.S. domestic monetary authority's powers to regulate the nominal quantity of money by holding money balances outside the control area. In sum, merely by shifting deposits between foreign and domestic transactors and between foreign and domestically located banks, the private sector is, in principle, able to resist some of the monetary authority's power to regulate the nominal quantity of money. The question remains as to how important these effects are.

While many potential sources for foreign-located U.S.-owned deposits exist, perhaps the single most important category is the euro-dollar market. This market is regionally diverse, extending to virtually every major country. Both assets and liabilities are denominated in U.S. dollars, which makes this market little different from U.S. dollar deposits.

Technically, it is really quite easy to expand the scale of the euro-dollar market. In fact, even if euro-dollar banks wish to keep reserves in the United States, the market is, for all intents and purposes, limitless in its expansion potential. The reserves of the euro-dollar system are more flexible than reserves backing U.S. demand deposits. To begin with, they are not held at the Federal Reserve. Rather, they are deposits held at ordinary private banks in the United States, basically to cover net dollar withdrawals. Secondly, the ratio of reserves in the euro-dollar market is determined chiefly by the business decisions of banks rather than the regulations of the U.S. monetary authority.

Suppose the euro-dollar market generally observes a reserve ratio of r.

Because U.S. Dollar deposits serve as euro-dollar reserves, a $1 increase in a domestic deposit held by a euro-dollar bank can support an amount of euro-dollar demand deposits equal to the reciprocal of the reserve ratio, $1/r$. A $1 shift in deposits in the U.S. to euro-dollar reserves will support $$(1/r - 1)$ in additional dollar balances. Since r is less than unity, a shift in deposits towards euro-dollar banks will lead to an increased capacity to support dollar deposits in total. Insofar as there are domestic balances not held as euro-dollar reserves, the expansion potential is not governmentally constrained.

From an individual bank's point of view, a $1 euro-dollar deposit requires less in the way of bank reserves held at the Federal Reserve than does a $1 domestic demand deposit. The difference in required reserve holdings is again dependent on the euro-dollar reserve ratio. Within the United States, each dollar's worth of deposits must be matched by some fraction of a dollar of reserves held in either vault cash or noninterest-bearing deposits at the Federal Reserve. To the extent that each dollar's deposit in the United States supports $1/r$ in euro-dollar deposits, the amount of U.S. bank reserves needed to support each euro-dollar deposit is substantially less than that required for a domestic dollar deposit. There is an additional pyramiding process. As long as all deposits are not located in the euro-dollar market, an increase in overall deposits can occur using the same amount of bank reserves held at the Federal Reserve.

. On the margin, one would expect euro-dollar money balances to be less convenient for domestic transactors than their domestic dollar counterpart. In order to entice domestic transactors to hold foreign deposits, the explicit net costs of holding foreign-located deposits has to be sufficiently smaller than those same costs for deposits located in the United States.

Thus, to offset the inconvenience of holding euro-dollars, explicit interest can be and is paid on these euro-dollar deposits.

The existence of the euro-dollar market and other non-U.S. deposit markets, as well as foreign holdings of U.S. balances, could well be a means of evading the control of U.S. monetary authorities. The existence of these markets may tend to weaken policy actions of the Federal Reserve and in the extreme could make the supply of money endogenous to the domestic economy.

In quantitative terms, it is difficult to know the potential (let alone the actual) magnitudes of the euro-dollar and other non-U.S. market effects. It is not the size of the euro-dollar and other markets that matters, but their responsiveness. Likewise in any quantitative evaluation, it is important to know which transactors are using the euro-dollar balances. The answers to these questions are not definitive, but we do have some crude estimates of the size and growth of euro-dollars and their relationship to U.S. deposits.

Euro-dollars, while available to U.S. transactors, also can be held for other purposes. However, to the extent that they support U.S. transactions, they cause the U.S. money supply to be more elastic.

In percentage terms, euro-dollar deposits have grown rapidly from the end of 1959 and, as of the end of 1973, were quite large in absolute volume.* While the data themselves are open to a great deal of question, the Bank for International Settlements' data suggest that euro-dollar deposits within a sample of eight European countries stood at roughly $90 billion at the end of 1972, up from about $1.5 billion at the end of 1959. This is an average growth rate of about 37 percent per annum. In relation to M_2 (demand plus time deposits and currency in circulation), these numbers represented about 0.7 percent of the size of the M_2 at the end of 1959 and over 17 percent of the M_2 by the end of 1972.

If euro-dollars are considered partial substitutes for domestic dollars, and there are shifts in the supply of domestic dollars, then we would expect non-U.S.-located money balances to move inversely with domestic money balances. An autonomous increase in U.S.-located balances should result in a fall in foreign-located balances and vice versa. In the limiting case where domestic and foreign deposits are perfect substitutes, U.S. government policies designed to increase the supply of domestic money balances should, *ceteris paribus,* result in a fully offsetting contraction of foreign-located balances. The money supply would be endogenous. Likewise, policy designed to contract the domestic money supply would lead to an expansion of foreign-located balances. In the graph shown in Fig. 1, the March to March annual percent change in the aggregate stock of euro-dollar deposits is plotted against time, as is the annual percent change in M_2 balances (with sign reversed). As is clear from the graph, there is a significant association between the growth rates of the two series.†

II.   The Balance of Payments and Money

The balance of payments has been noted as a source of leakage for domestic monetary policy. In recent years, the "monetary approach" to the balance of payments, which traces this leakage explicitly, has again gained favor among economists. Historically, the monetary approach is associated with David Hume, while the more recent association would be with Robert Mundell [3].

In the simplest form of the monetary approach, the overall balance of

---

*External dollar deposit liabilities of banks of eight European countries; Bank for International Settlements.

†Using simple correlations, the same results appear with either. M_1 or M_2. With M_2, the elasticity is -2.85 with a t score of 3, and with M_2, the elasticity is -3.15 with a t score of 4.6.

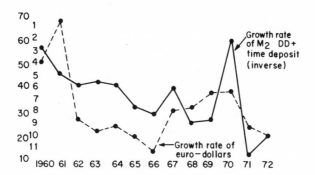

FIGURE 1. Graphed growth rates of M_2 (inverse) and euro-dollars versus time (March 1960-March 1972).

payments represents net flows of reserve money into or out of a country. The monetary approach to the balance of payments views money as an international commodity and not as a nontraded commodity. Under fixed exchange rates the domestic stock of money is in part (and, in the limiting case, fully) endogenous to an individual country. According to this view of the balance of payments, the domestic monetary authorities lose control over the stock of money since the actions of the U.S. Federal Reserve are reversed in part by net movements of money among the countries. Thus, under fixed rates, the Federal Reserve shares control of both the balance of payments and the domestic quantity of money. Discrepancies between demands and supplies of money will, if not accommodated in some other way, result in balance-of-payments flows.

It is easy to see how balance-of-payments surpluses or deficits could result in net changes in the domestic money supply. In order to have surpluses or deficits in the overall balance of payments, all that is required is that one or both of the governments in question agree to buy and sell the one currency for the other.

Imagine for the moment that an American borrows 100 German marks from a private German. The transaction is balanced since the American has increased his assets by holding a 100-D.M. demand deposit and simultaneously increased his liabilities by issuing debt to the amount of 100 D.M. Imagine that the American goes to the German central bank, the Bundesbank, and exchanges his D.M. demand deposit for a $35 U.S. demand deposit. The Bundesbank is obliged to execute the transaction since it has agreed to fix the exchange rate. The central bank then acquires the 100 D.M. demand deposit and gives up $35 worth of its holdings at the Federal Reserve in the U.S. The private American has acquired a $35 demand deposit in the U.S., which augments the domestic U.S. money supply. The Bundesbank has reduced its holdings of U.S. dollar demand deposits by $35, which does not affect the U.S. money supply. In Germany the reverse has occurred. Privately held German D.M. deposits have fallen by 100 D.M. In all, the domestic money supply of Germany has fallen by 100 D.M. and the U.S. money supply has risen by $35.

The results of this example are not materially altered whether the American sells goods or issues debt. The effect is the same whichever central bank carries out the intervention. In each and every case, the domestic money supply of the U.S. increases, while that of Germany falls. Money has literally been exported from Germany to the U.S. So long as at least one of the central banks fixes the exchange rate, this transfer of money will occur.

Under a flexible exchange-rate system, the above mechanism cannot operate. In general, for any one private person to increase his dollar balances, there must be one other private person willing to give up his balances. Only when the government specifically intervenes will total dollar balances held by the private sector increase.

As could be expected, the smaller the country in question, the less its central bank will be able to control its money supply. In the limiting case, shifts in the private domestic demand for and supply of money balances will elicit swings in the balance of payments in such a way as to offset the changes in excess demands without necessarily affecting prices. To the extent that the balance of payments is reserve movements, domestic money balance effects of movements in the balance of payments are magnified. The degree of magnification depends directly on the size of the domestic money multiplier, i.e., the ratio of total bank money to reserves.

On an "official settlements" basis, the U.S. has balance-of-payments data going back to 1960. Even for so few years, however, there have been large fluctuations in the balance of payments, as measured by this definition. In 1971, for example, the U.S. had a $30 billion deficit in the official settlements account. This alone represents more than a 10 percent change in U.S. M_1 (the total of demand deposits plus currency in circulation). Given the typical range of swings in monetary policy, these data demonstrate that even small swings in the balance of payments can materially alter the effects of Federal Reserve policies.

There has been empirical work on the monetary approach to the balance of payments. In general, the results support the view that the balance of payments responds swiftly and definitively to changes in the demand for or supply of money within a country. This responsiveness is illustrated in the graph of Fig. 2 in which a proxy for the U.S. excess demand for money is plotted against the balance of payments of the U.S. divided by GNP.

While not conclusive, the work to date does support the theory of a

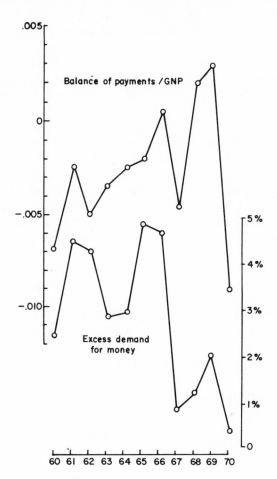

FIGURE 2. The balance of payments and the excess demand for money [4]. U.S. balance of payments (O.S.) as a ratio to GNP (left). Growth rate of GNP less growth rate of money supply (right).

relatively endogenous money supply by suggesting that, through changes in the balance of payments, the Federal Reserve may have less than complete control over the quantity of money.

III.   Private Actions and Bank Money

Even within a purely domestic framework, there are channels through which the money supply may be endogenous. Historically, the money multiplier was considered the principle conduit for any and all private effects to occur. Perhaps more effort has been expended on research on the money multiplier than on any other single source of endogeneity of the money supply. Clearly, private individuals and firms can potentially alter the money supply held in banks by shifting their deposits between demand and time deposits or even by withdrawing their deposits in the form of currency. A dollar of time deposits, demand deposits, or currency uses up different amounts of the reserves provided to the overall banking system. Given current law, each dollar of time deposits requires less in the way of reserves than a dollar of demand deposits which, in turn, uses less reserves than a dollar of currency. Therefore, shifts into and out of those three assets can affect the total available stock of money.

Similarly, banks can potentially alter the nominal stock of money. If, for example, banks choose to hold more reserves per dollar of either time or demand deposits, or if they choose to borrow reserves from the Federal Reserve, they can alter the money supply. In sum, it is conceivable that banks and other private economic agents can influence the nominal stock of bank money.

Putting the relationships a little more formally, we can define the bank money supply as equalling the entire reserve base times the money multiplier. Here the reserve base would include both borrowed and unborrowed reserves and would equal all deposits held by banks at the Federal Reserve plus the total amount of currency in circulation. In a highly simplified banking system, the M_1 money multiplier would be:

$$m = \frac{1 - t + c}{rd + r't + c}$$

where

t = ratio of time deposits to the sum of time and demand deposits
d = ratio of demand deposits to the sum of time and demand deposits, or $1 - t$
c = ratio of currency in circulation to the sum of time and demand deposits
r = ratio of desired or required reserves per dollar of demand deposits
r' = ratio of desired or required reserves per dollar of time deposits

The total reserve base would, in this instance, equal $R_u + R_b$, where the subscripts u and b indicate unborrowed and borrowed, respectively. Finally, the bank money supply as represented by M_1 would equal:

$$M_1 = (R_u + R_b) \left(\frac{1 - t + c}{rd + r't + c} \right)$$

Were we to use the M_2 concept of bank money, the numerator of the money multiplier would be $1 + c$ as opposed to $1 - t + c$. For the purposes of this discussion, I will stay with the M_1 version of bank money, recognizing, of course, that similar statements could be made with reference to M_2 or any other form of bank money.

For the purposes of trying to separate the effects on the money supply caused by the monetary authorities and those caused by the public, it is necessary to determine whether it is the Federal Reserve or a private entity that controls the relevant factor. In several cases it is by no means obvious whether the factor is controlled primarily by the monetary authority or the public.

Based on institutional considerations, it seems reasonable that the general public would be the primary controller of the time deposit/total deposit ratio, the currency in circulation/total deposit ratio, and the demand deposit/total deposit ratio. Commercial banks, it would appear, would be the primary agent operating on borrowed reserves; and would probably share evenly with the central bank control over reserves per dollar of both time and demand deposits. Perhaps in the short run, banks have primary responsibility over the reserve ratios, while over longer periods of time the monetary authority's power to regulate these reserve ratios increases. The monetary authority clearly has primary control over unborrowed reserves. Whether one agrees or disagrees with the designation of each of these categories, the Federal Reserve does not have complete hegemony over the bank money supply.

The time frame of the analysis is extremely important. Over short periods, underlying time trends tend to be dominated by short-term variations. Over longer periods, however, variables with more dominant trends tend to overpower stationary variables. In the specific case of M_1, over long periods of time, the monetary base has a significant trend, while the money multiplier tends to be far more stationary. Thus, one would expect that the monetary base would dominate long-run money supply changes more than it would short-term fluctuations.

The simplest question is whether the reserve base or the money multiplier dominates movements in the money supply. Both Brunner [5] and Cagan [6] found that over long periods of time the monetary base did dominate overall movements of the money supply. However, the money multiplier was a significant factor.

In an unpublished student paper at the University of Chicago, Marc Miles [7] carried the Brunner-Cagan partitions out on a monthly level. The period Miles covered was from January 1947 through June 1969. As would be expected, on a monthly basis the importance of the monetary base diminishes relative to the money multiplier. Miles also found that the relative importance of these factors varied substantially over different subperiods. In many of the subperiods, the base was found to be quite closely related to the money supply and not the multiplier. Miles contrasted the relative importance in determining the money stock of the ratio of currency to total deposits plus the ratio of demand deposits to total deposits with all other factors—r, r', R_u, and R_b. For the entire period he found that those variables assumed to be under the direct control of the Federal Reserve accounted for roughly the same percentage of the variation in the money supply as those assumed to be under the control of the public.

While the specifics of the Miles-Brunner-Cagan results are, for our purposes, not very important, what does matter is that the public can exercise control over the quantity of bank money. While this proposition is clearly true on a conceptual level, there is some evidence to suggest that it may also be true in practice.

Even if the Federal Reserve were to have complete control over the bank money supply, problems still exist in the implications for income stabilization purposes. In the first place, it is necessary to assume that the Federal Reserve behaves in such a way as to make the money supply exogenous. Even if the money supply were under the Federal Reserve's control in a technical sense, specific decision rules on the part of the Federal Reserve could make the money supply endogenous. If, for example, the Federal Reserve always increased the money supply whenever the demand for money rose (say, by using an interest-rate target), then the supply of money would be virtually endogenous.

Secondly, in order to have a controlled money supply, it is also necessary to have a relevantly defined money supply to control. Actions have to be geared to specific measured quantities. Therefore, the empirical counterpart to the appropriate monetary aggregate has to be reasonably precise. Even in the narrow domain of bank money aggregates, it is difficult to determine the appropriate measure of the money supply.

In an examination of the demand-deposit component of the bank money supply, Levin points out some of the conceptual as well as empirical problems [8]. He compares and contrasts four basic concepts of demand deposits, showing the conditions under which each would or could be the appropriate measure. The four major concepts include bank records, bank records minus uncollected funds, bank records minus bank float, and finally holder records. While Levin specifically discusses both the conceptual and empirical discrepancies among these four concepts, he makes it clear just how sensitive different empirical estimates of money are to the specific assumptions.

To the extent that relevant categories are not specifically controlled, the bank money supply tends to become more endogenous. This is true even if the relevant categories could be controlled but are, out of either ignorance or lack of concern, left uncontrolled.

IV. Price Flexibility and Money

In a classical economist's monetary framework, monetary policy would have no direct effect on aggregate economic activity. According to classical assumptions, the price level is perfectly flexible. This means that any change in the nominal quantity of money will be fully offset by changes in the price level. Therefore, the real quantity of money—the nominal stock of money divided by the price level—will remain unchanged. Real output in the classical system is, on the first level of analysis, independent of the nominal stock of money. Basically, price-level flexibility makes the real quantity of money strictly endogenous, even though the monetary authorities may control the nominal quantity of money. Again in a classical framework, only real factors can affect real magnitudes and only nominal factors can affect nominal magnitudes. Real and nominal elements of the economy are presumed independent of each other.

While few economists today would disagree with the proposition that over a long period of time price levels do tend to be flexible in both upward and downward directions, the essence of the theory that the money supply is controlled by the monetary authorities presumes, among other things, that price levels are less responsive to excess demand pressures in the short run. With rigid or sticky prices, changes in the nominal quantity of money may also result in changes in the real quantity of money.

However, to the extent that prices are flexible, the private sector may retain control over the real money stock by altering the prices it pays. Were the demand for money to increase, the price level would fall. This fall in the price level would result in an increase in the real stock of money even though the monetary authorities literally did nothing. If, on the other hand, the demand for money were to decrease, the price level would rise. This rise in the overall level of prices would elicit a fall in the real quantity of money. Again, all this could occur without any explicit action by the monetary authorities. In a world where prices were perfectly flexible, the Federal Reserve would have no control over the real money supply. In such a world, the sole function in controlling the nominal quantity of money would be to determine the price level.

From this analysis it is apparent that the Federal Reserve loses control over the real money supply to the extent that prices are flexible. The effect of price-level flexibility is precisely analogous to the situation in which the private sector controls the production of money. The only difference between price flexibility as a source of endogeneity and the other sources of endogeneity discussed in this chapter is that, for the other sources, the nominal as well as the real money supplies are endogenous. With price-level flexibility, only the real money supply need be endogenous.

If price levels are not perfectly flexible in the very short run, yet eventually become perfectly flexible, then the time frame of the analysis of the money supply is critically important. Vis-a-vis price-level flexibility, the more time that elapses, the more flexible most economists feel prices become. Therefore, the longer the period of analysis, the more endogenous the real money supply. These results are diametrically opposed to the conclusions reached in the previous section. In that section the Federal Reserve appears to have more control over the nominal quantity of bank money the longer the period of analysis.

Numerous empirical problems arise whenever an attempt is made to estimate the degree of price-level flexibility. The results hinge in part on the unit of time selected. More important, however, the selection of the appropriate measure of the price level borders on the impossible.

Existing price indices are woefully inadequate for this task. Many prices are list prices and only change when the price lists themselves change, even though the prices at which transactions have occurred have moved substantially. Several of the methods used to collect price data in and of themselves introduce a smoothing process in the data and thus distort the responsiveness of the measured price indices versus actual prices. In addition, some price data are imputed and not measured directly. To compound the problems even further, we don't know how the individual prices should be weighted in order to get the relevant price index for monetary income stabilization purposes.

However bad the data are, we can at least see in general terms the degree of price level flexibility as reflected in the principal indices. In the graph shown in Fig. 3, rates of growth of the nominal M_1 money supply are

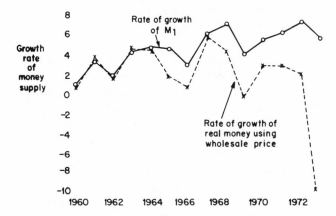

FIG. 3. Graphed rates of growth. Based on averages of last three months' data for year—seasonally adjusted year over year comparison. *Source*: Data Resources Inc., Data Bank.

plotted against rates of growth of the real M_1 money supply calculated using the
Wholesale Price Index. These same figures are presented in tabular form in Table
1 using the Consumer Price Index and the Gross National Product deflator,
respectively. These data support the proposition that the private sector does
have some control over the real stock of money.

V. Unutilized Trade Credit Available and Money

Still another means by which the private sector can evade the Federal Reserve's
power to control the nominal supply of money is through the trade credit and
other related markets. Firms and individuals can choose to substitute credit for
other forms of money [9]. The development of credit relationships can alter the
amount of other monies the private sector needs to hold to support a given level
of transactions. In other words, they can supplement their holdings of money
balances with unutilized trade credit available. Irrespective of the name one
gives it, the existence of a trade credit market could vitiate the control that the
monetary authority has over the relevant money supply.

TABLE 1

Rates of Growth

Year	M_1 (%)	M_1/CPI (%)	M_1/GNP deflator (%)
1960	0.4	−1.0	−1.4
61	2.8	2.1	1.7
62	1.4	0.1	0.3
63	3.9	2.5	2.5
64	4.4	3.1	2.7
65	4.3	2.5	2.5
1966	2.1	−0.8	−0.7
67	6.1	3.4	2.7
68	7.2	2.6	3.2
69	4.1	−1.6	−1.1
70	5.6	0.1	0.4
1971	6.3	2.9	2.8
72	7.5	4.1	4.2
73	5.9	−2.2	−1.1

Without going through elaborate examples, it is apparent that the un-utilized portion of the trade credit market acts as a privately determined sub-stitute for bank money. If we define trade credit as being the sum of trade debt plus unutilized trade credit available, then unutilized trade credit available represents the power to acquire goods and services by incurring debt. Trade debt, on the other hand, represents the net debt associated with prior acquisitions of goods and services. If demand deposits and currency (which like unutilized trade credit represent the power to acquire goods and services directly in the future) is defined as money, then by deduction unutilized trade credit can also be considered available money.

To the extent that an excess demand for money arises, the private sector could conceivably increase the amount of unutilized trade credit avail-able and thereby offset the incipient excess demand for money. The increase in the amount of unutilized trade credit available could result from an increase in the amount of credit available to transactors or an increase in the number of transactors with unutilized trade credit. Either way, the excess demand for money would be eliminated. By increasing the use of trade credit the private market can mesh receipt and outlay streams more precisely.

The exact opposite would occur were the money supply to increase. In this instance the use of credit would fall. Again, the trade credit market, specifically through unutilized trade credit available, has offset any tendency toward excess in the money market. All has occurred without any explicit actions by the Federal Reserve. To the extent that this market does function efficiently, the monetary authority's power to regulate the quantity of money has been evaded.

As with the other sources of endogeneity for the money supply, the empirical proposition takes on a great deal of importance. While it should be clear that unutilized trade credit available would be source of evasion of the Federal Reserve's power to control, we must also know just how important this source is. Very little empirical work has been done directly on this proposition, but to the extent it has, the findings seem to support the notion that unutilized trade credit available is a viable source of domestic money [9].

VII.   A Glimpse at the World of Endogenous Money

The last five sections of this chapter have outlined several situations in which actions on the part of the private sector could lead to a fully endogenous money supply, i.e., one that is outside the control of the domestic monetary authorities.

While this image of the world is clearly extreme, the extent to which the money supply is even partially endogenous causes interesting questions to be raised. If the nominal quantity of money is endogenous, what determines the price level? What factors enter the supply functions for money, and specifically under competitive conditions, what is the role played by the nominal rate of interest?

Few economists have tackled these questions directly. Under traditional assumptions, Friedman lays out his full system in his "Optimum Quantity of Money" essay. The importance of an exogenous money supply, the prohibition of interest payments to money, and sticky prices are fully investigated [10]. Gurley and Shaw, and more recently Black, developed some of the implications of the assumption that the nominal quantity of money is endogenous [11].

Under the usual equilibrium conditions in the money market, an endogenous money supply and a flexible price level leave us with one equation and at least two unknowns. Depending on one's perception of real output, it is conceivable that we could have one equation and three unknowns. However, even if we appeal to something akin to Say's law, we are still left with one equation and two unknowns. In order to obtain any sort of uniqueness in the price level and the nominal quantity of money, we have to appeal further to outside factors.

In an economy where all money earns interest, inflation no longer is a tax on the holdings of money. With increasing inflation, not only do the yields on bonds and other alternative assets rise, but so does the yield on nominal money balances. In such a world the sacrifice one makes in holding money balances is strictly the difference between the lending and the borrowing rates of interest. This differential is in no obvious way affected by the overall rate of price increase.

To date, Black is the only economist actually to appeal to some exogenous force to make the price level unique. He views prices as completely determined outside the money market. Thus, with an overall price level given and a predetermined demand for real money, the supply of money becomes determined. A unique solution results.

Irrespective of whether Black's view is valid, the important point to note is that he is one of the few economists to even consider these propositions since they were raised by Gurley and Shaw some 15 years ago. Given the conceptual ease with which we can conjure an endogenous money supply, and also given the lack of empirical refutation of these conceptual possibilities, far too little work has been done on the implications of models where money is endogenous. Fruitful research in the future will take us along the path of the Gurley and Shaw work and bring us to a point where we analyze money as an ordinary commodity.

ACKNOWLEDGMENTS

The author is indebted to Fischer Black, C. Robert Coates, R. David Ranson, and P. Kahn for helpful comments and suggestions.

REFERENCES

1. John G. Gurley and Edward S. Shaw, *Money in a Theory of Finance,* Brookings Institution, Washington, D.C., 1960.

2. Robert J. Barro, "Are Government Bonds Net Wealth?" *Journal of Political Economy,* Vol. 82, December 1974, pp. 1095-1117.

3. Jacob Frenkel, "Adjustment Mechanisms and the Monetary Approach to the Balance of Payments: A Doctrinal Perspective," *Scandinavian Journal of Economics* (Forthcoming).

4. Arthur B. Laffer, "Monetary Policy and the Balance of Payments," *Journal of Money, Credit, and Banking,* February 1972, p. 19.

5. Karl Brunner, "The Role of Money and Monetary Policy," *Federal Reserve Bank of St. Louis Review,* July 1968.

6. Phillip Cagan, *Determinants and Effects of Changes in the Stock of Money 1875-1960,* National Bureau of Economic Research, New York, 1965.

7. Marc Miles, "The Relative Effect of the Monetary Authorities and the Public on Monthly Changes in the Money Supply," University of Chicago, 1970.

8. Fred Levin, "An Examination of the Demand Deposit Component of the U.S. Money Supply," University of Chicago Thesis Prospectus, June 8, 1970.

9. Arthur B. Laffer, "Trade Credit and the Money Market," *Journal of Political Economy,* 78, 1970, pp. 239-267.

10. Milton Friedman, "The Optimum Quantity of Money," *The Optimum Quantity of Money and Other Essays,* Aldine, Chicago, 1969, Chap. 1.

11. Fischer Black, "Banking and Interest Rates in a World Without Money," *Journal of Bank Research,* 1, Autumn 1970, pp. 8-20.

Comment

DONALD J. MATHIESON

International Monetary Fund
Washington, D.C.

In many respects, I am the wrong person to comment on Arthur Laffer's chapter. I have always believed that to be a good discussant one should disagree with the author's fundamental hypothesis. Since I was born and raised in Chicago, however, I have believed since childhood that the real money supply is an endogenous variable.

In commenting on Laffer's chapter, I would first like to contrast his reasons for the endogenous nature of the real money supply with those of earlier writers. I want then to turn to the implications of his analysis for the feasibility of short-run stabilization policy. And finally, I am going to consider what Laffer's analysis implies for the present international monetary system.

Laffer stresses the fact that the real money supply is an endogenous variable, not only because of the presence of price-level flexibility but also because the nominal money supply may at times be endogenous. Theorists like Patinkin and Friedman have generally accepted the idea that the monetary authorities control the nominal money supply. In these theories, the real money supply is an endogenous variable because of price-level movements. Laffer's message is that the nominal money supply is also endogenous. This endogenity results from either changes in the nominal quantity due to such factors as balance-of-payments surpluses or deficits, or by substitution of different "monies" for the domestic currency. This substitution can take the form of the use of euro-dollars instead of U.S. dollars or the use of trade credit instead of deposits.

Although Laffer's analysis provides us with a menu of possible channels through which the real money supply becomes endogenous, it fails to explain the factors that would influence the private sector to pick one channel or another. If one were to consider a large, open economy with a fixed exchange rate and a substantial nontraded-goods sector that exists in a world of capital mobility, any number of routes could be used to endogenize the real money supply. And policymakers would probably not be indifferent to the routes selected by the private sector.

His analysis also carries the implicit message that monetary policy cannot be used for short-run stabilization purposes. In the long run, the monetary authorities do have substantial influence over some monetary variables—especially the trend value of the reserve base. In the short run, however, the private sector can offset many of the changes the central bank produces in the nominal money supply. In terms of the nominal-money supply function, we can summarize Laffer's position as follows. In the long run, the nominal-money supply function is dominated by official choices; but real money supply is endogenous through price-level movements. In the short run, however, the price level may be "sticky;" but the nominal money supply function is dominated by private-sector choices.

If this analysis is correct, however, it should not be taken as comforting for advocates, such as Friedman and Shaw, of the constant rate of growth in the money supply. If the monetary authorities try to follow a constant rate of growth rule for M_1, this may be quite difficult if the nominal money supply function is as unstable as Laffer believes. This seems to present somewhat of a dilemma for the monetary authorities. Do they simply generate a constant rate of growth in the reserve base and allow M_1 to jump around (if either the demand for money or the supply of money functions are unstable)? Or do they attempt to keep the rate of growth of M_1 constant, which may mean that the reserve-base growth rate may have to jump around. This does not seem to be an issue that is easy to resolve, for the above policies may imply fundamentally different growth paths for the economy.

Laffer's analysis also has some interesting implications for the problem of controlling the world money supply over the next 12 to 18 months. Let me define the world money supply as simply the total stock of dollars in private hands (a somewhat narrow definition). As I look at the current international monetary situation, it appears that a highly inflationary situation is about to develop—in fact, the short-run nominal money supply may be indeterminant. But let me explain why this appears to be true.

Recently, the U.S. federal reserve has been increasing the U.S. reserve base at a rate of 8 to 10 percent a year. While this is inflationary, it is not the source of my major concern. I am more concerned with the potential increase in the world reserve base that is about to be generated as foreign

central banks use their previously accumulated dollar balances to meet their
countries' higher anticipated oil import bills. Even though we now exist in a
world of "floating" exchange rates, a number of central banks (especially
those of Germany and Italy) have indicated that they will use their accumulated dollar balances to prevent any "adverse" movements in their exchange
rates. During the three-month period ending in February 1974, the
Economist reports that the official reserves of the EEC and Japan fell by
about $5.5 billion or 6.8 percent of total reserves. If this decline were to be
sustained for a full twelve months, this would mean a decline of $20 to 25
billion. Since central banks have been speculating on the future of the
official price of gold, these changes in official reserves have reflected movements in dollar assets.

To understand the inflationary impact of these official reserve movements, one must first recognize that most foreign central-bank dollar reserves
are held as U.S. treasury bills. At various times in the past few years, foreign
central banks have held one-third or more of all outstanding U.S. treasury
bills. To liquidate its dollar holdings, a foreign central bank simply sells its
treasury bills on the open market or allows them to mature and receives payment from the U.S. Treasury. If the U.S. Federal Reserve would do nothing
while this conversion was taking place, the conversion need not by itself
be inflationary. If foreign central banks are going to liquidate $20 to 25
billion of their treasury bill holdings, however, this would mean a substantial
rise in treasury bill rates. My fear is that the Federal Reserve will not be
willing to tolerate treasury bill rates of 15 to 20 percent. If the Fed
therefore buys these treasury bills, then this will involve an open market
purchase of $20 to 25 billion. Given a U.S. reserve base of about $100
billion, we could therefore see a 20 to 25 percent increase in the reserve base
of the world money supply.

Even if the Federal Reserve does not purchase all $20 to 25 billion of
the treasury bills, there is another factor at work that will also serve to increase the world money supply. The world supply of privately held dollars
can be envisioned as having three main components. The base of this world
money supply is the U.S. stock of high-powered money. Built on this base
are the deposits in U.S. commercial banks. But while these dollar deposits
are low-powered money in the United States, they also can serve as the reserve
base (or stock of high-powered money) for the euro-dollar market. As the
Arabs receive payment for their oil in dollars, some will be used to purchase
goods, some to purchase short- and long-term financial assets, and some will
be held as euro-dollar deposits. Even if we assume that the euro-dollar
multiplier is low (around 1), there could be a considerable expansion in the
euro-dollar market. And these flows will also raise the size of the euro-
dollar multiplier by closing some of the leakages from the system.

This growth in the world "dollar" supply will not only be inflationary by itself, but it also could generate unforseen movements in exchange rates. How will this excess stock of real money be worked off? What sorts of trade and capital flows will be generated? Until we know the answer to these questions, we really cannot project the nature of the exchange rate and price-level movements that will take place.

General Discussion

Jacob Frenkel raised two issues. First, he wondered whether or not one should worry excessively about which channels the private sector will use to bring about an endogenous real-money supply. He contrasted what he called the "black box" and "channels" approaches to monetary theory. In certain cases, one need not worry excessively about the channels used to produce a result, when only the end result itself matters. Second, he argued that endogenity is just a fact of life; and we must be concerned with identifying just what variables the monetary authorities can control.

In responding to Frenkel's comments, Laffer raised the point that one could consider the case of completely endogenous money—the free banking case. This illustrates one basic difference between Friedman and Shaw. In Friedman's optimal monetary system, there would be 100% reserve ratios for banks; whereas in Shaw's optimal system, there would be free banking with no required reserve ratios.

Richard Stillson pointed out that Karl Brunner's empirical work suggests that while the nominal money supply is endogenous to some degree, it is still controllable by the monetary authorities.

Chapter 12

International Financial Integration: Long-Run Policy Implications

MICHAEL G. PORTER

Department of Economics
Australian National University
Canberra, Australia

I. Background and Brief Summary

The monetary theory of open economies has, with notable recent exceptions [1, 2; chapter 7 of Ref. 3 offers a clear analysis of the context of development], been based on the assumption of fixed prices and conducted in terms of nominal magnitudes such as nominal money balances, nominal interest rates, and nominal exchange rates. The key analytical issues have been the relative efficacy of monetary and fiscal policies in achieving joint internal and external balance under alternative exchange-rate policies. The inferences drawn from these comparative-static models had been generally useful in earlier years, thanks partly to the absence of widespread inflation in much of the industrial world [4-6]. In other words, the fixed-price assumption was a reasonable simplification.

However, it is the burden borne by the analysis which follows that no real choice of exchange rate *and* monetary policy exists; that in fact for all but the short run, choice of a monetary policy allows no degree of freedom for exchange-rate policy. This basic point becomes clear when exchange and monetary policies are expressed in the appropriate dimensions. These considerations, plus the empirical facts of the persistent yet variable nature of

At the time this chapter was presented, the author was a member of the Priorities Review Staff of the Australian Government, on leave from the Australian National University. The views expressed in this chapter are those of the author and not necessarily of his respective employers. The author's present address is: Department of Economics, Monash University, Clayton, Australia.

the recent worldwide inflation, and the resulting variability of the relative prices of national currencies, suggest a need for setting theory and policy discussions in terms of real balances, real interest rates, and rates of change of (effective) exchange rates.

Despite the overwhelming academic rejection of nominal monetary theory [7, 8, 9] and its misleading implications for setting monetary policy in terms of nominal interest rates, we still find ourselves in a world in which many monetary authorites are attempting to peg nominal interest and exchange rates despite variable expectations regarding inflation. Similarly, they are continuing to set nominal exchange rates against a particular currency, despite variability in effective exchange rates. The consequences of these misplaced interventions are often misunderstood. The most important misunderstanding would appear to be the self-destructive nature of "fixed price" intervention; with authorities often being trapped into buying (selling) ever rising volumes of bonds or foreign exchange whenever the interest rate or foreign currency price is set too low (high). Unless the authorities are blessed with perfect foresight, fixed-price intervention is fundamentally unstable and in current circumstances, tends both to aggravate inflation and destabilize reserves. In the case of nominal interest rates that are artificially low, the authorities end up buying bonds from a private sector convinced that yields will rise. Thus the money supply expands and inflation is aggravated.

Another, less discussed misunderstanding is of the massive income redistribution resulting from fixed-price interventions in money and exchange markets. The magnitudes involved in these distortions at times of inflation make tax progression and welfare intervention look trifling in their effects on income redistribution.

A lesson of real monetary theory, to be set out below, which I first came to fully appreciate under the tutelage of Edward Shaw, would seem to be that the authorities are continually attempting to *over-determine* the system. In an integrated world economy there is no scope in the long, or medium, run for independently controlling the (rate of change of the) exchange rate, the interest rate, and the (rate of change of the) money supply. Yet is is precisely these attempts to regulate two or three of these factors independently which, it can be argued, are the root cause of many of our current disturbances in the world economy. Illusions of independent assignment of monetary instruments are a predictable outgrowth of direct controls on foreign and domestic borrowing, but the reality of such "price suppression" is eventually manifested in the massive and inequitable evasion of controls.

Section II of the chapter introduces the general issues by emphasizing the relevance, in the long run, of the monetary approach to balance-of-payments theory. This approach stresses the tendency for independent monetary policies to be frustrated by induced changes in the *overall* balance of payments. The monetary approach also helps to explain the transmission of inflation between countries, offers a world quantity theory of money, and leads to a more general theory of the demand for reserves.

In order to clarify the linkages between exchange rate, interest rate, and other monetary policies in the long run, a simple neoclassical monetary framework is developed in Section III. The object here is to present a theoretical analysis of the long-run implications of international financial integration by focusing particular attention on what I call "the overdetermination problem." The authorities may only exercise independent control over one of the following: the exchange rate, the money supply, or the interest rate. Once the time path of this control is set, the equilibrium values of the other "instruments" are also determined, along with the associated rate of change of prices. Thus, the authorities must choose among an exchange-rate, an interest-rate, and a money-supply policy, despite the impossibility, over time, of controlling more than one of these independently. The analysis in Section III then includes some implications of alternative strategies regarding the exchange-rate and monetary policy.

The chapter is concluded, in Section IV, by extending the discussion to cover the "real balance effect" as applied to national behavior, and this leads naturally to a discussion of the transmission of world inflation. The final conclusion includes some brief comments on the implications of the analysis for international monetary reform.

II. The Monetary Approach to Long-Run Balance-of-Payments Theory

This theory has been summarized with typical clarity by Harry Johnson [1] so that only the bare essentials need be noted here. Following the Scottish philosopher, David Hume, it is argued that the balance of payments is ultimately a monetary phenomenon reflecting the interplay of domestic and foreign *money* markets.

An open economy with a fixed exchange rate may adjust its stock of real money balances by running a balance-of-payments surplus or deficit, since prices will tend to be set externally. In the case of David Hume's specie-flow mechanism, an excess demand for money would be satisfied by a trade surplus (reflecting an excess supply of goods) in the form of specie, with this specie then serving as national money. With the emergence of gold exchange and dollar standards the same process is observed, but it is complicated by fractional reserve banking, exchange intervention, and other such practices. With a *flexible* exchange rate, real balances are also adjusted in an open economy by independent changes in the *price* level facilitated by exchange-rate movements.

The monetary model, as developed by Johnson, following earlier work of Mundell, Polak, and others, does not segregate the balance of payments into current and capital accounts, and assumes a fixed exchange rate, one world price level, and a common interest rate. The driving force of the model is the assumed stability of national demand for money functions, which have as arguments the level of nominal national income and the level of nominal deposit and other interest rates. The authorities control the domestic part of the monetary base, but the remainder is the result of balance-of-payments flows, and thus the nominal money supply is endogenous.

Johnson [1, p. 219] obtains a solution that "indicates that a country's reserves will grow faster the lower its initial reserve ratio, the faster the growth of total world reserves, the higher its income elasticity of demand for money and its real growth rate relative to other countries, and the lower its international reserve ratio and rate of domestic credit expansion relative to other countries." A feature of the model is that in the long run, monetary policy is totally offset in its effect on the money supply by induced movements in the balance of payments.

The model is indifferent to whether equilibrium in national money markets is restored via current or capital accounts, since it aggregates the two and analyzes the economy in terms of goods and money markets. An extension of the model to allow capital movements [2] yields similar results, i.e., with fixed rates monetary policy is completely offset in the long run, with the extent of the offset in the short run depending on the precise degree of capital market integration. The Dornbusch model is supported by evidence presented with the Kouri and Porter short-term model [10, 11], which has been applied to a variety of industrial countries. Other theoretical models offering variations on this theme are Mussa [12], Dornbusch and Swoboda [13], Swoboda [14], Mundell [4], and Laffer [15]. Parkin [16] develops a two-good model in the same tradition, but focuses on a quite different question, namely the paradox that inflation rates differ sharply across countries that share fixed exchange rates.

A further extension of the monetary model under perfect integration is to allow divergent nominal interest rates and price levels in the different countries. So long as price changes are correctly anticipated, then (the term structure of) interest rates will diverge across countries to reflect the anticipated divergences in prices and the associated expected time paths of the exchange rates.

A country expected to pursue a relatively expansionary monetary policy will exhibit a higher expected rate of inflation, a higher interest rate, and an associated depreciating value of the domestic currency. Countries expected to inflate at a consistently higher rate will have nominal yield *curves* that are on a higher plateau, and the compounded yield differential for a particular maturity will reflect the expected international differential in inflation rates over that time horizon. But real interest rates, the relative price of domestic and foreign goods (measured in either currency) will, in the neoclassical economy, remain unchanged. This situation is readily analyzed in terms of the theory of the term structure of exchange-rate expectations set out in [17], an extension of interest parity theory;

$$(1 + R_n^X)^n K_{t+n}^E = (1 + R_n^W)^n K_t$$

where R_n^X, R_n^W are domestic and foreign yields on n period bonds; K_{t+n}^E and K_t are the expected future exchange rate and current rate, respectively. The assumption is simply that a dollar must offer equal yields whether invested for n periods in X or W.

The exchange rate and price level are assumed, in Fig. 1a, to change symmetrically and exponentially (see left-hand side) and the associated term structure of international interest rate ratios is one of constancy (right-hand side).

In Fig. 1b the assumption is of a price level that is expected to converge

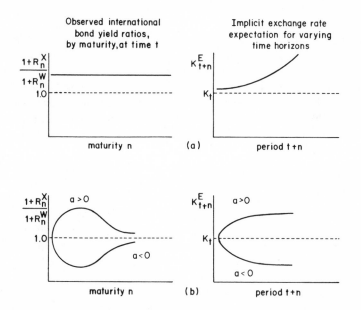

FIGURE 1. (a) Constant expected rate of change of exchange rate (i.e., steady depreciation or appreciation); (b) expected asymptotic converge to a new value of the exchange rate. It is assumed that $n > 1$, where the unit is the shortest quoted maturity. The letter e represents the base of natural logarithms.

(asymptotically) to a stable value relative to the foreign price level. In this case the domestic yield curve displays a "humped" shape relative to foreign yield curves. Again, real interest rates and effective exchange rates are unchanged, and are independent of the nominal magnitudes (rate of change of money, prices, and the exchange rate).

The examples in Fig. 1 illustrate how the simplifying assumptions of the monetary model of the balance of payments can be relaxed so as to incorporate more detail of behavior without changing the essence of the analysis.

III.   A Neoclassical Sketch of a Small, Open Economy

Recent economic events are suggestive of a strong trend toward real and financial integration. The theoretical section that follows draws some secular implications of these trends and focuses on *long-run* equilibrium real values of the key variables in a small, open economy. Thus analysis is cast in terms of real money balances, real foreign and domestic yields, real deposit rates, and real financial wealth. It can be shown that the equilibrium set of real values allows only one degree of freedom in nominal magnitudes. Analysis of the long-run properties of this fictitious economy is suggestive of how the authorities may tend to over-determine the system, thereby generating disequilibrium in the world economy. In the long run the authorities can be shown to exercise independent influence over the equilibrium level of nominal interest rates *or* the rate of change of the nominal money supply *or* the rate of change of the exchange rate. Given this choice and the foreign interest and inflation rates, the authorities face an associated equilibrium rate of change of domestic prices and the corresponding equilibrium values of the other nominal "instruments." Once this instrument has been chosen, then the goal of price stability will imply unique values for this instrument at each point in time.

The key to the argument is extremely simple; that in the long run money is neutral in open economies in the Patinkin [8] sense, and does not affect real magnitudes so long as nominal bond and deposit rates are flexible and the price level and the exchange rate are free to adjust. Constraining more than one of these prices will overdetermine the system and so generate disequilibrium. In particular, choice of fixed exchange rates and an independent monetary (or interest-rate) policy will generate disequilibrium in goods, money, and bond markets.

We make numerous abstractions in order to focus on the points of central importance. In particular we follow Patinkin and ignore the labor market and assume that real physical output is exogenously determined. We abstract from population growth and technical progress, and so assume steady per capita income. The focus is on monetary, price, and exchange-rate strategies in a fully employed economy. Actual and expected changes in the price level are assumed to be equal and the same assumption is applied to the exchange rate. The full system is specified in Table 1. In Table 1, dot over a variable indicates the expected domestic rate of inflation. Expected and actual changes are assumed to be equal, i.e., there are no systematic forecast errors.[1]

Partial derivatives are assumed to be as follows:

$$C_1 > 0, \ C_2 < 0, \ C_3 < 0, \ C_4 < 0, \ C_5 > 0, \ C_6 < 0$$

$$L_1 > 0, \ L_2 < 0, \ L_3 < 0, \ L_4 > 0, \ L_5 > 0, \ L_6 < 0$$

$$F_1 > 0, \ F_2 < 0, \ F_3 > 0, \ F_4 < 0, \ F_5 > 0, \ F_6 > 0$$

TABLE 1

Excess Demand Functions

1. Goods

$$C\left(\frac{W}{P}, \ i - \dot{P}, \ i_f + \dot{K} - \dot{P}, \ d - \dot{P}, \ Y, \ \frac{P}{KP_f}\right) - Y = E$$

2. Money

$$L\left(\frac{W}{P}, \ i - \dot{P}, \ i_f + \dot{K} - \dot{P}, \ d - \dot{P}, \ Y, \ \frac{P}{KP_f}\right) - \frac{M}{P} = 0$$

3. Net holdings of foreign bonds

$$F\left(\frac{W}{P}, \ i - \dot{P}, \ i_f + \dot{K} - \dot{P}, \ d - \dot{P}, \ Y, \ \frac{P}{KP_f}\right) - \frac{KB}{i_f P} = 0$$

Identities

4. Money supply $M = D - \dfrac{KB}{i_f} - \displaystyle\int_0^T E\, dt$

5. Real financial wealth $\dfrac{W}{P} = \dfrac{M}{P} + \dfrac{KB}{i_f P_f}$

where

E	=	net imports
W	=	financial wealth
P	=	domestic price level
i	=	domestic nominal consol yield
i_f	=	foreign nominal consol yield
K	=	domestic price of foreign currency
d	=	nominal deposit rate on money balances
Y	=	real income
M	=	nominal money supply
B	=	initial consol income flow (measured in foreign currency)
D	=	domestic credit component of money supply.

where the subscript refers to the ordering of the arguments in the demand functions. Thus C_5 is equal to $\partial E/\partial Y$, the partial derivative of the demand for net imports with respect to a change in real income.

The excess demand for (composite) goods, identically equal to net imports, is a function of real financial wealth W/P, the domestic real rate of interest $i - \dot{P}$; the foreign real rate of interest $i_f + \dot{K} - \dot{P}$ (note we adjust the foreign yield for expected appreciation of foreign currency, and depreciation of domestic currency, as measured by $\dot{K}$); the real deposit rate $d - \dot{P}$; real income Y; and the relative price of domestic and foreign goods P/KP_f. We abstract from the income effects of interest payments on foreign assets.

The excess demand for real money balances is a function of the same set of real values, as is the excess demand for foreign bonds. For simplicity, foreigners are assumed to abstain from holding domestic bonds, but the analysis could readily be extended to cover this case, with no new consequences. [2] The model may be reduced to two dimensions, thereby facilitating diagrammatic analysis, by assuming that in equilibrium there will be international arbitrage between both domestic and foreign bonds and goods at all points in time such that:

Bond arbitrage $\qquad i_f + \dot{K} = i \qquad\qquad$ (1)

and

Goods arbitrage $\qquad \dot{P} = \dot{P}_f + \dot{K} \qquad\qquad$ (2)

These two conditions imply that real interest rates are equalized across countries over time regardless of whether they are evaluated in domestic or foreign goods:

$$i - \dot{P} = i_f - \dot{P}_f = i_f + \dot{K} - \dot{P}$$

The loci of points of zero excess demand in the goods, money, and bond markets (CC, LL, and FF) are graphed in Fig. 2, with the arrows indicating the direct effect of excess demand on the relevant price or yield.

Fixing the exchange rate forces all relative price adjustment to be via domestic prices. Thus the economy adjusts to the exchange rate, and not vice versa. A further implication of the adjustment process implied in the model is that if K is flexible, but monetary expansion excessive, than adjustment *will* be via domestic inflation.

CC is the locus of points of zero excess demand for goods; thus a rise in real balances must, in equlibrium, be offset by a rise in the real rate of interest. LL is the locus of points of zero excess demand for money and hence a rise in the real interest rate must be offset by a fall in M/P if equilibrium is to be maintained. Thus CC slopes upward to the right, and LL to the left. FF is

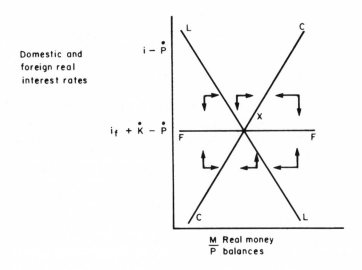

Domestic and
foreign real
interest rates

$i - \dot{P}$

$i_f + \dot{K} - \dot{P}$

$\frac{M}{P}$ Real money
balances

FIGURE 2

the locus of points of bond market equilibrium and the assumption of perfect
capital mobility implies a horizontal function at the world real rate of interest.

Points to the right of *CC* imply an excess demand for goods and hence
both a falling nominal money supply (trade deficit) and rising prices and,
thereby, a tendency for real balances to fall. To the left of *CC* real money
balances are rising due to the trade surplus caused by the excess supply of
goods. This relationship between excess demand in the goods market and the
endogenous adjustment of real money balances in an open economy is crucial
to understanding the adjustment process in the long run.

Below (above) *FF* nominal yields will be bid up (down) to obtain the
equilibrium real yield, and the speed of adjustment in the foreign bond market
is assumed to be such that these yield effects will dominate any contrary
effects due to an excess demand for or supply of money. The economy can
thus be shown to have a unique and stable real equilibrium at X, but this
allows only *one* degree of freedom in the assignment of $\dot{M}$, $\dot{P}$, $\dot{K}$, or i.

A simple way of summarizing the above is as follows: our arbitrage
conditions in the bond and commodity markets conditions 1 and 2, combine
with the existence of a stable stock of real balances M/P, to provide three
conditions in four unknowns, $\dot{M}$, $\dot{P}$, $\dot{K}$, and i, as follows:

$$i = i_f + \dot{K}$$
$$\dot{P} = \dot{P}_f + \dot{K}$$
$$\dot{M} = \dot{P}$$

The externally determined values are i_f and $\dot{P}_f$, and hence the world real rate of interest is the ultimate real constraint on the domestic economy.

A. Policy Implications

In order to understand the above conclusions, consider the following conceptual experiment undertaken in an economy that starts from equilibrium: The domestic authorities double the rate of expansion of the money supply, allowing interest rates, prices, and the exchange rate to freely adjust. It can readily be shown that the equilibrium real values of *all* parameters will be unchanged so long as:

1. The resulting inflation is correctly anticipated.

2. The deposit and nominal bond rates are allowed to rise by the increased rate of inflation.

3. The rate of depreciation of the currency increases by the same amount.

The solution to the above real system thus has a degree of freedom in nominal magnitudes such that the authorities may independently set equilibrium values to *one* of the following:

$\dot{K}$ = rate of change of the exchange rate

i = nominal bond rate (and associated deposit rate)

$\dot{M}$ = rate of change of the money supply

Once the choice has been made the *equilibrium* values of the other two are determined along with the equilibrium rate of change of the domestic price level. A qualification, however, is that a rise in the value M, i, and K, that is *not* matched by a rise in the nominal deposit rate d will reduce the equilibrium stock of real balances and increase the equilibrium stock of real foreign claims and cause minor changes in net exports to allow for the changed flow of real income from foreign bonds.

B. Exchange-rate Policy

The implications of this long-run model are that if the authorities choose a fixed exchange regime, $\dot{K} = 0$, in face, say, of foreign inflation (deflation), then we can readily solve for the implied equilibrium values of the other variables and "instruments." Thus if $\dot{K} = 0$, then

$$\dot{P} = \dot{P}_f \qquad \text{[we inflate (or deflate) with the rest of the world]}$$
$$\dot{M} = \dot{P} \qquad \text{[our money supply grows with world inflation]}$$
$$i = i_f \qquad \text{[we share common nominal and real interest rates]}$$

In other words, a fixed exchange-rate policy constrains the monetary growth, interest, and inflation rates to values set in the outside world. The transmission process involves transitory surpluses on current and capital accounts, which in turn generate the equilibrating rate of expansion of the money supply such that prices increase at a rate sufficient to restore full equilibrium in the balance of payments.

C.   Price Policy

If we choose price stability, $\dot{P} = 0$, then our (per capita) monetary policy in equilibrium requires $\dot{M} = 0$. The other equilibrium conditions then follow from the assumed exchange, interest, and monetary flexibility, that is,

$$\dot{K} = -P_f \qquad \text{[we appreciate (depreciate) with the world inflation (deflation)]}$$
$$i = i_f + \dot{K} \qquad \text{[we maintain interest rates that diverge from foreign rates by the expected rate of appreciation or depreciation]}$$

Thus, in general, price stability requires floating exchange rates and market-determined interest rates, that fall *below* (above) world levels by the rate of appreciation (depreciation) of the currency.

D.   Monetary Policy

If we choose a particular rate of expansion of the (per capita) money supply, $M = g_m$, then in the long run

$$\dot{P} = g_M \qquad \text{[prices expand at the same rate]}$$
$$\dot{K} = g_M - \dot{P}_f \qquad \text{[we depreciate at a rate equal to the difference between domestic and foreign inflation rates]}$$
$$i = i_f + \dot{K} \qquad \text{[our interest rate exceeds the world level by the rate at which our currency depreciates]}$$

The monetary policy could, or should, perhaps be chosen in order to achieve the objectives of the previous policy of stable prices.

E. Interest-rate Policy

If the authorities choose to peg interest rates (that is, $i = i*$) while allowing
free capital inflow, with M and P adjusting, then this predetermines the
equilibrium values of the rest of the system. Thus we obtain:

$$\dot{K} = i* - i_f \qquad \text{[we eventually depreciate at the excess of our interest rate over the foreign rate]}$$

$$\dot{P} = \dot{P}_f + \dot{K} \qquad \text{[we eventually inflate by the sum of foreign inflation and exchange depreciation]}$$

$$\dot{M} = \dot{P} \qquad \text{[our money balances expand with prices]}$$

The transmission process in this case may be drawn out by the authorities trying to sterilize the monetary consequences of balance-of-payments
surpluses. Thus high interest rates may *initially* dampen inflation if inflow is
sterilized. However, experience suggests that eventually the gain in reserves
that follows aggressive independent interest-rate policy, precipitates specu-
lative inflow that swamps earlier sterilization attempts. German and
Australian experiences in 1970-72 are evidence for this.

The above analysis is highly oversimplified, and ignores the many and
varied factors that may explain the nature of the adjustment process. Factors
such as union bargaining power, price controls, temporary unemployment, and
errors in expectations will undoubtedly be important in explaining inflation
in the short run. The burden of the above is that monetary forces will
ultimately manifest themselves in he various markets so that the world real
rate of interest is transmitted to the domestic economy, with the world rate
of inflation manifesting itself either in domestic inflation or exchange-rate
appreciation.

IV. Real Reserves, the Transmission of Inflation, and
Monetary Reform

It is a simple extension of the monetary theory of the balance of payments
to argue that countries behave much like individuals and aim to hold real
reserves in some fairly stable relationship to the volume of transactions in
international trade. With fixed exchange rates, the precise magnitude of real
reserves at any level of trade will be a function of the opportunity cost of
holding money in foreign balances relative to the direct rate of return on
these balances. A rise in inflation will not of its own tend to cause a substitution by countries away from reserve holdings unless the interest rate

earned on reserves is sticky, which does not appear to be the case; witness the extreme market sensitivity of euro-dollar rates.

Over the long run, there has been a strong tendency for the velocity of circulation of official international money holdings to increase. This trend reflects the increasing integration of international capital markets as domestic and foreign moneys have become better substitutes, and as private holdings are substituted for official reserves, enabling governments to economize on reserve holdings.[2]

Increased acceptance of exchange rate flexibility also reduces the need for official reserve holdings, since there is no need to support the rate. But private firms and individuals will aim to hold foreign balances, probably aggregating to larger amounts, given the economies of scale in holdings of transactions balances.

There is evidence, set out in the table below, of a secular rise in the velocity of international circulation, but this trend has been reversed in the last for years despite the increased exchange rate flexibility. Broadly the reason for this would appear to be the excessive injections of international liquidity coming through massive U.S. balance-of-payments deficits and broad access to euro-dollar borrowings, with a further factor being some issue of SDRs by the IMF. Thus, if we can assume that a velocity of around 3 is "reasonable" in light of earlier evidence and continued exchange rate rigidity, then the existing velocity in mid-1973 of about 1.74 is indicative of a chronic excess supply of real reserves in the world economy. Given the lags in transmission of excess reserves to net imports, often thought to be around two years, the data revealed in Table 2 would seem to suggest the presence of the basis for yet further substantial inflation generated from excessive real international reserves. It is unlikely that a velocity of 1.74 is sustainable, i.e., that countries really need to maintain reserves adequate to finance eight months of imports. This is particularly true given the ready access to borrowing in the increasingly efficient international capital market.

The foregoing argues strongly for continuance of the existing inflationary pressures originating from the excessive level of real reserves in relation to transactions, and if so will constitute evidence of the broad relevance of the quantity theory approach to the determination of domestic and world inflation.

A. Monetary Reform

We also observe, as an outcome of this recent experience, that a large amount of energy is being expanded on international reform of the exchange regime and the so-called "adjustment process." Unfortunately, what is not well

TABLE 2

World International Reserves, Trade, and Velocity

	Reserves (U.S. $ billion) (1)	Imports (U.S. $ billion) (2)	Velocity[b]
1950	49.0	58.2	1.19
1955	54.0	88.6	1.64
1960	60.4	119.4	1.97
1966	72.6	192.5	2.65
1967	74.3	202.6	2.73
1968	77.4	225.4	2.91
1969	78.3	257.1	3.28
1970	95.1	294.6	3.10
1971	140.3	329.0	2.34
1972	192.0	385.0	2.01
1973 (June)	292.3	508.0	1.74

[a] Adjusted for market valuation of official gold holdings, 1969-72. Market values for gold were:

	U.S. $
December 1969	35.20
December 1970	37.38
December 1971	43.63
December 1972	64.90
June 1973	123.25

[b] $\dfrac{\text{Col. 2}}{\text{Col. 1}}$

Source: IFS 1972 Supplement.

understood is that a country's choice of an exchange-rate strategy implies at the same time a choice for its monetary strategy. Thus the choice of a set of fixed rates is, over the long run, a choice that implies acceptance of common rates of monetary expansion, with the rate itself reflecting the aggregate outcome of national monetary increases. But there is no simple relationship between world monetary expansion and its components, given the uneven substitutability of national moneys. Since there was no agreement on rates of monetary expansion within the Committee of Twenty, or any other groups, agreement on exchange-rate "fixity" amounted to little more than misplaced wishful thinking. Fixed relative prices of various currencies with no control on relative money supplies is doomed to the fate of all price-fixing arrangements that ignore quantities.

Again we find that the central proposition advanced in the earlier theoretical section of the chapter appears to hold true; that in the long run the authorities may only exercise independent control of the money supply *or* the exchange rate, unless they wish to suppress the workings of the market economy.

V.   Concluding Remarks

The chapter began with a review of the long-run theory of the balance of payments and noted the contribution of monetary theory in this area. Following, a theory of the long-run relationships between interest rates, the time path of the money supply, the exchange rate, and the price level was developed. The key argument was that authorities tend to overdetermine the system by choosing to set more than one of these values independently, thereby generating disequilibrium in the domestic and world economies. Exchange-rate strategies imply particular monetary policies and vice versa, and thus governments can only choose both in a very short-run sense. This line of reasoning is implicitly critical of those, including official institutions, who would urge countries and groups of countries to adopt a pattern of fixed exchange rates independently of a monetary strategy that would be broadly compatible. Trying to set both the price of international money and the quantity of domestic money independently is really rather like telling the left leg to stay put while inviting the right leg to go wherever it sees fit.

Finally, it is to be stressed that the analysis is of a fictional economy in which transactions are costless, factors mobile, etc., whereas in fact the world economy is otherwise. The question is whether or not the implications of this simplified analysis offer reliable insights rather than whether or not the world is a frictionless machine.[4]

ACKNOWLEDGMENTS

I would like to thank Ken Mahar and Richard Snape for their comments.

NOTES

1. Clearly, one way in which monetary policy may have real, but perhaps undesired, effects is when actual and anticipated price changes differ.

2. More formally, by Walras' law we may eliminate one market (say bonds) and analyze the equilibrium properties of the system in terms of goods

and money markets, with real balances and real interest rates being the endogenous variables.

3. Most studies of the demand for international reserves (e.g., Clark [19]) omit the impact of increasing financial integration on the need for reserves.

4. See ref. 18 for analysis of money and barter with transactions costs. In the limiting case this model obtains the conventional result of money being neutral in the sense of Patinkin [8].

REFERENCES

1. H. G. Johnson, "The Monetary Approach to Balance of Payments Theory," in *International Trade and Money*, M. B. Connolly and A. K. Swoboda (eds.), University of Toronto Press, Toronto, 1973, pp. 206-224.

2. R. Dornbusch, "A Portfolio Balance Model of Macroeconomic Policies in the Open Economy." Paper presented to the Fourth Konstanzer Seminar on Monetary Theory and Monetary Policy, Konstanz, W. Germany, June 1973.

3. Edward S. Shaw, *Financial Deepening in Economic Development,* Oxford, London, 1973.

4. R. A. Mundell, *International Economics,* MacMillan, New York, 1968.

5. R. I. McKinnon, "Portfolio Balance and International Payments and International Payments Adjustment" in R. A. Mundell and A. Swoboda (eds.), *Monetary Problems of the International Economy,* University of Chicago Press, Chicago, 1969.

6. R. I. McKinnon, "Monetary Theory and Controlled Flexibility in the Foreign Exchanges," *Essays in International Finance,* No. 84, Princeton University, Princeton, N. J., April 1971.

7. Milton S. Friedman, *The Optimum Quantity of Money and Other Essays,* Aldine Publishing Company, Chicago, 1969.

8. Don Patinkin, *Money, Interest, and Prices,* Harper and Row, New York, 1965.

9. J. G. Gurley and E. S. Shaw, *Money in a Theory of Finance,* Brookings Institution, Washington, D.C., 1960.

10. Pentti J. K. Kouri and Michael G. Porter, "A Monetarist Model of Canadian Capital Flows." Paper presented to the Canadian Economics Association Meetings, Kingston, Ontario, June, 1973.

11. Pentti J. K. Kouri and Michael G. Porter, "International Capital Flows and Portfolio Equilibrium," *Journal of Political Economy,* 82, May/June, 1974.

12. Michael Mussa, "A Monetary Approach to Balance of Payments Analysis," *Journal of Money, Credit and Banking,* **6**, 3, 1974, pp. 333-335.

13. A. K. Swoboda and R. Dornbusch, "International Adjustment, Policy, and Monetary Equilibrium in a Two Country Model," in M. J. Connolly and A. K. Swoboda, eds., *International Trade and Money,* University of Toronto Press, Toronto, 1973, pp. 225-261.

14. A. K. Swoboda, "Monetary Policy Under Fixed Exchange Rates: Effectiveness, The Speed of Adjustment and Proper Use," *Economics,* New Series, **40**, 158, May 1973.

15. A. B. Laffer, "The Anti-traditional General Equilibrium Theory of the Rate of Growth and the Balance of Payments Under Fixed Exchange Rates," mimeo, December 1968.

16. J. M. Parkin, "Inflation, the Balance of Payments, Domestic Credit Expansion and Exchange Rate Adjustments," in R. Aliber, ed., *National Monetary Policies and the International Financial System,* University of Chicago Press, 1974.

17. Michael G. Porter, "A Theoretical and Empirical Framework for Analysing the Term Structure of Exchange Rate Expectations," IMF *Staff Papers,* July 1972.

18. J. Niehans, "Money and Barter in General Equilibrium with Transactions Costs," *American Economic Review,* **61**, 5, December 1971.

19. P. B. Clark, "The Demand for International Reserves: A Cross-Country Analysis," *Canadian Journal of Economics,* November, 1970.

Comment

HARRY G. JOHNSON

Department of Economics
University of Chicago
Chicago, Illinois

It is a great pleasure to me, and to the other members of the "Chicago contingent" to be present at this intellectual festival in honor of Edward S. Shaw —the Stanford Shaw festival. I am particularly fortunate in that the paper on which I have to comment is so clear and straightforward that it requires little in the way of detailed comment, so that I can take some of the time for a personal tribute to Ed Shaw.

I first met Ed Shaw at a seminar in Chicago in '55, while I was teaching at Northwestern. The occasion was slightly unreal; here was this tall, handsome, tanned Californian, dressed casually but impeccably in a more expansive style than the mid-West affected, who talked good monetary economics with a sense of humor utterly alien to the Miltonian majesty of Chicago. Here also was an ambiguous quantity—a monetarist who not only might differ from the local grand master, but was quite capable of being right. It was no wonder that, when I joined the Chicago faculty five years later, the chief article of faith in the Chicago workshop was that financial intermediation could not possibly affect the demand for money. Alvin Marty won local fame by catching Gurley and Shaw out on the technical question of whether a reduction of demand due to the innovation of a substitute necessarily increased the elasticity of demand on the new demand curve, while one non-party liner, Ed Feige, was smart enough to compute clandestinely so many regressions at the expense of the Federal Reserve before submitting his prospectus that he had to be allowed to go on to a Ph.D. and a Ford prize, and another, Joe Burns, spent an extra year of data-gathering before he was allowed to escape with a thesis devoted to the important message that sophistication of financial intermediation is part of the process of real economic growth.

From Chicago I went to Stanford for the summer, during which time I taught a course on money from Shaw's book. Being at that time a Cambridge Keynesian of the most arrogant sort, I chafed under the obligation of understanding how money-supply statistics are constructed—enough to teach the courses; and I was only dimly aware of the personal contributions Ed Shaw had made to the development of what was then an art but is now a profession, albeit still poorly understood in the United Kingdom. But some sense of the importance of the subject must have rubbed off on me, for I went back to the U.K. with a project for constructing a U.K. money-supply series—only to be told by Brian Reddaway, Director of the Cambridge Department of Applied Economics, that the results would not be worth the £500 I estimated it would cost to do it properly. (I later completed the project at Manchester, where as Professor I had a little money to waste on fractious frivolity.)

Turning back to Ed Shaw, I think that his contributions on financial intermediation have shown, on a far grander scale than the earlier work on money supply, a deep sense of relevance to the long-run development of better and more useful monetary economics. It was, I think, very unfortunate that monetary theory came to be dominated for about a quarter of a century by two 1930s developments: the Keynesian claim that there was a fundamental logical error in classical monetary theory, and the Hicksian naivete of assuming that money (and, for that matter, saving) could be introduced into general equilibrium theory as just another good. The assertion of fundamental logical error has since been reduced to the demonstration that some early contemporary mathematical economists were pretty stupid; and the present generation of high-powered mathematical economists have begun to build their analysis—with results whose usefulness is still to be assessed—on the assumption that money actually does something distinctive. Be that as it may, what I consider to be the important contribution of Gurley and Shaw—a proposition about the nature of economic growth that stands in confrontation both with at least the vulgar Keynesianism that concentrates on aggregate real saving and investment, and the classical monetary-theoretic view that "money is merely a veil over the barter economy"—was temporarily smothered by logical dispute firmly constrained within the ground rules of neoclassical general-equilibrium monetary theory. Nevertheless, the central message has taken hold in empirical research and policy thinking; and it has been attracting increasing attention as contemporary "secular inflation" has begun to crack the molds of traditional financial organization in the advanced industrial countries. Ed Shaw deserves great scholarly credit for keeping a fundamental idea alive and kicking for a long and thankless period during which the Keynesian-monetarist debate was crowding the other players off the center-stage.

I turn from this conference to the particular chapter I have been deputized to discuss. I have only three brief comments to make. First, I think Porter has done a very useful service in dramatizing so starkly the fact that the national policymakers have only one degree of freedom in monetary policy, as regards the four superficially possibly independent targets of the nominal interest rate, the rate of monetary growth, the rate of change of the price level, and the rate of change of the exchange rate, and attributing many of the world's monetary problems to failure to appreciate this constraint on policy freedom. I would object only that he sometimes carelessly mentions level when he means rate of change of level, and that on his first page he somewhat misleadingly refers to analysis in nominal terms when he really means that nominal analysis is identified with real analysis on the erroneous assumption that nominal prices are fixed and independent of monetary developments.

Second, in describing my own work Porter elides part of the analysis in a potentially confusing way. One can only discuss money magnitudes independent of real if one assumes either that real output, etc. is fixed (the static full-employment assumption), or that the income elasticity of demand for real balances with respect to real income or a similar scale variable is unity. The general analysis allows for the possibility of nonunitary income elasticity of demand for money, but a unitary elasticity seems a good empirical approximation—contrary to the empirically erroneous Friedman view that colored Chicago research in the early 1960s, that "money is a luxury good"—and is introduced as a supplementary empirical assumption for its mathematical convenience. I would add that some recent research suggests that the unitary elasticity assumption, and specifically its implication of the irrelevance of financial innovation to the demand for money, is not incontrovertibly established; and that the possibility of changes in demand due to financial innovation is, as Porter suggests, particularly important with respect to international reserve-holding behavior, where the number of effective asset holders is small and the speed and magnitude of the effects of innovation—such as the recent recourse of the British authorities to the euro-dollar market for a $2.5 billion loan—cannot safely be assumed to be absorbed into the trend term in the regression.

This brings me to my final point. Porter is quite right in criticizing current concepts of international monetary reform for their failure to couple the desire for rate stability with the need for appropriate money-supply management. But I think he presents too simple a view of the problem. It would be nice if the problem were, say, for the IMF to determine an appropriate rate of SDR creation and for national monetary authorities to link domestic credit creation to SDR reserve holdings, i.e., to construct a fractional reserve world banking system like the traditional picture of the gold standard but based on a rationally-managed international reserve base. But the actual problem is, as just suggested, greatly complicated, and maybe even made insuperable, by the twin phenomena of financial intermediation, represented notably but not exclusively by the use of the dollar as a reserve currency and by the euro-dollar market, and of financial innovation, represented by "swap facilities," longer-term balance-of-payments loans on central bank or government account, and intervention by central banks in commercial banking behavior, including what Dennis Robertson once called "ear-stroking," to distinguish it from the traditional use of the carrot and the stick to control the motion of the stubborn donkey of free enterprise. It may well be that the structure of international monetary organization will begin to crumble as soon as we attempt to use it, or reform it to be suitable to use, for rational world monetary management.

Chapter 13

Coordination of European Macroeconomic Policies

DONALD R. HODGMAN

Department of Economics
University of Illinois
Urbana, Illinois

Since the adoption in February 1971 of the EEC's (European Economic Community's) plan for economic integration and monetary union, the goal of coordination or harmonization of national macroeconomic policies of member states has been accepted in principle and endorsed in official agreements. Most recently the EEC Council of Ministers, at its meeting of February 18, 1974, adopted a series of decisions and directives expressing the official intention of member states' governments of seeking greater coordination of economic policies through a variety of measures to be described in this chapter.

It is important to realize that Council decisions and directives are supposed to register commitments by the governments of the respective member states to the decisions taken. Thus, such decisions carry far more weight than the recommendations, frequently more ambitious, of the EEC Commission to the Council for the latter's action. Nevertheless, the record of past postponements and broken commitments by member states in implementing Council decisions and directives calling for coordination of macroeconomic policies raises the question of credibility.

This chapter seeks to assess the prospects for macroeconomic policy coordination within the EEC. First, we review the economic and political rationale for such cooperation within the framework of plans for economic integration and monetary union. Second, we explore the substantive content of macroeconomic policy cooperation and analyze its implications for the ability of national governments to fulfill their normally accepted policy responsibilities. Third, we examine briefly possible Community-level alternatives to national policies for internal and external balance. Finally, we offer some conclusions concerning the future of efforts to harmonize macroeconomic policy within the EEC.

I.   The Uneasy Economic Case for Integration

The underlying economic rationale for coordination or harmonization of macroeconomic policies among the member states of the EEC derives from the high and increasing degree of interdependence of their economies through mutual trade in goods and services and through international capital movements, especially short-term capital movements via the Euro-dollar market (see Tables 1a and 1b).[1] The existing degree of interdependence that has been fostered by the EEC's customs union will be sharply increased by the commitment to internally fixed exchange parities and other measures to create a common market called for in the Community's program to achieve economic integration and monetary union by 1980. These other measures include the removal of administrative impediments to intra-EEC freedom of capital movements (presumably combined with effective controls over capital movements between the Community and the rest of the world); and removal of those barriers to the free movement of labor, capital, and entrepreneurship posed by national tax and social welfare systems. In the common market that would be created by these measures goods, services, labor, and capital would be able to move readily among closely linked national markets. Inflationary or recessionary tendencies generated in one country would spread with ease to partner countries. The capacity of national authorities to influence domestic conditions by means of independent national policy measures would be further impaired. The required degree of acceptance of mutual responsibility for economic welfare in partner countries would need to rise to a new level.

These implications of monetary union and economic integration within a common market have been analyzed in theoretical terms in the writings of numerous economists including among others Balassa [1], Johnson [2, 3], McKinnon [4], Meade [5], Mundell [6, 7], and Scitovsky [8]. Criteria and conditions for optimum currency areas have been set out by McKinnon [4] and Mundell [6]. The problem of having sufficient policy instruments appropriately assigned to achieve targets of internal and external balance has been treated extensively. Particular emphasis has been placed on the desirability of exchange-rate flexibility to preserve external balance while freeing monetary and budgetary policy to concentrate on domestic full employment at stable prices. The potential increase in allocative efficiency achievable in a common market as compared to a customs union has been analyzed.

TABLE 1a

Imports from Member Countries (EEC 6) as Percentage Share of Total Imports, 1962-1971

Country (1)	1962 (2)	1963 (3)	1964 (4)	1965 (5)	1966 (6)	1967 (7)	1968 (8)	1969 (9)	1970 (10)	1971 (11)
Germany, F. R.	32.5	33.4	34.9	38.1	38.5	39.6	41.5	43.6	44.4	46.8
France	33.6	35.8	37.4	38.8	40.9	43.4	47.5	50.5	48.9	50.1
Italy	31.2	33.0	32.7	31.3	32.5	34.6	36.2	38.7	41.1	42.4
Netherlands	50.2	51.6	52.0	53.4	54.0	54.5	55.4	56.7	55.9	54.5
Belgium } Luxembourg	51.0	52.5	53.3	54.5	56.0	55.6	54.9	57.4	58.8	63.0
United Kingdom	15.8	16.0	16.6	17.3	18.5	19.6	19.8	19.4	20.1	21.4
Ireland			15.6	15.3	13.4	14.6	16.4	15.5	16.5	16.5
Denmark	37.8	35.9	35.4	35.6	34.4	32.7	32.7	33.6	33.2	31.8

Source: Basic Statistics of the Community, Statistical Office of the European Communities. Columns 2 and 3, 1967 edition, 112-113; columns 4 to 11, 1972 edition, pp. 86-87.

TABLE 1b

Exports to Member Countries (EEC 6) as Percentage Share of Total Exports, 1962-1971

Country (1)	1962 (2)	1963 (3)	1964 (4)	1965 (5)	1966 (6)	1967 (7)	1968 (8)	1969 (9)	1970 (10)	1971 (11)
Germany, F.R.	34.0	37.3	36.4	35.2	36.3	36.8	37.6	39.8	40.2	40.1
France	36.8	38.2	38.8	41.0	42.3	41.3	43.0	47.8	48.8	49.4
Italy	34.8	35.5	37.8	40.2	40.6	38.7	40.1	42.5	43.0	44.7
Netherlands	49.2	53.3	55.7	55.7	55.6	54.9	57.4	60.1	62.0	63.7
Belgium Luxembourg	56.8	60.8	62.6	61.9	62.9	63.0	64.3	67.6	68.5	68.6
United Kingdom	19.3	21.1	20.6	20.0	19.2	20.2	20.2	21.6	21.8	21.0
Ireland			11.5	12.9	11.0	8.5	9.0	11.1	11.6	8.5
Denmark	28.4	28.8	28.1	27.4	25.4	22.9	23.3	23.0	22.7	22.4

Source: Basic Statistics of the Community, Statistical Office of the European Communities. Columns (2) and (3), 1967 edition, p. 116. Columns (4) to (11), 1972 editions, pp. 90-91.

Johnson [2, p. 8] has made the point that the cost in national sovereignty arising from the frustration of national preferences on income redistribution via budget expenditures and taxes may offset the welfare gains attributable to allocative efficiency in a full union.

The thrust of such economic analysis has been to emphasize the severity of the constraints imposed on independent actions on the part of national economic authorities by membership in a common market and the demanding requirements for harmonization of national monetary and budgetary policies implied by monetary union. Moreover, analysis suggests that the level of economic efficiency achievable in a common market may not exceed that in a customs union by enough to justify the loss in national economic sovereignty involved.

Despite such views of academic economists, the political leaders of the member states of the European Economic Community have continued to re-affirm the goal of economic integration and monetary union even in the face of increasing operational difficulties encountered in its progressive imple-mentation. Various reasons have been advanced for this apparent neglect of expert economic advice by the political leadership. It has been suggested that the subtleties of economic analysis of comparative advantage and of the ad-justment process permitted by flexible exchange rates surpass the comprehen-sion of national politicians and their economic advisers [2, p. 5]. But it is acknowledged that there are some economic arguements that favor monetary and economic union. These include improved allocative efficiency resulting from increased factor mobility within the common market [2, p. 11] and the greater influence and economic independence of the EEC in international monetary and economic affairs [7]. Flexible exchange rates among the member countries of the EEC are handicaps in achieving both these objectives. There is the further argument, advanced by proponents of political union of Western Europe, that economic union can force the pace of political unifica-tion, regarded by some as indispensable to Europe's future.

Thus, the economic integration and monetary union of Europe may confer both economic and political benefits on the members of the EEC, but these benefits may come at high cost in the yielding of national economic and even political sovereignty. In Section II of this paper we examine in greater detail one aspect of this problem, namely the implications for member states of Community efforts to coordinate national monetary and budgetary policies by means of guidelines for such policies.

II. Guidelines for Coordinating National Monetary and Budgetary Policies

The EEC plan for monetary union and economic integration calls for a variety of implementing measures, most of which are under active study and discussion, and some of which have been undertaken with varying degrees of success. Study and negotiation are proceeding in a number of areas related to allocative efficiency and the fostering of competitive market conditions in industry, finance, and factor markets. Examples include changes in tax structure and financial regulation, and harmonization of social security and social welfare benefits with equal treatment for foreign and domestic workers. We shall leave aside these measures to improve allocative efficiency and concentrate on the macroeconomic areas of monetary and budgetary policy as related to exchange-rate policy.

The EEC agreement to narrow the bands within which exchange rates among Community currencies should be allowed to fluctuate is well known, as is the progressive breakdown of this agreement with the independent floating of the British and Irish pounds, Italian lira, and French franc. Any resumption of the commitment to narrower bands together with joint floating in relation to non-Community currencies (particularly the dollar) implies serious mutual commitments to coordinated policy action to maintain these parities. If exchange parities are to be fixed permanently, alternative mechanisms must be found to cope with national balance-of-payments deficits and surpluses and their effects on the internal balance of national regions. Awareness of the need for these mechanisms accounts for arrangements for short-term mutual credit and the Commission's recommendation for pooling of reserves in the recently created European Monetary Cooperation Fund. The call for coordination of national monetary and budgetary policies (discussed in the following) is linked to balance-of-payments effects of these policies, to the initiation and dissemination of recession and inflation in the Community, and to the distribution of the real economic benefits of reserve pooling.

The proposed and much debated Community regional fund has its primary rationale in aid to historically depressed regions rather than in facilitating adjustment by depressed regions that may be newly created by competitive forces within a tighter economic union. But clearly such a fund, if so authorized, might well serve to channel investment capital from surplus to deficit regions within the union and thus aid in the adjustment process. Likewise, removal of barriers to a Community-wide capital market might facilitate flows of private capital to aid in the economic recovery of depressed regions.

At its meeting of February 18, 1974 the EEC Council reaffirmed the commitment of member states to economic integration and monetary union and agreed on certain procedures and measures of implementation. The Council agreed to set aside a specific day each month for consultation on economic and monetary matters. The structure of EEC committees dealing with economic matters was simplified by combining into a newly designated Economic Policy Committee the functions formerly exercised by the EEC's committees concerned with short-term economic policy, budgetary policy, and medium-term economic policy. The aim of economic convergence was endorsed and is to be guided by medium-term economic forecasts and programs. At this meeting the Council also approved certain measures for the coordination of macroeconomic policies of member states. Governments are called upon to provide their monetary authorities with discretionary authority to apply reserve requirements to the liabilities and credits of monetary institutions, to employ open-market policy in a comprehensive manner, to set and alter rediscount ceilings with the central bank, and to modify the various intervention rates practiced by the monetary authorities.[2]

In the realm of budgetary policy the Council directs the member states to provide their competent authorities with power if the need arises "to slow down or accelerate the rate of public spending and to modify direct or indirect taxes within not more than 90 days." Competent authorities also are to be empowered, without prior authorization, "temporarily to freeze the yield of excess tax revenue or of loans and to release such funds at a later date" and to be able to control the indebtedness of local authorities and of social security agencies.[3]

The manner in which these instruments of monetary and budgetary policy are used and their relationship to the goal of macroeconomic policy coordination has not been specified or analyzed by the Council or by the staff of the EEC Commission. They are simply a standard toolbag of instruments, each of which is currently in use in some of the member states. Moreover, no allowance is made for the different institutional and behavioral environments in which national authorities may be called upon to use these instruments in support of Community-agreed policy. Thus, there is little evidence to suggest that careful analysis rather than considerations of administrative comparability lies behind their selection.

The Council's February-1974 decisions gave a fresh emphasis to certain *goals* for both monetary and budgetary policies. Central bankers were invited to coordinate their monetary policies, especially in the development of the money supply, bank liquidity, conditions for granting credit, and the level of interest rates.[4] The Council agreed to lay down guidelines for the main elements of preliminary national economic budgets. "Within this framework, quantitative guidelines for the draft of public budgets for the following year shall be fixed before these budgets are finally adopted and shall cover developments in government expenditure and revenue, the nature and extent of budget surpluses, and deficits and the way the latter are to be financed or used."[5]

Although the rationale for these goals is not made explicit, it can be deduced. Coordination of monetary policies is intended to support a fixed-exchange-rate system within the Community by preventing monetary policies from giving rise to interest-rate and price-level differentials between countries that will stimulate disequilibrating current and capital account deficits and surpluses. Concern for the nature and extent of budget surpluses and deficits and their use or mode of financing likewise has its rationale in a desire to prevent inflationary budget financing that would add to the domestic money supply or supply of liquid assets at an excessive rate. A deeper rationale for both sets of goals stems from awareness of the importance of differential inflationary trends for the spread of inflation to partner countries, for balance-of-payments disequilibria internal to the Community, and for the distribution of real income among member states under a system of extensive official credits or pooled reserves to preserve fixed exchange rates. Thus, the key purpose of proposals for the coordination of monetary and budgetary policies among EEC member states is to establish a Community policy for the rate of monetary expansion in each member state that is judged consistent with a goal of some rate of price inflation that is common throughout the Community. In addition, the monetary authorities are encouraged to cooperate to minimize interest-rate differentials that may stimulate short-term capital flows, giving rise to balance-of-payments disequilibria among member states.

Under the proposed guidelines what degree of independence is retained by monetary and budgetary authorities in pursuing national goals of economic stabilization and in aiding in the balance-of-payments adjustment process? The call for cooperation among monetary authorities does not, per se, impose onerous limitations on their freedom of action. However, to the degree that a common capital market is achieved within the Community, the capacity of monetary authorities to exercise independent national monetary policies will be neutralized by intra-Community capital flows. Moreover, as is clear from guidelines calling for noninflationary budget financing, Community-level controls over expansion of national money supplies are contemplated. Once such controls become effective monetary policy will cease to be an independent national instrument for achieving national economic balance, either internal or external.[6]

If monetary policy ceases to be an effective instrument of national economic policy, what about budgetary policy? When monetary policy cannot be used to achieve internal balance under fixed exchange rates because of perfect international capital markets, budgetary policy usually can be recommended as a feasible alternative. Does this conclusion hold under the EEC's proposed guidelines for national budgetary policies?

Published references to budgetary guidelines cited above have stressed Community-level intent to specify quantitative limits for "government expenditure and revenue, the nature and extent of budget surpluses and deficits and the way the latter are to be financed or used." Unpublished study papers prepared by the Commission staff provide some further evidence on the direction of discussion at the staff level. A distinction is drawn between conjunctural and "structural" budget strategies. Structural considerations refer to the medium-term effects of the budget with particular reference to the balance of saving and investment in the economy.[7] Budget deficits of the government sector over a medium-term period should not exceed the net savings of other domestic sectors with allowance for savings invested abroad through a surplus in the current account of the balance of payments. Moreover, the pressure of government borrowing in the capital market on interest rates and thus on investment by the private sector must be weighed. The structural role of the government budget involves a choice concerning the division of the national product between private and collective needs. This choice is political rather than technical. In the initial stages of Community efforts at budgetary co-ordination, attention should be directed primarily to the question of budget balance, the size of surpluses or deficits, and their effects on the money supply or supply of liquid assets in the national economy rather than to the absolute size of the government budget or to specific tax revenues and expenditures. The Community-level assessment of national budgetary policies should make some allowance for the conjunctural or cyclical situation during the year in question.

A major concern in Community thinking is for the potentially inflationary effects of deficit financing. In the medium term the state should refrain on balance from inflationary or deflationary financing. It is recognized that even a balanced government budget may have inflationary effects by squeezing the private sector to the point that counter pressure is provoked through increases sought in money wages. Staff working papers also refer to difficult technical problems that must be met in formulating recommendations for the coordination of budgetary policies. These include problems of substantive comparability among national budgets, institutional differences, and the need for improved analytical methods in assessing national economic trends.

From this glimpse of the Commission's thinking on budgetary coordination it should be obvious that technically analyzed and validated Community-level guidelines for national budgets are not feasible in the near future. Nevertheless, it is of interest to examine the discretion left to national governments for compensatory budgetary policies under guidelines of the kind being discussed. More particularly, what are the implications for national budgetary policy if a government yields the right to increase or decrease the money supply as an aspect of budgetary finance?

In such a circumstance budget deficits and surpluses remain possible. Deficits must be financed by borrowing without recourse to an expansion of the monetary base. Thus, the national central bank may not feed reserves to the banking system or purchase government securities to support the issue

of debt by the Treasury. Nor may net purchase of government debt by
foreigners be permitted. Indeed, there is an implication that controls over
capital movements through the balance of payments will be required to prevent
the rise in domestic interest rates, that could be caused by Treasury borrowing,
from attracting a capital inflow from outside the Community that would increase the domestic money supply if the exchange rate with the outside world
were fixed. Similar restrictions would have to apply to the uses made of budget surpluses to prevent these from altering the money supply: namely, no net
retirement of debt held by the central bank or by foreigners.

    If a Community-wide capital market should be created, the debt opera-
tions of national governments would take place in this market. Securities
issued by one national government would be available for purchase throughout
the Community by lenders other than central banks. What factors will influence the terms such a market would impose on securities issued by different
governments? In the absence of the capacity to create money to service the
national debt, the attractiveness of government debt would depend on lenders'
assessments of a government's ability to pay and of the permanence of the rate
at which the exchange rate was fixed. Ability to pay is influenced by such
factors as national tax base and tax discipline; the size, rate of capacity
utilization, and rate of growth of the national economy; and the burden of
service costs on outstanding debt (see Table 2).[8] The credibility of a fixed
exchange rate depends on trends in various indicators of national economic
performance such as the gross national product, rate of unemployment, price
trends, and trends in the national balance of payments. Credibility of the fixed
exchange rate also could be influenced by arrangements for help from Community sources to nations experiencing balance-of-payments deficits including
the availability of official credits or pooled reserves, and a government's
access to a share in monetary expansion under Community control. Factors
influencing ability to pay are similar to those determining the credit ratings
of state and local governments, which likewise lack the power to create
money.

    Deficit finance for compensatory purposes might require a government
to borrow at high rates of interest when the market assessment of these factors
was unfavorable. Moreover, there is a question as to the effectiveness of
government spending financed in this manner for stimulating aggregate demand.
To what extent will the rise in market rates of interest required to absorb the
increased volume of government borrowing with a fixed money supply
occasion an offsetting decline in private-sector expenditures? This is the
"squeezing out" phenomenon alluded to by monetarists in their questioning of
the effectiveness of pure budgetary policy (unaccompanied by monetary expansion) as a stimulus to aggregate demand. Of course, to the extent that
purchasers of a particular government's securities are distributed throughout a

TABLE 2

Central Government Debt (National Debt) as Percentage of GNP
in Member Countries, 1967-1972

Country (1)	1967 (2)	1968 (3)	1969 (4)	1970 (5)	1971 (6)	1972 (7)
Germany, F. R.	16.2	16.2	14.4	12.2	12.4	11.6
France	15.8	15.6	13.0	12.1	10.7	8.6
Italy	15.3	16.0	15.9	16.5	18.6	21.2
Netherlands	31.4	31.3	30.0	29.1	27.4	24.4
Belgium	53.9	54.8	52.0	48.2	46.5	44.9
Luxembourg[a]	35.4	32.8	31.8	29.5	31.8	26.8
United Kingdom					59.0	57.6

[a] The GNP figures for Luxembourg are uncertain or estimated.
Sources: Author's computations. Figures for total central government debt and for GNP are taken from *Basic Statistics of the Community,* Statistical Office of the European Communities. Columns 2 and 3, debt figures, p. 110; GNP p. 22, 1968/69 edition. Column 4, p. 22, 110, 1970 edition. Column 5, pp. 22, 112, 1971 edition. Columns 6 and 7, data taken from *Monthly Statistics,* #11, 1973, Eurostat, pages 8 and 70.

Community-wide capital market, the rise in interest rates may be moderated by the breadth of the market. On the other hand, the multiplier effects of government expenditures in a particular state will be reduced by the higher marginal propensity to import in the more highly integrated Community economy. On balance the effectiveness of compensatory budget policy in stimulating aggregate demand on a national basis would appear likely to suffer serious impairment under budgetary guidelines contemplated by the EEC Council.

III.   Remaining Policy Possibilities

If neither monetary nor budgetary policies may be expected to survive within a monetary and economic union as effective instruments of *national* economic policy in coping with *national* problems of internal and external balance, what policy instruments and adjustment processes remain? Insofar as the problem may be viewed as one of disparate trends in national price levels of partner countries, there may be room for national price controls and incomes policies. However, past experience with both kinds of policies does not permit optimism regarding their effectiveness, and their distorting effects on economic allocative efficiency are well known.

Policies to encourage factor mobility, particularly that of labor, likewise have a potential contribution to make. International mobility of labor in Western Europe faces major barriers of language, custom, and national psychology. Numerous institutional and legal barriers also remain, including problems relating to equality and transferability of social welfare benefits, and equal treatment of foreign and domestic workers as to union membership, property rights, and similar aspects of economic status. Labor mobility may easy adjustment problems within the EEC in the long run, but will scarcely make more than a modest contribution in the near future.

The major kinds of policies that remain as alternatives to national policies are Community-level policies that involve the sharing of real income among member states. These include the potential of the Community budget to act as a federal budget in redistributing income among member states, creation of a regional fund to channel Community investment to economically depressed regions, pooling of foreign-exchange reserves (tantamount to non-repayable grants) and long-term loans from member countries with balance-of-payment surpluses to those with deficits. Since these policies explicitly influence the distribution of real income among member states, agreement on such policies has been difficult to reach.

The general Community budget underwent a staged reform intended to culminate in the introduction on January 1, 1975 of a federal budget financed by federal revenues in order to free the Community from the vagaries of State contributions. The structure and operation of the previous Community budget prevented it from functioning as an instrument of stabilization policy within the Community or from aiding specific member states in coping with economic recession or balance-of-payments problems. Some 96.5 percent of the Community budget's expenditures are governed by existing treaties and legal regulations and thus are not subject to discretionary management.[9] For example, in 1973 77 percent of forecast Community budget expenditures were for outlays related to the Community's Common Agricultural Policy.[10] Other stipulated expenditures are to cover administrative expenses of the European Parliament, Court of Justice, Council of Ministers, the Commission, the European Coal and Steel Community, the Economic and Social Committee, the Audit Committee, and the research and investment budget of the European Atomic Energy Community.

In the spring of 1973 the Commission proposed to the Council the establishment of a European Regional Development Fund to aid in diminishing regional imbalances in the Community by offering aid on a case-by-case basis following an assessment of need and in support of Community objectives. This Fund has not yet been approved by the Council in view of substantial disagreements among the member states over the size of the Fund, the contributions to the Fund to be made by specific member states, and the principles that would govern the distribution of aid. A compromise version of the Regional Fund appears possible sometime during the spring of 1974. Even if approved, however, the Fund, as presently conceived, is not intended to meet the needs of member nations for compensatory budget policy or for aid in meeting persistent balance-of-payment deficits.[11]

Pooling of foreign-exchange reserves in the European Monetary Cooperation Fund (established in April 1973) was proposed to the Council by the Commission in June 1973 and again in more modest form in November 1973. To date the Council has not acted on this proposal. Objections to reserve pooling have been raised precisely on the grounds that such automatic grants from surplus to deficit member nations would permit the latter to avoid or delay the national adjustment processes needed to restore equilibrium in their balance of payments.

Similar objections have been proffered to more generous terms and more extensive facilities for the extension of medium-term credit to aid deficit countries. Under the existing agreement such credits may be extended by a decision of the EEC Council for a period of two to five years. Such aid is conditional upon economic policy commitments to be negotiated between the recipient of aid and its partners. Thus, far from being a substitute for adjustment mechanisms, the medium-term credit arrangements available within the Community include provisions intended to compel debtor states to follow economic policies to activate these mechanisms with effects on price trends, interest rates, and trade flows.

IV. Concluding Remarks

The preceding discussion leads to a series of conclusions that bear on the future of economic integration and monetary union in the EEC. First, the technical and analytical basis needed for specification of appropriate guidelines to coordinate national monetary and budgetary policies within the Community does not exist at present. Second, coordination of the kind contemplated in Council decisions and Commission proposals and study papers, if it could be strictly implemented, would greatly impair the capacity of national authorities to engage effectively in aggregate-demand management as a sphere of national economic policy. Third, national governments and populaces are not prepared to transfer to Community-level authorities monetary and budgetary powers equivalent to those at the command of sovereign national governments. The frontier of cooperation at which progress has halted (except for the Common Agricultural Policy, which is under review) is characterized by reluctance to engage in deliberate transfers of real income among member states on a significant scale. This is illustrated by current debates and disagreements over the Regional Development Fund and over the pooling of foreign-exchange reserves in the Monetary Cooperation Fund. Moreover, even if member nations agreed on the transfer of such powers to the Community, the issue of democratic political control over such powers and the inadequacy of the technical and analytical foundation needed to guide their use would remain as major problems.

In the absence of willingness to confer on Community authorities the capacity to conduct compensatory monetary and budgetary policies and to transfer real resources to aid in intra-Community balance-of-payments adjustments, the common market, which is the goal of monetary and economic union, will not be viable and would be inferior in terms of the economic welfare of its members to a looser customs union. On present evidence, such a union is the most probable outcome in the foreseeable future of the Community's plan for economic integration and monetary union. As a corollary, Europe's influence in international monetary and economic affairs will continue to be fragmented and thus inferior to that of the superpowers, particularly the United States.

ACKNOWLEDGMENTS

The author gratefully acknowledges financial support from the National Science Foundation for the body of research from which this chapter is drawn.

NOTES

1. The high and increasing share of trade of EEC members (the original six) with each other is shown in the tables cited.

2. Council Directive of 18 February 1974 on stability, growth, and full employment in the Community, article 9.

3. Note 2, articles 7 and 8.

4. Council decision of 18 February 1974 on the attainment of a high degree of convergence of the economic policies of the member states of the European Economic Community, article 8.

5. Note 2, article 3.

6. At present and during the period covering transition to a Community-controlled monetary authority, the diversity of financial institutions and markets and the variety of central banking techniques in member states will complicate greatly the use of any simple guidelines for monetary coordination.

For a detailed discussion of the national settings for monetary policy see my *National Monetary Policies and International Monetary Cooperation,* Little, Brown and Co., Boston, 1974.

7. The concept of a "structural" budget is Dutch in origin.

8. There are substantial differences among member countries in the volume of central government debt outstanding in relation to the level of gross national product as shown in Table 2. Owing to complex problems of comparability (for example debudgetization and differences in the degree of centralization of governmental functions), these figures should be considered merely indicators of general orders of magnitude.

9. European Communities-Directorate General Press and Information, *Newsletter on the Common Agricultural Policy,* No. 5 "Financing the Common Agricultural Policy and the Community's own Resources", (13428/X/70-E), p. 11.

10. According to figures given in the Community's projected budget for the year 1973, outlays in support of the Common Agricultural Policy were estimated at 3,262,210,000 units of account compared to an overall budget total of 4,245,282,241 units of account. Source: *Journal officiel des Communautés européennes,* 15e année No. £307, 31 décembre 1972, pp. 47, 188-189.

11. On March 18th, 1975, the EEC Council approved a Regional Development Fund with initial resources in units of account as follows: 1975, 300 million; 1976, 500 million. To date (Febraury 1976) there has been no agreement for pooling of foreign exchange reserves.

REFERENCES

1. Bela Balassa, *The Theory of Economic Integration,* Irwin, Homewood, Ill., 1961.

2. Harry G. Johnson, "The Implications of Free or Freer Trade for the Harmonization of Other Policies," in Harry G. Johnson, Paul Wonnacott, and Hirofumi Shibata, (eds.), *Harmonization of National Economic Policies Under Free Trade,* published for the Private Planning Association of Canada by University of Toronto Press, Toronto, 1967.

3. Harry G. Johnson, "Problems of European Monetary Union," *Euromoney,* April 1971, pp. 39-43, reprinted in Robert E. Baldwin and J. David Richardson, eds., *International Trade and Finance, Readings,* Little, Brown and Company, Boston, 1974.

4. Ronald I. McKinnon, "Optimum Currency Areas," *American Economic Review,* September 1963, pp. 717-25.

5. J. E. Meade, *The Theory of Customs Unions,* North Holland, Amsterdam, 1955.

6. Robert A. Mundell, "A Theory of Optimum Currency Areas," *American Economic Review,* September 1961, pp. 657-65.

7. Robert A. Mundell, "A Plan for an European Currency," and "Uncommon Arguments for Common Currencies", in Harry G. Johnson and Alexander K. Swoboda, eds., *The Economics of Common Currencies,* George Allen and Unwin Ltd., London, 1973.

8. Tibor Scitovsky, *Economic Theory and Western European Integration,* Unwin University Books, London, 1958.

Comment

EDWARD J. RAY

Department of Economics
Ohio State University
Columbus, Ohio

Hodgman establishes quite clearly in his chapter that the EEC is entering a critical period of transition. As the community becomes more integrated, the need for coordinated monetary and fiscal policies increases and the ability of national governments to pursue independent monetary and fiscal policies diminishes. Yet, despite the common objective of economic unity and the diminished effectiveness of national macropolicies, individual countries are reluctant to surrender macroeconomic decisions to the community as a whole.

The requirement that monetary and fiscal policies be coordinated can easily be appreciated if we permit ourselves a simple fiction. Suppose the EEC is fully integrated in the sense that products and factors move relatively freely, much as they do within the United States. In fact, think of the problems that would arise if the United States were divided into nine regions each choosing its own monetary and fiscal policies. Each region has its own central bank authorized to pursue its own monetary policies with respect to interest rates, money supply, etc. Each region has its own central government with authority to run budget surpluses or deficits, to issue securities, and to legislate taxes and credits to influence private consumption and investment expenditures. Furthermore, assume that fixed exchange rates are maintained among regions.

Both monetary and fiscal policy will be somewhat ineffective at the regional level and inappropriate from the national standpoint. Monetary policy will be ineffective within any region because of the offsetting capital flows from other regions generated in response to the local money expansion or contraction. And, on the national level, it is unlikely that the aggregate rate of change in the money supply resulting from the collective effect of nine regional banks operating independently will be optimal. However, one suspects that Milton Friedman could argue pursuasively that nine bankers working at odds would be preferable to a single banker with discretionary powers.[1]

To the extent that fiscal policies such as deficit spending at the regional level induce capital flows viz-a-viz other regions, such policies will be effective. However, other regions might well impose capital controls to maintain balance-of-payments equilibrium and to promote their own regional investment plans. Capital controls and fixed exchange rates are no strangers. Without capital inflows from other regions, expansionary policies by the regional government would be largely offset by corresponding reductions in private expenditures and therefore rendered ineffective. From the perspective of the nation as a whole, the lack of coordination of fiscal policies such as investment taxes and credits, income taxes, welfare programs, etc., would promote factor flows that are inefficient and therefore inappropriate.

So, the need to coordinate monetary and fiscal policies among regions in the country seems clear. However, neither the present discussion nor Hodgman's discussion of the EEC indicates the composition of an appropriate program for policy coordination during the period of transition from regional independence to national unity.[2] Hodgman observes at several points in his discussion that the analytical bases for appropriate monetary and fiscal-policy coordination do not exist. He suggests that this lack is a critical failing of the current system and an obstacle to the development of appropriate programs in the future, but does not choose to pursue the matter further.[3]

In terms of efforts to coordinate monetary policies, he points out the difficulty that the Community has been having in maintaining fixed exchange rates, as indicated by the independent float of the British and Irish pounds, the Italian lira, and the French franc. Recommendations to pool reserves in the European Monetary Cooperation Fund and to channel long-term loans from surplus to deficit countries through a Regional Development Fund are largely offered to make the fixed exchange-rate system workable. Professor Hodgman correctly states that flexible exchange rates could handicap factor mobility as well as the economic and political influence of the EEC. Yet, we are all familiar with the grief generated by a system of fixed exchange rates when monetary authorities choose to act independently. Whether fixed or flexible exchange rates or something in between is most appropriate for the EEC depends on such factors as the degree of openness and freedom of factor flows between countries as well as economic conditions and price stability within countries. Some discussion of economic conditions, monetary policies, and institutional arrangements in the member countries might help determine the appropriate exchange-rate system for the current period of transition.

The actual guidelines proposed by the EEC Commission for monetary coordination are rather vague. Again, a discussion of economic conditions, policy objectives, and financial institutions within member countries might help determine the most promising avenues for monetary cooperation. In order to develop and assess programs for moving from independent to integrated monetary policy, we need to know our starting point.

The Commission's guidelines for coordinating fiscal or budget policies are also vague. The impetus for controlling budget surpluses and deficits within the EEC is to prevent differential inflationary trends from generating inappropriate monetary expansion for the community as a whole and to avoid balance-of-payments deficits and surpluses among the members of the fixed exchange-rate system.

So, the Commission's concern with both monetary and budget-policy coordination in the EEC rests largely on the desire to make a fixed exchange-rate system work within the community. Therefore, in assessing these policies, we should at least be clear as to whether we want fixed exchange rates within the EEC.

Hodgman tells us that he does not intend to discuss attempts at co-ordinating monetary and fiscal policies to improve allocative efficiency within the common market. I would suggest that a discussion of those attempts and an appraisal of the areas in which cooperation seems promising would be useful. What we miss in this discussion is a careful assessment of the degree to which policies can be coordinated and whether or not the guidelines suggested by the EEC Commission are in any sense realistic and/or appropriate.

Accepting the fact that Hodgman wishes to "concentrate on the macro-economic areas of monetary and budget policy as related to exchange rate policy," I would suggest that a discussion of the appropriateness of fixed exchange rates during the transitional period should be pursued in greater depth. I suspect that greater reference to relevant empirical evidence would aid us considerably in gaining a proper perspective on the EEC Commission guidelines with respect to both feasibility and desirability.

In summary, Hodgman has focused on the conflicts that exist between the Commission's guidelines to achieve the long-run objective of full economic integration in Europe and the short-run determination of member nations to make their own macroeconomic decisions. He persuades us that the conflict is real and that its resolution is critical if the program of economic integration is to proceed. He poses the problem but stops short of discussing the appropriate policies to deal with it.

NOTES

1. Jacob Frenkel suggested that the position attributed to Milton Friedman would be more appropriate if there were an even rather than an odd number of regions since policies would cancel each other out more easily with an even number. Hugh Patrick suggested that Belgium and Luxemburg be counted as one region reducing the total number of regions from nine to eight.

2. Jacob Frenkel pointed out that the conditions for a customs union and an optimum currency area differ. In effect, though the EEC countries may define an appropriate group to form a customs union, they may not correspond to an appropriate group for a single currency area.

3. Both Hugh Patrick and Tibor Scitovsky suggested that Europe has been prodded in the direction of integration with little analysis of its desirability from an economic standpoint.

Numbers in brackets are reference numbers and indicate that an author's work is referred to although his name is not cited in the text. Italic numbers give the page on which the complete reference is listed.

A

Adelman, Irma, *118*
Alcazar, Marco, 115 [9], *119*
Alchian, Armen A., 192 [24], *194*
Arrow, K. J., 209 [1], *220*
Aubey, Robert T., 115 [10], *119*
Auernheimer, Leonardo, 178 [3], 180 [3], *193*, 196 [6], *198*
Averitt, R., 118 [52], *122*

B

Bach, G. L., 192 [25], *194*
Baer, Werner, 73 [3], *74*
Bahl, R. W., 101 [24], *120*
Bailey, Martin J., 178 [4], 180 [4], 192 [4], *193*, 196 [1], *198*
Balassa, Bela, 131 [113], *137*, 304 [1], *317*
Baltensperger, Ernest, 108 [39], *121*
Barro, Robert J., 178 [5], 180 [5], *193*, 261 [2], *276*

C

Basch, Antonin, 67 [34], *70*
Baumol, William J., 108 [38], *121*
Benston, George J., 117 [42], *121*
Bernstein, E. M., 129 [9], *137*
Black, Fischer, 275 [11], *276*
Brimmer, Andrew F., *21*, 115 [12], *119*
Brunner, Karl, 269 [5], *276*

C

Cagan, P., 180 [16], 184 [17], 191 [17], *194*, 205 [2], *220*, 269 [6], *276*
Cameron, Rondo, 111 [1], *118*
Campbell, Colin D., 65 [14], *68*
Cass, David, 26 [3], 33 [3], *34*
Cassel, Gustav, 184 [19], *194*
Cathcart, Charles D., 192 [27], *195*, 196 [7], *198*
Child, Frank C., *124*
Chiu, J. S., 117 [46], *121*
Christian, James W., 116 [34], *120*

Clark, P. B., 296[19], *297*
Cooley, D. E., 117[46], *121*
Corredor, J., 73[4], *74*

D

Davis, Lance E., 111[50], 112[31],
    116[31], *120, 121*
Davis, Tom E., 109[41], *121*
Dean, W., 115[7], *119*
Deaver, John V., 65[15], *68*
Despres, Emile, 64[7], *68*
Diaz-Alejandro, Carlos F., 104[32],
    120
Diz, Adolfo Cesar, 65[16], *68*
Dornbusch, Rudiger, 192[22], *194,*
    252[2], *257,* 281[2], *296,*
    284[2,13], *296, 297*
Dutton, Dean S., 65[17], *68*

E

Eckaus, R. S., 118[5], *119*
Eshag, E., 108[37], 117[37], *121*
Exter, John, 129[8], *137*

F

Frenkel, Jacob A., 187[20], 188
    [20], 192[20,22], *194,*
    261[3], 264[3], *276*
Friedman, Milton, *21,* 32[9], *34,*
    128[5], *137,* 178[6], 180[6],
    182[6], *193,* 275[10], *276,*
    282[7], *296*

G

Goldman, S. M., 209[3], *220*
Goldsmith, Raymond W., 106[33],
    107[33], 117[33], 118[48],
    118, 120, 121, 130[10], *137*
Gonzalez-Vega, Claudio, 31[8], *34*

Greaves, Ida, 129[6], *137*
Griliches, Zvi, 65[21], *69*
Gurley, John G., 17[4], *21, 22,* 75
    [1], 76[2], *91,* 260[1],
    261[1], *276,* 282[9], *296*

H

Hadjimichalakis, M. G., 209[4], *221*
Hanson, James S., 56[24], 65[23],
    69, 72[1], *74*
Harberger, Arnold, 64[8], *68*
Hazari, R. K., 115[14], *119*
Heeyhm, Song, 81[5], *91*
Hinshaw, Randall, 252[1], *257*
Hymer, Stephen, 101[4], 117[4],
    118
Hynes, A., 65[18], *68*

I

Ingram, James E., 129[7], *137*
Iyoha, Milton A., 102[26], *120*

J

Je, Kim Mahn, 81[5], *91*
Johnson, Harry G., *22,* 23[1], 33
    [1], *34,* 35[4,6], 64[4], *67,*
    68, 128[2], *136,* 178[7],
    179[12], 180[7], *193, 194,*
    239[4], *249,* 281[1], 283[1],
    284[1], *296,* 304[2,3], 307
    [2], *317*
Jucker-Fleetwood, E., *121*

K

Kafka, A., 102[28], *120*
Kapur, B. K., 208[5], 218[6], 219
    [6a], 220[6a], *221*
Kerstenetsky, Isaac, 73[3], *74*
Kessel, Reuben A., 192[24], *194*

Keynes, John M., 177[1], 184[1], 193

Kindleberger, Charles P., 103[29], 120, 133[14], 137

Komiya, R., 116[30], 120

Koot, Ronald, 65[20], 69

Kouri, Pentti J. K., 284[10,11], 296

Kuh, Edwin, 65[23], 69

Kuznets, Simon, 99[20], 119

Kybal, Milic, 67[34], 70

L

Laffer, Arthur B., 267[4], 273[9], 274[9], 276, 284[15], 297

Laidler, D., 248[6], 250

Lauterbach, A., 115[8], 119

Leff, Nathaniel H., 104[18], 107 [35,36], 115[18,19], 116 [27], 119, 120

Levhari, David, 64[5], 67, 192[26], 195

Levin, Fred, 270[8], 276

Levy, Haim, 118[53], 122

Lewis, W. A., 201[7], 221

Lintner, John, 38[11], 64[11], 68

M

McKinnon, Ronald I., 15[10], 22, 29[7], 34, 35[1], 46[1], 49[1], 57[25], 62[1], 67, 69, 80[6], 83[6], 91, 115[6], 116[6], 119, 128[4], 136, 199[8], 200[8], 201[8], 208 [8], 215[8], 221, 249, 281 [5,6], 296, 304[4], 317

Maddala, G. S., 65[22], 69

Marty, Alvin L., 178[8-10], 180 [8-10], 182[10], 192[8,9], 193, 196[2,4], 198

Marwah, K., 116[22a,22b], 120

Maynard, Geoffrey, 67[31], 69

Meade, J. E., 304[5], 317

Meiselman, David, 184[18], 194

Meltzer, Allan, 128[5], 137

Mikesell, Raymond, 59[29], 69

Miles, Marc, 269[7], 276

Modigliani, Franco, 117[45], 121

Monsen, R. J., 117[46], 121

Morley, Samuel A., 67[30], 69

Morris, Cynthia Taft, 118

Mundell, Robert A., 131[12], 137, 178[10a], 180[10a] 193, 196[3], 198, 209[9], 221, 281[4], 284[4], 296, 304 [6,7], 307[7], 317, 318

Mussa, Michael, 192[23], 194, 284[12], 297

N

Nafziger, E. W., 115[17], 119

Nam, Woo H., 79[8], 91

Nerlove, Marc, 112[51], 118[51], 121

Nichols, D. A., 116[23], 120

Niehans, J., 297

North, Douglass C., 111[50], 121

P

Pagoulatos, Emilio, 116[34], 120

Papanek, Gustav, 115[15], 119

Parkin, J. M., 239[5], 248[5], 249, 284[16], 297

Patinkin, Don, 64[5], 67, 282[8], 286[8], 296[8], 296

Patrick, H. T., 76[2], 91

Pazos, Felipe, 116[25], 120, 169

Peltzman, Sam, 64[13], 68

Phelps, Edmund S., 20[12], 22, 33 [10], 34, 180[13], 194

Polack, J. J., 233[1], 249

Porter, Michael G., 284[10,11],
    285[17], *296, 297*
Porter, Richard C., 66[28], *69*,
    118[47], *121*

R

Resnick, Stephen, 101[4], 117[4],
    118
Reynolds, C., 73[4], *74*
Rosen, G., 115[13], *119*

S

Sarnat, Marshall, 118[53], *122*
Scitovsky, Tibor, 304[8], *318*
Selowsky, Marcelo, 67[32], *69*,
    201[10], *221*
Sharpe, William F., 64[12], *68*
Shaw, Edward S., 17[4], *21, 22,*
    29[6], 32[6], *34*, 35[2],
    49[2], 56[2], 64[9], *67, 68*,
    75[1,10], 76[2], *91*, 116[21],
    119, 127[1], *136*, 178[2], *193*,
    199[11], *221*, 260[1], 261[1],
    276, 281[3], 282[9], *296*
Sheshinski, Eytan, 192[26], *195*
Sidrausky, Miguel, 26[4], *34*, 192
    [21], *194*
Siegel, Jeremy, J., 191[15], *194*
Silveira, Antonio M., 65[19], 66
    [26], *68, 69*
Simonsen, Mario Henrique, 66[27],
    69
Sinai, Allen, 117[40], *121*
Singh, S. K., 110[43], *121*
Sjaastad, Larry A., 180[14], 193
    [14], *194*

Solow, Robert M., 25[2], *34*
Spellman, Lewis, 21[14,16], *22*
Stammer, D. W., 115[11], *119*
Stephenson, James B., 192[25],
    194
Stokes, Houston, 117[40], *121*
Suk, Kim Kwong, 81[4,5], *91*
Swoboda, A. K., 284[13,14], *297*

T

Thorp, Rosemary, 67[33], *70*
Tobin, James, *22*, 35[3], 38[10],
    46[3], 64[3], *67, 68*
Tower, Edward, 178[11], 180[11],
    194, 196[5], *198*

V

van Rijckeghem, Willy, 67[31], *69*
Vogel, Robert C., 56[24], 65[24],
    69, 72[1], 73[2], *74, 148*

W

Wan, Henry Y., 26[5], *34*
White, Lawrence J., 115[16], *119*
White, William F., 231[7], *250*
Williamson, J. G., 117[44], *121*
Williamson, John, 130[11], *137*

Y

Yaari, Menahem E., 26[3], *34*

Z

Zinser, James, 59[29], *69*

Subject Index

A

Argentina
  inflation, 51, 147, 148, 154
  measures of instability, 152, 157

B

Balance of payments
  the budget and, 231-247
  inside money and, 264-267
  as instruments of stabilization,
    166-167
  long-run, 283-286
  trade credit and, 264-267
Bank money, private actions and,
    267-270
Belgium
  debt as percentage of gross
    national product, 313
  exports, 306
  imports, 305

Bolivia
  inflation, 50, 51, 147, 153
  measures of instability, 151,
    157
Bond illusion, 261
Brazil
  complementarity hypothesis, 37
  financial intermediation, 72, 74
  inflation, 50, 51, 147, 148, 201
  measures of instability, 152
  monetary instruments of
    stabilization, 164
  recession (1964-67), 208
Budget, the
  balance of payments and, 231-
    247
  case studies, 235-247
  cash, 231
  Community, 314
  coordinating monetary policies
    and, 307-313
  domestic, 231
  foreign, 231

327

[Budget]
  money market and, 231-247
  taxes and, 232-233

C

Cameroon
  inflation, 147
  measures of instability, 151
Canada
  inflation, 146
  international financial inter-
      mediation, 132-134, 139
  measures of instability, 149
Capital
  accumulation through a
      financial system, 17-19
  aggregate accumulation of,
      47-48
  demand, inflation and, 49, 57
  equilibrium marginal
      productivity of, 25
  expected real rate of return on,
      43-44
  foreign income, 230-247
    balance of payments and,
      231-247
    the budget impact, 231-247
    money market and, 231-247
  intensity, 18
    interest rate and, 16
    population growth and, 16-17
  technology and, 28-29
  variability of the real rate of
      return on, 44
  working
    defined, 201
    holding of, 204
Capital flight, the Group principle
    and, 102-104
Capital flows, foreign, 227-257

[Capital flows]
  case studies, 235-247
  monetary disturbances in an
      open economy, 227-230
  policy considerations, 233-235
Capital formation in Latin
      America, 35-74
  the aggregate economy and,
      46-48
  complementarity hypothesis,
      36-48
  expected real rate of return,
      43-44
  financial growth and, 58-62
  financial repression and,
      58-62
  inflation and, 57-58
  the portfolio constraint and,
      45-46
  return and, 36-48
  risk and, 36-48
  variability of the real rate of
      return, 44
Capital inflows
  loans and, 234-235
  policy and, 233-235, 254-256
Capital/labor ratio, 13-15, 24
Capital markets, the Group
      principle, 97-126
  aggregate saving, 106-107, 110
  capital flight, 102-104
  capital/market reform, 110-111
  distortions, 104-106
  equity/debt ratios, 108-109
  government policy implications,
      109-111
  the Groups, 98-100
  the Groups' structure, 107-108
  inflation, 102, 103, 109
  investment rates, 106-107
  limitations, 100-104
  portfolio composition, 100-102

[Capital markets]
  potential private savings, 104-105
  reform, 110
  segmentation, 100
  two principal functions of, 97-98
Capital/output ratio, 25, 30
Cash budget, 231
Ceylon
  inflation, 147
  measures of instability, 150, 157
Chile
  inflation, 51, 147, 148, 154, 201
  measures of instability, 152, 157
China
  inflation, 146
  measures of instability, 150
Colombia
  inflation, 51, 147
  measures of instability, 151, 157
Commodity supply as an instrument
  of stabilization, 167-168
Community budgets, 314
Complementarity hypothesis, 36-48
  the aggregate economy and,
    46-48
  the portfolio constraint and,
    45-46
  return and, 36-48
    expected real rate on capital,
      43-44
    expected real rate on money,
      39-41
    variability of the real rate on
      capital, 44
    variability of the real rate
      on money, 41-43
  risk and, 36-48
Consumption per capita, 13-15,
  25-26
Costa Rica
  inflation, 51, 146
  measures of instability, 150

Cuba, international financial intermediation, 132
Cyprus
  inflation, 146
  measures of instability, 149
  price stability, 155

D

Debt
  as percentage of gross national
    product, 313
Debt/equity ratios, 108-109
Debt-intermediation view (DIV) of
  money, 2, 177-178
Deflation
  increasing demand for money,
    214-218
  reducing supply of money, 212-
    214
Denmark
  exports, 306
  imports, 305
  inflation, 146
  measures of instability, 149
Deposit rate ceilings, 19-20
Domestic budget, 231-233
Dominican Republic
  inflation, 146
  measures of instability, 151, 157

E

Economic repression from deposit
  and loan rate ceilings, 19-20
Economy
  aggregate, complementarity
    hypothesis and, 46-48
  open, monetary disturbances in,
    227-230

[Economy]
open, neoclassical sketch of, 286-
292
exchange rate policy, 290-291
interest rate policy, 292
monetary policy, 291
policy implications, 290
price policy, 291
Ecuador
inflation, 51, 147, 153
measures of instability, 150
El Salvador
inflation, 51, 146
measures of instability, 150, 157
Endogenous money, 274-275
Equity/debt ratios, 108-109
Ethiopia
inflation, 146
measures of instability, 151
Euro-dollar market, 262-265
Exchange rate
depreciation of, 230
fixed, 128
flexible, 128, 283-284, 307
open economy policy, 290-291
Exchange reserves, variability of,
154-155
Exports, 85-89, 306

F

Financial integration, international,
281-301
background of, 281-283
long-run balance of payments
theory, 283-286
monetary reform, 293-295
open economy, neoclassical
sketch of, 286-292
exchange rate policy, 290-291
interest rate policy, 292

[Financial integration]
monetary policy, 291
policy implications, 290
price policy, 291
real reserves, 292-293
transmission of inflation, 292-
293
Financial intermediation, 17-18,
72-74, 127-141
fixed exchange rates, 128
flexible exchange rates, 128
liquidity in, 130-131
reserve money and, 131-132
Financial intermediation, macroeconomic system with,
11-34
analysis of the model, 15-17
capital intensity, 16-17
population growth, 16-17
saving behavior, 15-16
capital accumulation through a
financial system, 17-19
capital/labor ratio, 13-15, 24
deposit and loan rate ceilings,
19-20
impact of interest rate ceilings,
30-32
impact of technology, 26-29
investment share of output,
13-15
per capita consumption, 13-15,
25-26
wealth demand model, 11-13
Financial repression from deposit
and loan rate ceilings,
19-20
Financial repression in Latin
America, 35-74
the aggregate economy and, 46-48
capital formation and, 58-62
complementarity hypothesis,
36-48

[Financial repression in Latin
        America]
    expected real rate of return on
        capital, 43-44
    expected real rate of return on
        money, 39-41
    inflation and, 48-62
    the portfolio constraint and, 45-46
    return and, 36-48
    risk and, 36-48
    variability of the real rate of
        return on capital, 44
    variability of the real rate of
        return on money, 41-43
Fiscal instruments of stabilization,
        164-166
Foreign budget, 231-233
France
    debt as percentage of gross
        national product, 313
    exports, 306
    imports, 305
    inflation, 146
    measures of instability, 149

                        G

Germany
    debt as percentage of gross
        national product, 313
    exports, 306
    imports, 305
    inflation, 146
    measures of instability, 149
Ghana
    inflation, 147
    measures of instability, 151
Government
    the budget
        balance of payments and, 231-
            247

[Government]
    case studies, 235-247
    cash, 231
    Community, 314
    coordinating monetary
        policies and, 307-313
    domestic, 231-233
    foreign, 231-233
    money market and, 231-247
    taxes and, 232-233
    policy
        capital inflows and, 233-235,
            254-256
        the Group principle and, 109-
            111
        open economy, 290-292
Great Britain
    debt as percentage of gross
        national product, 313
    exports, 306
    imports, 305
    inflation, 146
    international financial intermedi-
        ation, 129, 133, 138
    measures of instability, 149
Greece
    inflation, 146
    measures of instability, 150, 157
Gross national product
    debt as percentage of, 313
    inflation and, 72
    Korea, 76-79, 83, 85-87
    Taiwan, 86
Group principle, 97-126
    aggregate saving, 106-107, 110
    capital flight, 102-104
    capital/market reform, 110-111
    distortions, 104-106
    equity/debt ratios, 108-109
    government policy implications,
        109-111
    the Group, 98-100

[Group principle]
  the Groups' structure, 107-108
  inflation, 102, 103, 109
  investment rates, 106-107
  limitations, 100-104
  portfolio composition, 100-102
  potential private savings, 104-105
  reform, 110
  segmentation, 100
  two principal functions of, 97-98
Guatemala
  inflation, 51, 146
  measures of instability, 150, 157
Guyana
  inflation, 146
  measures of instability, 150
  price stability, 155

H

Honduras
  inflation, 51, 146
  measures of instability, 150, 157

I

Imports, 305
Income
  foreign capital, 230-247
    balance of payments and,
      231-247
    the budget impact, 231-247
    money market and, 231-247
  money equilibrium ratio, 78, 80-82
Income/wealth ratio, 19
India
  inflation, 147
  measures of instability, 151, 156
Indonesia
  capital flow, 236-238, 240

[Indonesia]
  commodity supply as an instru-
    ment of stabilization, 168
  fiscal instruments of stabilization,
    165
  inflation, 147, 148
  measures of instability, 152
  monetary instruments of stabil-
    ization, 163
Inflation
  approaches to ending, 199-223
    the basic model, 203-212
    fall in output during a mon-
      etary contraction, 200-203
    increasing demand for money,
      214-218
    reducing supply of money,
      212-214
  capital demand and, 49, 57
  capital flight and, 103
  comparative rates of, 145-148
  comparative variability of, 148-154
  the Group principle and, 102, 103,
    109
  investment and, 57
  in Latin America, 35-74, 146-148,
    153, 154, 201
    the aggregate economy and,
      46-48
    capital formation and, 57-58
    complementarity hypothesis,
      36-48
    demand for real monetary
      assets and, 52-56
    expected real rate of return on
      capital, 43-44
    expected real rate of return on
      money, 39-41
    financial repression and, 48-62
    gross national product and, 72
    the portfolio constraint and,
      45-46

[Inflation]
  rate of, 50-52
  real size of financial sector
    and, 53-56
  return and, 36-48
  risk and, 36-48
  variability of the real rate of
    return on capital, 44
  variability of the real rate of
    return on money, 41-43
  major evils of, 35-36
  transmission of, 292-293
  welfare cost of, 177-178
    expectations function, 185-190
    extension to a dynamic frame-
      work, 183-185
    the steady state, 178-182
Inside money, 259-280
  balance of payments and,
    264-267
  endogenous, 274-275
  euro-dollar market, 262-265
  non-U.S. deposits as, 261-264
  price flexibility and, 271-273
  private actions and bank money,
    267-270
  unutilized trade credit available
    and, 273-274
Instability, 143-174
  causes of, 155-159
  design of stabilization policies,
    170-171
  exchange reserves variability,
    154-155
  inflation
    comparative rates of, 145-148
    comparative variability of,
      148-154
  instruments of stabilization, 159-
    169
    balance of payments, 166-167
    commodity supply, 167-168

[Instability]
  fiscal, 164-166
  jawboning, 169
  monetary, 160-164
  taxes, 165
  wage adjustments, 169
Integration, economic case for,
    304-307
Interest rates
  capital intensity and, 16
  ceilings, impact of, 30-32
  Korea, 85-89
  open economy policy, 292
Investment
  inflation and, 57
  in land, near urban areas, 100-
    101
  share of output and, 13-15
Investment rates, the Group
    principle and, 106-107
Iran
  inflation, 146
  measures of instability, 150,
    157
Iraq
  inflation, 146
  measures of instability, 150
  price stability, 155
Ireland
  exports, 306
  imports, 305
Israel
  inflation, 147
  measures of instability, 151
Italy
  debt as percentage of gross
    national product, 313
  exports, 306
  imports, 305
  inflation, 146
  measures of instability,
    149

Ivory Coast
    inflation, 147
    measures of instability, 151

                        J

Jamaica
    inflation, 147
    measures of instability, 150
Japan
    inflation, 146
    measures of instability, 149
Jawboning as an instrument of
        stabilization, 169
Jordan
    capital flow, 239-242, 244
    inflation, 147, 153
    measures of instability, 150

                        K

Kenya
    inflation, 146
    measures of instability, 150, 157
Korea
    complementarity hypothesis, 37
    financial structure, 36
    fiscal instruments of stabilization,
        165
    gross national product, 76-79, 83,
        85-87
    jawboning as an instrument of
        stabilization, 169
    measures of instability, 151, 156-
        157, 159
    monetary instruments of
        stabilization, 160-163
    monetary reform, 75-93
        export financing, 85-89
        inflation, 85-89, 147, 153-154

[Korea]
    interest rates, 85-89
    money/income ratio, 80-82
    private saving, 77-80
    real rates of return on holding
        money, 82-85
    real stock of money, 77-80

                        L

Labor
    population growth and, 16-17
    rate of growth of, 25-26
    technology and, 27-29
Labor/capital ratio, 13-15, 24
Land investment near urban areas,
        100-101
Latin America
    capital formation in, 35-74
        the aggregate economy and,
            46-48
        expected real rate of return,
            43-44
        financial growth and, 58-62
        financial repression and, 58-
            62
        inflation and, 57-58
        the portfolio constraint and,
            45-46
        return and, 36-48
        risk and, 36-48
        variability of the real rate of
            return, 44
    complementarity hypothesis, 36-
        48
        the aggregate economy and,
            46-48
        expected real rate of return on
            capital, 43-44
        expected real rate of return on
            money, 39-41

[Latin America]
the portfolio constraint and, 45-46
return and, 36-48
risk and, 36-48
variability of the real rate of return on capital, 44
variability of the real rate of return on money, 41-43
financial repression in, 35-74
fiscal instruments of stabilization, 164
inflation, 35-74, 146-148, 153, 154, 201
capital formation and, 57-58
demand for real monetary assets and, 52-56
gross national product and, 72
rate of, 50-52
real size of financial sector and, 53-56
measures of instability, 149-152, 156, 157
money in, 35-74
the aggregate economy and, 46-48
expected real rate of return, 39-41
the portfolio constraint and, 45-46
return and, 36-48
risk and, 36-48
variability of the real rate of return, 41-43
wage adjustments as instruments of stabilization, 169
See also names of countries
Lebanon
inflation, 146
measures of instability, 150
Libya
inflation, 147, 153

[Libya]
measures of instability, 150
Loan rate ceilings, 19-20
Loans
capital inflows and, 234-235
rationing mechanisms, 31-32
Luxembourg
debt as percentage of gross national product, 313
exports, 306
imports, 305

M

Macroeconomic policies, 303-322
case for integration, 304-307
coordinating monetary and budgetary policies, 307-313
possibilities for, 313-315
Macroeconomic system with financial intermediation, 11-34
analysis of the model, 15-17
capital intensity, 16-17
population growth, 16-17
saving behavior, 15-16
capital accumulation through a financial system, 17-19
capital/labor ratio, 13-15
economic repression from deposit and loan rate ceilings, 19-20
financial repression from deposit and loan rate ceilings, 19-20
impact of interest rate ceilings, 30-32
impact of technology, 26-29
investment share of output, 13-15
per capita consumption, 13-15, 25-26
wealth demand model, 11-13

Malaysia
    inflation, 146
    measures of instability, 150
Mexico
    financial intermediation, 73-74
    inflation, 51, 146
    measures of instability, 149, 157
Monetary instruments of stabiliza-
        tion, 160-164
Monetary reform
    international financial integration,
        293-295
    Korea, 75-93
        export financing, 85-89
        inflation, 85-89, 147, 153-154
        interest rates, 85-89
        money/income ratio, 78, 80-82
        private saving, 77-80
        real rates of return on holding
            money, 82-85
        real stock of money, 77-80
Money
    debt-intermediation view (DIV),
        2, 177-178
    excess demand for, 228-230
    excess supply of, 228-230
    expected real rate of return on, 39-41
    fall in output during a contraction,
        200-203
    holding, real rates of return on, 82-85
    income equilibrium ratio, 78, 80-
        82
    increasing demand for, 214-218
    inside, 259-280
        balance of payments and, 264-
            267
        endogenous, 274-275
        euro-dollar market, 262-265
        non-U.S. deposits as, 261-264
        price flexibility and, 271-273
        private actions and bank
            money, 267-270

[Money]
        unutilized trade credit avail-
            able and, 273-274
    in Latin America, 35-74
        the aggregate economy and,
            46-48
        complementarity hypothesis,
            36-48
        expected real rate of return,
            39-41
        the portfolio constraint and,
            45-46
        return and, 36-48
        risk and, 36-48
        variability of the real rate of
            return, 41-43
    outside, 261
    reducing supply of, 212-214
    as a store of value, 83, 84
    trade credit and, 264-267
    variability of the real rate of
        return on, 41-43
Morocco
    inflation, 146
    measures of instability, 151, 156,
        157
    price stability, 155

N

Netherlands, the
    debt as percentage of gross
        national product, 313
    exports, 306
    imports, 305
Nicaragua
    inflation, 51, 146
    measures of instability, 150, 157
Nigeria
    inflation, 147
    measures of instability, 151

Norway
    inflation, 146
    measures of instability, 149

O

Oman, capital flow, 241-247
Output
    during a monetary contraction,
        200-203
    investment share of, 13-15
Output/capital ratio, 25, 30-31
Outside money, 261

P

Pakistan
    inflation, 147
    measures of instability, 151,
        157
Panama, international financial
        intermediation, 128, 129,
        132
Paraguay
    inflation, 50, 51, 146
    measures of instability, 151, 157
Per capita consumption, 13-15, 25-
        26
Peru
    inflation, 51, 147
    measures of instability, 151
Philippines, the
    inflation, 147
    measures of instability, 151, 157,
        158
Population growth
    capital intensity and, 16-17
    labor and, 16-17
Portfolio composition, the Group
        principle, 100-102

Portfolio constraint, complementarity
        hypothesis and, 45-46
Portugal
    inflation, 147, 153
    measures of instability, 150, 157
Price
    flexibility, money and, 271-273
    open economy policy, 291
    stability, 155
Puerto Rico, international financial
        intermediation, 129

R

Return
    complementarity hypothesis, 36-
        48
    expected real rate on capital,
        43-44
    expected real rate on money,
        39-41
        variability of the real rate on
            capital, 44
        variability of the real rate on
            money, 41-43
    high rates of, 16
    increasing rates of, 16
    real rates on holding money,
        82-85
Risk, complementarity hypothesis,
        36-48

S

Saving
    aggregate, the Group principle
        and, 106-107, 110
    behavior, 15-16
    compulsory private, 90
    potential private, 104-105

[Saving]
    propensities and the Korean
        monetary reform, 75-92
    export financing, 85-89
    inflation, 85-89, 147, 153-
        154
    interest rates, 85-89
    money/income ratio, 78, 80-
        82
    private saving, 77-80
    real rates of return on holding
        money, 82-85
    real stock of money, 77-80
Separation property, 38-39
Sierra Leone
    inflation, 147
    measures of instability, 151,
        157
Singapore
    inflation, 146
    measures of instability, 149
Stabilization
    design of policies, 170-171
    instruments of, 159-169
        balance of payments,
            166-167
        commodity supply, 167-
            168
        fiscal, 164-166
        jawboning, 169
        monetary, 160-164
        taxes, 165
        wage adjustments, 169
Steady state inflation, 178-182
Sweden
    inflation, 146
    measures of instability, 149
Switzerland, international financial
        intermediation, 135-136
Syria
    inflation, 146
    measures of instability, 151, 157

T

Taiwan
    financial structure, 86
    gross national product, 86
    inflation, 89
    real rates of return on holding
        money, 82-85
Taxes
    the budget and, 232-233
    as an instrument of stabilization,
        165
Technology
    capital and, 28-29
    impact of, 26-29
    labor and, 27-29
Thailand
    inflation, 146
    measures of instability, 150, 157
Trade credit, 259-280
    balance of payments and, 264-267
    endogenous money, 274-275
    euro-dollar market, 262-265
    money and, 264-267
    non-U.S. deposits as money, 261-
        264
    price flexibility and money, 271-
        273
    private actions and bank money,
        267-270
    unutilized available, money and,
        273-274
Trinidad and Tobago
    inflation, 147
    measures of instability, 150
Tunisia
    inflation, 147
    measures of instability, 150,
        157
Turkey
    inflation, 147, 153
    measures of instability, 151

U

Uganda
    inflation, 147
    measures of instability, 151
United States of America
    fiscal instruments of stabilization,
        166
    inflation, 146
    international financial intermed-
        iation, 128, 132-135, 138
    non-U.S. deposits as money,
        261-264
Uruguay
    inflation, 50, 51, 147, 148, 154
    measures of instability, 152,
        156, 157

V

Venezuela
    inflation, 51, 146

[Venezuela]
    measures of instability, 150, 157
Vietnam
    inflation, 147, 148, 154
    measures of instability, 152

W

Wage adjustments as instruments of
        stabilization, 169
Wealth/demand function, 25-26
Welath/demand model, 11-13
Wealth/income ratio, 19
Welfare cost in inflation, 177-198
    expectations function,
        185-190
    extension to a dynamic frame-
        work, 183-185
    the steady state, 178-182
Working capital
    defined, 201
    holding of, 204